5/09

ENCYCLOPEDIA OF THE AGE OF THE INDUSTRIAL REVOLUTION, 1700–1920

ENCYCLOPEDIA OF THE AGE OF THE INDUSTRIAL REVOLUTION, 1700–1920

Volume 2   O–Z and Primary Documents

Edited by **Christine Rider**

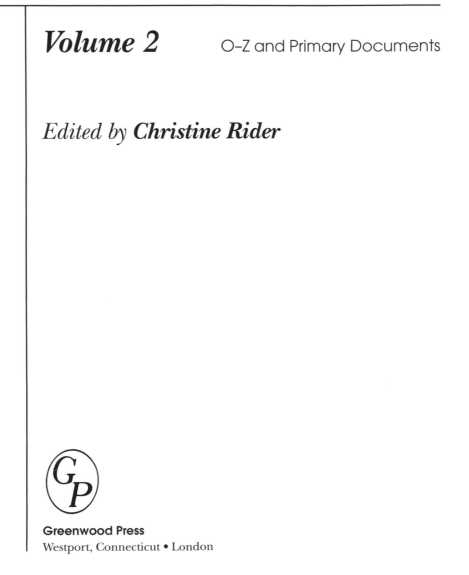

Greenwood Press
Westport, Connecticut • London

Library of Congress Cataloging-in-Publication Data

Encyclopedia of the age of the industrial revolution, 1700–1920 / edited by Christine Rider.
    p. cm.
  Includes bibliographical references and index.
  ISBN-13: 978-0-313-33501-3 (set : alk. paper)
  ISBN-10: 0-313-33501-X (set : alk. paper)
  ISBN-13: 978-0-313-33502-0 (v.1 : alk. paper)
  ISBN-10: 0-313-33502-8 (v.1 : alk. paper)
  [etc.]
  1. Industrial revolution—Encyclopedias. 2. Technological innovations—
Encyclopedias. 3. Economic history—Encyclopedias. I. Rider, Christine.
  HD2324.E545 2007
  330.9'03403—dc22   2007001830

British Library Cataloguing in Publication Data is available.

Library of Congress Catalog Card Number: 2007001830

ISBN-13: 978-0-313-33501-3 (set)
ISBN-10: 0-313-33501-X
ISBN-13: 978-0-313-33502-0 (vol. 1)
ISBN-10: 0-313-33502-8
ISBN-13: 978-0-313-33503-7 (vol. 2)
ISBN-10: 0-313-33503-6

First published in 2007

Greenwood Press, 88 Post Road West, Westport, CT 06881
An imprint of Greenwood Publishing Group, Inc.
www.greenwood.com

Printed in the United States of America

The paper used in this book complies with the
Permanent Paper Standard issued by the National
Information Standards Organization (Z39.48-1984).

10 9 8 7 6 5 4 3 2 1

CONTENTS

LIST OF ENTRIES

LIST OF PRIMARY DOCUMENTS

1. Excerpts from Sir Isaac Newton's *Mathematical Principles of Natural Philosophy* (Great Britain, 1687)
2. Excerpts from *The Wealth of Nations* by Adam Smith (Great Britain, 1776)
3. Excerpts from Alexander Hamilton's *Report on Manufactures* (United States, 1791)
4. Excerpts from Thomas Malthus's "Essay on the Principle of Population" (Great Britain, 1798)
5. Combination Acts (Great Britain, 1799, 1800)
6. The Embargo Act (United States, December 22, 1807)
7. Luddite Writings (Great Britain, ca. 1812)
8. Excerpts from the Writings of David Ricardo on Free Trade (Great Britain, 1817)
9. "Memoirs" of Prince Metternich (Austria, 1820)
10. The Monroe Doctrine as Expressed in President James Monroe's Annual Message to Congress (United States, 1823)
11. Report to Parliament of the Sadler Committee on Working Conditions in Textile Mills (Great Britain, 1833)
12. Excerpts from Alexis de Tocqueville's *Democracy in America* (United States, 1835)
13. The Chartists' First Petition to Parliament (Great Britain, 1838)
14. Louis-René Villermé on Poverty ("La Misère") (France, 1840)
15. Friedrich List Argues for a Protectionist Policy for Germany (Germany, 1841)
16. Sir Robert Peel's Speech to the House of Commons Supporting Repeal of the Corn Laws (Great Britain, 1846)
17. Excerpts from *The Communist Manifesto* by Karl Marx and Friedrich Engels (1848)
18. Commodore Matthew Perry's Instructions Regarding His Mission to Japan (United States, 1852)
19. Excerpt from *Bleak House* by Charles Dickens (Great Britain, 1852–1853)
20. Czar Alexander II's Decree Emancipating the Serfs (Russia, 1861)
21. Excerpt from *London Labour and the London Poor* by Henry Mayhew (Great Britain, 1861)
22. Report on the Fabian Society by George Bernard Shaw (Great Britain, 1896)
23. Samuel Gompers on the Principles of the American Federation of Labor (United States, 1903, 1914, 1920)
24. Excerpts from John Mitchell's *Organized Labor, Its Problems, Purposes, and Ideals* (United States, 1903)

GUIDE TO RELATED TOPICS

Business and Trade

Antitrust Policy in the United States
Banking
Bimetallism
Carnegie Steel Corporation
 (1892–1901)
Cobden-Chevalier Treaty (1860)
Continental System (1806–1813)
Corn Laws
Credit
Economies of Scale
Erie Canal
Gold Standard
Great Depression (1929–1939)
International Trade
Krupp Iron Works
Mercantilism
Ocean Transportation
Port of New York
Railroads
Seaports
Smoot-Hawley Tariff (1930)
Tariff Policy
Terms of Trade
Trust-Busting
Waltham-Lowell System

Countries and Regions

Asia, Industrial Revolution in
Austria-Hungary (ca. 1800–1914),
 Industrial Revolution in
Britain, Industrial Revolution in
Canada, Industrial Revolution in
Central and Eastern Europe, Industrial Revolution in
France, Industrial Revolution in
Germany, Industrial Revolution in
Japan, Industrial Revolution in
Japan, Industrial Revolution in: The Political Aspect
Meiji Restoration (1867)
Polish Lands, Industrial Revolution in
Russia, Industrial Revolution in
Spain, Industrial Revolution in
United States, Industrial Revolution in
Zaibatsu

Individuals of Note

Bakewell, Robert (1725–1795)
Bell, Alexander Graham (1847–1922)
Bellamy, Edward (1850–1898)
Boulton, Matthew (1728–1809)
Brunel, Isambard Kingdom (1806–1859)
Carnegie, Andrew (1835–1919)
Darby, Abraham (1678–1717)
Dickens, Charles (1812–1870)
Edison, Thomas Alva (1847–1931)
Faraday, Michael (1791–1867)
Ford, Henry (1863–1947)
Fourier, Charles (1772–1837)
George, Henry (1839–1897)
Gilbreth, Frank (1868–1924)
Gompers, Samuel (1850–1924)
Hertz, Heinrich Rudolf (1847–1894)
List, Friedrich (1789–1846)
Malthus, Thomas Robert (1766–1834)

Marx, Karl (Heinrich) (1818–1883)
Morgan, John Pierpont (J. P.) (1837–1913)
Mullaney, Kate (1845–1906)
Owen, Robert (1771–1858)
Peel, Robert (1788–1850)
Ricardo, David (1772–1823)
Rockefeller, John D. (1839–1937)
Siemans, Ernst Werner von (1816–1892)
Smith, Adam (1723–1790)
Stephenson, George (1781–1848)
Taylor, Frederick (1856–1915)
Tesla, Nikola (1856–1943)
Tristan, Flora (1803–1844)
Tull, Jethro (1674–1741)
Watt, James (1736–1819)
Wedgwood, Josiah (1730–1795)

Labor

American Federation of Labor (AF of L)
British Labour Party
Child Labor and Child Labor Laws
Cigar Makers International Union of
    America (CMIU)
Congress of Industrial Organizations (CIO)
Gompers, Samuel (1850–1924)
Grand National Consolidated Trades Union
    (GNCTU)
Great Railroad Strike (1877)
Homestead Strike (1892)
Industrial Workers of the World (IWW)
Labor and the Industrial Revolution
London Working Men's Association (LWMA)
New Model Unions
Rochdale Pioneers
Sweated Labor and Sweatshops
Syndicalism
Working-Class Protest Movements

Organizations, Firms, Associations, and Unions

American Federation of Labor (AF of L)
Carnegie Steel Corporation (1892–1901)
Cigar Makers International Union of Amer-
    ica (CMIU)
Congress of Industrial Organizations (CIO)
Friendly Societies
Grand National Consolidated Trade Unions
    (GNCTU)
Guilds, Decline of
Industrial Workers of the World (IWW)
Krupp Iron Works

London Working Men's Association (LWMA)
Lunar Society
New Model Unions
Rochdale Pioneers

Politics, Law, and Philosophy

Antitrust Policy in the United States
British Labour Party
Chartism
Child Labor and Child Labor Laws
Cobden-Chevalier Treaty (1860)
Combination Acts (1799, 1800)
Communes
Communism
Continental System (1806–1813)
Corn Laws
Democracy
Fabian Society
Factory Acts
Meiji Restoration (1867)
Mercantilism
Paris Commune (1871)
Progressive Era
Revolution of 1848
Socialism
Tariff Policy
Trust-Busting

Professions, Industries, and Fields of Endeavor

Architecture
Art
Automobiles
Aviation
Banking
Coal Mining
Cotton
Electrical Industry
Flour Milling
Iron Industry
Iron Production in Merthyr Tydfil
    (Wales)
Muckraking Journalism
Music
Newspapers
Ocean Transportation
Petroleum Industry
Psychiatry
Railroads
Shipbuilding
Urban Transportation

Ocean Transportation

The Industrial Revolution had a dramatic impact upon the international movement of cargoes, passengers, mails, and military forces throughout the world by seafaring ships. The invention of the **steam engine** and other innovations resulted in larger, faster, and safer ships, carrying a constantly growing volume of **international trade**. The enlarged volume of international trade throughout the nineteenth century also strongly affected the course of the Industrial Revolution. Larger and faster steamships brought increasing amounts of **cotton** and other raw materials to growing numbers of expanding factories and carried away similarly increasing amounts of textiles and other manufactured goods to foreign markets.

Ocean Transport before the Industrial Revolution

During the two centuries before the Industrial Revolution, ocean transport had been carried on by relatively small wooden sailing ships. These ships usually had a length of 100 feet or less and rarely exceeded 200 feet. They carried approximately 100 tons of cargo (the amount carried by five or six contemporary cargo containers) and had crews of 20 to 30 men.

Ownership of commercial sailing ships usually was divided into fractional shares: one-half, one-quarter, one-sixteenth, and so on. These shares of ownership were usually owned by individual merchants or partnerships of merchants, with a minority share of ownership frequently held by the ship's captain and officers. Most of the cargo space was devoted to the merchant-owners' goods, and any unused space was rented out to other merchants. Ships sailed when their holds were filled, with no scheduled arrival or departure dates and few set routes.

Most ocean transport was concentrated in the North Atlantic, either between European coastal nations or between Europe and the American colonies. European nations also carried on a smaller amount of waterborne trade with the **seaports** in Africa, the Middle East, and Asia. Non-European empires and states had few seafaring vessels, mostly concentrated in the coastal states bordering the Indian Ocean.

Technological Innovation: Steamships and Metal Hulls

The first technological innovation of water transport resulting from the Industrial Revolution was the adaptation of steam engines to provide propulsion for small boats and larger ships. Initially, steamboats ran only on the sheltered inland waters of rivers, lakes, and canals. By the 1820s and 1830s, however, larger steamships were beginning to cross the Atlantic Ocean. Transatlantic voyages of sailing ships would take between three weeks and three months, depending upon prevailing winds and weather. Steamships using engines powered by coal, or so-called bought wind, could make the voyage in two weeks. Further advances in steam-engine technology and the adoption of the screw propeller in place of wooden paddles increased steamships' speed and shortened the crossing time. By the late 1800s, transatlantic voyages took less than a week.

During the mid-1800s, advances in mining and metallurgy led to the replacement of ships' wooden hulls with metal: initially iron, later steel. Metal was more expensive than wood and required more energy-intensive methods of preparation, but metal ships also were more durable and much safer in event of collisions. The use of metal for ship construction also led to the construction of much larger ships. The largest possible wooden ship could not exceed 300 feet in length, as a result of structural weaknesses caused by the pounding of waves. Ships constructed of iron and steel, however, could withstand the impact of waves, so there was no structural limit upon their size. By the late 1800s, the largest metal steamships were nearly 1,000 feet long.

The development and improvement of portable steam engines altered the course of land transport as well as water transport. The growing networks of **railroads** in Britain and other coastal industrial nations focused upon major seaports. They facilitated the rapid movement of ever-increasing amounts of freight and passengers from the ports' hinterland to outgoing steamships and the rapid transportation of freight and passengers from incoming vessels.

Organizational Innovation: Steamship Lines

The Industrial Revolution's impact on ocean transport was not limited to the invention of the steamship; it also involved the creation of a new type of business organization, the shipping line. This new type of company specialized in the ownership, operation, maintenance, and coordination of multiple steamships, which sailed on fixed schedules between major seaports.

The introduction of steam engines and metal hulls resulted in seafaring ships that were much faster and larger than traditional wooden sailing ships. The metal steamships cost more to build than wooden sailing ships and were more expensive to operate. They needed a constant supply of coal and also engineers and crew with mechanical training. The steamships' ability to carry more passengers and cargo more rapidly, however, also resulted in a faster throughput, lower per-unit costs, and higher profits. Merchants were willing to pay premium rates to transport their manufactured goods to foreign markets more quickly than in slower sailing ships. Earlier arrival meant earlier sales and more rapid receipt of revenues and profits.

The increased costs of constructing and running steamships were beyond the capacity of any single merchant or partnership. This led to the creation of corporations that specialized in owning and operating steamships. The competitive advantage of providing frequent service caused these firms to acquire multiple steamships, allowing several departures each week for major seaports. This increased the shipping lines' need for capital investment and eventually led to the consolidation of most of the industry into a small number of large firms.

A large majority of the large shipping lines were British, most of which had started operations during the 1830s and 1840s. Samuel Cunard pioneered steamer service between Britain, Canada, and the United States with the Cunard Line, which soon obtained a dominant position along the North Atlantic routes. Its major British competitor was the White Star Line, owner of the *Titanic*. The Peninsular and Orient Navigation Company (P&O) became a major line on routes to the Middle East, Asia, and Australia.

Most other industrial nations soon developed major shipping lines, frequently using subsidies for carrying the mail and other forms of government assistance. France had Compagnie Generale Transatlantique (also known as the French Line), the Netherlands had the Holland America Line, and Germany had the Hamburg America Line. The latter was the largest shipping line in 1910, when measured in number of ships (126).

The United States was the only industrial nation without a major shipping line. High labor costs and other factors led the nation's investors and entrepreneurs interested in transportation to focus upon railroad companies and continental land development, rather than international shipping. U.S. shipping lines either focused upon the nation's coastal trade, which was limited by law to U.S. ships manned by U.S. crews, or were adjuncts of larger corporations such as the United Fruit Company.

The Japanese government gave a very high priority to the development of steamships and shipping lines after the 1868 **Meiji Restoration**. The government fostered the consolidation of smaller lines into the Japan Mail Steamship Company (Nippon Yusen Kaisha, or NYK) in 1885. This line soon expanded its operations to seaports in India and then to Europe and the United States in the 1890s.

Ocean Transport and Global Economics

The development of metal steamships resulted in a rapid and steady decline in the cost of ocean shipping throughout the entire nineteenth century and an accompanying growth in the volume of waterborne international trade. By the end of the century, the annual volume of international trade (most of which was carried by ships, rather than by railroads and other land transport) was nearly twenty times greater than at the beginning of the century.

The growing volume of international trade facilitated the growth of factories and other aspects of industrialization in Britain, northwestern Europe, and North America. Ocean shipping brought larger and larger amounts of cotton and other raw materials from nonindustrial nations and regions to the factories in Britain and Europe. The same steamships also exported the increasing volume of textiles and other manufactured goods produced by industrial nations' factories. Some of these manufactured goods were exported to nonindustrialized lands, and other manufactured goods were sold to consumers in other industrialized nations.

The growing volume of raw materials and manufactured goods carried by shipping lines hastened the division of the world into industrialized and nonindustrialized regions. The former were characterized by numerous factories, a relatively small agricultural workforce, high per capita fossil fuel consumption, large imports of raw materials, and large exports of manufactured goods. The latter had few factories, a large proportion of population involved in agriculture, low fossil fuel consumption, and a reversed pattern of imports and exports.

The increased amount of international shipping was facilitated by changes in the major nations' attitudes regarding the benefits of removing restrictions on international trade. Starting in the early 1800s, adherents of the free trade movement in Britain persuaded the government to remove prohibitions against imports of grain and other raw materials. Afterward, the British government actively negotiated a series of treaties and trade agreements with other nations, which decreased import tariffs and other barriers to international trade throughout the mid-1800s.

The later growth of economic nationalism in a newly united German Empire and other nations resulted in opposition to unfettered international trade during the late 1800s and early 1900s. The outbreak of **World War I** in August 1914 completely disrupted the flow of international trade. When the war ended, the volume of international trade remained at a low level than during the prewar era. Many nations attempted to limit imports and become more economically self-sufficient during the 1920s, a trend that increased during the **Great Depression** of the 1930s.

Ocean Transport and Global Governance

The development of rapid and inexpensive ocean transport had two important consequences for the global political system: First, it led to the implementation of a rudimentary system of international regulation, and, second, it strongly altered the balance of power between the industrialized and the nonindustrialized states.

Prior to the Industrial Revolution, the prevailing means of (peaceful) international politics was the bilateral negotiation of treaties and other international agreements between sovereign states. Nations handled most aspects of international trade and shipping on a nation-by-nation basis, using treaties of friendship, commerce, and navigation. The decreasing cost and increasing speed of ocean transport led to an immense increase in the size and number of steamships as well as an increase in the number of people, foodstuffs, and germs crossing international borders. These led to new international agreements, initially bilateral and later multinational, that sought to regulate such transactions and minimize their dangerous consequences.

The growth in the size, speed, and sheer number of steamships led to increased dangers of collisions at sea. During the mid-1800s, there were between 1,000 and 2,000 recorded collisions and shipwrecks annually. Britain and France led the move for safety regulations, initially negotiating bilateral treaties and then sponsoring international conferences. These set standards for ships' lights (to help avoid collisions with other ships), codes and distress signals, and movement in fog. They also established sets of sea-lanes for eastbound and westbound travel along the major transatlantic routes.

The large number of people moving across the oceans also raised dangers about spread of disease, particularly bubonic plague, cholera, typhoid, and tuberculosis. British ships carried the most passengers, and Britain again prompted international conferences regarding uniform rules for the inspection of immigrants, quarantine of incoming ships, and other public health issues. These conferences were paralleled by others coordinating international communications by mails, telegraph, telephone, and wireless **telegraphy** (radio). After the end of World War I, virtually all these regulatory functions and the small number of international bureaucracies that implemented them were consolidated in the newly created League of Nations.

The first set of changes involved peaceful negotiation of issues between nominally equal powers. The second set of changes dealt with the forceful imposition of changes in the relationships between industrialized nations and the nonindustrialized empires and states—very unequal powers.

The large seafaring metal steamships were not limited to carrying civilian passengers and commercial cargos; they also could carry naval weapons and military forces. The technological innovations that resulted in the development of large fleets of merchant steamships also led to the development of large fleets of steam-powered naval warships on the part of most industrial nations. Britain already had a large navy (of wooden sailing ships) at the onset of the Industrial Revolution. Its early development of steam power and other technologies resulted in Britain possessing the largest naval fleet throughout the nineteenth century.

During most of the nineteenth century, there were few naval battles (or major wars) between the industrial nations. Most naval battles were between industrialized nations and nonindustrialized states, with consistent results: Small contingents of a few armed steamships could easily defeat much larger numbers of wooden sailing ships. Steamships transporting troops armed with rifles, artillery, and other modern weapons could be rapidly dispatched to the nonindustrialized regions of the world, where they easily defeated much larger native forces armed with less-advanced weapons.

Advances in ocean transport (combined with the development of modern weapons) strongly altered the balance of power between industrial and nonindustrialized states. Governments and military leaders of industrialized states obtained greater capacity to impose their will upon nonindustrialized states. During most of the nineteenth century, however, Britain and the other great powers chose not to conquer and directly rule most nonindustrialized states. Britain primarily followed a policy of simply forcing China and other nonindustrial states to open their borders to international (i.e., British) trade.

The growth of nationalistic rivalry between the industrial nations that followed the formation of the German Empire in 1870, however, led to changes in policy regarding nonindustrialized regions. Britain, France, Germany, and other major powers began using their naval and military power to conquer large areas of Africa and Asia and set up colonial governments.

The Japanese government that came into power by the Meiji Restoration of 1868 avoided the threat of foreign conquest by giving high priority to the development of steamships and modern weapons. By the late 1800s, Japan defeated the army and navy of the much larger, but nonindustrialized, Chinese Empire. The Japanese navy later defeated the Russian fleet in the 1905 Russo-Japanese War and thereby joined the ranks of the world's major powers.

Ocean Transport and Global Cultures

The vast increase of transoceanic shipping also strongly affected the various cultures around the world. Improved ocean transport increased the dissemination of (primarily European) mail, books, and other printed matter around the world. It also facilitated the movement of doctors, missionaries, teachers, and other proselytizers of European religion and culture to Asia, Africa, and the Middle East.

Other important cultural changes resulted from the integration of nonindustrialized states into a global market economy. Nonindustrial economies that previously had been based upon barter and exchange, or politico-religious tribute, were altered by the introduction of market transactions. Some states accepted these changes voluntarily; others, for example China and Japan, had them forcibly imposed by warships and military forces. Native merchants and other groups serving as intermediaries with industrial nations gained increased influence by their role in the increasing exports of raw materials, imports of manufactured goods, and corresponding flow of revenues.

The advent of cheap ocean transport of passengers also altered the composition of regional populations. The industrialization of Britain and Europe and the accompanying import of agricultural goods decreased the need for a rural workforce. Some nonemployed rural workers migrated to the growing industrial cities, whereas many others migrated overseas, to North America, South America, Australia, and other recently acquired colonies. The largest passenger ships of the Cunard Line, the Hamburg America Line, and other shipping firms each could carry several thousand passengers on each voyage in their communal steerage quarters.

The international migration of millions of Britons and Europeans to the west and south throughout the nineteenth century was paralleled by a smaller but still substantial movement of Chinese and Japanese emigrants eastward and southward at the end of the 1800s, primarily by new Japanese shipping lines. The U.S. enactment of racial restrictions upon Asians' entry during the 1880s channeled much of this eastward migration toward Argentina and other nations of South America.

FURTHER READING: Boyce, Gordon. *Information, Mediation and Institutional Development: The Rise of Large-Scale Enterprise in British Shipping, 1870–1919.* Manchester, U.K.: Manchester University Press, 1995; Fox, Stephen. *Transatlantic: Samuel Cunard, Isambard Brunel, and the Great Atlantic Steamships.* New York: Harper, 2004; Hugill, Peter J. *World Trade since 1431: Geography, Technology, and Capitalism.* Baltimore: Johns Hopkins University Press, 1995; O'Rourke, Kevin H., and Jeffrey G. Williamson. *Globalization and History: The Evolution of a Nineteenth-Century Atlantic Economy.* Cambridge, MA: MIT Press, 2001; Starkey, David J., and Gelina Harlaftis, eds. *Global Markets: The Internationalization of the Sea Transport Industries since 1850.* St. John's, NF: International Economic Maritime History Association, 1998; Sugiyama, Shinya. *Japan's Industrialization in the World Economy, 1859–1899: Export Trade and Overseas Competition.* Atlantic Highlands, NJ: Athlone Press, 1988. WEB SITES: http://www.cronab.demon.co.uk/marit. htm; http://www.kipnotes.com/Shipping.htm; http://www.mightyseas.co.uk/; http://www. tc.umn.edu/~tmisa/biblios/8-global_culture.html.

STEPHEN G. MARSHALL

Owen, Robert (1771–1858)

Robert Owen was a curious combination: a successful British industrialist whose employment practices contrasted with those of most of his contemporaries and who also was critical of industrial capitalism. Owen became a manager of a textile mill at age 20, later becoming cofounder of the New Lanark textile mills in Scotland, which he operated to show that good practices were compatible with profitability.

The early years of the Industrial Revolution continued the long hours, hard work, and drudgery of the average worker's life, except that it was now taking place in the new environment of the factory. Factories were built to get the best use out of machines and were not intended to provide a pleasant work environment for employees. Early factories often were unheated in winter, suffocating in summer, and were unventilated and cramped places where the cutting edges of machines were unguarded. The workforce included children as young as six years old, and working hours were long, with only brief periods allowed for meals. These conditions persisted because employers believed that competitive pressures forced them to work their employees as hard and as long as possible, for the sake of survival; if any one tried to improve conditions, employers' costs would rise and profits disappear, forcing the companies out of business.

Owen, in contrast, was an altruist who believed that environment played a large part in forming character and deliberately set about changing the work environment in his mills. He refused to employ children younger than 10, paid high wages, built houses (with sanitation) for his workers, and provided schools for their children. Workers also had access to stores selling good products at reasonable prices. His profits did not suffer; essentially (as later theorists would put it), his investments in human capital paid off in worker productivity.

Owen's campaigns for the reorganization of society focused on the establishment of self-governing producer cooperatives to replace private property and self-interest. He believed that in combination with continuing scientific and technological progress, human productivity, creativity, and material well-being would increase. He founded a cooperative in New Harmony, Indiana, in 1814, but it failed in 1831, lacking Owen's leadership. In England, he formed the **Grand National Consolidated Trades Union** (GNCTU) in 1832, which was open to all employees irrespective of trade or industry. The GNCTU's goal was to replace competitive capitalist industry by a cooperative system of worker control, but it met intense employer resistance in the form of lockouts, and it collapsed in 1834.

Owen's legacy of what could be called pre-Marxian **socialism** influenced later legislative action to achieve social change; his belief in the cooperative movement was not influential.

FURTHER READING: Morton, A. L. *The Life and Ideas of Robert Owen*. London: Lawrence & Wishart, 1962; Podmore, Frank. *Robert Owen*. 2 vols. Des Moines, IA: Meredith, Appleton-Century-Crofts, 1907.

CHRISTINE RIDER

P

Paris Commune (1871)

The Paris Commune was a mostly working-class rebellion that gained control of the French capital from March to May 1871. The Commune began as a spontaneous political demonstration by working-class Parisians against a national government that had recently lost a short and painful war against Prussia and her German allies and was attempting, in March 1871, to reassert national control over the capital. Very soon after coming to power, the Commune demonstrated its sympathy toward the working class as well as a broad grasp of the impact that the processes of industrialization and capitalism had had on the city during the preceding decades. In the end, however, the Commune was not able to devise a coherent social and economic program to address those aspects of the age of industry that had had a negative impact on the city. This inability no doubt resulted partly from the fact that the insurrectionists were preoccupied with the need for defense during the military siege of the city by the national government—which, in fact, eventually defeated the Commune.

The word *commune* describes a municipal entity in France of any size, from village to city. The term was adopted by the Parisian government that came to power in an election in late March following the rebellion of March 18, 1871, and the ensuing evacuation of the city by the regular army and the national government headed by Adolphe Thiers. Communards were supporters of the Commune, most of whom, to judge by the records of those who joined the National Guard (*fédéré*) or were arrested in the wake of its defeat, were skilled workers in the building and metal trades. Unskilled workers, along with clerks, also participated at substantial, though lower, rates. Many of the workers who signed on with the National Guard were migrants from the provinces, both seasonal workers and those who had moved permanently to the city. Workers such as these had been drawn to Paris in large numbers during the Second Empire (1852–1870) by the promise of work and good wages brought on by the rebuilding of the city under the prefect Baron Georges Haussmann (1809–1891). Even by this late date in the age of industry, the Parisian working class was made up mostly of skilled or semiskilled workers in artisanal trades and employed in thousands of comparatively small firms. Paris in 1871 was not an industrial hub like London or Manchester in England, or even like the French cities of Lille or Saint-Etienne. Thus, proletarian factory workers of the type envisioned at the time by Karl **Marx** were not especially prominent in the Commune. Dedicated Communards—particularly those who fought against the troops of the national government through the final, terrible Bloody Week street battles of May—were no doubt motivated in part by the desire to initiate social and economic reforms that could ameliorate aspects of the paternalist and capitalist system of the Second Empire, recently defeated in the war against Prussia. Even more crucial in fomenting rebellion was resentment by ordinary Parisians at the French government for the military defeat of 1870–1871, the desire to establish a federalist system of government for the nation that would allow more local autonomy, and, as the end of the Commune came into sight, the desire by neighbors and coworkers to defend neighborhoods against the Versaillais, the French national army that was attempting to retake the capital (and which was named after the city of Versailles, just west of Paris, where Thiers's government was headquartered).

The Commune was in power just three months and during this period was preoccupied with the imperative of defending itself against the national government and the Versaillais army. This is worth emphasizing because at the time and ever since there was criticism of the Commune, even among its supporters (notably Karl Marx, whose *The Civil War in France* became a classic of contemporary history), for its seeming slowness in enacting reform. Nonetheless, in its short life, the Commune, operating through an executive commission and nine subordinate commissions and dominated by political factions that included Jacobin socialists, Proudhonists, and followers of the radical Louis-Auguste Blanqui, did in fact pursue a handful of progressive social and economic policies. The Commune attempted to alleviate financial hardships for ordinary Parisians through several means: extending an earlier moratorium on debts, providing pensions for the families of National Guardsmen who had been killed, and decreeing easy terms for persons who had pawned their goods with the city's pawnshops. The Commune abolished night work in bakeries (an issue that bakers had complained about for years) and allowed some women workers to organize and have a kind of monopoly on the production of military uniforms. The Commune also underwrote the creation of workers' cooperatives (most of which focused on the production of military goods) and transferred control of several shops and factories that had been shut down during the recent war with Prussia to the workers who had been employed in them. Even as members of the Commune's executive commission reasserted a commitment to the idea of an organization of labor, small businesses were encouraged to continue to produce and sell. Despite the claims of some of its opponents and later critics, the Commune never demonstrated an intention to expropriate property nor, despite the opportunity to do so, did it seize the substantial assets of the Bank of France—a failure noted with special bitterness by Marx. Most Communards were not communists, though many were socialists, Blanquists, or advocates of association or of the Proudhonist variety of anarchism. These tendencies were all very much within the mainstream of leftist thought in nineteenth-century France.

Yet the Commune did not articulate a clearly defined industrial policy, and though signs of its socialistic impulses are apparent in any number of its economic decrees, most of its policies were of a political and military cast, directly geared toward defending the city against the Versailles government and its military forces. The Declaration to the French People of April 19, 1871, which became the sharpest manifesto of the Commune's program and goals, spoke eloquently to individual and communal rights, though the document devotes only scant attention to matters of taxing and finances and offers nothing about industry. The hints of the proletarian state, and with it a new, progressive, noncapitalist economic superstructure, which some—again, most famously, Marx—saw in the history of the Paris Commune, were stillborn in 1871.

Paris, *ville libre*, the short-lived vision of a free and autonomous city within a federated French national state, was crushed in the fighting of Bloody Week (May 21–28, 1871). Skirmishing between Versaillais and Communard forces had begun on April 2, even as German occupation forces, which had been in France since summer 1870, remained in positions to the east, blocking escape from or entry to the city. By the end of this French civil war, as many as 20,000 persons, most of them Communards, were killed—often through summary execution—and more than 40,000 arrested. Many of those sentenced were sent to overseas penal colonies in Algeria or New Caledonia. The last of the Communards were granted amnesty in 1880.

The Commune was the longest-lived, but also the most tragic and violently repressed, of all nineteenth-century European revolutions. Though it had its origins in politically progressive ideals and had attempted to enact a handful of reformist economic policies, given its precarious situation and France's humiliating defeat, it is not surprising that during its short life the Commune focused more on political and military matters than economic or industrial policies.

FURTHER READING: Gould, Roger V. *Insurgent Identities: Class, Community and Protest in Paris from 1848 to the Commune.* Chicago: University of Chicago Press, 1995; Jellinek, Frank. *The Paris Commune of 1871.* New York: Grosset and Dunlap, 1965; Lissagaray, Prosper-Olivier. *History of the Commune of 1871.* Trans. Eleanor Aveling Marx. New York: Monthly Review Press, 1967 [1886]; Tombs, Robert. *The Paris Commune 1871.* London: Longman, 1999.

CASEY HARISON

Pauper Children

Pauper children were British children who were orphans or children whose parents could not afford to support them. Their numbers increased during the Industrial Revolution. Under the English Poor Laws (the great law of the 43rd year of Elizabeth I), children and orphans could be apprenticed to employers. Previously, charity for the poor had been made available by religious institutions, but this ended following Henry VIII's dissolution of the monasteries. Following passage of this law, the poor received assistance from their local parish with funding that was supervised by a Board of Guardians. The system of relief to the poor was changed again following the Poor Law Amendment Act of 1834, which defined three classes of poor individuals: able-bodied adults, children, and elderly or non-able-bodied who were referred to as *impotent*. The lawmakers' explanation was that because pauperism was the result of idleness, vice, or alcoholism that resulted in an immoral state of existence, paupers required supervision. If an able-bodied person wanted assistance, they would have to leave their home to live in a workhouse, an institution designed to promote productivity. This system destroyed extended families by requiring men, women, children, and grandparents to live in separate quarters.

Government officials were supposed to arrange for pauper children to learn a trade, become apprentices, and be cared for until age 21. Many children were sold or given to factory or mill owners, however, where they worked unreasonably long hours, had no health care, were deprived of education, and often died or acquired a handicap because of working conditions. Others were forced to work alongside their parents or were leased to mill owners for a period of years like servants. These children were allegedly better off than pauper children because they were considered free-labor children but often were subjected to the same abuses. Sometimes money that children earned was given to the parents.

Although poor children had always existed, one unfortunate consequence of the Industrial Revolution was that their numbers increased in urban areas. As factories replaced cottage industries, farm families and peasants migrated to the cities. At the same time, urban populations were feeling the consequences of the new enclosure laws passed by Parliament in the early nineteenth century. These laws had allowed private farms to take over land that had been held in common by tenant farmers who subsequently lost their livelihood. The change created new social classes that widened the gap between the rich and the poor.

It is estimated that for every 200 farmers who lost their farms, from 2,000 to 3,000 laborers were now without work and, by extension, 5,000 to 6,000 wives and children were without support. When this happened, the unemployed farmers and peasant laborers were driven off the land. As the peasants left their farms with no place to go, they migrated into the cities to live in slums. Because of steam-powered mechanization, the textile industry's factories replaced cottage industries in rural areas.

When David Dale (1739–1806) founded a factory in Glasgow for cotton spinning and was unable to find enough adult laborers to work for him, he sought permission from workhouses and charities to obtain children as young as five, six, and seven. He purchased them and moved them into a residence he built, large enough to hold 500 of them. Originally, he had promised to feed, clothe, and educate them as well as provide them with medical care and high-quality instruction, and once he established the workhouse, he hired servants to care for them. Although he rarely visited to check on their welfare, Sir Thomas Bernard, in *Society for Bettering the Condition and Increasing the Comforts of the Poor*, praised his establishment as providing fresh air, clean clothing, an ample diet, as well as educational instruction after 7.00 P.M. His manufactory was reputed to be radically different from others in the United Kingdom; however, not all sources praise his mills so highly. According to other sources, the children were forced to work from 6:00 A.M. until 7:00 P.M. with only two bathroom breaks. And although they were scheduled to receive an education after hours, the children were so exhausted that they could barely learn anything. Robert **Owen**, who married David Dale's daughter, Caroline, in 1799, later testified that after he purchased the New Lanark workhouse, he found that the children were not thriving or as well nourished as they previously had been described.

In general, most children worked in cramped and crowded positions that caused their bodies to become stunted in growth. Robert Owen's testimony to Sir Robert **Peel** in 1816 confirmed this as he described children with deformed limbs and stunted growth.

Pauper children often ran away from cruel bosses and, when they were caught, were returned to be punished and endure worse working conditions. They suffered unconscionable horrors because of immigration into cities and living conditions in workhouses. Workhouse administrators bought children from and sold them to factories as needed. Two literary giants, Frances Trollope and Charles **Dickens**, wrote from personal knowledge. Trollope's *Michael Armstrong: Factory Boy* (1840) was written after she read an article about Robert Blincoe, a pauper child who started work at the age of four, first as a chimney boy then in a cotton mill. His miseries were well documented. She visited textile mills in Manchester and Bradford to see conditions firsthand. Trollope's *Jessie Phillips* (1843) was about the English Poor Laws of 1834. Dickens himself was a pauper child; *Oliver Twist* (first appearing serialized 1837–1839) is a semiautobiographical account of an orphan who is placed in a workhouse at the age of 12 because his family had been forced into debtor's prison.

The conditions that Dickens and Trollope wrote about, as fiction, can be found in primary documents about the London poor. Some pauper children worked in coal mines, others did various work on the streets. In 1851, it is estimated that of the more than 40,000 street people, 12,000 were children. Some children sold whatever they could: rags, squirrels, fish, salt, sand, shells, fruits and vegetables, secondhand clothing, old metal articles, glass, and crockery. Times were so dire that everything from a dead horse, from skin to offal, was sold. Children performed tasks such as sweeping crossings so that the gentry would not dirty their feet when walking from carriage to business establishment. Climbing boys or chimney sweeps worked as apprentices to master sweepers. They were required to be older than eight, but rarely did anyone pay attention when they were younger. Parents could, and did, employ their own children. Children as young as four-and-a-half were working in this unwholesome occupation. Then there were mud-larks, children who rummaged through the rivers or standing water for bits and pieces of metal, wood, or coal that they could sell. Many of these children were less than six years of age, wore rags, carried baskets for their accumulated finds, and could neither read nor write. Worse yet were sewer hunters, children who stood in raw sewage shoveling wet drainage into sifters in hopes of finding something they could sell.

Occupational hazards were rampant. Testicular cancer, the first work-related cancer to be discovered, was found in men who had been chimney sweeps as youths. Chemical poisoning in young girls from the white phosphorus used in making matches caused so-called phossy jaw, a necrosis of the jawbone.

Children were useful to employers because they were small enough to do intricate work and could be forced to endure long hours. The **cotton** industry wreaked havoc on the lives of families. Children often began work at age four or five and were stunted in both spirit and body. As scavengers in textile factories, their job was to salvage loose cotton from under machinery. Their tiny fingers could slip in between moving parts, but because the machines remained running, they frequently lost fingers or their hair slipped into machines that then drew them in and crushed them. Often young girls were sexually abused, beaten, or tortured.

In the coal mines, children often were stripped of their clothing, girls and boys together. The young girls were forced to wear belts and chains around their waists and drag coal tubs underground, on all fours like an animal. The youngest children were entrusted with jobs in which they had to sit in the dark and control trap doors that allowed ventilation into coal mines.

Pottery factories used white lead, a carcinogen, as an element in the glazes in which pots were dipped. Although there was more space between people in these factories, the toilet facilities were such that they were located in unwholesome locations with no privacy. Girls and women were subjected to lewd comments and staring by the men and boys. Boys turned the jiggers (horizontal wheels) in rooms that were as hot as 120 degrees. Large cast-iron stoves heated the rooms to temperatures so hot they broke thermometers. Temperatures out of doors were below zero at times, so that when these children ran between buildings, poorly clothed for cold weather, they often contracted pneumonia, tuberculosis, or other infections.

The fate of pauper children began to improve starting in the 1820s after the **Factory Acts** shortened hours, raised the legal age at which children could work, and introduced effective enforcement. Often, however, children became unemployed with no other means of support, so the laws did nothing to really help the poor. It was not until adult labor was sufficient to meet the needs of industry that children were no longer employed.

FURTHER READING: Hammond, J. L., and Barbara Hammond. *The Village Labourer: 1760–1832.* New York: Augustus M. Kelley. 1987 [1913]; Jackson, Lee. "Match Girls." In *Victorian London, Down East.* At http://www.victorianlondon.org/publicationsroundlondon1-2.htm; Mayhew, Henry. *London Labour and the London Poor. A Cyclopaedia of the Condition and Earnings of those that will work, those that cannot work, and those that will not work.* London: Frank Cass and Company Limited. 1967 [1851]; McElroy, Wendy. *Legal Child Abuse,* 2001. At http://www.zetetics.com/mac/mises/legalchildabuse.html; Pike, E. Royston. *Hard Times: Human Documents of the Industrial Revolution.* New York: Frederick A. Praeger. 1966; Toynbee, Arnold. "Lectures on the Industrial Revolution in England: The Growth of Pauperism." In *The Industrial Revolution,* pp. 67–78. Boston: Beacon, 1956 [1884]. WEB SITES: http://www.spartacus.schoolnet.co.uk/Lpoor1834.htm (1834 Poor Law); http://www.cottontimes.co.uk; http://www.workhouses.org.uk/; http://victorianlondon.org.

LANA THOMPSON

Peel, Robert (1788–1850)

Robert Peel, a nineteenth-century British prime minister, was born on February 5, 1788, in Bury, Lancashire, to cotton baron Robert Peel and Ellen Yates. After completing his education at Harrow and Oxford University, he entered Parliament as a member of the Tory Party in 1809. Peel was prime minister for five months from December 1834 to May 1835 and again from September 1841 to July 1846. He is remembered for his policies establishing the London Metropolitan Police Force, repeal of the **Corn Laws**, passage of various **Factory Acts**, and the Catholic Emancipation Bill.

Peel's financial reforms helped stimulate trade during the Industrial Revolution. As chairman of the currency committee, he restored the Bank of England's cash payments in 1819 and later in 1844 passed the Bank Charter Act regularizing the issue of banknotes as an anti-inflation measure. As a believer in free trade, he reduced tariffs in 1842: Duties on 600 goods were abolished and reduced on 1,000 items, which revived trade. Tax reforms eased the burden on the working class by utilizing direct taxation in the form of an income tax, then set at seven pence to the pound.

Peel opposed the earlier Tory positions, which favored maintaining the status quo and opposing reform. He recognized the changing circumstances accompanying the Industrial Revolution and initiated reforms. For him, the interests of the party should be subordinated to those of the nation. This resulted in the Conservative Party's new principles as set out in the Tamworth manifesto of 1834, which supported the Reform Act of 1832 and promised a series of reforms.

Peel's father was noted for reforms aimed at improving the conditions of his workers, and his son continued this tradition. Working conditions in mines were appalling, and the Collieries Act of 1842 banned the employment of women and boys younger than 10 underground. The Factory Act of 1844 limited the working hours of women to 12 hours and those of children younger than 13 to 6.5 hours in the textile industries. Children and women working in factories related to printing designs benefited from the Calico Print Works Act of 1845, which prohibited the employment of children younger than 8 and eliminated night work for women and children younger than 13.

Ireland desperately needed to import cheap corn after the potato blight, but the Corn Laws did not allow grain imports. Peel's party, however, was composed mainly of landholders who opposed the repeal of the Corn Laws. An ongoing campaign raged for its repeal in order to reduce the price of grain and thus benefit workers, which met success with repeal in 1846 but also ended Peel's career as prime minister. He was accused of betraying his party, but Peel was convinced of the rightness of his action in the interests of the nation. He continued to serve as a member of Parliament, offering advice as an elder and respected statesman. Peel died on July 2, 1850, following a horse-riding accident.

FURTHER READING: Crosby, Travis L. *Sir Robert Peel's Administration, 1841–1846.* London: David & Charles, 1976; Gash, Norman. *Sir Robert Peel: The Life of Sir Robert Peel after 1830.* 2nd ed. London: Longman Group, 1986; Hobsbawm, Eric. *Industry and Empire: The Birth of the Industrial Revolution.* Rev. ed. New York: New Press, 1999; Jenkins, T. A. *Sir Robert Peel.* Basingstoke, UK: Palgrave Macmillan, 1998; Ramsay, A.A.W. *Sir Robert Peel.* New York: Barnes & Noble, 1971.

PATIT PABAN MISHRA

Penny Dreadfuls

Penny dreadfuls were inexpensive magazines published during the mid-nineteenth century directed particularly toward working-class boys. They had dramatic, eye-catching covers with ornate letters and artful illustrations. The stories were action-packed and geared to be read in a short period of time. The appellation is misleading because, although the serializations were cheap, they did not cost a penny and were not dreadful. In addition to stories, they included letters, poems, articles on sports or hobbies, and contests that offered prizes.

The first penny dreadful, *The Boys of England,* was written by Charles Stephens in 1866 and published by Edwin J. Brett (1828–1895). Brett loosely patterned his page formats on the *London Journal* and *Reynold's Miscellany,* which were mainstream publications.

Previous magazines, called penny bloods, were intended for adult audiences. They catered to prurient interests with themes of prostitution, murder, kidnapping, robbery, or criminal acts committed by unsavory characters and were sometimes modeled after actual events. For example, Sweeney Todd, a serial killer, was drawn wearing a white apron and clutching a large curved razor, glaring down at his murdered victim lying in a pool of blood. The words *Sweeney Todd* were written above and *demon barber of Fleet Street* below that scenario. Surrounding this picture were four scenes from the other stories inside. Another subject was Spring-Heeled Jack, a Batman-type character with pointed ears, black clothing, a cloak, and the ability to vault or jump huge distances; unlike Batman, his motives were evil. *Varney the Vampyre; or The Feast of Blood* showed a crouching, fanged, bearded man carrying an obviously unconscious woman, arms outstretched, eyes closed, and head fallen back. These were all penny blood fodder.

As adult tastes grew more sophisticated and more selective, Brett saw an opportunity to expand the scope and improve the circulation of his publications. His initial success had inspired competitors who were copying his themes and writing similar stories, making it difficult for Brett to remain unique. By shifting his focus to youth and developing more respectable and uplifting content, he accomplished two goals. Rather than be criticized for the content of his publications, he now joined the expressed outrage at the indecency of his competitors. As soon as sales of his new genre were adequate, he publicly criticized his rivals, Emmett Brothers and Hogarth House, for pandering to the tastes of the slum dwellers.

During the Industrial Revolution, population expanded, and large numbers of young people in cities created a new market. Brett wanted to provide reading material to those who otherwise might not develop reading habits. Covers now showed the triumph of good over evil, respectable everyday people involved in school or work, challenged with antisocial influences, their contrasts apparent by their clothing and postures. One popular theme was that of an ordinary person, denied rights to an inheritance or a position because of someone in power. Through trials of endurance and tests of character, the protagonist eventually would survive, overcoming misfortune and gaining what was rightfully his or hers. This was important to Victorian society because it reinforced the belief that with hard work and honesty, one could overcome the burdens of one's circumstances.

An interesting social phenomenon grew as boys formed reading groups, sharing publications for discussion afterward. The books also featured female heroines who as a last resort called upon their male friends to help them. Heroines, or strong female characters, in these stories for girls challenged existing nineteenth-century values in which men previously had been expected to rescue women in perilous situations. Examples include *Queen of the Road, May Turpin* (1864); *Rose Mortimer; or The Ballet Girls' Revenge* (1852), and *The Pretty Girls of London* (1869) were written specifically for girls. *Ela the Outcast; or The Gipsy of Rosemary Dell* (1841) sold 30,000 copies.

Their content was designed for reading enjoyment rather than the moralizing so common in Victorian literature, a prelude to an era when a leisure class with time to read would emerge. Yet their messages were consonant with established values. Serialization appealed so much to one religious society, The Religious Tract Society, that they published their *Boys Own Paper,* a spiritual tract, which appeared regularly in serial form between 1879 and 1967.

Penny dreadfuls were deliberately published in serial installments to ratchet up the suspense and interest of the young reader. One needed to buy the next issue to find out what happened in the story. Some evolved into books. One of the longest was Bracebridge Hemyng's Jack Harkaway series, published by M. A. Donohue and Company between 1871 and 1910. Works such as *Jack Harkaway and School Days, After School Days, Afloat and Ashore, At Oxford, Adventures at Oxford, Among the Brigands of*

Italy, Escape from the Brigands of Italy, and *Adventures around the World* traced Jack's life as he matured from a boy to a man, unlike most comic book heroes. In the later stories, Jack died, his son carried on, and then his grandson became the protagonist. These titles were hardly the sort that would lead to crime, perversion, or violent behavior. When Alfred Saunders, a 13-year-old errand boy was charged with stealing from his father, however, he admitted buying penny papers with the money. The evidence used to convict him was serialized books with the titles of *The Young Briton* (first published in 1869), *Sons of Britannia* (first published in 1870), and *Boys of England* (first published in 1866). The toy pistol, lantern, and cigar holder in his possession when he was caught by the police were regarded as further proof of his guilt. His father told the magistrate that he considered *The Young Englishman* (first published in 1867) "filthy." The magistrate was convinced and sentenced Saunders a severe punishment: three years of industrial school.

A moral panic appeared to hang over the masses as the popularity of these writings increased from 150,000 per week to 250,000 in 1871. Between 1866 and 1900, 96 commercially oriented periodicals for boys had been published or reissued. Penny dreadfuls, some said, influenced youth to adopt the immoral behaviors of the characters and reenact episodes, even though the glorification of crime was not their focus. Critics were eager to publicize so-called proofs of the damage to young minds whenever dreadfuls were found in the possession of young boys caught for the commission of some crime.

The popularity of these publications spread to the United States, where Frank Leslie (1821–1880) owner of *Frank Leslie's Illustrated Newspaper* pirated them for his *Boys and Girl's Weekly.* Norman Munro followed suit and began *The Boys of New York,* which lasted 19 years. Leslie convinced Hemyng to come to the United States, where he continued to write about Jack Harkaway.

In the United States, as the Industrial Revolution transformed industry, immigrants from the British Isles arrived to find better lives and formed communities in eastern seaboard regions. As they assimilated U.S. culture, they added to the already growing urban areas to compete for jobs with workers who had moved from farms and rural areas. Interest in reading increased in these new areas. The steam rotary press increased the numbers of books that could be printed. Dime novels, as they were called in the United States, began regular publication in the 1860s. They satisfied a reading audience that was unable to afford traditional hardbound volumes. Erastus Beadle, a former miller's apprentice and self-taught printer, opened a print shop and began to write, first magazines then music and then dime novels. They, like penny dreadfuls, were cheap and paper-covered with highly detailed illustrations. Newsstands displaying such titles as *The Young Mountaineer* (1870); *Myrtle, the Child of the Prairie* (1863); and *Quindaro; or The Heroine of Fort Laramie* (1870) would capture the imagination of the tired traveler or young person who had never been in a library. The subject matter was the United States, historical figures, or the wild West, with graphic pictures of knife-bearing white men fighting savages with exaggerated postures and facial expressions.

After the genre gained popularity in the United States, Anthony Comstock, the postal office employee who considered himself a decency crusader, attempted to quash anything considered obscene. He regarded dime novels equivalent to children's pornography. His voice was so powerful that he was able to ban or suppress dime novels in Massachusetts, California, Connecticut, Maine, New Hampshire, South Carolina, Tennessee, and Washington without ever reading any of them.

Because penny dreadfuls and their successor dime novels were popular rather than formal literature, they were subject to many criticisms. Like subsequent popular-culture inventions (movies, comic books, television, video games, and the Internet), crime, social problems, and delinquency were blamed on their influence.

The Industrial Revolution and its major categories of transportation, machine power, and factories located in cities that used mass production as opposed to cottage industries facilitated the spread of popular-culture literature. It was not until the next technology—moving pictures—gained popularity in the late 1890s that penny dreadfuls and dime novels lost their readership.

FURTHER READING: Anglo, Michael. *Penny Dreadfuls and Other Victorian Horrors.* London: Jupiter, 1977; *The Beadle Collection of Dime Novels.* Given to the New York Public Library by Frank O'Brien. 1922; *History of British Comics 1866–1870 (Story Papers) Part 3.* At http://www.comicsuk.co.uk/History/HistoryMain.asp?PassedEra=Story%20Papers203; Holmes, Michael. *Penny Dreadfuls and Penny Bloods.* 2005. At http://www.collectingbooksandmagazines.com/penny.html; Jones, Daryl. *The Dime Novel Western.* Bowling Green, OH: Popular Press, 1978; Pearson, Edmund. *Dime Novels or Following an Old Trail in Popular Literature.* Port Washington, NY: Kennikat Press, 1968 [1929]; *Peeps into the Past.* At http://www.geocities.com/justingilb/texts/PEEPS.htm; *Penny Dreadfuls: I.* At http://www.bl.uk/collections; Springhall, John. "Disseminating Impure Literature: The Penny Dreadful Publishing Business since 1860." *Economic History Review* 3 (1994): 567–84; Springhall, John. *Youth, Popular Culture and Moral Panics: Penny Gaffs to Gangsta-Rap, 1830–1996.* New York: St. Martin's Press, 1998.

LANA THOMPSON

Petroleum Industry

The modern petroleum industry commenced in the mid-nineteenth century just as the United States began to industrialize. Although coal was the primary fuel in the industrial era, petroleum gradually supplanted coal for many purposes, and it has been an integral and essential part of the development of modern industrial society. Episodes of boom and bust, intense competition, merger and consolidation, the promise of great wealth, and governmental efforts to either regulate or control it have characterized the industry's history. In the latter part of the twentieth century, the oil industry confronted an environmental movement that sought to reduce fossil fuel consumption and prevent toxic wastes from polluting human and animal habitats.

Petroleum refers generally to crude oil and its by-products. It is popularly referred to as a fossil fuel because it derives originally from organisms such as plankton and algae compressed under high pressure over very long periods. Chemically, petroleum is a hydrocarbon composed of hydrogen and carbon compounds. Petroleum is refined into a broad range of products, including various grades of gasoline, fuel oil, and kerosene, as well as lubricating fluids and other compounds used in the manufacture of many products, including plastics, cosmetics, medicines, fertilizers, insecticides, waxes, floor coverings, road pavement, roofing materials, and synthetic fibers.

Petroleum before the Industrial Revolution

Coal fueled the initial phase of the Industrial Revolution in both Britain and the United States, and until the mid-nineteenth century, oil was not a significant source of energy, although it had served some limited purposes for many centuries. Since ancient times, petroleum in very limited quantities had been used for heating and lighting. In addition, asphaltic bitumen, a form of petroleum, was used in architecture, roadwork, medicine, and in waterproofing ship hulls as well as in baskets and mats. During the Middle Ages, soldiers sometimes used oil in projectiles to create fires used against opposing armies and their fortifications.

In North America during the colonial era, European explorers noted that Native Americans used petroleum as a curative. This practice was adopted by some Europeans who used petroleum as a treatment for headaches, rheumatism, and toothaches among other ailments. The supposed medicinal use of petroleum in the United States spawned the new breed of snake oil salesman. One of these, the canal boat operator Samuel Kier, realized an opportunity and began manufacturing and marketing Rock Oil—or oil from the ground—as a cure for a wide variety of ailments, including blindness. Although he was by no means the first such promoter, he was one of the most successful. Kier later claimed to have sold approximately 240,000 half-pint bottles of medicinal oil for $1.00 each. Kier's marketing efforts brought increased attention to petroleum and its possible uses, if not misuses.

The possibility that oil had more practical uses attracted other entrepreneurs who had greater visions. One of these was George H. Bissell, a young New York lawyer who suspected that rock oil was similar in chemical composition to coal oil (oil extracted from bitumen or bituminous shale) that was used in the mid-nineteenth century for illumination. Coal oil already had begun to displace whale oil as a fuel for illumination in large part because of the high cost of the latter. Whale oil was the first illuminating and lubricating oil to achieve widespread commercial viability.

Bissell understood that if petroleum could be refined into an illuminant, there would be a huge and ready market for it. He also believed that large underground oil supplies were located in eastern Pennsylvania. He and a partner, J. G. Eveleth, formed an investor group to help finance the purchase of oil properties at Titusville, Pennsylvania. The investors wanted assurances, and they demanded that the partners visit the land and contract for a scientific report on the oil there. Bissell asked Benjamin Silliman Jr., a Yale University professor, and Luther Atwood, a chemist and pharmaceutical manufacturer, to draft a scientific report on the oil, and the two scientists produced their report in April 1855. It confirmed Bissell's belief that oil could be used as an illuminant. Now satisfied, the New Haven investors required that the new oil firm, to be named the Pennsylvania Rock Oil Company, be incorporated in Connecticut. They formed the company on September 18, 1855, and leased 1,200 acres of land at Titusville.

James M. Townsend, president of Pennsylvania Rock Oil Company, hired Edwin L. Drake to drill for oil. Drake, currently a conductor for the New York, New Haven, and Hartford Railroad, was a 38-year-old former dry-goods salesman and express agent for the Boston and Albany Railroad; he had no real experience with oil drilling. He did accept the assignment and moved to Titusville, where Townsend sent mail addressed to "Colonel" Drake to improve Drake's standing among Titusville's residents. Drake then hired W. A. "Uncle Billy" Smith, who was an experienced salt-well operator, to drill for oil. On August 28, 1859, they struck oil at 69.5 feet.

The Titusville oil discovery marked the beginning of the modern oil industry. Crude oil, however, was not easily utilized. First, it had to be refined into a more usable form, such as kerosene for lighting. The first major kerosene refinery in the United States was formed in 1861 by D. S. Stombs and Julius Brace of Virginia, and many more followed soon thereafter. Once large volumes of kerosene became commercially available, petroleum quickly supplanted the more expensive whale oil, fortunately for the whale species, which more than likely would have been driven to extinction with continued harvesting.

By the 1870s and into the early 1880s, kerosene lamps along with gas lighting provided much of the domestic illumination for Americans. With Thomas **Edison**'s incandescent light bulb (1879) and first electric power-generating station on Pearl Street in New York City (1882), however, electric lighting quickly displaced kerosene lamps as well as gas lights. Petroleum also proved to be a very useful lubricant in a wide assortment of machinery and displaced some whale oil used for this purpose as well. For the remainder of the nineteenth century, petroleum was used primarily as a lubricant for machinery and railroads and kerosene for lighting when electricity was not available and as a general fuel oil. These uses constituted large markets for petroleum, and the industry continued to expand rapidly even though coal continued to be the primary fuel for railroads and steamships.

Industrial Organization and Monopoly

The oil industry is highly capital intensive. Immense sums of money are required to finance oil discovery, exploration, and development projects. Marketing, transportation, and distribution systems likewise require substantial sums of money as well as engineering expertise. The oil industry became a new industrial sector in the United States that emphasized scale and scope in order to maximize profits.

The burgeoning oil industry, and particularly the refining sector, attracted increasing attention from entrepreneurs. In 1863, a partnership of Maurice B. Clark, Samuel Andrews, and John D. **Rockefeller** formed the Excelsior Works refinery. Rockefeller bought out Clark in 1865, the same year in which their refinery became the biggest in Cleveland, Ohio. By 1869, the Cleveland refinery complex had become the largest in the world, and it produced one-tenth of the nation's refined petroleum output. In 1870, a variety of related partnerships were consolidated into the Standard Oil Company (Ohio) with John D. Rockefeller as president.

Rockefeller was a ruthless businessman who aggressively sought to buy out competitors. As Standard Oil grew in size and financial power, Rockefeller became more able to force competitors to sell out to him. By 1872, Standard Oil controlled virtually all of Cleveland's daily refining capacity of 12,000 barrels, or one-fourth of the industry's total refining capacity. Pittsburgh and the New York-New Jersey area also were large petroleum-refining centers in the late nineteenth century.

Standard Oil quickly became the largest oil company in the United States as it absorbed smaller firms and expanded operations. Standard Oil's corporate growth and organizational structure provided a model for other large firms. Structurally, Standard Oil developed its business first by expanding horizontally into refining and then consolidating its legal and administrative functions. Subsequently, Standard Oil integrated vertically into production as well as transportation and marketing.

Standard Oil's monopolization of the U.S. oil industry also can be viewed as an attempt to bring stability to a potentially chaotic industry as the firm was involved in numerous and ongoing attempts to bring supply and price stability to the otherwise volatile industry. One method to make the industry more stable was the pooling agreement. In 1871, Tom Scott of the Pennsylvania Railroad invited several petroleum refiners, including Standard Oil, to participate in an oil pool. Under the auspices of the South Improvement Company (SIC), the Pennsylvania planned to coordinate oil shipments with selected oil refiners. SIC members would receive rebates and commissions on their shipments, and nonmembers would pay the full published rates. After this scheme became public, disgruntled oil producers and other refiners attempted to boycott SIC members. The SIC never transacted any oil, but the scheme and other cases of rebating and cutthroat competition helped define Standard Oil's public image for years to come.

Rockefeller and Standard Oil continued to pursue control over production and prices in the late nineteenth century. One group of refiners formed the National Refiners Association in 1872 with John D. Rockefeller as president. This organization sought to make pricing agreements with the Petroleum Producers Association. The arrangement also was short-lived as new producers continued to bring more oil to the market, effectively nullifying any agreement.

Pools and associations proved inefficient and problematic, so Standard Oil then sought to control the market through the strength of its own corporate and financial power. The firm gained control over petroleum pipelines and railroad transportation routes and then could squeeze other refiners financially and force them to merge with Standard. By 1879, Standard Oil controlled more than 90 percent of total U.S. refining capacity. As the firm increased its dominance in refining operations, it began integrating vertically into petroleum pipelines and wholesale marketing. Standard Oil's monopolistic position allowed it to gain favorable rates for railroad transportation as well.

Standard Oil pioneered the trust corporate form in 1882. The Standard Oil Trust was based on a legal agreement in which trustees managed all Standard Oil properties. From 1882 through 1911, Standard Oil's Executive Committee set the trust's business policies. Following organization of the trust, Standard incorporated subsidiaries in many other states. Rockefeller also moved Standard Oil's headquarters from Cleveland into new offices at 26 Broadway in New York City.

By the end of the nineteenth century, Standard Oil was one of the largest and most highly integrated companies in the world. In 1899, Standard Oil of New Jersey became the new holding company for all of the Standard Oil divisions. Although its market share of U.S. refining capacity dropped to 82 percent in 1899, Standard Oil's vertically integrated structure gave it a strong competitive advantage. Standard Oil also then controlled about 87 percent of domestic oil production and 85 percent of the domestic petroleum marketing business.

Standard Oil's dominance of the oil industry as well the industry's increasing political and economic influence brought calls for government regulation. Ongoing problems with rebates led congress to begin imposing more federal controls over interstate business transactions. Congress created the Interstate Commerce Commission (ICC) in 1887 to regulate railroad transportation. Later, the Elkins Act (1903) and the Hepburn Act (1906) enhanced the ICC's regulatory power to prohibit rebates and impose penalties on firms that offered them. The Hepburn Act also expanded the scope of the ICC over interstate oil pipelines.

Standard Oil faced public detractors who contributed to the call for increased governmental scrutiny and more direct regulation. Ida Tarbell's *The History of Standard Oil Company* (1904) exposed Standard Oil's business practices and fomented anti–Standard Oil public opinion. Then, in 1906, the U.S. Justice Department filed an antitrust suit against Standard Oil. In 1909, a U.S. circuit court ruled that Standard Oil was in violation of antitrust laws, and in 1911, the U.S. Supreme Court heard Standard Oil's appeal. The Supreme Court affirmed the circuit court's ruling, and Standard Oil subsequently was divided into 26 separate firms. These new firms included Standard Oil of New Jersey (Exxon); Standard Oil of New York, or Socony (Mobil); Standard Oil of California, or Socal (Chevron); Standard Oil of Indiana (Amoco); Standard Oil of Ohio, or Sohio (later part of British Petroleum); Continental Oil (Conoco); and Atlantic (ARCO).

Standard Oil already had begun to lose market share in the early twentieth century for reasons beyond its control. The discovery of massive southwestern oil fields in states where Standard had little or no business presence or influence led to the emergence of powerful competitors. On January 10, 1901, Anthony F. Lucas and Al and Curt Hamill discovered oil at Spindletop, a salt dome formation south of Beaumont, Texas. John H. Galey and James M. Guffey, Pittsburgh-based wildcatters associated with the Mellon interests, financed Lucas's efforts. When his well struck oil at a depth of 1,139 feet, so-called black gold blew more than 100 feet into the air. Oil continued to flow until it was capped nine days later. The Lucas gusher produced an estimated 100,000 barrels per day and marked the beginning of the Texas oil boom as well as the decline of Pennsylvania dominance in oil. New companies that emerged after Spindletop included the Texas Company (Texaco) and Gulf Oil (later merged with Chevron).

The demand for oil, and particularly gasoline, increased rapidly during the early twentieth century. Mass production of the internal combustion, gasoline-powered automobile produced in large numbers by automobile entrepreneurs including Henry **Ford** and Louis Chevrolet created an ever-increasing demand for gasoline as a fuel and oil as a lubricant. Affordable automobiles helped create a mass market for them as well as the oil products necessary to fuel and maintain them. By **World War I**, gasoline-powered tractors, trucks, and later airplanes also increased demand, and after the war, oil-burning steamships became more common, thereby displacing coal. Oil played an extremely crucial role in the Allied victory during World War II, and after the war, **railroads** began converting from coal to diesel fuel, thereby creating more demand for petroleum. During the twentieth century, the oil ndustry continued to develop new petroleum-based, or petrochemical, products. These included a huge array of goods, from pesticides and fertilizers to cosmetics and contact lenses to plastics and rubber products, among many more.

Despite its apparent abundance, oil is a limited natural resource. Although it has been a major oil producer, the United States has relied on imported oil in increasing volumes since World War II. Imports in 1950 accounted for approximately 14 percent of total U.S. consumption; 20 percent in 1960; 23 percent in 1970 (when U.S. production peaked at 9.4 million barrels per day); 40 percent after the 1973 embargo; and about 50 percent by the mid- to late 1990s. As more easily produced oil is utilized, oil firms will spend increasing amounts of time exploring for and producing oil that is more difficult and costly to locate and produce.

Worldwide oil consumption continues to increase. New global oil discoveries of about 9 billion barrels annually were more than offset by increasing annual global consumption of 28 billion barrels (2003), about half of which represents gasoline consumption. Under the current world oil-consumption rate, some estimates indicate that human society no later than the mid-twenty-first century will have consumed approximately half of the 2.4 trillion barrels of consumable oil on earth. Estimates vary considerably regarding the actual volume of known and unknown recoverable oil reserves, but there is some concurrence that by the mid-twenty-first century world oil production will have peaked.

More oil is consumed in the United States than in any other nation. The United States consumed 20.7 million barrels of oil per day in 2004, more than half of which (12.1 million barrels per day net) came from imports. The United States has attempted to redress some of this oil-supply problem through policy. The Energy Policy Act of 1992 sought to restructure U.S. energy markets to revitalize the industry. The act mandated new energy efficiency programs, use of alternative fuels and renewable energy, research and development programs, and various tax credits and exemptions. Some oil firms claimed, however, that the Clean Air Act Amendments of 1990 and other initiatives impinged on industry business and profitability.

Most of the world's crude oil reserves are known to be located in relatively few regions. The Middle East contains about 65 percent of the worlds' crude oil reserves, and Saudi Arabia alone accounts for approximately 262 billion barrels of oil; Iran, Iraq, Kuwait, and the United Arab Emirates each claim an amount in the range of 100 billion to 130 billion barrels. Venezuela and Russia have about 50 billion to 70 billion barrels each. The United States has approximately 22 billion barrels of crude oil reserves.

By the end of the twentieth century, a new round of mergers and acquisitions brought more change to the industry. Consolidations resulted in a decline in the total number of major U.S. energy companies from 19 in 1990 to 10 in 2000. The world's largest publicly traded energy company emerged in 1999 when Exxon and Mobil merged as Exxon Mobil Corporation. Two years later, Chevron and Texaco merged. Continuing oil-market volatility, environmental constraints, and supply issues most likely will prompt additional mergers in the future.

FURTHER READING: Hidy, Ralph W., and Muriel E. Hidy. *Pioneering in Big Business, 1882–1911*. New York: Harper & Brothers, 1955; Nevins, Allan. *John D. Rockefeller: The Heroic Age of American Enterprise*. New York: Charles Scribner's, 1840; Pratt, Joseph A. *The Growth of a Refining Region*. Greenwich: JAI Press, 1980; Sampson, Anthony. *The Seven Sisters: The Great Oil Companies and the World They Shaped*. New York: Viking, 1975; Vietor, Richard H. K. *Energy Policy in America since 1945*. New York: Cambridge University Press, 1984; Williamson, Harold F., and Arnold R. Daum. *The American Petroleum Industry: The Age of Illumination, 1859–1899*. Evanston, IL: Northwestern University Press, 1959; Williamson, Harold F., and Arnold R. *The American Petroleum Industry: The Age of Energy, 1899–1959*. Evanston, IL: Northwestern University Press, 1963; Yergin, Daniel. *The Prize: The Epic Quest for Oil, Money and Power*. New York: Simon & Schuster, 1991. WEB SITE: http://www.eia.doe.gov (U.S. Energy Information Administration).

CHRISTOPHER J. CASTANEDA

Polish Lands, Industrial Revolution in

In the second half of the eighteenth century, Poland's neighbors, Austria, Prussia, and Russia, partitioned Poland three times, in 1772, 1793, and 1795, and annexed its land. Between 1772 and 1918, the Polish state formally did not exist, and thus in relation to that period of time, the term *Polish lands* is used instead of *Poland.* Austria annexed the most populous region of Galicia; Prussia annexed the more industrialized region of Silesia and agricultural Greater Poland; Russia took the largest part of central Poland. As a result of these partitions, Polish lands entered the sphere of influence of these three large economies, and their different status had a tremendous impact on the advent and progress of the Industrial Revolution. Though the economy did not attain its economic potential, it is believed that the period was important for maintaining national identity and unity. Thus, industrialization had a patriotic meaning for the Poles and was realized after Poland was officially declared an independent state by the treaties ending **World War I**.

The Austrian Part of Poland

Galicia initially fell under the liberal mercantilist policy of Austria. Administrative constraints that had been imposed on small cottage industries were removed, and technological change occurred. Due to the new borders (the old northwestern markets were cut off and southern ones opened), traditional markets for Galician goods were blocked, and competitive imports from Bavaria and Prussia entered. After the Napoleonic Wars, the economic condition of rural Galicia worsened, especially in 1844–1845, a time of poor harvests and floods. Widespread starvation occurred in 1847, and protests and riots by an impoverished rural population increased. Revolution in Vienna in 1848 made things worse. All these events sped up the beginning of the end of serfdom and the enfranchisement of peasants.

An important technological invention took place in Galicia in that time: While experimenting with oil distillation, pharmacist Ignacy Lukasiewicz extracted kerosene. He started the construction of Europe's first oil refinery in 1856, and industrial-scale oil extraction and refining began; it was the first step out of Galician poverty. A new, efficient Canadian stroke method of drilling wells was adopted in 1862, and the first steam-powered drills were used. Soon afterward, the region became a technologically advanced center of the oil industry, the first in that part of the world. Oil production expanded a hundredfold in the period before 1880, with local refineries processing 25 percent of crude oil.

The booming **petroleum industry** attracted international capital to Galicia: 17 German oil companies, 14 English ones, three Hungarian ones, two Belgian, and one Italian. English capital accounted for the largest share, with 51 percent of the total, and German capital accounted for 45 percent. The developing oil industry employed new workers and encouraged the growth of other industries. At the end of the nineteenth century, steam engines and steam-powered machines were produced in neighboring Krakow, railway coaches were produced in Sanok, and textile machines and the best-quality woolen fabrics were made in Bielsk. The local sugar industry became equipped with technologically advanced machines and produced 93 percent of the sugar to satisfy the growing demand of the Galician population.

The developing oil industry could not absorb the large number of rural workers who moved to seek a better life in urban centers, however, and although industrial Silesia did attract seasonal immigration, Galicia experienced significant emigration, mainly to Canada and Brazil.

The Prussian Part of Poland

The Prussian section of the Polish lands introduced technological changes much earlier than the other sections, and even before the partitions, the then-independent Kingdom of Poland saw industrial change. Iron ore smelting, the key Silesian industry, was a motor of this economic development. New technologies were imported, mainly from England. As early as the period from 1750 to 1760, 28 more advanced charcoal-smelting furnaces, 12 technologically modern large furnaces, and several ironworks using older technologies operated in Upper Silesia. A large governmental ironworks was built in Mala Panew in 1754 and another in Kluczbork in 1755, and a zinc- and lead-smelting works in the Tarnowskie Mountains followed.

The eighteenth-century Prussian king, Frederick II (the Great, 1740–1786), implemented many policies to support industrialization in the form of grants, loan reductions, and special preferences for business. In addition, a large government bank was established to finance initiatives in industry and trade. A new governmental ironworks, the King's Smelting Works, was built in Gliwice in 1795, with four large technologically advanced furnaces. The first coke furnace on the European Continent was installed in Upper Silesia at that time, and the use of mineral fuel became more common. Smelting works and armament factories were located near the iron and coal mines. The first steam-powered machines were used to drain mines, which enabled excavation of deeper seams of coal and ores.

After 1808, iron ore smelting slowed due to the low quality of iron, and it was not until about 1830 when the new technologies of puddling, the hot-air blast, and steam-powered machines were introduced to the industry that it started developing again. The puddling method was used for the first time in the ironworks near Katowice, introduced by a Scottish industrialist in 1828. In 1846, as many as 18 large coke furnaces, 40 charcoal furnaces, 50 rolling mills, and 191 modern coke furnaces operated in Upper Silesia. Growth accelerated following adoption of the **Bessemer process**, the first converter installed in the King's Iron Works in 1865, and of the Martin furnace, two of which were installed in 1872. In 1866, 90 percent of the ironworks used mineral fuel, 68 percent of total iron production was produced in coke furnaces in 1861, and 98 percent of bar iron was produced by the puddling method in the region in 1867. Iron mining and smelting encouraged technological changes in other industries, and significant development of the metal and machine industries occurred in the second half of the nineteenth century. Steam engines, cranes, gauge railways, conveyer belts, and separation belts were supplied. Steam engines and steam-powered machines were produced for the mines and iron and coke works in the region. Railways were built across the entire region, inducing technological changes in the methods of transportation.

Starting in 1789 and throughout the period of the Napoleonic Wars, the prices of farm products rose due to the increased demand for grain by the belligerents in Europe. The demand for food stimulated technological change in Greater Poland's agriculture, and both agriculture and the food-processing industry adopted more mechanized techniques. The famous machine works, Cegielski, in Poznan was built in 1855 to supply the farm sector with tools and machinery. An economic association and land credit associations were established to support the dissemination of technological knowledge and progress in agriculture.

The Russian Part of Poland

In 1815, the Congress of Vienna established the Polish Kingdom under the rule of the czar of Russia. It consisted of most of the Polish territory formerly held by Prussia and Austria as well as Russian Poland. A new constitution started the process of abolishing serfdom and preparing for the later enfranchising of peasants. The implementation of Napoleonic civil and commercial codes meant that benefits derived from property, and not only birth. Although the new government was politically constrained, it continued to be active in the economy. The Polish Kingdom took advantage of its geopolitical location: Austrian and Prussian goods faced a tariff barrier, but local goods enjoyed almost free access to the vast Russian markets. Governmental policy, represented by the very active Treasury Ministry under Xavery Drucki-Lubecki, attracted a large influx of foreign industrialists, craftsmen, and qualified workers. It granted loans, free housing, benefits, and privileges for immigrants from nearby Silesia, Saxony, and Bohemia as well as France, Belgium, and England. The government provided a large market for many different goods. The Bank of Poland was established in 1828 with government funds to provide loans for various economic activities, and it followed protectionist policies for many years. Also, landowners were interested in the development of industry as it provided a large outlet for their agricultural goods, chiefly wool and flax for the linen industry.

The textile industry became the key one: It utilized the growing free rural labor and an increasing volume of marketable agricultural goods. The Lodz region was traditionally a textile center, previously dominated by old-style cottage industry. A technological acceleration occurred in 1842, however, following the resumption of exports of textile machines from England and after the subsequent removal of tariffs between the Polish Kingdom and Russia in 1851. The textile industry consisted of three branches: cotton, wool, and linen. The cotton industry became the largest and the most efficient as it was based on the best available technology, meeting a rapidly growing demand for cotton goods. The first fully mechanized spinning factory was built in 1839, using 7,584 spindles. The most dynamic technological changes were introduced in the period from 1865 to 1880, when the number of spindles increased from 190,000 to 540,000 and the number of power looms rose from 500 to 10,000. Large, technologically advanced factories were built; for example, Karol Scheibler's factory with self-actors had 158,000 spindles in Lodz in the 1880s. In the wool sector, the first power looms were installed much later, after 1865, but became more common in the 1870s, and by 1880, 55 percent of total wool output was made on power looms. The largest linen factory, Zyrardow, employed as many as 8,000 workers, and its manager invented and installed the first spinning machine for flax.

The capacity of textile machines increased from 851 to 25,833 horsepower from 1864 to 1888, accounting for 51 percent of all industrial capacity in the Polish Kingdom. The iron-smelting sector was second with 10,294 horsepower, or 20 percent of the total capacity. This sector replaced the use of charcoal by mineral fuel on a large scale. The puddling and hot-air blast technologies were adopted in the 1830s; a Bessemer converter was installed in the Warsaw Iron Works and a Martin furnace in the Bank Iron Works in 1878. By 1887, 19 of 24 large furnaces used the hot-air blast technology to produce 94 percent of iron; by 1890, mineral fuel was used to produce 65 percent of the iron and 96 percent of the steel. The most rapid technological change in mining took place between 1864 and 1880, when the capacity of the steam engines in use increased from 400 horsepower to 5,126 horsepower. The sugar industry benefited the most of all the food-processing industries, using 288 steam engines and 340 steam-powered machines with a total capacity of 3,360 horsepower, or almost half of the total capacity in food processing, in the 1880s. It used 13 percent of the country's total machine capacity, and its level of technology equaled that of Western Europe.

The industrialization of the Polish Kingdom was based initially on Western European technologies, but as more and more local machine and metal works were built, it became more self-sufficient. The Warsaw region was the center of the metal and machine industries. At the beginning of the twentieth century, these industries employed 33,000 workers, 55 percent of the total number of workers in the metal and metallurgy industries of the entire country. For example, the Warsaw machine factory, owned by the joint stock company Lilpop, Rau, and Loewenstein, was technologically advanced and one of the largest factories in the entire Russian Empire. The Rudzki Company was the largest metal factory in the Warsaw region, employing 9,000 workers in 1914. Only 61 Warsaw factories used steam power in 1867, but 332 did in 1903. Warsaw then looked like a forest of chimneys, because every factory was required to build at least one. The dynamic development of the city caused a rapid increase of the price of building land, so new factories were built around the city (where labor was cheap), creating a large urban agglomeration. The urbanization process was accompanied by the development of railways, and the rail network was built selectively to connect industrial centers with their markets.

The developing banking system provided financial support for industrialization, and eight large banks were established in the Polish Kingdom. The largest in Warsaw were the Commercial Bank (established in 1870) and Discount Bank (1871), and another large bank was the Commercial Bank in Lodz (1872). Most of these banks belonged to the well-developed European network.

Growing trade triggered the demand for new machines, semimanufactured goods, and new materials, which encouraged production specialization, and a trend toward the concentration of industry occurred soon afterward. Four large industrial centers emerged in the Polish Kingdom: Lodz, Warsaw, Sosnowiecko-Czestochowski, and Staropolski. The Lodz region produced one-third of the total industrial output of the Polish Kingdom and employed more than one-third of the labor force; the Warsaw region produced one-fourth of it and employed slightly under one-fourth; the Sosnowiecko-Czestochowski region, being the best equipped, accounted for more than 40 percent of machine capacity; whereas the Staropolski region lagged but was on the verge of prosperity after 1918 and the establishment of an independent Poland. In the period from 1870 to 1913, the rate of employment in the Polish Kingdom doubled. The capacity of industrial machines and engines increased more than 50 times, and output increased tenfold. In particular, coal output increased 20 times, iron output increased 15-fold, and steel output rose by a factor of 36. The rate of growth of the Polish Kingdom was significant, reducing the gap between it and the more developed Western European countries, and overtaking Russia and Austrian Galicia.

Workers' wages were low, with women and children working at the lowest wages, but permanent employment was important. There were frequent social conflicts and strikes. Because the standard of living was better, industrial centers experienced a demographic explosion. For example, in the period from 1850 to 1913, the population of Lodz increased from 18,000 to 506,000. Population increase created a large market for consumer goods: In 1913, the per capita consumption of domestic cotton in the Polish Kingdom was three times higher than in Russia and almost the same as in France or Germany.

A rapid process of the concentration of industry in fewer hands was beginning to be apparent at the end of the nineteenth century. In the main industries (textiles, iron smelting, and mining), large companies, those employing more than 500 workers, dominated the economy. The largest ones were joint-stock companies. Some sectors of industry became monopolies at that time, and only the sugar industry remained dispersed.

In conclusion, although manual cottage industry marked large parts of the economy, and the agricultural sector still retained its importance, the Polish lands were taking the initial steps toward the widespread industrialization that occurred following Poland's independence after **World War I**.

FURTHER READING: Jezierski, Andrzej, and Cecylia Leszczynska. *Economic History of Poland.* Warsaw: Kent Text, 2003; Kostrowicka, Irena, Zbigniew Landau, and Jan Tomaszewski. *Economic History of Poland.* Vols. 19 and 20. Warsaw: Ksiazka i Wiedza, 1975; Pus, Wieslaw. *Industry of the Polish Kingdom in the Period of 1870–1914: Problems of Structure and Concentration.* Lodz, Poland: Lodz University Publishers, 1984; Skodlarski, Janusz. *Economic History of Poland, Outline.* Warsaw: Science Publishers of PWN, 2005.

HELENA SINORACKA

Port of New York

During most of the nineteenth and twentieth centuries, New York City was the largest city in the United States and, for most of this period, the nation's leading seaport. The city's excellent harbor, large industrial base, and role as terminus for major **railroads** made it the leading destination and point of departure for most shipping lines serving the Atlantic coast. By the end of the nineteenth century, more ships would enter and leave the Port of New York than the combined total of ships using the next three largest seaports. By the end of the twentieth century, however, technological innovations had caused virtually all commercial shipping operations to abandon New York City. The development of containerization caused cargo ships to move their operations to container terminals in New Jersey, and the development of passenger jets eliminated almost all the business of transoceanic passenger liners.

Port of New York in the Early 1800s

During the early American colonial period, the ports of Boston and Philadelphia initially had more shipping operations than New York (which was then limited to

Manhattan Island). New York had several important natural advantages, however, including an excellent deepwater harbor and its central position along the Atlantic coast. In addition, the Hudson and Mohawk River valleys provided an easy, low-elevation route through the Appalachian Mountains, and the later construction of the Erie Canal in the early 1800s provided a direct water route to the Great Lakes.

Britain's recognition of American independence had removed imperial restrictions forbidding settlement of Indian lands of the Northwest Territory (now Ohio, Indiana, Illinois, Michigan, and Wisconsin). The new (non-Indian) settlement of the Northwest Territory made it part of the hinterland of the Port of New York and encouraged the economic growth of New York City. By the time of the census of 1810, New York's population surpassed that of Philadelphia; thereafter it remained the nation's largest city.

British colonial policies also had been designed to inhibit the growth of American manufacturing, and even until the War of 1814, almost all coal used in the United States was imported from Britain. Afterward, the development of coalfields in eastern Pennsylvania spurred U.S. industrialization. Although Philadelphia was closer to the coal mines, new canals (Morris, Delaware and Hudson, and Delaware and Raritan) and then new railroads transported larger volumes of coal to New York City. Its growing population and increasing number of factories caused a steadily expanding demand for the new fuel.

New York's growing number of residents, factories, and other businesses also made it a magnet for shipping operations. The port's competitive advantage over other U.S. **seaports** also grew as a result of three innovations after the War of 1812. The first was the introduction of scheduled packet service between New York and Britain. Previously, ships had waited for a full load of cargo before sailing. The new service involved ships departing on a fixed schedule, which attracted many new customers. The second factor was the construction of the **Erie Canal** (opened in 1825), which provided a cheap means of transportation between the coast and the nation's interior. The third reason was establishment of a three-way routing of cotton from southern states to England via New York.

By the 1820s, New York shipping operations (which extended into the Brooklyn waterfront) were double that of Boston, the nation's next largest port city. The port's lead increased as New York became the nation's largest manufacturing city with the rise of the factory system.

The trend continued with the construction of railroads. New York's central coastal position and relatively easy access for railroads to the Great Lakes attracted more railroad traffic to New York than to Boston, Philadelphia, or other coastal cities. Eventually, a total of nine railroad lines (New York Central; Erie; Pennsylvania; Jersey Central; Reading; New York, Susquehanna, and Western; New York and Ontario; Lehigh Valley; and Baltimore and Ohio) made New York their terminus. New York's large number of railroad facilities, in turn, attracted more ocean shipping operations than any other U.S. city.

Development of Railroad-Ship Facilities

Although New York had excellent advantages that made it a leading seaport, it also had a strong disadvantage. For almost all of the nineteenth century (until united with Brooklyn in 1898), New York meant Manhattan, and Manhattan was an island separated from the continental United States by the mile-wide Hudson River. Only one railroad (the New York Central routed along the Hudson River until it crossed a bridge at Poughkeepsie) provided a direct land link with the nation's interior. All the other railroads terminated in New Jersey or Staten Island.

Ships docking at the Port of New York (essentially the marine terminals along the Manhattan and Brooklyn waterfronts) carried cargoes and passengers with destinations or origins in the continental United States, rather than New York City itself. The result was that the Port of New York was, in effect, two ports. Major ships docked in Manhattan or Brooklyn, and although part of their cargoes came from, and went to, these locations, the large remainder was reloaded onto a fleet of barges, lighters, and car floats and sent across the river to railheads in New Jersey for carriage to and from the rest of the nation.

Initially, the cargoes were carried in barges pulled by steamers and tugboats. During the mid-1800s, certain railroads began using new vessels called car floats. These were barges containing rails upon their decks, so several railroad cars could be rolled upon them and then carried across the Hudson River

Further Innovations

The Port of New York also changed in response to changes in ships' technology, particularly the development of larger and faster metal **steamships** that gradually replaced wooden sailing ships. The steamships were more expensive to run, and owners demanded quicker turnaround time, which required more efficient loading and unloading. This led to the construction of warehouses on the many long and narrow finger piers that ringed the waterfronts of Manhattan and Brooklyn. The evolution of piers containing large warehouses, however, limited their use to steamships because large sailing ships with wide masts could not come close enough to the shedded piers to load and unload cargoes.

The larger ships required deeper waters, which led to expensive channel dredging. In the mid-1800s, the U.S. Army Corps of Engineers began a process of dredging channels through the series of submerged sandbars that ringed the entrance to New York Bay. They started with 20-foot cuts and then expanded them over the next century to 30 feet and 40 feet.

The larger ships also required longer piers as ships grew longer. By the late 1800s, the largest passenger liners were approaching 1,000 feet in length. The *Titanic*, which had been planning to dock in New York after its initial transatlantic voyage, was 883 feet long.

Important innovations of the late 1800s that would alter the form of the Port of New York and other major seaports were the development of specialized ships designed to transport a particular type of bulk cargo and of complementary specialized dock facilities. The process started with the development of colliers, specialized ships designed to carry only coal, in the early 1800s. The trend accelerated in the late 1800s, with the development of iron-ore ships and docks in the Great Lakes and then with petroleum tankers for transatlantic routes.

The specialized port facilities usually took up extensive space, and the petroleum ones were efficiently located next to petroleum processing and storage facilities. Most of these were located in New Jersey and on Staten Island for direct connections to the nation's interior. These facilities were mechanized and required much less labor, but more skilled labor, and were very capital-intensive.

At the time, the diversion of bulk cargoes from the waterfronts of Manhattan and Brooklyn were not noticed, because they were counterbalanced by the constantly increasing amounts of break-bulk cargoes, which continued to be handled at Manhattan and Brooklyn piers.

Wartime Mobilization, Unionization, and the Port of New York Authority

The onset of **World War I** initially caused a decline in shipping operations in general and at the Port of New York in particular. Britain and its allies set up a naval blockade against Germany and Austria. The enemy responded by starting a submarine campaign that attacked ships carrying cargoes to Britain and its allies.

After the U.S. entry into the war in 1917, the federal government took over the U.S. railroads. The government permitted union organization of railroad workers, including those manning the fleet of hundreds of barges and car floats that carried cargoes across the Hudson River between New York and New Jersey. At the end of the war, frequent strikes led to disruptions in cross-Hudson shipments and prompted New York and New Jersey to cooperate on the construction of the Holland Tunnel, the first of several trans-Hudson bridges and tunnels that provided alternate routes between New York and the continental United States.

The end of the war also was followed by the establishment of a bistate Port of New York Authority (PNYA), composed of several commissioners and modeled after the Port of London Authority. The PNYA, however, had limited power over the actual waterfront facilities, and its attempts at coordinated development were strongly opposed by most of the railroads serving the port. The PYNA soon shifted its focus to developing bridges and tunnels to cross the Hudson River as well as nascent airplane facilities.

After the war, devastated economic conditions in Europe combined with a growing atmosphere of economic nationalism and attempted self-sufficiency. The prewar consensus of free trade was almost entirely abandoned, which led to a sharp decline in international trade and shipping. Shipping operations at the Port of New York declined somewhat, although a growing trade in petroleum products (prompted by the development of refineries along the Arthur Kill between Staten Island and New Jersey) mostly offset the decline in traditional break-bulk cargoes. The 1929 economic crash and subsequent **Great Depression** further lessened international trade and shipping. The Port of New York operations further declined, as did most of the nation's other ports.

The outbreak of World War II temporarily disrupted international shipping after the Germans began submarine warfare. In response, the U.S. Navy adopted a convey system, which channeled almost all transatlantic shipping through the Port of New York. Its shipping operations revived to match levels of the 1920s.

After the war, another series of strikes by railroad workers and longshoremen continually disrupted port operations. In addition, members of organized crime became leaders of many longshoremen's unions. Theft and pilferage of cargoes became a serious issue, and insurance firms estimated that such losses amounted to as much as one-fifth the value of cargoes handled on the New York waterfront. The problem was popularized by the 1954 film *On the Waterfront* and led to the creation of a bistate New York Waterfront Commission of New York Harbor designed to fight organized crime.

The Creation of the Port of New York and New Jersey

Despite losses due to waterfront theft and strikes, the first decade after World War II saw port operations increase to major new levels, largely due to shipping for European reconstruction and revival of the U.S. economy. More and more of the port's cargoes were being handled at New Jersey, rather than at Manhattan or Brooklyn.

The PNYA and the city of Newark negotiated an agreement whereby the Port Authority would take over and modernize the operations of Port Newark in 1948. New Jersey began constructing the New Jersey Turnpike in 1949, along a route that gave Port Newark immediate access. This gave trucks carrying cargoes to and from Port Newark easy access to the port's hinterland. The Port Authority soon expanded Port Newark's operations into the adjacent city of Elizabeth, creating Port Newark-Elizabeth, which covered two square miles.

Trucking entrepreneur Malcom McLean chose Port Newark as the site of the first shipment of cargo containers in 1956. During the early 1960s, McLean and the Port Authority collaborated on the design and construction of the world's first specialized container terminal at Port Newark-Elizabeth. Containerization eventually evolved into the dominant form of shipping after 1966. This involved shipment of cargoes in standardized containers, with specialized container ships and container terminals characterized by giant cranes and large areas for temporary storage of containers. These required much less labor but were very much more capital-intensive and energy-intensive and were much faster and efficient than traditional waterfront loading practices and facilities. By the early 1970s, almost every shipping line had left Manhattan and Brooklyn for new container terminals at Port Newark-Elizabeth, Port Jersey in Bayonne, or Howland Hook in Staten Island.

In recognition of this spatial change in operations, the Port Authority changed its name in 1972 to the Port Authority of New York and New Jersey. Almost all of the port's shipping operations were now at New Jersey, although the city of New York forced the Port Authority to subsidize the continued operations of undersized and unprofitable minicontainer ports in Brooklyn to the tune of several millions of dollars per year. Despite this expensive subsidization, many New Yorkers still resented the Port Authority and blamed it for the abandonment of the New York waterfront.

FURTHER READING: Albion, Robert Greenhalgh, and Jennie Barnes Pope. *The Rise of the Port of New York, 1815–1860.* Repr. ed. Hamden, CT: Archon Books, 1961; Bone, Kevin, ed. *The New York Waterfront: Evolution and Building Culture of the Port and Harbor.* New York: Monacelli Press, 2003; Buttenwieser, Ann L. *Manhattan Water-Bound: Manhattan's Waterfront from the Seventeenth Century to the Present.* Syracuse, NY: Syracuse University Press, 1999; Condit, Carl W. *The Port of New York.* 2 vols. Chicago: University of Chicago Press, 1980–1981; Doig, Jameson W. *Empire on the Hudson: Entrepreneurial Vision and Political Power at the Port of New York Authority.* New York: Columbia University Press, 2001; Matteson, George. *Tugboats of New York: An Illustrated History.* New York: New York University Press, 2005. WEB SITES: http://www.gothamcenter.org/festival/2001/confpapers/marshall.pdf; http://www.nan.usace.army.mil/harbor/index.htm; http://www.panynj.gov/; http://www.southstseaport.org/.

STEPHEN G. MARSHALL

Poverty

See Wealth and Poverty in the Industrial Revolution

Progressive Era

The Progressive Era was a time of remarkable reform in the United States. Beginning around 1890 and lasting until approximately 1920, the era was shaped by campaigns against political corruption, industrial exploitation, urban poverty, and vice. Numerous reformers sought help from politicians, successfully winning legislation that improved workplace conditions for employees, banned the sale of alcohol, protected women and children from immorality and workplace exploitation, and preserved the natural environment and wildlife. Other reformers sought political power themselves, ultimately using their influence to improve municipal conditions for ordinary people. Some reformers were highly moralistic and passionate, seeking to shock Americans into demanding change from employers and politicians. Others were university-trained so-called experts who documented and offered hardheaded solutions to a wide-range of economic, social, and political problems. In light of this broad array of causes and participants, historians have debated and discussed the precise meaning of the Progressive Era more fervently and thoroughly than virtually any other period in U.S. history.

Reformers

The most influential progressive reformers were white, middle-class Protestants. Journalists, scholars, religious leaders, and social workers responded anxiously to increases in immigration, the growth of the urban population, and the seemingly uncontrollable expansion of industrialization. Immigrants from Eastern and Southern Europe settled in the nation's burgeoning cities, where they lived in run-down homes and worked in grimy factories. Working conditions were generally difficult; most labored long hours with little pay. Additionally, few factory owners approached workplace safety systematically. Strikes by workers often failed. Living conditions also were troubling; many lived in crowded, unsanitary tenement homes.

Several muckraking journalists led the way in raising the nation's consciousness about these societal ills, spotlighting expressions of poverty, social inequality, dishonest businessmen, and the extreme concentration of wealth in the hands of few. Seeking to alarm middle-class audiences about the rampant poverty in New York City's Lower East Side, Jacob Riis's *How the Other Half Live* (1890) included dramatic pictures showcasing the hardships of tenement life. Lincoln Steffens wrote popular articles about citywide corruption, culminating in *The Shame of the Cities* (1904), whereas socialist-novelist Upton Sinclair's *The Jungle* (1906) exposed the plight of meatpacking workers and the unhealthful condition of factory-processed meat. In several magazine articles, Ida Tarbell noted the unscrupulous business decisions made by the nation's most powerful tycoons. Many muckraking writers denounced leaders of big business as robber barons.

Middle-class white women were the most influential progressive reformers. Individuals such as Jane Addams, Ellen Gates Star, and Frances Kelley sought to improve living and working conditions while also expanding educational opportunities for immigrants and African Americans. Such women worked intimately with those whom they sought to help. Jane Addams was an especially influential reformer; she opened Hull House, a settlement home modeled on London's Toynbee Hall, in Chicago in 1889. Thousands of working-class neighborhood residents enjoyed Hull

House's cafeteria, gymnasium, libraries, and meeting spaces. Following the opening of Hull House, hundreds of settlement homes emerged in urban areas throughout the country. Dozens of settlement-home activists like Jane Addams sponsored adult education programs, lobbied politicians, and promoted public health. Following the work done by settlement-house volunteers, a number of women engaged in the new occupation of social work.

Women also were highly active in national reform organizations. They served in leadership positions and as rank-and-file activists in the Woman's Christian Temperance Union (WCTU), the Women's Trade Union League (WTUL), the National Consumers League (NCL), and the National Conference of Charities and Corrections (NCCC). Through these organizations, women crusaded against alcohol abuse, lobbied for suffrage rights, and walked picket lines demanding greater fairness for workers and consumers.

City and State Reforms

Several cities became bastions of Progressive reform in large part because of the activities of reform-oriented mayors. Cleveland's Tom Johnson, Detroit's Hazen Pingree, and Toledo's Samuel "Golden Rule" Jones were intrepid fighters for greater public control over utilities. All three political leaders challenged private business interests for what they believed was the good of the community. By the second decade of the twentieth century, a growing number of mayors helped make electricity, gas, and water more financially accessible to ordinary people. On the eve of **World War I**, a majority of waterworks were owned by municipalities, and cities owned more than 25 percent of urban-based electric plants.

The political landscape also changed considerably on the statewide level. During the 1910s, a number of states implemented the referendum and allowed its citizens the right to recall politicians. Such reforms made political leaders more accountable to voters. Furthermore, a handful of states prohibited the sale of alcohol and allowed women the right to vote. Several states also approved labor laws. Following the Supreme Court's *Muller v. Oregon* ruling (1908), numerous states passed laws regulating the number of hours women were permitted to work. By 1912, a majority of states had enacted basic child labor laws. Several employed workplace inspectors to ensure compliance with labor regulations. One of the first inspectors was Florence Kelley. A former Hull House volunteer, Kelley served as the chief workplace examiner for the state of Illinois from 1893 to 1896.

National Changes

Municipal and statewide reforms coincided with political changes nationally. Republican President Theodore Roosevelt was one of the most high-profile reformers. Born into an upper-class family in New York, Roosevelt was a former police commissioner, assistant secretary of the Navy, New York governor, and friend of muckraking journalist Lincoln Steffens. As president, Roosevelt challenged trusts, passed laws protecting consumers from contaminated food, set aside land for parks, and regulated railway companies. But Roosevelt was far from a socialist. In labor-management disputes, he took a middle-of-the-road approach, promoting the interests of both labor and capital. In 1902, during a massive anthracite coal strike, Roosevelt approved the formation of a commission to help settle the conflict. Following the strike, miners earned pay raises but failed to achieve recognition for their union, the United Mine Workers of America (UMWA).

Americans had to wait out the presidential years of Republican William Howard Taft before another progressive leader emerged. Elected president in 1912, Democrat Woodrow Wilson continued the reform tradition made famous by Theodore Roosevelt. In 1913, Wilson created the Federal Reserve Act (establishing the Federal Reserve System as the nation's central bank) and the Department of Labor (DOL), appointing William B. Wilson, a former UMWA leader, as head. Also in 1913, the Seventeenth Amendment to the Constitution transferred the election of U.S. senators from state legislators to the voters, one of the most significant advances of democracy in U.S. history.

In 1917, the president sent U.S. troops to fight in World War I, believing idealistically that U.S. military intervention in the European conflict would end future wars and promote democracy internationally. In return for organized labor's promise not to strike during the war, Wilson recognized trade unions as legitimate collective-bargaining entities. In 1918, he created the National War Labor Board, which consisted of members of both labor and business, in an effort to create industrial efficiency and workplace stability. Some labor leaders, including **American Federation of Labor** (AF of L) chief Samuel **Gompers**, celebrated this period as an era of industrial democracy.

The immediate postwar period represented a time of both victory and defeat for progressive activists. In 1919, temperance advocates celebrated the Eighteenth Amendment to the Constitution, which banned the sale and consumption of alcohol. A year later, in 1920, women won national suffrage rights. There were signs, however, that the postwar period constituted the decline of progressivism. In international affairs, Woodrow Wilson failed to win congressional approval for U.S. participation in the League of Nations. Domestically, a massive strike wave pitted workers and employers against one another in industrial cities and towns throughout much of the country. Yet in the 1930s, a number of the social welfare programs promoted by some Progressive Era politicians and grassroots reformers, including restrictions in hours and minimum-wage laws, became national policy.

Advances in education around the turn of the century complemented official political changes. Several research universities, including Johns Hopkins, Harvard, Clark, Columbia, and Chicago, began offering advanced degrees and churning out innovative scholars. Developments in the social sciences, including economics, psychology, and sociology, posed a challenge to traditional views on wage labor, the role of the state in the economy, and childhood education. Richard Ely, one of the founders of the American Economic Association (AEA) and an influential Johns Hopkins professor, attacked laissez-faire capitalism and supported unionization, and John Dewey and his mentor, psychologist G. Stanley Hall, pioneered changes in early childhood education.

Some university-trained academics conducted both paid and voluntary work outside of the academic environment. John Dewey toiled alongside Jane Addams at Hull House, where he practiced his educational methods with neighborhood children. Fredrick Howe and Edward Bemis, two Johns Hopkins–educated economists, worked as experts under Tom Johnson in Cleveland, Ohio, during his mayoral years. Howe lived briefly in a Cleveland settlement home, and Edward Bemis served as Cleveland's waterworks superintendent.

Urban areas benefited from the work of Progressive Era architects. Architect Daniel Burnham impressed thousands who visited the World's Columbian Exposition in Chicago in 1893. As chief designer of the exposition, known as the White City, Burnham won praise for starting the City Beautiful Movement. Burnham helped design sections of several cities, including Cleveland (1903) and San Francisco (1905). Urban park designer Fredrick Law Olmsted, famous for his majestic work in the late nineteenth century, continued designing massive urban parks in cities throughout the nation during the early twentieth century. Inspired by both nature and technology, architect Frank Lloyd Wright designed hundreds of impressive structures, including prairie-style homes and magnificent buildings in Oak Park, Illinois, and Buffalo, New York.

FURTHER READING: Finegold, Kenneth. *Experts and Politicians: Reform Challenges to Machine Politics in New York, Cleveland, and Chicago.* Princeton, NJ: Princeton University Press, 1995; Hofstadter, Richard. *The Age of Reform: From Bryan to F.D.R.* New York: Vintage Books, 1955; Kolko, Gabriel. *The Triumph of Conservatism: A Reinterpretation of American History.* Chicago: Quadrangle Books, 1967; McCartin, Joseph A. *Labor's Great War: The Struggle for Industrial Democracy and the Origins of Modern American Labor Relations, 1912–1921.* Chapel Hill: University of North Carolina Press, 1997; Rogers, Daniel T. *Atlantic Crossings: Social Politics in a Progressive Age.* Cambridge, MA: Harvard University Press, 1998; Stromquist, Shelton. *Re-Inventing "The People": The Progressive Movement, the Class Problem, and the Origins of Modern Liberalism.* Urbana: University of Illinois Press, 2006; Wiebe, Robert H. *The Search for Order, 1877–1920.* New York: Hill and Wang, 1967.

CHAD PEARSON

Protestant Ethic and the Industrial Revolution

The Industrial Revolution resulted, at least in part, from a coming together of capitalist methods and continuous technological innovation in manufacturing. The thesis that a type of Protestantism stimulated capitalism, the first element of the two, has a long history. A similar thesis argues that the same type of Protestantism also encouraged empirical (observation-based) science and practical education, thereby stimulating technological innovation. As the Industrial Revolution matured late in the nineteenth century, however, the value system that supported industrial capitalism ceased to rely on religion. For its part, Protestant support of industrial capitalism ceased to be unanimous.

The Industrial Revolution began in the mid-eighteenth century in Britain when a series of innovations transformed the textile industry. Water-powered or steam-powered machinery was applied to spinning and weaving, greatly increasing output and quality. As larger machines were integrated with larger labor forces and power supplies and as comparable changes occurred in other industries, such changes called on the organizational and financial skills of capitalists.

The Industrial Revolution also required continuous innovation of productive technology. Although early innovation did not necessarily require high-order science, it required an interest in practical problems and an ability to conceptualize a problem, the ability to learn from observation and experimentation, mechanical and technical skills, and ability to formulate mechanical solutions. In support of manufacturing, civil-engineering skills also were required to enhance transportation and urban infrastructure.

It is possible, if unlikely, that the capitalistic and technological competence needed for an Industrial Revolution emerged roughly simultaneously by coincidence. The Protestant-ethic thesis, however, proposes that both capitalism and science were promoted by the rise of seventeenth-century Calvinist culture in those places that subsequently were the first to experience the Industrial Revolution.

The Protestant Ethic and Early Capitalism

In a pair of renowned journal articles (1904–1905), the German sociologist Max Weber presented the thesis that Calvinist Protestantism, during the seventeenth century, put the moral force behind what ultimately would develop into modern capitalism. Weber agreed that love of profit and some capitalistic and financial techniques had existed in pre-Protestant and non-Protestant cultures. He denied claiming that Calvinism was either a necessary or sufficient condition for capitalism. Rather, he suggested that Calvinism was equivalent to a catalyst, whose theology and moral values vastly speeded capitalist development.

A century-long literature has debated Weber's thesis without reaching a verdict. Various researchers have raised questions such as the following. Can the Weber thesis convincingly explain apparent exceptions to the Protestant-capitalist link? Did the antiaristocratic business class in Britain naturally gravitate to dissenting Protestant churches, bringing their ideology with them, rather than having their values formed by the churches? Did Puritanism simply stimulate existing trends, rather than introducing them? The debate continues, with recent research seeking statistical evidence that modern cultural values, similar to those once associated with Calvinism, have measurable impacts on economic development.

Calvinist theology had several elements that supported the values of capitalism. In Calvinism, God's salvation of humans was not mediated by church or clergy or earned by pious deeds. Salvation was given, as God chose, directly to individuals. This central doctrine simultaneously devalued religious intermediaries and authorities and exalted the individual. It additionally placed a strong expectation on the individual, for the elect of God normally would be known by lives that glorified God. Glorifying God in upright living would never earn salvation, which always was held to be a divine gift, but God's elect would naturally find upright living to be congenial.

Although much of this was shared by other Protestants, the uniquely Calvinist doctrine was that God's grace was bestowed only on some, the elect. One consequence of this doctrine (not emphasized by Weber) was a sense of mission to reform society. The elect believed themselves obliged to enforce God's laws on all of society, a tendency very evident in societies dominated by Calvinistic Puritans (e.g., Oliver Cromwell's era in England or the New England colonies). Weber mostly emphasized, however, that the doctrine of election made many Calvinists anxious whether they were indeed among the elect. Seeking to relieve anxiety, Weber reasoned, they would seek signs that they really were among the elect, signs such as a life that glorified God.

The stereotypical anxious Calvinist of Weber's theory needed some way to live a life glorifying God and in that life find some assurance of election. Protestantism largely devalued formal religious institutions and religious duties, however, closing religious service as a channel to glorify God. The major channel for most Calvinists was a person's work in the everyday world. In fact, the English Puritans, who were Weber's favorite example, believed that God assigned a vocation to each person, thus sanctifying work. To truly glorify God through one's vocation, one should labor with diligence, honesty, thrift, and systematic (or rationalized) effort. Weber called these the ascetic virtues of the Protestant ethic. Finally, success in a vocation might allay anxiety about one's salvation.

According to Weber, pre-Protestant capitalism and commerce had been content to operate without great intensity in cultures that devalued economic activity. After the Calvinists energized it, capitalism became known for its unremitting rationalizing of the productive process, its drive for ever greater efficiency, its constant search for economic opportunities, and its willingness to innovate. In the extreme, production was valued as an end in itself, rather than for the benefits it could provide to people. Once such capitalism succeeded in a culture, capitalist values and habits would become entrenched even if Protestant doctrines were to change or people ceased to follow the faith.

Protestantism and Technology

The Industrial Revolution also required continuous technological innovation in manufacturing. Attitudes and values friendly to science and technology, some argue, also were linked to Calvinism. Puritanism reached its zenith in England in the seventeenth century about the same time as modern science made its initial, large advances there. The intervening decades before the Industrial Revolution began may have permitted the spread of technological competence.

The case for a Calvinism-science link was made by U.S. sociologist Robert K. Merton (first in 1938, again in 1970). Merton argued that English Puritans (and German Pietists, who were Protestants sharing certain traits with the Puritans) strongly valued empirical science and produced large proportions of scientists from their ranks. One may argue that a bias toward empirical science is logically consistent with fundamental Protestant premises. Protestantism, as noted previously, devalued authority in matters of religion; it replaced authority with the individual's direct understanding of God often through personal interpretation of scripture. The parallel of this principle in the study of nature would be the rejection of ancient authorities, such as Aristotle, and the resort to direct observation, or empiricism.

One stimulus to empiricism, argued Merton and others, came from belief that God was revealed in his works (nature), not only in scripture. The seventeenth-century Puritan confidently believed that the lessons of nature would complement the revealed truths of scripture. A second reason for the appeal of science was the Puritan sense of vocation, which naturally served the welfare of oneself and of fellow humans. Science and empirical knowledge were of utility in achieving this end.

These tendencies also influenced the Protestant approach to education, according to Merton. English Puritanism and European Pietism valued practical and empirically oriented learning over speculative reasoning or authoritative tradition. A curriculum heavily weighted toward science, developed by Peter Ramus in the sixteenth century, was widely adopted by Puritan and Pietist universities. Below the university level, these groups also favored technical studies, as shown in statistics quoted by Merton. Late in the seventeenth century, John Amos Comenius, educational philosopher and exiled bishop of the pre-Reformation Protestant Unitas

Fratrum, advocated pragmatic and utilitarian approaches to education. His ideas, too, were well accepted in Puritan England.

Merton also reported the results of many studies showing that scientists of the seventeenth century were disproportionately of Calvinist backgrounds. He argued that working scientists in the newly created Royal Society in Britain often were Puritans and interpreted their work in religious terms that far exceeded what mere lip service to religion would have required. He also cited studies covering Continental Europe that showed a correlation of scientists and Protestant populations.

Post-Protestant Ethics and the Late Industrial Revolution

By the late nineteenth century, the matured industrial economy found moral support from sources other than religion. The maturing discipline of political economy, along with Enlightenment legal doctrines and political thought, had coalesced as laissez-faire doctrine. Laissez-faire was a mixture of economic laws, legal doctrines, and moral concepts that provided a favorable interpretation of industrial capitalism. Even newer ideas, such as Darwinian evolution and natural selection, were put in the service of industrial capitalism as social Darwinists (e.g., Herbert Spencer or William Graham Sumner) promoted the value of competitiveness, economic freedom, private property rights, freedom of contract, the beneficial effects of inequality, and so on. Industrialist Henry **Ford** forcefully inculcated disciplined work values in his immigrant workforce.

For their part, Protestants of the late nineteenth century were divided in opinion about industrial capitalism. The century had seen the rise of non-Calvinist denominations, especially in the United States, which held a variety of economic views. In denominations descended from the Calvinist tradition, some preachers such as Henry Ward Beecher still advocated a harsh version of the Protestant ethic, which blamed urban poverty on the vices of the poor, promoted the ascetic virtues, and morally endorsed capitalism. Conservative denominational colleges still used the texts such as those of Francis Wayland, which blended laissez-faire economics and Protestant values.

A different opinion within Protestantism arose under the name the *Social Gospel*, which was given its fullest expression by Walter Rauschenbusch, an urban pastor turned seminary professor, around 1900. Questioning the extreme individualism of earlier Protestant thought, he argued that cultural and economic systems also have moral dimensions. Social systems, he held, should respect human potential in all participants. Despite progress such as the rise of democratic governments, Rauschenbusch concluded that the industrial capitalism of his era failed to respect human dignity. His thought was influenced by the then-new German methods of analyzing scripture, evolutionary ideas from biology, and ideas from the U.S. land reformer Henry George as well as from socialists.

Despite clear differences with the old Puritanism, Rauschenbusch's work manifested some traditional Protestant principles. He rejected received authority on economic matters and replaced it with empirical observation. He credited as true what he had observed as pastor of a church in an impoverished section of New York City, and he rejected what he thought were but speculative justifications of the industrial system pronounced by laissez-faire economics.

At about the same time, the academic economist Richard Ely credited a family heritage of New England Yankee (Puritan) morality for his reformist inclinations.

He rejected laissez-faire theory, which he found to be disconnected from measurable facts. As a central figure in reform economics in the late nineteenth century, Ely worked to start professional associations that, among other goals, would promote statistical studies as being integral to economic practice. He believed that actual economic data would document facts that laissez-faire could not explain away.

The Social Gospel reflected the reforming Puritan instinct, but not in the old sense that the elect should enforce their view of divine laws on a sinful culture. Instead, Rauschenbusch concluded that if an economic system harmed human life, then a change of the system could free people to rise to full human potential. Rauschenbusch never rejected the material benefits of the Industrial Revolution, instead proposing social entitlements for everyone to these benefits, reducing the disproportionate costs of industry borne by some, and democratizing industry.

FURTHER READING: Ely, Richard T. *Ground under Our Feet: An Autobiography*. New York: Macmillan, 1938; Frey, Donald E. "Individualist Economic Values and Self-Interest: The Problem in the Puritan Ethic." *Journal of Business Ethics* 17 (October 1998), p. 1573–1580; Landes, David S. *The Unbound Prometheus: Technological Change and Industrial Development in Western Europe from 1750 to the Present*. Cambridge: Cambridge University Press, 1969; Merton, Robert K. *Science, Technology and Society in Seventeenth Century England*. New York: Howard Fertig, [1938] 1970; Rauschenbusch, Walter. *Christianizing the Social Order*. New York: Macmillan, 1912; Sumner, William Graham. *What the Social Classes Owe to Each Other*. New York: Harper and Brothers, [1883] 1920; Wayland, Francis. *The Elements of Political Economy*. Boston: Gould, Kendall and Lincoln, 1845; Weber, Max. *The Protestant Ethic and the Spirit of Capitalism*. New York: Scribner's, [1930] 1958.

DONALD E. FREY

Psychiatry

Prior to 1800, persons with mental illness did not receive much effective treatment. They were basically warehoused in big asylums as a way to keep them separated from the rest of society. That started changing in the late 1700s at the York Retreat in England and La Biletre in Paris.

The York Retreat was set up by an English Quaker named William Tuke, who differentiated it from the more indifferent and sometimes inhumane treatments that people with mental illness suffered up until that time. It was a pleasant country house where mental patients lived and rested in a kindly, religious atmosphere. At about the same time the York Retreat opened, a hospital in Paris (La Biletre) was undergoing a transformation to make it a more positive treatment environment. Phillipe Pinel, its administrator, asked the government's permission to remove chains from the people housed there. Until that time, the people there (often called *inmates* as a reflection of the way there were treated) were chained as a way to keep their behavior under control. If this method did not work, then more extreme measures such as starvation, solitary confinement, or ice-cold baths were used. Pinel not only asked to remove the inmates' chains but also undertook steps to treat them more like sick patients than criminals.

Both the York Retreat and La Biletre methods were considered successful enough in terms of treating people with mental illnesses that other institutions started using similar methods. In fact, so many institutions undertook similar changes that the end of the eighteenth and beginning of the nineteenth centuries are known as the beginning of the humanitarian movement in mental health treatment. As this movement grew, so did the use of so-called moral therapy. Moral therapy was an approach to treating mental illness that focused on relieving patients' symptoms by the use of friendly associations, discussions of the patient's difficulties, and engaging them in purposeful activities. This therapy spread in Western countries through the first half of the 1800s and was found to be quite successful. Some mental institutions were finding discharge rates of more than 50 percent, even for patients who had their symptoms for years.

Although more humanitarian treatments of mental illness showed success in the early nineteenth century, other changes associated with the Industrial Revolution also had major effects on the treatment of mental illness. One such change associated with the Industrial Revolution was the population growth in Britain and the United States, especially in and around industrial centers. This led both to a rise in some illnesses (including smallpox and typhoid fever) but also a rise in effective medical care for treating these illnesses. Just as the factory system emphasized efficiency in making and using machinery, medical care during the Industrial Revolution emphasized more efficient means of delivering treatment. People were seen in more mechanical ways in order to try to develop the most efficient methods of addressing problems; this emphasis on the physical led to a more body-centered and medical-centered approach to treating mental illness.

Mental Hygiene

The so-called mental-hygiene movement of the late 1800s was a movement that emphasized medical treatments for mental illness, and it became the primary approach within facilities for mentally ill patients. Humanitarian approaches were emphasized less as the medical approaches were emphasized more. Because of the success of the more humanitarian treatments used earlier, psychiatric institutions were viewed more and more as the most appropriate form of care for people with mental illness. These institutions, however, were emphasizing instead medical treatments as opposed to the humanitarian supportive approaches as the mental-hygiene movement progressed. Unfortunately, the medicines, surgeries, and other medical treatments used were not found to be as effective as the moral therapy used earlier. In addition, as more patients were sent to these institutions, the staffs were less able to provide the individualized supportive care needed for the humanitarian treatment approaches. As the institutions grew and the treatment focused more on medical approaches only, the quality of care and the number of successes suffered.

One other issue that played a significant role in the deteriorating effectiveness of mental-health treatment throughout the mid- to late nineteenth century was the role of court-ordered institutionalization. The early humanitarian facilities like the York Retreat mainly treated patients who were admitted voluntarily (either by themselves or family). As the medical treatment of psychiatric illness became more and more accepted, however, there were more referrals of people involuntarily committed by the court system. When this happened, the patient mix in psychiatric facilities contained more violent criminals among the relatively nonviolent patients. In addition, racial and ethnic prejudice played a role in psychiatric hospitals' populations. Behaviors that were different among members of different ethnic groups often were seen as signs of abnormalities by members of a country's dominant racial and ethnic groups. These differences often were addressed by sending people to psychiatric institutions. Such behaviors often would be considered a problem whenever they caused disruption or just seemed too different to allow the person to fit into what people deemed normal society. This additional mix into the population of psychiatric institutions added to the difficulties of trying to treat the patients who had definite mental illnesses. As psychiatric facilities became the place to send more types of people who just did not fit into typical Western society, it became more difficult to treat the types of patients who originally made up these facilities' patient populations.

It is also worth noting that outpatient treatment did not make up a large portion of psychiatric care in the 1800s. Some facilities tried to provide supportive services for people living outside their facilities, but most treatments were limited to residential care. Some data suggests that symptoms of anxiety and depression were more prevalent throughout industrialized countries as more people lived closer together and as finding work meant more people had to separate from extended families. Overall, any formal treatment for these problems had to wait until the person required some sort of institutionalized care. Modern psychiatry typically utilizes outpatient care as a way of preventing the person from becoming so dysfunctional that a hospital stay is required. Very little data from the1800s suggests how much institutionalized care might have been prevented if outpatient care had been more available. It is quite possible the difference could have been substantial if only because outpatient care would have allowed many treatments to begin sooner.

By the end of the nineteenth century and into the early twentieth century, psychiatric care did not look very promising. A large number of psychiatric institutions throughout the industrialized world provided primarily inpatient treatment to a number of patients, but there was little proven success in terms of the patients in these institutions getting better. In fact, psychiatric institutions at the end of the 1800s became once again primarily warehouse-type facilities for people with mental illnesses. Ironically, in many ways, psychiatric care had not progressed much in terms of effectiveness from the late 1700s.

The mental-health community in the late 1800s knew that their treatments could be more successful; the promise of the early 1800s was not lost even in the dismal late 1800s and early 1900s environments. In the early 1900s, some professionals took paths that would modify the mental-hygiene emphasis on physiological treatments by combining it with some of the more humane, individual-centered treatment methods from the late 1700s. For instance, Sigmund Freud became famous for emphasizing a supportive so-called talking cure for mental illness. Freud was a neurologist, however, and he strongly insisted that the reasons his treatments worked were ultimately medical. In several of his articles and books, he expressed his expectation that some day a neurological explanation for all his theories would be found. Consequently, his approach was an example of a treatment method and theory of mental illness that combined medical aspects and humane treatment methodology.

The late nineteenth and early twentieth centuries also saw the birth and growth of the profession of psychology. The American Psychological Association started in the late 1800s and grew in size and prominence throughout the 1900s. This is important because psychology is the field of study that emphasizes nonmedical treatments of mental illness. The early years of psychology again put the emphasis on physiological explanations for behavior and mental illness, however, even as the treatments proposed were nonmedical. The first psychology laboratories studied physiological processes, but psychology practitioners eventually incorporated these findings into nonmedical theories about treating problems. Psychology as a clinical profession grew as a combination of both humanitarian and physiological views of human behavior.

Psychiatry during the Industrial Revolution could not by itself be deemed a success. Historical data shows little change in discharge rates for mental patients toward the end of the 1800s compared to 100 years earlier. The middle period during which there were some notable increases in success rates did not last long, but the approaches to mental-health treatment during that time did set the stage for more successful approaches throughout the next century.

FURTHER READING: Coleman, J. C., J. N. Butcher, and R. C. Carson. *Abnormal Psychology and Modern Life.* Chicago: Scott, Foreman, 1984; Montoux, P. *The Industrial Revolution in the 18th Century.* New York: Harper & Row, 1965; Office of the Surgeon General. 2006. *History of Mental Health Treatment.* At http://www.surgeongeneral.gov/library/mentalhealth/chapter2/sec7.html/.

DANIEL C. MARSTON

Public Health

Public health refers to health problems pervasive in a particular society and the measures taken by the society to address and prevent those problems. In Europe and the Americas, the Industrial Revolution heightened awareness of both aspects of public health. **Urbanization** and large-scale industry generated a wide range of maladies. Simultaneously, enthusiasm for reform through civic institutions and science spurred medical research, legislation, and public works projects conceived to bring about large-scale improvements in the health of the public.

The growth of economies based on industrial manufacturing affected health on many levels. Large-scale manufacturing directly precipitated a variety of health crises. Miners who labored to satisfy the ever-increasing demand for coal were at constant risk of injury or death and developed pneumoconiosis (black lung disease) from coal dust. The smokestacks of coal-powered factories spewed ash, sulfur, carbons, and other toxins that lingered in the haze hanging over manufacturing towns, exacerbating respiratory diseases. Production of textiles, ceramics, and metals used poisons that pervaded the ground and water. Byssinosis, a fatal scarring of lung tissue among textile workers, resulted from the constant inhalation of cotton particles. Constantly moving fan belts and machines could maim or kill factory workers whose vigilance slackened, exhausted by long shifts and the accelerating pace of production known as *speedup.*

The rapid and poorly planned growth of manufacturing towns and commercial cities, and the unprecedented urban concentrations they produced, also imperiled health in ways that extended beyond the factory workers to the general population. In Britain, approximately 3 million people lived in urban areas in 1801, but by 1901, 28.5 million people were city dwellers. In the United States, the population of New York, the largest city, grew from 123,706 in 1820 to almost 3.5 million in 1900. Manufacturing towns could grow even more explosively: Lowell, Massachusetts, went from being a village of 2,500 residents to a city of 33,000 in less than twenty-five years. The industrial poor were especially vulnerable to the consequences of urbanization: Workers and the unemployed typically crowded into housing that had been hastily and cheaply constructed, with little attention to ventilation, sanitation, or water supplies. Infectious diseases, including influenza, tuberculosis, and smallpox, swept through densely populated neighborhoods, among people whose resistance often was eroded by malnutrition and overwork. Contaminated drinking water transmitted typhoid, dysentery, and cholera. The spread of disease was hastened by the increased mobility that the industrial economy demanded; intercontinental travel, mass immigration, and swift transportation by **railroads** and **steamships** were efficient vectors for pathogens.

An Asiatic cholera pandemic, killing hundreds of thousands between 1829 and 1832, terrified industrialized nations as the disease rampaged from India through Russia, Germany, France, Britain, Canada, and the United States. The epidemic precipitated some of the first organized, large-scale attempts at the amelioration of public health as many municipalities took formal measures to avoid the disease. Although affluence was no safeguard against the disease, it did not escape observation that it spread most rapidly in crowded, dirty slum districts. Some communities therefore attributed the disease to degenerate habits or foreign vices, attempting to control its spread by restricting access to ports, quarantining suspect districts, or containing patients in specialized hospitals. Other observers suspected some aspect of impoverished living conditions as the culprit and attempted to ameliorate the overcrowding, air pollution, or bad water. A controversial but dramatically effective long-term response to the epidemic in the United States was the construction, beginning in 1837, of the Croton Water System for New York City. This vast infrastructure of reservoirs, pipes, and sewers brought clean water to the city from distant rural areas and separated New York's principal water supply from human wastes.

The premise that governments could take deliberate action to improve the health of the general population remained controversial throughout the 1830s and 1840s. Many leaders of public opinion asserted that disease and destitution resulted from moral impurity, calling for spiritual uplift rather than physical intervention; others debated whether the root of illness lay in contagion, the transmission of germs from one person to another, or miasma, the effect of breathing tainted air. In the 1830s, planned industrial model cities such as Lowell, Massachusetts, and Saltaire in England offered evidence that environments could be constructed to benefit workers both physically and morally. In 1842, an English royal commission headed by Edwin Chadwick reported that "drainage, street and house cleansing by means of supplies of water and improved sewerage, and especially the introduction of cheaper and more efficient modes of removing all noxious refuse from the towns" were the "great preventives" of disease. In response, the Health of the Towns Association and various private organizations, such as the Ladies National Association for the Diffusion of Sanitary Knowledge, attempted to disseminate principles of domestic hygiene to the general population.

Acknowledging by 1848 that inadequate urban infrastructure rather than slovenly habits underlay the filth of industrial cities, the British Parliament passed a Public Health Act establishing a General Board of Health empowered to inspect communities, evaluate their "sewerage, drainage, and supply of water, the state of the burial grounds, the number and sanitary condition of the inhabitants," and monitor compliance with or violation of the policies in place. Although in the form in which the act was passed, it merely facilitated sanitary improvements without power of enforcement, it laid the foundation for subsequent legislation, including the Second Public Health Act in 1872, requiring the appointment of a medical inspector responsible for the sanitation in each region, and the more comprehensive Third Public Health Act in 1875, which extended the power of local authorities to enforce regulations regarding lighting, water supplies, sewage disposal, food, public parks, and housing. The sewer systems installed in response to the acts were far from perfect; most urban municipalities flushed raw sewage directly into nearby rivers, with dire consequences for marine habitats. The Thames, and most other rivers adjacent to large cities, remained heavily contaminated with fecal matter well into the twentieth century. Nevertheless, the sewer systems dramatically reduced the numbers of deaths from cholera, typhus, and other bacterial diseases. Other industrial nations undertook similar measures. Led by Max Von Pettenkofer, the Bavarian court of Maximilian II instituted a public-health initiative comprising improvements in housing, health education, and supervision of food quality as well as pure water and effective waste disposal. In France, the Third Republic of 1870 instituted a Bureau of Public Health and Hygiene to oversee sewage and water systems, make smallpox vaccination widely available, record instances of infectious disease, and register the causes of all deaths. The Third Republic simultaneously created the Consultative Committee on Public Health that included Louis Pasteur among its members.

Attempts to contain infection or contagion were highly controversial, both because of the lack of scientific consensus regarding the source of disease and because surveillance and incarceration conflicted with notions of self-determination and individual rights. Consequently, policies to limit contagion typically targeted underclass groups such as prostitutes or immigrants rather than mainstream populations. Government acts constructing hospitals, chartering medical schools, or supporting medical science enjoyed broader support across social classes, and donations by capitalists endowed and supported many medical institutions. Both medicine and surgery, which had been a less professional branch, gained in prestige and scholarly stature over the nineteenth century. The Medico-Chirurgical Society of London, which later became the Royal Society of Medicine, was founded in 1805; the University College of Medicine in London was chartered in 1833. In addition to the Royal Free Hospital, founded in 1828, and the University College Hospital, founded in 1833, more than seventy specialized hospitals opened in Britain between 1800 and 1860. In Lowell, Massachusetts, the consortium of textile manufacturers provided a hospital for workers by 1839.

Measures to limit industrial pollution were far less potent. The Town Improvement Causes Act of 1847 requiring factory smokestacks to be constructed "so to consume the smoke arising from the combustibles used" was widely ignored, as were provisions in 1866 and 1875 forbidding smoke nuisances. Although the Rivers Pollution Act in 1876 forbade the "disposal of solid matter, liquid or solid sewage, or drainage from mines and factories into streams," the act exempted any district whose economy relied on manufacturing industries, "unless satisfied that no material injury will be inflicted on such industries."

Amelioration of working hours and conditions was still more problematic: It was obvious that long hours of factory work were more taxing than traditional farm labor and that speedup increased the likelihood of injury from factory machinery, but legislators desiring the support of industrial leaders were reluctant to enact policies that would limit hours or workloads. In Great Britain, child labor was officially limited to 12 hours per day as early as 1800, although compliance was seldom enforced. The Prussian Child Labor Law of 1839 prohibited factory labor for children younger than 9 years old and limited workers younger than 16 years to 10 hours per day; similar legislation was enacted in Massachusetts and Connecticut in 1842. Mill workers in New England's textile mills advocated a 10-hour working day for adults as well, but effective legislation to limit the working hours of adults met with substantial resistance from industrialists. The eight-hour day urged by the Welsh reformer Robert Owen as early as 1817 did not become widespread in developed nations until the 1930s.

FURTHER READING: Bennett, James T., and Thomas J. DiLorenzo. *From Pathology to Politics: Public Health in America.* New Brunswick, NJ: Transaction, 2000; Chadwick, Edwin. *Edwin Chadwick: Nineteenth Century Social Reform.* Ed. David Gladstone. London: Routledge/Thoemmes Press, 1997; Duffy, John. *The Sanitarians: A History of American Public Health.* Urbana: University of Illinois Press, 1990; Melosi, Martin V. *The Sanitary City: Urban Infrastructure in America from Colonial Times to the Present.* Baltimore: Johns Hopkins University Press, 2000; Smith, F. B. *The People's Health, 1830–1910.* New York: Holmes and Meier, 1979; Wohl, Anthony S. *Endangered Lives: Public Health in Victorian Britain.* Cambridge, MA: Harvard University Press, 1983.

JANE WEISS

R

Radio

In the midst of the Industrial Revolution, radio emerged as a composite of a number of landmark inventions: the telegraph by Samuel F. B. Morse (1791–1872) in 1836, the telephone by Alexander Graham **Bell** (1847–1922) in 1876, and the phonograph by Thomas Alva **Edison** (1847–1931) in 1877.

Technical Developments

The story of radio is one that begins nearly a century before its invention. When philosopher Gian Domenico Romagnosi (1761–1835) reported in an Italian newspaper in 1802 that he had discovered a profound relationship between electricity and magnetism, there was no fanfare from the scientific community. Years later in 1820, Danish scientist Hans Christian Ørsted (1777–1851), then unaware of Romagnosi's earlier findings, discovered the same principle of electromagnetism unintentionally as he was preparing for one of his lectures. A compass needle jumped and sealed the fateful relationship when he turned the battery current off and on. English scientist Michael **Faraday** (1791–1867) experimented further with this concept in 1831. Morse, a Massachusetts native, relying on Ørsted's prior work, invented the electric telegraph in 1837. Charles Wheatstone (1802–1875) also filed a patent that same year in Great Britain. Morse would continue to increase the signal of the telegraph with the assistance of a colleague at New York University, chemistry professor Leonard Gale.

In the late nineteenth century, British, U.S., and Indian scientists and inventors from around Europe invested time and money into understanding the principles and practice of reception and transmission of radio waves, what would become known as radio. It was not until 1878 that David E. Hughes (1831–1900) discovered noise from radio waves as they emitted from his telephone receiver, and this spurred others toward the goal of radio communication. He invented the microphone in the same year. As an avid musician from his youth, he sought a way to reproduce **music**. Scientists, inventors, and entrepreneurs in Europe and the United States competed to unravel the mysteries of sound transmission over the next two decades. At the 1881 Paris Exposition International d'Electricité, opera was transmitted through several strategically placed microphones and listener headsets. This so-called theatrophone paved the way for long-distance transmission of entertainment and speeches.

The contributions of different inventors to the discovery of radio has been a source of contention among historians. As the nineteenth century came to a close, Guglielmo Marconi (1874–1937) received accolades for his telegraph message sent without wires. In 1893, Nikola **Tesla** (1856–1943) presented and published his blueprint for wireless radio across the United States. On May 7, 1895, Russian physicist Alexander Popov (1859–1906) demonstrated radio-wave transmission and reception to his peers (on what later became designated as the annual Radio Day). One year later, a British radio patent was awarded to Marconi, and by 1897, he had established an experimental radio station on the southern coast of the United Kingdom. Tesla also applied for two radio patents in the United States, but these were later overturned by the U.S. Patent Office in favor of Marconi in 1904. The U.S. Supreme Court reinstated Tesla's patent in 1943 after a long court battle, unfortunately after his death.

Quebec native Reginald Fessenden (1866–1932) is often credited with airing the first radio broadcast. At age 20, he was hired by Edison and is believed to be the first person to relay voice and music over the airwaves with wireless technology. On December 24, 1906, at 9:00 P.M., several ships at sea heard the broadcast as he played a recording of Handel's "Largo" from Brant Rock, near Boston, Massachusetts. He then followed it by playing the melody of "Oh, Holy Night" on his violin.

Programming Developments

The nineteenth century was dominated by a thrust toward mass production, yet romanticism in the arts and technical improvements to woodwind and brass instruments and the piano served to liberate musicians. Philosophers like Henry David Thoreau (1817–1862) feared that the quest for progress was draining the human soul and passion. Thoreau espoused the virtues of sound and solitude from his cabin near Walden's Pond in Concord, Massachusetts, against a backdrop of increasing industrialization. He was fascinated by the sound of the train that ran along the borders of his property and believed it symbolized the arrival of a new era of commerce and communication. He described technology as a beast that roared through his woods and wrote of a solitude that he believed was becoming extinct. The human voice would be manufactured and duplicated through technology in the coming years thanks to inventors like Edison, and radio ultimately would be the result of the synthesis of these inventions.

Edison made history with his recording of "Mary Had a Little Lamb" on the first tinfoil cylinder phonograph in 1877. His phonograph was intended as a dictation device to provide authenticity to legal documents, and the reproduction of music was an unintended consequence. By the early 1900s, factory foremen would play music to increase their workers' production. The music industry flourished as entrepreneurs and competitors rushed to seize their share of the market. Radio station owners soon realized that records would provide an efficient means of filling air time, without the expense of live programming. Early radio was initially experimental, but it became increasingly limited to classical music, educational programming, and some jazz. Radio offered a way to manage and organize music in society: Because it developed within the context of industrialization, it emerged as an industry of efficiency, production, and sales.

In the early years of the twentieth century, Marconi had opened a radio factory in England, and Tesla built a radio antenna tower on Long Island, New York, that he envisioned would evolve into a universal center for transmission across the globe. The very act of transmission had become a commodity. Tesla failed to achieve the success he dreamed of, however, after investors backed away from his project's escalating costs. Since its inception, the radio industry measured its success in production units, originally determined by the number of radio sets sold and then by the number of commercials aired on a specific radio station. Radio's drive toward commercialism would make it more difficult for nonmainstream expressions of music to find outlets across commercial and public airwaves.

For example, Luigi Russolo's *Art of Noises* (1913) attempted to expand the definition of music to include industrial noise, going beyond traditional forms such as classical and jazz. Russolo (1885–1947) performed a series of concerts using what he called Intoners, or sound machines, as he attempted to incorporate the culture of industrialization into music. He positioned noise as a logical progression in music, and in this way, art would imitate the sounds of the era. Industrialization produced a new type of modern noise that challenged prior ways of interpreting life through one's acoustical environment. Emily Thompson demarcates this transition as the beginning of the sound scale of modernity, which ultimately created a unique culture of listening—and cultivated a new breed of visionaries—that began at the turn of the twentieth century.

Before his death, Russian futurist Velimir Khlebnikov (1885–1922) became known as the Great Sorcerer of radio. In essays such as "The Radio of the Future," he envisioned the medium as the central disseminating point for all world knowledge and a means to send messages of healing. In 1933, F. T. Marinetti and Pino Masnata's manifesto *La Radia* called for the reinvention of radio as a medium and space for creative authorship. In the years between the two world wars, radio in Europe offered a plethora of experimentation and potential, more so than in the United States, where broadcasting was shaped into an industry.

U.S. radio was soon programmed to assimilate national and local audiences and create a universal popular culture, or in some cases, propaganda. Music playlists were comparatively limited in relation to the wide variety of songs and genres in existence. The earlier vaudeville skits heard on the phonograph in the late nineteenth century had introduced audiences and investors to audio theater's possibilities, and radio drama emerged as a new form of entertainment and political expression in the United States and Europe by the early 1920s. Europe's early legendary experiments with radio included Radio Berlin's many *Playhouses*. In the United States, black radio drama such as *Destination Freedom* would serve as a political and creative expression in the 1940s, although Jack L. Cooper already had made history as the first African American talk radio personality with his debut in 1929. Cooper envisioned his role as one of empowering his listeners at a time of limited minority access to the airwaves.

As radio began to mature, its power became evident during the war years. Radio had the power to make stars and villains, protagonists and antagonists, in a moment. A series of broadcasts during World War II, with anti-U.S. propaganda aimed at American forces in the South Pacific, gave rise to subsequent public clamor to hunt down the culprit. Iva Ikuko Toguri d'Aquino, a young American woman, became inadvertently identified as Tokyo Rose, a fabricated name for the

English-speaking female Japanese propagandists. She was fined and imprisoned for treason based on false testimony but eventually was pardoned by President Gerald Ford.

During the same period of time, British Broadcasting Corporation (BBC) Radio rose in power as a credible voice to listeners and became the primary broadcast weapon to counter Nazi propaganda across Europe. A number of listeners complained about the BBC's dull programming, yet World War II had solidified the state-controlled corporation as a voice of uncompromising social responsibility, in contrast to the corporate U.S. model reliant on fickle network ratings and program sponsorship. In the same postwar period, U.S. government-funded Radio Free Europe was founded in New York in 1949, with headquarters in Munich, Germany. Its broadcasts were financed by the Central Intelligence Agency (CIA) and designed as part of the nation's psychological Cold War campaign. The first program aired on July 4, 1950, on U.S. Independence Day, launching a new chapter in radio's history.

FURTHER READING: Archer, Gleason L. *History of Radio to 1926*. New York: American Historical Society, 1938; Fessenden, Helen. *Fessenden, Builder of Tomorrows*. New York: Coward-McCann, 1940; Harding, Robert S. *George H. Clark Radioana Collection, 1880–1950*. Washington, DC: Smithsonian Institution, National Museum of American History, 1990. At http://invention.smithsonian.org/resources/fa_clark_index.aspx; Marvin, Carolyn. *Thinking about Electric Communication in the Late 19th Century*. Oxford: Oxford University Press, 1998; Newman, Mark. *Entrepreneurs of Pride and Profit: From Black-Appeal to Radio Soul*. New York: Praeger, 1988; Sterne, Jonathan. *The Audible Past: Cultural Origins of Sound Reproduction*. Durham, NC: Duke University Press, 2003; Thompson, Emily Ann. *The Soundscape of Modernity: Architectural Acoustics and the Culture of Listening in America, 1900–1933*. Boston: MIT Press, 2002; Walker, Jesse. *Rebels on the Air: An Alternative History of Radio in America*. New York: New York University Press, 2001.

PHYLIS JOHNSON AND JAY NEEDHAM

Railroads

Cheap, efficient land transportation was an essential need of the Industrial Revolution, as existing road transportation by wagon was too slow and expensive. Although English shippers had experimented with man-made canals from the middle of the eighteenth century, they were expensive to build and maintain and still slow because mule-drawn boats moved at only three miles per hour, and using steam power was impractical. In fact, they provided the main competition with railroads until well into the 1840s in both England and the United States.

With its extensive river system, the United States supported a large array of steamboats that effectively competed with railroads until the 1870s. The canals and steamboats lost out because of the dramatic increases in efficiency of the railroads, in terms of speed, scheduling, and costs per ton-mile. In Germany, on the other hand, parts of its well-integrated system of rivers and canals remained competitive into the early twenty-first century.

Railroads originated in England, which had created an elaborate system of canals and roadways to haul coal for the new steam engines. The engineers and businessmen needed to create and finance a railway system also were available. The first high-pressure **steam engine** locomotive was developed by Richard Trevithick in

1802; a locomotive using smooth wheels on an iron track could pull cars of freight a few hundred yards. In 1815, George **Stephenson** built the prototype of the modern steam locomotive, starting a technological race over the next century to build locomotives with more power at higher steam pressures. Stephenson himself was one of the major innovators. His decisive breakthrough came in 1825 when he built the Stockton and Darlington line, 12 miles long, that proved it was commercially feasible to have a system of usable length. On his first run, his locomotive pulled 38 freight and passenger cars at speeds as high as 12 miles per hour. Stephenson's *Rocket* was the locomotive for the Liverpool and Manchester line, which opened in 1830. Stephenson went on to design many more railways and is best known for standardizing designs, such as the standard gauge of rail spacing, at 4 feet, 8.5 inches.

Thomas Brassey was even more prominent, operating construction crews that at one point in the 1840s totaled 75,000 men throughout Europe, the British Empire, and Latin America. He and thousands of British engineers and crews went all over the world to build new lines. In the process, they invented and improved thousands of mechanical devices and developed the science of civil engineering to build roadways, tunnels, and bridges. **Telegraphy**, although invented and developed separately, proved essential for the internal communications of the railways because it allowed a central control station to track all the trains in the system, shifting slower trains to a siding as a fast train went by, warning of hazards, and sending orders to fix or work around troubles. Most important for efficiency, the telegraph allowed a system to use a single track for two-way traffic.

Britain had a superior financial system based in London that funded the railways in Britain as well as those in many other parts of the world, including the United States, up until 1914. The boom years were 1836 and 1845–1847, when Parliament authorized 8,000 miles of lines at a projected cost of £200 million, which was about the same value as the country's annual gross domestic product (GDP) at that time. A new railway needed a charter, which typically cost more than £200,000 (about $1 million) to obtain from Parliament, but opposition could effectively prevent its construction. The canal companies, unable or unwilling to upgrade their facilities to compete with railways, used political power to try to stop them. The railways responded by purchasing about a fourth of the canal system, in part to get the right of way and in part to buy off critics. Once a charter was obtained, there was little government regulation, as laissez-faire and private ownership had become accepted practices. The railways largely had exclusive territory, but given the compact size of Britain, this meant that two or more competing lines could connect major cities. George Hudson became known as the railway king of Britain as he amalgamated numerous short lines and set up a clearinghouse in 1842 that rationalized the service by providing uniform paperwork and standardized methods for transferring passengers and freight between lines and loaning out freight cars. By 1850, rates had fallen to a penny a ton-mile for coal and speeds had increased to fifty miles per hour. Thus, Britain had a well-integrated, well-engineered system that allowed fast, cheap movement of freight and people. The system directly or indirectly employed tens of thousands of engineers, mechanics, repairmen, and technicians, bringing a new level of technical sophistication that could be applied to many other industries and helping many small and large businesses expand their role in the Industrial Revolution. Thus, railroads had a tremendous impact on industrialization. By lowering transportation costs, they reduced costs for all industries moving supplies and finished goods, and they increased demand for the production of all the inputs needed for the railroad system itself. By 1880, there were 13,500 locomotives that each carried 97,800 passengers a year or 31,500 tons of freight.

Europe

In France, railways became a national medium for the modernization of backward regions, and a leading advocate of this approach was the poet-politician Alphonse de Lamartine. One writer hoped that railways might improve the lot of "populations two or three centuries behind their fellows" and eliminate "the savage instincts born of isolation and misery." Consequently, France built a centralized system that radiated from Paris (plus lines that cut east to west in the south). This design was intended to achieve political and cultural goals rather than maximize efficiency. After some consolidation, six companies controlled monopolies of their regions, subject to close control by the government in terms of fares, finances, and even minute technical details. The central government department of Ponts et Chaussées (Roads and Bridges) brought in British engineers and workers, handled much of the construction work, and provided engineering expertise and planning, land acquisition, and construction of permanent infrastructure such as the track bed, bridges, and tunnels. It also subsidized lines along the German border, which were considered necessary for the national defense. Private operating companies provided man

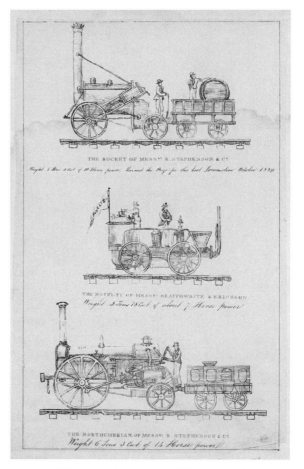

Drawing of three early locomotives, 1831. Science Museum/ Science & Society Picture Library.

agement, hired labor, laid the tracks, and built and operated stations. They purchased and maintained the rolling stock: 6,000 locomotives were in operation in 1880, which averaged 51,600 passengers per year or 21,200 tons of freight. Much of the equipment was imported from Britain and therefore did not stimulate machinery makers. Although starting the whole system at once was politically expedient, it delayed completion and forced even more reliance on temporary experts brought in from Britain. Financing was also a problem. The solution was a narrow base of funding through the Rothschild family and the closed circles of the Bourse in Paris, so France did not develop the same kind of national stock exchange that flourished in London and New York City. The system did help modernize the parts of rural France it reached, but it did not help create local industrial centers. Critics such as Emile Zola complained that it never overcame the corruption of the political system, but rather contributed to it.

The railways probably helped the Industrial Revolution in France by facilitating a national market for raw materials, wines, cheeses, and imported manufactured products. Yet the goals set by the French for their railway system were moralistic, political, and military rather than economic. As a result, the freight trains were shorter and less heavily loaded than those in such rapidly industrializing nations such as Britain, Belgium, or Germany. Other infrastructure needs in rural France, such as better roads and canals, were neglected because of the expense of the railways, so it seems likely that areas not served by the trains suffered net negative effects.

Belgium, on the other hand, provided an ideal model for showing the value of the railways for speeding the Industrial Revolution. After breaking with the Netherlands in 1830, the new country decided to stimulate industry. It planned and funded a simple cross-shaped system that connected the major cities, ports, and mining areas and linked to neighboring countries. Belgium thus became the railway center of the region. The system was very soundly built along British lines, so profits were low, but the infrastructure necessary for rapid industrial growth was put in place.

In Germany, political disunity (Germany did not become unified until 1870) and deep conservatism made it difficult to build lines in the 1830s. By the 1840s, however, trunk lines did link the major cities, although each German state was responsible for the lines within its own borders. Economist Friedrich **List** summed up the advantages to be derived from the development of the railway system in 1841: "First, as a means of national defense, it facilitates the concentration, distribution and direction of the army. 2. It is a means to the improvement of the culture of the nation. . . . It brings talent, knowledge and skill of every kind readily to market. 3. It secures the community against dearth and famine, and against excessive fluctuation in the prices of the necessaries of life. 4. It promotes the spirit of the nation, as it has a tendency to destroy the Philistine spirit arising from isolation and provincial prejudice and vanity. It binds nations by ligaments, and promotes an interchange of food and of commodities, thus making it feel to be a unit. The iron rails become a nerve system, which, on the one hand, strengthens public opinion, and, on the other hand, strengthens the power of the state for police and governmental purposes" (quoted by Simon Sterne, p. 118).

Lacking a technological base, the Germans imported their engineering and hardware from Britain but quickly learned the skills needed to operate and expand the railways. In many cities, the new railway shops were the centers of technological awareness and training, so by 1850 Germany was self-sufficient in meeting the demands of railroad construction, and the railways were a major impetus for the growth of the new steel industry. Observers found that even as late as 1890, their engineering was inferior to Britain's; however, German unification in 1870 stimulated consolidation, nationalization into state-owned companies, and further rapid growth. Unlike the situation in France, the goal was support of industrialization, and heavy lines crisscrossed the Ruhr and other industrial districts and provided good connections to the major ports of Hamburg and Bremen. By 1880, Germany had 9,400 locomotives pulling 43,000 passengers or 30,000 tons of freight.

Throughout Western Europe, railway construction was the main engine of economic growth in the 1840s and into the 1850s, stimulating growth in **coal mining**, iron mongering, machinery making, and civil engineering. By speeding up turnover, the railways made wholesaling and manufacturing more profitable and brought remote farmlands closer to markets and thus much more profitable. The creation of complex business organizations led to the multiplication of new managerial and engineering skills that spread from railways to other technologically oriented industries. As T. H. Ashton concluded, "The locomotive railway was the culminating triumph of the technical revolution: its effects on the economic life of Britain and, indeed, of the world, have been profound" (Ashton, p. 71).

Russia was a latecomer, building a private system in the 1870s and 1890s. The state nationalized most of the lines, with military goals in mind, as exemplified by the Trans-Siberian Railroad, and with the aid of foreign funding. Although the modernizing dreams of Count Sergius Iulevich Witte in the early twentieth century were not fully realized, the lines did give an impetus to the metallurgical industry, as a major new industrial area grew in the south, based on the coal mines of the Donetz basin and the iron ore of Krivoi Rog, which were linked by rail lines.

In Spain, the railways were designed by the government to foster industry, but setting the hub in Madrid for political reasons negated much of the advantage. The lines were poorly built and poorly managed and probably slowed industrialization by diverting capital and talent. In Italy, the railways were a political necessity to bind the new nation. The equipment, expertise, and funding was imported, but the main export, silk, was too light to make the system profitable.

When Austria and Hungary united in 1867, there were only 3,700 miles of railways, two-thirds of them in the more industrialized Austria. To integrate the large country, the lines were doubled in length, linking all the major cities and assisting in the industrialization of Vienna, Bohemia, and Silesia. The downturn of 1873 ended the boom and led to nationalization of the lines around 1880. The opening of the Oriental Railways link from Vienna to Constantinople in 1888 excited Berlin more than Vienna, and Germany then took the lead in developing the rail system in the Ottoman Empire. The Austro-Hungarian system doubled in size again by 1914, by which time it was carrying thousands of peasants one way from hundreds of villages to the growing cities or, more likely, to the ports from which steamships took them to North America. Although not as well built or as well managed as the German lines, the Austro-Hungarian system played a major role in supporting the war effort during **World War I**, even as its equipment was being run down and cannibalized. With half the rolling stock reserved for the army, and the rest breaking down, the transportation system virtually collapsed in 1918, and the cities ran short of food and coal. In 1919, the lines were divided among the successor states to the Austro-Hungarian Empire.

Asia

India provides an example of the British Empire pouring its money and expertise into a very well-built system designed for military reasons (after the Mutiny of 1857) and with the hope that it would stimulate industry. The system was overbuilt and much too elaborate and expensive for the small amount of freight traffic it carried. It did capture the imagination of the Indians, however, who saw their railways as the symbol of an industrial modernity—but one that was not realized until a century or so later.

In Japan, by contrast, railways were part of the stunningly successful industrial transformation of the late nineteenth century. Between 1870 and 1874, railway building accounted for nearly a third of all state investment in modern industry, augmented by large British loans. Profits were high as the lines facilitated the rapid growth of textiles, cement, glass, and machine tools as well as civil engineering.

North America

In Canada, the federal government strongly supported railway development for political goals. First, it wanted to knit together the far-flung provinces, and second, it wanted to maximize trade inside Canada and minimize trade with the United States, to avoid becoming an economic satellite. The Intercolonial Line, finished in 1876, linked the Maritime provinces to Quebec and Ontario and contributed to an ice-free winter route to Britain. No less than three transcontinental lines were built to the west cost, but that was far more than the traffic would bear, making the system simply too expensive. The federal government was forced to take over the lines, one after another, and cover their deficits. Because most of the equipment was imported from Britain or the United States and most of the products carried were from farms, mines, or forests, there was little stimulation to manufacturing. On the other hand, the railways were essential to the growth of the wheat regions in the Prairie provinces and to the expansion of coal mining, lumbering, and paper making. Improvements to the St. Lawrence waterway system continued apace, and many short lines were built to river ports.

In the United States, railway mania began in the 1830s and persisted through the 1870s. A large number of short lines were built, but thanks to a fast-developing financial system based on Wall Street and oriented to railway securities, the majority were consolidated into 20 trunk lines by 1890. State and local governments often subsidized lines but rarely owned them. The federal government operated a land-grant system between 1855 and 1871, through which new railway companies were given millions of acres they could sell or pledge to bondholders. A total of 129 million acres were granted to the railroads before the program ended, supplemented by a further 51 million acres granted by the states and by various government subsidies. This program enabled the opening of numerous western lines, especially the Union Pacific-Central Pacific with fast service from Omaha, Nebraska, to San Francisco in 1869. Although the transcontinentals dominated the media, with the completion of the first in 1869 dramatically symbolizing the nation's unification after the divisiveness of the U.S. **Civil War**, most construction actually took place in the industrial Northeast and agricultural Midwest and was designed to minimize shipping times and costs. West of Chicago, many cities grew up as rail centers, with repair shops and a base of technically literate workers. The U.S. imported British technology in the 1830s but was soon self-sufficient, as thousands of machine shops turned out products and thousands of inventers and tinkerers improved the equipment. The U.S. Military Academy at West Point saw most of its graduates become civil engineers in the private sector. This was a better-paying, higher-status job than army officer, in stark contrast to the preeminence of military officers in Europe. The result was that the Americans became enamored of engineering solutions for all economic, political, and social problems, combined with an unusually strong financial system that grew out of the railways. As the railways grew larger, they devised increasingly complex forms of management and invented middle management, setting up career paths and establishing uniform bureaucratic rules for hiring, seniority, firing, promotions, wage rates, and benefits. By 1880, the nation had 17,800 locomotives carrying 23,600 tons of freight but only 22,200 passengers. The effects of the U.S. railways on rapid industrial growth were many, including the opening of hundreds of millions of acres of very good farmland ready for mechanization, lowering costs for food and all goods, opening a huge national sales market, creating a culture of engineering excellence, and creating the modern system of management.

FURTHER READING: Ellis, Hamilton. *British Railway History.* London: George Allen & Unwin, 1959; Fremdling, Rainer. "Railways and German Economic Growth: A Leading Sector Analysis with a Comparison to the United States and Great Britain." *Journal of Economic History*

37, no. 3 (September 1977), p. 583–604; Jenks, Leland H. "Railroads as an Economic Force in American Development." *Journal of Economic History* 4, no. 1 (May 1944), p. 1–20; Nock, O. S. ed. *Encyclopedia of Railways*. London: Octopus Press, 1977; O'Brien, Patrick. *Railways and the Economic Development of Western Europe, 1830–1914*. London: Palgrave Macmillan, 1983; Simmons, Jack, and Gordon Biddle, eds. *The Oxford Companion to British Railway History: From 1603 to the 1990s*. 2nd ed. Oxford: Oxford University Press, 1999; Sterne, Simon. "Railways." In *Cyclopedia of Political Science, Political Economy, and the Political History of the United States by the best American and European Writers*. New York: Maynard Merrill & Co., 1881, vol. 3, p. 118; Stover, John. *American Railways*. 2nd ed. Chicago: University of Chicago Press, 1997.

RICHARD JENSEN

Repeating Rifles

John Hall, an American, was the first to patent an effective breech-loading rifle in 1811. By 1819, Hall had overcome various technical and patent obstacles and had developed a weapon using interchangeable parts. He was then employed by the federal government's Harpers Ferry Arsenal in Virginia as an armorer. The introduction of interchangeable parts in U.S. gun making brought about revolutionary changes in the early nineteenth-century United States and European industrial technology, because it permitted the later development of mass-production techniques. A number of inventors, notably Christian Sharps, Horace Smith, David Wesson, B. Tyler Henry, and Christopher Spencer, developed breech-loading repeating rifles of differing calibers in the late 1850s and early 1860s, most of which employed various lever actions to pump cartridges into the firing chamber. Metallic cartridges of copper were introduced in the mid-1850s but were too soft, and it took some years before refillable brass cartridges became standard.

Repeating rifles were first used in quantity during the U.S. **Civil War** (1861–1865) but had to overcome opposition from the leaders of the Army Ordnance Department, who argued that they wasted ammunition, that they had not undergone trials in the civilian market, that they cost too much, that they were suitable only for cavalry, and that their designers could not manufacture them quickly enough and in sufficient numbers. Further, coping with metal cartridges would overburden the already sorely taxed department. In the early months of the war, the Ordnance Department focused on securing weapons in quantity: hundreds of thousands of long-standard muzzle-loading weapons employing paper or cloth cartridges, single-shot Springfield rifles (models 1855 and 1861), and European-made single-shot rifles for the Army. Not until after September 1863 were thousands of new repeaters produced and put into service by the U.S. Army and Navy, many of them produced by Henry, Sharps, Spencer, Oliver Winchester, and others. The ammunition-wasting arguments made were largely disproved. These weapons, particularly the Spencers, were popular with troops and quickly proved their utility on the battlefield.

The last Henrys were produced in 1866, however, and the last Spencers in 1868, there being no significant U.S. military market for them after the Civil War. Most remaining Spencers ended up in the U.S. gun trade, and U.S. soldiers armed with single-shot weapons often found themselves fighting hostile Indians utilizing repeating rifles. Some Spencers were eagerly purchased by European governments for their armies. Winchester produced a repeating rifle employing a center-fire primer and brass cartridge in 1866, which largely superseded earlier weapons. Although many postwar

U.S. Ordnance Department leaders convened rifle selection boards, the models chosen by these conservative entities were invariably single-shot weapons, not repeaters, and most proved unequal to newly designed competitors being produced in Europe. Despite their proved utility, the Army discontinued the use of all repeating rifles, hence frustrated U.S. inventors sold their devices to eager European governments. Colonel Theodore Roosevelt's famed charge up San Juan Hill in 1898 in the Spanish-American War succeeded, despite the fact that Spanish defenders were armed with repeaters and Roosevelt's men were not. The model 1895 lever-action Winchester designed by John Browning was the last such weapon employed in combat—by the Russian Army during **World War I**.

Late nineteenth-century European repeating rifles, notably the British Lee-Enfield and German Mausers, outperformed the U.S. single-shot 1888 model Springfield and—after the U.S. Army began utilizing smokeless powder, first developed in France in 1884—the Danish Krag-Jorgensen, first improved and then adopted by the U.S. Army in 1892. The development of smokeless powder forced armies around the world to make radical changes in military tactics.

Blanchard copy-turning lathe, 1857, used for forming gun stocks. Science Museum/Science & Society Picture Library.

The conservative position taken by U.S. Ordnance Department leaders meant that the U.S. military forces were less well armed going into World War I. Some soldiers were issued manual bolt-action 30.06 caliber 1903 model Springfield rifles—yet another single-shot weapon—which continued to be standard until the 1930s. Others were issued European-made British Enfields. The Army Ordnance Department designed a repeating rifle closely resembling the contemporary German Mauser, but protracted legal wrangling over patent infringements with German manufacturers resulted. The U.S. government was obliged to pay substantial sums to satisfy these claims in the early 1920s.

The Browning Automatic Rifle (1917) did not see wartime service. In the 1920s, U.S. ordnance men experimented with rifles using .276 caliber cartridges. Canadian-born John Garand's M-1, with its seven cartridge clip using .30 caliber cartridges, was finally adopted by the U.S. Army in 1936. It replaced the 1903 model Springfield. U.S. infantrymen were armed with 4 million of these highly respected M-1s in World War II, and it was also used in the Korean and Vietnam Wars. A number of mass-produced European weapons saw wartime use in the 1940s, notably the German .31 caliber Sturmgewehr (assault rifle) StG 43 and StG 44 with their 30-round detachable box magazines, the Russian 7.62 caliber (54 millimeter) SVT 40 (Takarev self-loading, semiautomatic rifle) with a 10-round detachable box magazine, and the Russian SKS (1945) .39 caliber semiautomatic carbine, utilizing a 10-round clip or 10-round magazine. The SKS was used in some Third World nations into the early twenty-first century.

The .39 caliber Russian AK-47 Kalashnikov, introduced in 1949 and many times modified, has enjoyed considerable popularity in many parts of the world. It combined many known features of the M-1, StG 44, and other competing makes in a new weapon. The U.S. Army adopted the .30 caliber M-14, with a 20-round magazine, in 1957, but this weapon was beset with persistent problems. The comparatively lightweight M-16 rifle (originally the Armalite A-15), adopted by the U.S. Air Force in 1964, was, after protracted testing and a number of modifications, also adopted by the U.S. Army and Marine Corps. It utilizes the NATO standard .556 millimeter (.223 caliber) round and was adopted by 15 NATO countries; some 8 million M-16 rifles have been produced worldwide. During the 1990s and early 2000s, efforts continued to develop a new Objective Individual Combat Weapon (OICW). Originally intended to both replace the M-16 and support the launching of small-caliber smart grenades, these two objectives have more recently been pursued separately.

FURTHER READING: Bilby, Joseph. *A Revolution in Arms*. Yardley, PA: Westholme, 2006; Clark, David C. *Arms for the Nation: Springfield Longarms*. Albany, NY: National Park Service, 1994; Coggins, Jack. *Arms and Equipment of the Civil War*. New York: Doubleday, 1962; Hallahan, William H. *Misfire: The History of How America's Small Arms Have Failed Our Military*. New York: Scribner, 1994; Hounshell, David A. *From the American System to Mass Production 1800–1932, The Development of Manufacturing Technology in the United States*. Baltimore: Johns Hopkins University Press, 1984; O'Connell, Robert. *Soul of the Sword: An Illustrated History of Weaponry and Warfare from Pre-History to the Present*. New York: Free Press, 2002; Smith, Merritt Roe. *Harpers Ferry Armory and the New Technology: The Challenge of Change*. Ithaca, NY: Cornell University Press, 1977.

KEIR B. STERLING

Revolutions of 1848

Revolutions swept across much of Europe in 1848. Though the revolutions had political causes and goals, they also were underlain by the important economic and social changes that had accompanied the Industrial Revolution in the preceding decades. Along with those political developments of 1848–1849 that sought to fulfill promises of the eighteenth century's Enlightenment and revolutions, governments in this period endeavored to address the social question that paralleled the rise of modern industry and capitalism. It is difficult to imagine the revolutions of 1848 occurring or taking the shape they did without the stimulus and conditions of the Industrial Revolution. Still, as with the political events of this period, in hindsight the responses of governments to the exploitative side of industrialization, which contributed much to the start of revolution, appear fleeting or premature.

The year of upheaval began with the February Revolution in France that brought down the monarchy and replaced it with a republic headed by a provisional government. Soon after, the contagion of rebellion moved eastward and southward, affecting Austrian territories in Central Europe and northern Italy and then numerous German states, including the largest and strongest of them, Prussia. England, which had been the main engine of industrialization since the eighteenth century, saw a brief resurgence of the reformist Chartist movement but otherwise avoided political turmoil in 1848. Likewise, economically progressive Belgium and the Netherlands and economically backward Spain and Russia experienced little disturbance. The most industrialized and the least industrialized of the European states avoided revolution in 1848.

Politically, revolutionaries in 1848 sought the right for males to vote and hold elected office (there were also advocates for female citizenship), constitutionally formed republican or parliamentary governments, better access to education, and more local government. In places such as Germany, Italy, and Hungary, political and economic aspirations also were joined with the desire for national independence.

The political drama of 1848 cannot be fully grasped without considering the economic and social impact of the Industrial Revolution. In many places where industry or modern capitalism were concentrated—in capital cities such as Paris, Berlin, Milan, Vienna, and Frankfurt and regions such as the Ruhr, Bohemia, and northern France—so, too, was revolution concentrated. The building of **railroads** in the 1830s and 1840s helped transform poor rural populations into urban proletariats resentful of the unmet political and economic demands of the era. Skilled workers felt threatened by the transition to factory work. Technological improvements in printing contributed to the mass production of **newspapers**, improved literacy, and the diffusion of the idea of revolution. Poverty and rural proletarianization were on the increase, fomenting rebellion against semifeudal land arrangements in German Posnan and Russian Poland, machine-breaking in Prussian Silesia in 1844, and a peasant uprising in Austrian-controlled Galicia in 1846. High food prices, economic stagnation, bankruptcy, and rising unemployment characterized the late 1840s across much of Europe. The crisis was worsened by potato blight and poor harvests.

The Industrial Revolution brought modern factory production, along with the reorganization of labor to fit what were viewed as natural economic laws, and with these came the substitution of the Old Regime's moral economy for one defined by laissez-faire. Such changes were felt in cities with large working-class populations like Paris, Vienna, Milan, and Berlin, where revolution also became a class rebellion against free-market practices. Almost everywhere, 1848's so-called springtime of revolution was marked by schemes to replace the new regime of free enterprise with a so-called organization of labor that would reassert collective aspirations over the ethic of egoistic individualism but without undoing the potential of modern technology. Other demands included improvements in working-class housing, better pay, and shorter working hours. In the end, such high-minded goals proved difficult to achieve and sustain.

Naturally, there were differences in how the convergence of industrialization and revolution played out. In France, where the season of revolution had started, the republic's provisional government quickly decreed a shorter working day and an end to exploitative subcontracting. It also charged a newly established Luxembourg Commission with advising on reforms related to the working class. Through spring and early summer, the French government investigated abusive labor practices and passed laws to ameliorate the harsher side of laissez-faire. In response to high unemployment, national workshops were established as a public works project to provide jobs at meager wages. The manual labor at the workshops could not have been very satisfying for out-of-work artisans, but for the time being, they helped stifle political unrest. The government also instituted a 45 centime tax to address the financial crisis, but because it fell mostly on landed property, it alienated many peasants. The national workshops were dissolved in June, a signal that the period of reform was coming to an end. The hoped-for democratic and social republic concluded tragically when Parisian workers rose against the state during the June Days rebellion (June 23–26, 1848). Political observers as far apart on the political spectrum as Karl **Marx** and Alexis de Tocqueville saw the June Days as an example of unfettered class warfare. In the end, the state triumphed—first by buying time with promises of reform and then aided in part by a central feature of industrialization, railroads, which were used to bring in troops to put down the rebellion—but at the cost of thousands of casualties and the stifling of an incipient labor movement.

In Milan and Piedmont in northern Italy, economic modernization for progressive-minded politicians like Emilio di Cavour was connected to independence from foreign powers—in northern Italy this meant the Austrian Empire—and the unification of the peninsula under an Italian government. Unification was the ideal of economic modernizers like Cavour as well as revolutionary thinkers and activists like Giuseppe Mazzini and Giuseppe Garibaldi. The period 1848–1849 saw a failed military campaign by the Piedmontese to drive out the Austrians and the creation of a short-lived Roman republic, which fell to French forces in 1849 following the election of the conservative Louis-Napoleon as president of France late in 1848. Though Piedmont under Cavour would continue to industrialize and operate under policies of laissez-faire, the political unification of Italy would have to wait a few more years.

In Vienna and the Czech city of Prague, the events of 1848 proceeded somewhat as they had in Paris, with bourgeois and working-class crowds demanding political and economic reforms. Unlike the French king, the Austrian Hapsburg emperor was not overthrown, though the challenge to his authority opened the gates for nationalist movements in Hungary, Italy, Galicia (the Polish territories), Bohemia (the Czech territories), and elsewhere to gain traction. Except for the Czech lands, modern industry could be found in only scattered pockets across the empire. Accordingly, many of the economic and social reforms of spring were directed toward peasants. In March 1848, feudal holdovers were abolished, including labor service *(robot);* later, serfdom was ended altogether. Eventually in the Austrian Empire, as elsewhere across Europe, the liberal **bourgeoisie** retreated from its early radicalism, siding with governments against the threat of lower-class disorder and supporting the repression of rebellion in Prague (June 1848) and Vienna (November 1848). The so-called genie's bottle of revolution proved frightening to many of the revolutions' original middle-class supporters. Wars of independence by the Italians and the Hungarians were defeated in 1849.

Early in 1848, revolution also spread across the German countryside and cities. An initial period of unity between working and middle classes forced governments to accede to popular demands. The Prussian king, Friedrich Wilhelm IV, promised a constitution. In March, reformers from western Germany met at Frankfurt and pushed forward a liberal economic platform drawn partly upon the model of the Zollverein customs union and called for national elections anticipating a unified Germany. This Frankfurt Assembly came apart, however, due to irresolution over the degree of democratic reforms to be instituted and the role to be played by the Germanic powers of Prussia and Austria. Friedrich Wilhelm let it be known that he would not accept the crown of a unified Germany if offered by a revolutionary assembly, and the Frankfurt Assembly was ignominiously dissolved in May 1849. Marx believed that in 1848 social and economic developments in Germany were still far behind those of Western Europe and the German bourgeoisie not yet ready to win out in revolution.

By 1849, counterrevolution had set in almost everywhere across Europe. Nationalist revolts were defeated, working-class rebellions repressed, and many of the reforms of the previous years began to unravel. The liberal middle classes had approached the revolutionary stage tentatively hoping to acquire more economic and political liberty but in the end sided with authoritarian governments as the social order was challenged by workers or peasants. Theirs was a typically ambiguous approach to liberty. Despite the political disappointments of 1848, the subsequent counterrevolution did not curb economic modernization, as the 1850s and 1860s witnessed the continued growth of European industry and capitalism.

FURTHER READING: Marx, Karl. *The Revolutions of 1848, Political Writings: Volume 1*. Ed. David Fernbach. New York: Penguin Books, 1973; Price, Roger. *The Revolutions of 1848*. Atlantic Highlands, NJ: Humanities Press International, 1988; Sperber Jonathan. *The European Revolutions, 1848–1851*. Cambridge: Cambridge University Press, 1994.

CASEY HARISON

Ricardo, David (1772–1823)

More than any other nineteenth-century classical economist, David Ricardo presented a complete theoretical framework for economic analysis and a justification for laissez-faire and free trade. Although Adam **Smith** rooted his economics in a historical and social setting, Ricardo isolated his. He came late to the study of economics and took a different approach to economic analysis, reducing the whole economic system to a few variables and then logically deducing conclusions from his initial assumptions. In particular, his theory of comparative advantage provided a forceful basis for removing restrictions from foreign trade and has formed the basis of international economic analysis ever since.

The Ricardo family of orthodox Jews originally lived in Spain but fled at the end of the fifteenth century to settle in Holland before moving to London. David Ricardo was born in 1772, the third of 17 children. He was not particularly well educated and was employed as a stockbroker at 14 by his father. When he was 21, he renounced Judaism, married a Quaker, became estranged from his father (and was reconciled only much later), and set himself up in business as an independent stockbroker, dealing mainly in government securities. He was extremely successful at this and, as a very wealthy man, retired in his early forties to become a prosperous landowner.

Ricardo started reading economic literature around the turn of the century. In 1808, when he was 36, he met James Mill (father of John Stewart Mill), who introduced him to Jeremy Bentham and the philosophical radicals. He also met Thomas **Malthus** in 1811, forming a lifelong friendship with him. Ricardo read Smith's *Wealth of Nations* in 1808 and, with encouragement from Mill, began writing pamphlets and papers on various issues such as bullion. Mill also encouraged him to write the major work with which Ricardo is associated, *Principles of Political Economy and Taxation*, which was published in 1817.

The next (and last) phase of Ricardo's career came in 1819, when he went into Parliament, representing a pocket borough in Ireland (reform of Parliament and elimination of these electoral anomalies did not come until after 1832). He was admired for his honesty and integrity, advocating many policies that clearly went against his own interests. He supported parliamentary reform, the secret ballot, and a tax on capital to pay off the debt resulting from the Napoleonic Wars and opposed the **Corn Laws**, which benefited landowners. In Parliament, he sided with the reformers, favoring greater freedom for religious opinions, abolition of the Poor Laws, a reduction in the number of crimes punishable by death, and other contentious issues of the day. An ear infection in 1823 resulted in his premature death in his early fifties.

Ricardo's Economics

Unlike Smith, who wanted to uncover the forces causing nations to become wealthy, Ricardo believed that the purpose of economic analysis was to uncover the laws regulating the distribution of income. His was a three-class system: Landowners received rent income, capitalists earned profits, and workers earned wages. Changes in the shares of income determined the rate of capital accumulation and, thus, the growth of the economy over time. These issues were clearly of concern in the early nineteenth century, as Britain shifted from being an exporter of grain to being a net importer and as the country became more industrialized, and his analysis led to some important policy implications.

In common with other nineteenth-century economists, he utilized a labor theory of value (the price of a product depended in some way on the quantity of labor required to produce it) and believed that, in equilibrium, wages tended to settle at the subsistence level that was sufficient to allow the labor force to reproduce itself over time. Given this, the really important issue was the share of income received by the landowners (assumed to be unproductive and merely spenders on luxury items), vis-à-vis the share received by capitalists, on whom capital accumulation and thus growth depended.

Dealing with these questions led to the idea of diminishing returns, the theory of differential rents, and the development of the theory of comparative advantage. In turn, all these had practical policy implications supporting laissez-faire and free trade. Ricardo's model of rent was based on the idea that more productive land paid a higher rent than less productive land and that the landowner (who rented the land to tenant farmers) could capture the difference. With trade restrictions in force, a growing population implied a need to increase domestic food production, which would bring more land into cultivation. Two further implications were involved, however. First, an attempt to increase output on existing fields runs into the problem of diminishing returns, that as more labor is used, the extra output of grain gets smaller and smaller. Second, to avoid this, more land will be brought into cultivation. As this happens, less productive land is used (as presumably farmers prefer to farm the best land first), which means that rents can be raised on the better land because it generates higher yields. Over time, this raises the cost of food, which means that the subsistence wage level must rise. Also, the rental share of national income rises; both effects squeeze profits, which will slow the rate of capital accumulation.

This analysis provided the basis for his opposition to trade restrictions in general and the Corn Laws in particular. If Britain, a small country with only a limited amount of good agricultural land available, permitted unrestricted imports of food, it could prevent the slowing of growth. Food could be produced more cheaply in larger countries where diminishing returns had not yet set in. Then the rent share of national income would not rise, and this would prevent the fall of profits. Thus the Corn Laws prevented resources from moving freely, tightened the squeeze on profits that slowed economic growth, and, for this reason, should be repealed.

This analysis also links with his analysis of **international trade** and a preference for the removal of restrictions. Smith saw trade as encouraging economic growth because it widened the market and helped manufacturers sell output that was surplus to domestic needs. Smith's analysis was based on the assumption that differences in absolute costs led to trade: Countries that could produce some goods more cheaply would sell these goods abroad. Ricardo's analysis was much more sophisticated. Even if one country was absolutely better at producing everything than another, because its absolute costs were lower, trade could still be advantageous to both. In a two-good, two-country example, if neither country trades, each produces a certain amount of both goods using all its available resources (labor and capital). The cost ratios of labor used in the production of each good in each country will differ, and it is this difference that gives rise to trade. The theory of comparative advantage holds that each country should specialize in the production of the good in which it has a comparative advantage and export some of it while importing the good it is comparatively disadvantaged in producing. This way, the total world output of both goods is greater than the total production with no trade, so consumption levels can be higher. (The exact division of the extra output depends on the prices at which the goods sell.)

For Britain, Ricardo advocated that trade patterns should encourage the export of manufactured goods and the import of food (in which it did not have a production advantage). Such a pattern would reduce the pressure on money wage rates and thus prevent the fall of profits. The full benefits of international trade, however, required not only the absence of restrictions but also a sound international financial system, another area in which Ricard influenced both theory and practice.

Ricardo adopted a bullionist position on money, and his work influenced the theory of the **gold standard** in the nineteenth century. He believed that a country's domestic money supply should be directly tied to its gold supply. This was so because he warned that an unwarranted increase in the issue of paper money would cause rising prices that would make exports less competitive and imports relatively cheaper, thus threatening the country's trading position. Under the strict gold standard, any unfavorable balance of trade would lead to an outflow of gold that would contract the supply of paper money (because importers would have to exchange their notes for gold at the central bank to pay their foreign suppliers). This outflow and money supply contraction would then lower the price level, result in a correction of the trade balance, and restore balance in the international accounts.

In summary, Ricardo's theory of comparative advantage, his position on international trade, and his analysis of income distribution's influence on economic growth were lasting contributions. (His development of a labor theory of value was not so clear cut and unambiguous.) He used his analytic ability to influence many of the controversial issues of his day.

FURTHER READING: Landreth, Harry. *History of Economic Theory: Scope, Method and Content.* Boston: Houghton Mifflin, 1976; Oser, Jacob, and Stanley L. Brue. *The Evolution of Economic Thought.* 4th ed. New York: Harcourt, Brace, Jovanovich, 1988; Ricardo, David. *The Works and Correspondence.* Ed. Piero Sraffa, with the collaboration of M. H. Dobb. 10 vols. Cambridge: Cambridge University Press, 1951–1955; Roll, Eric. *A History of Economic Thought.* 4th ed. London: Faber & Faber, 1973; Spiegel, Henry William. *The Growth of Economic Thought.* Rev. ed. Durham, NC: Duke University Press, 1983. WEB SITES: http://www.eh.net/encyclopedia/article/stead.ricardo; http://www.econlib.org/library/Ricardo/ricP1.html.

CHRISTINE RIDER

Rochdale Pioneers

The Rochdale Society of Equitable Pioneers, usually known simply as the Rochdale Pioneers, is usually considered the world's first cooperative enterprise and has thus become the foundation of the modern cooperative movement. The Rochdale Pioneers are best known for devising a set of principles that still form the basis upon which all modern co-ops operate.

Friendly Societies, corresponding societies, labor unions, and consumer cooperatives were the primary methods of secular working-class self-help in nineteenth-century Britain. All were intended to improve the standard of living of the working class: unions by improving the money wages of workers, mutual aid Friendly Societies and corresponding societies by helping with the unexpected risks associated with a market economy, and consumer cooperatives by focusing on the prices and quality of the goods that workers and their families bought. The Rochdale Pioneers, the first successful consumer cooperative, was founded in Rochdale, Lancashire, in 1844.

Most people associate the British cooperative movement in the nineteenth century with Robert **Owen** (1771–1858) and Owenism. Initially, Owen advocated the establishment of labor exchanges in which commodities would be produced by individuals and then evaluated by strict rules to determine their labor-hour content. Worker-producers would then be able to exchange their accumulated labor hours for goods produced by other workers. Problems developed because some products, especially agricultural goods, simply were not available, and there was not enough variety of the goods that were available. Essentially dependent upon the work of more skilled, rather than factory-based, labor, these labor exchanges were also of little benefit to the poorer sections of the working classes.

Following the collapse of the labor-exchange concept, and influenced by his utopian beliefs, Owen traveled to North America to supervise the establishment of a cooperative community. Owen believed that these communities would be secular, based upon the notion of cooperation in production and consumption. They were envisaged as self-sufficient economic, social, and political formations, as compared to the severe exploitation of the developing factory-based system of production. Although a brilliant visionary and a competent entrepreneur, he was unprepared for the planning and commitment that these communities required, and they were notorious failures.

In Owen's absence, the cooperative movement continued the establishment of cooperative societies that included consumer cooperatives and production units. Under the influence of William King, many of these societies rejected Owen's belief that cooperation should be externally financed. The formation of a consumer cooperative required each member to contribute to its initial financing in order to stock the shelves of the resulting store. There were difficulties ensuring a decent range and quality of goods, however, and financial problems arose from the extension of credit to members during periods of instability in employment.

A serious problem in the nineteenth century for working-class consumers was the existence of the truck system and Tommy shops. These involved workers being either paid in kind or in tickets or chits redeemable only at Tommy shops, which were often run by factory managers or foremen at a profit. Goods sold at these establishments were often of substandard quality or adulterated. Moreover, they liberally extended credit to consumers, leading to a cycle of indebtedness by consumers dependent upon the state of the local and general economy. The Truck Act of 1831 made it illegal to pay wages in kind or by chits, which made the system more difficult to operate, especially in large towns where there was a variety of different shops. In coal and iron mining towns and isolated factory towns, however, this system could still operate.

The Rochdale Pioneers were essentially pragmatists. The movement initially shared some of Owen's utopian vision and in their formative statement advocated setting aside a portion of earnings for the establishment of cooperative communities and the provision of education for members of the society and their families. The consumer cooperative movement, however, was deliberately limited in scope. Its primary aim was to supply safe and fairly priced goods to members, with the secondary aim being the education of members and their families. What made these stores cooperative was the distribution of profits in the form of the dividend, or divi, which was distributed to members based on the amount of purchases they made each year. The stores were extended to provide wholesale goods to other cooperative societies, and production was started with the opening of a bakery and the production of cloth (although these operations were not run as cooperatives and the workers were not paid especially well).

The Rochdale Cooperative Store on Toad Lane opened its doors in 1844. The success of the store was dependent upon the stability of employment and incomes of its members and a short improvement in the economic situation in 1844–1846. Given that the Rochdale Cooperative Store prohibited the extension of credit and that it initially only sold to members, it required a core membership of the more affluent sectors of the working class. Subsequently, cooperative societies and stores were set up in many different parts of the country, and shopping in them was open to all and no longer restricted to members.

FURTHER READING: Brown, W. Henry. *The Rochdale Pioneers: A Century of Co-operation.* Manchester, U.K.: Co-operative Union, 1944; Cole, G.D.H. *A Century of Co-operation.* Manchester, U.K.: Co-operative Union, 1944; Cole, John. *Conflict and Co-operation: Rochdale and the Pioneering Spirit 1790–1844.* Littleborough, U.K.: George Kelsall, The Bookshop, 1994;

Halevy, Elie. *The Age of Peel and Cobden: A History of the English People, 1841–1852.* London: Ernest Benn, 1947; Hopkins, Eric. *Working Class Self-Help in Nineteenth-Century England.* London: UCL Press, 1995.

SUSAN PASHKOFF

Rockefeller, John D. (1839–1937)

John Davison Rockefeller, the U.S. capitalist, was born on July 8, 1839, in Richford, New York. The family moved often before finally settling in Cleveland, Ohio, in 1853. At the age of 16, Rockefeller became assistant bookkeeper with Hewitt and Tuttle, a firm of commission merchants. Then he formed a company, Clark and Rockefeller, in partnership with Maurice Clark, which sold agricultural products and miscellaneous goods. During the U.S. **Civil War**, he went into the oil business, and his company began to invest in an oil refinery in 1862. Oil had been discovered in the Titusville area, resulting in a boom in northwestern Pennsylvania. The demand for kerosene for lighting purposes (to replace whale oil) boosted the new oil industry. On January 10, 1870, the Standard Oil Company was formed with Rockefeller, who controlled 30 percent, as its president. The company was worth $1 million and had 10 percent of the U.S. oil business at that time.

The Standard Oil Company along with its subsidiaries became successful in Cleveland, Pittsburgh, Philadelphia, and New York City. Rockefeller's ideas and strong-arm tactics in eliminating competition made the company extremely profitable. He wanted to create a vertically integrated, big company in the **petroleum industry**, dominating production, refining, and distribution. His ruthless business practices resulted in Standard Oil controlling the oil business in the Cleveland area within two years. He purchased and controlled refineries in the East and Midwest of the United States and even controlled the ancillary market for making oil barrels so that other companies could not bring their products to market. The company cut oil prices and used intimidating tactics against its competitors. The company expanded and prospered. In 1882, its properties were merged into the Standard Oil Trust, which had an initial capital of $70 million and was one of the biggest companies in the United States. Rockefeller was the richest man in the world, worth $900 million by 1901, and his company controlled 90 percent of the U.S. oil business.

He ran into legal problems, however. An Ohio court decision dissolved the trust, so Rockefeller formed the Standard Oil Company (New Jersey) in its place. Rockefeller's success and tactics came under attack from different quarters. Ida Tarbell's classic *History of the Standard Oil Company* (1904) revealed the methods used by Standard Oil in achieving its monopoly. Press campaigns were unleashed against Rockefeller, calling him the "dominating commercial man" and making him a hated figure. Then, on May 15, 1911, the Standard Oil monopoly was dissolved by the U.S. Supreme Court on the grounds that it violated the 1890 Sherman antitrust law. As a result, the parent New Jersey company was split into 38 individual firms.

After 1896, Rockefeller began many philanthropic activities and established institutions in various fields such as science, education, medicine, and public health that are still in existence today. He died on May 23, 1937, at his home in Ormond Beach; he was worth $1.4 billion at that time.

FURTHER READING: Abels, Jules. *The Rockefeller Billions: The Story of the World's Most Stupendous Fortune.* New York: Macmillan, 1965; Chernow, Ron. *Titan: The Life of John D. Rockefeller, Sr.* New York: Random House, 1998; Nevins, Allan. *John D. Rockefeller: The Heroic Age of American Enterprise.* New York: Charles Scribner's, 1941; Rockefeller, John D. *Random Reminiscences of Men and Events.* New York: Doubleday, Doran, 1933. WEB SITE: http://merlin.alleg.edu/employee/h/hmccull/tarbell/index.html.

PATIT PABAN MISHRA

Russia, Industrial Revolution in

The British Industrial Revolution of the eighteenth and nineteenth centuries opened the age of industrialization all over Europe and partly also on other continents. Although several Western European continental countries followed in the footsteps of the British, the northern, southern, and eastern parts of Europe responded belatedly and began industrializing only in the middle to late nineteenth century. Russia belonged to the latter group of peripheral countries. This giant empire, which was radically enlarged by occupying and absorbing neighboring territories and countries in the east, south, and west during the eighteenth and nineteenth centuries, remained frozen in a feudal order. Untouched by the Enlightenment and the so-called dual revolution, the combined impact of the sociopolitical French Revolution and the British Industrial Revolution that had taken place in the West, czarist Russia remained autocratic, despotic, and economically backward. The economy preserved its medieval character, the village community remained intact, and approximately 80 percent of the population was illiterate at the end of the nineteenth century. A military giant that had earlier triumphed over Napoleon, Russia with its approximately 70 million inhabitants in the 1850s was unable to mobilize its army in the Crimean War, suffering a humiliating defeat at the hands of the allied British, French, and Piedmont armies of 65,000 men in 1855. This defeat acted as a wake-up call.

Early Transformation

Reforms began, and in February 1861 the serfs were emancipated in most of the European parts of the empire, freedom of trade and commerce and security of property were recognized and guaranteed, and a somewhat semiautonomous civil administration was introduced. Reforms from above, however, were very limited. Two-thirds of the land remained in the hands of landlords, and, even 30 years after the emancipation, one-third of the peasants still had to pay feudal rents. The reform process proceeded gradually and overcautiously. Censorship was abolished in 1865, urban self-government was introduced in 1870, the noble military system was replaced with compulsory military service in 1874, and state education was established. Another humiliating military defeat, this time from Japan in 1905, was followed by a revolution that radicalized reforms, divided up communal land, and established private ownership. These and other measures gradually set in place the minimum internal political and social prerequisites for a modern economic transformation.

Starting in the 1880s, the first sign of transformation came in the form of a very belated and limited agricultural modernization. Extensive grain cultivation dominated, with 97 percent of the arable land given to grain and the ancient three-field rotation system still in use. Although yields reached only 25 percent to 30 percent of Western levels, grain output more than doubled between 1864–1866 and 1906–1910. The state introduced excessive taxation to force peasants to sell their products, which made it possible to dramatically increase grain exports by more than five times. Russia exported nearly half of its wheat output in the 1880s, and still nearly one-third of it at the turn of the century, and delivered approximately one-quarter of the world's grain exports. European exports increased by an annual 2.8 percent between 1860 and 1910, whereas Russian exports increased 3.8 percent per year. Growth was premised on starvation because the peasants had to decrease family consumption to be able to pay taxes. Although this controversial policy destroyed Russia's solid domestic market by depriving peasants of purchasing power and became an obstacle to the modernization of the countryside, export incomes served as the most important internal source of accumulation and investment.

Internal sources, however, as in many other cases in the peripheries, were not sufficient. From the time of the Russian reforms of the 1860s and 1870s onward, the leading capitalist countries of Europe significantly increased their capital exports to establish markets for their industrial products and to obtain access to food and raw material resources. Political considerations also played a role. France desperately worked on building an alliance system against Germany, and Russia played a major part in the French plans. Having a modern transportation system and military industry to transport and equip a modern army thus became crucially important.

Foreign Investment. Foreign investments, especially French, became, consequently, another decisive factor of economic modernization in postreform Russia. French and German capital exports accounted for one-third of capital exports by advanced European countries, and they targeted Russia: 27 percent of French and 15 percent of German capital exports were channeled into Russia, which received 7.6 billion rubles between 1861 and 1914. The greatest part, amounting to 3.5 billion rubles, was invested into **railroads**, and another 1.6 billion rubles were invested in state loans. On that basis, with three-quarters of its construction financed by foreign capital, Russia built the world's second-longest railroad system, increasing from only 1,000 miles in 1860 to 43,600 miles by 1913. The railroad connected Russia's agricultural areas as well as all the important raw-material resources of the Urals and Caucasus to its urban centers and to Europe. The railroad itself created a huge market for various industrial products. In the first period, almost all of the materials and engines were imported. From 1860 to 1880, imports of iron and engineering products increased 20 and 7 times, respectively. At the end of the 1870s, however, the government banned the importation of foreign goods for the railroads. After a few decades, Russia successfully supplied its huge railroad system. Foreign investment played an important role in this development, too: Around the turn of the century, one-third of total foreign investment was already channeled into industrial projects; by 1900, 42 percent of industrial stock was in foreign hands. Moreover, the share of foreign capital reached 72 percent in the mining, iron, and steel industries and 71 percent in engineering.

Banks also started to play an active role in industrialization. The capital of the banking institutions, rather modest until the mid-1880s, had increased approximately five times by **World War I** and reached more than 3.6 billion rubles. Between 1861 and 1881, domestic sources amounted to only about 18 percent of foreign investments, but by 1900–1914, domestic capital surpassed foreign investments by

124 percent. Between 1900 and 1914, 60 percent of new investments were financed by domestic sources. Nevertheless, 45 percent of the capital of the 10 largest Russian banks was in the hands of foreign investors. In the case of the four biggest banks, this percentage reached 60 percent.

Industrialization

Industrialization gained momentum. Russian industrial output until the mid-nineteenth century was produced by small-scale peasant, so-called *kustar,* industries and by the industrial activity of the boyar landlords, who used serf labor to extract and process the raw materials of their estates, mostly in the iron and timber industries. Until 1890, two-thirds of the Russian **iron industry** in the Urals still used the obsolete method of smelting with charcoal. Although pig-iron production stagnated in the 1860s and increased by only 33 percent during the 1870s, it more than doubled during the 1880s and again increased threefold during the 1890s. This breakthrough was the result of massive French investment and the establishment of the modern coal and iron industries of the Donyec Basin, which absorbed 40 percent to 45 percent of foreign investments. Until 1870, only 2 percent to 3 percent of coal and iron in Russia were produced in that area; by the turn of the century, this proportion had increased to more than 50 percent.

The turning point in industrialization occurred during the 1890s. Before that, only the textile industry around Moscow experienced real prosperity. In one single decade, between 1885 and 1895, the number of big industrial companies increased by 26 percent, their labor force by 60 percent, and the value of production by 112 percent. From that time onward, the annual growth rate of the Russian industry varied between 6 percent and 9 percent. Between 1900 and 1914, coal output more than doubled, iron and steel production increased by 50 percent to 60 percent, and textile output by 130 percent. Between 1860 and 1913, the entire value of Russian industrial production increased nearly 12-fold. During the half-century of modern transformation before World War I, Russia's gross domestic product (GDP) increased nearly threefold. Because the population of the country rapidly increased, however, per capita income increased by less than 50 percent. The $1,488 per capita GDP in 1913 remained somewhat behind the world average and reached only 40 percent of the Western European and 28 percent of the overseas (U.S., Australian, etc.) level.

Before World War I, 32 percent of Russian industrial output was produced by the coal, iron, steel, oil, and chemical industries, whereas textiles and food processing each contributed 28 percent. Unlike several other economically backward countries, Russia developed a relatively balanced structure of industry. Some modern branches of industry present in Western Europe at the turn of the century, nevertheless, were missing. Engineering was underdeveloped and did not produce modern machinery, the chemical industry could not produce finished products, and Russia did not have a technological edge in any of the industrial fields. The machine park with its 1.2 million horsepower capacity remained far behind the 7.9 million horsepower capacity in Germany. Great Britain's industrial output was 4.6 times greater than Russia's, Germany's 6 times greater, and the United States more than 14 times greater. In spite of making the first important steps, per capita industrial production in Russia reached only one-third of middling industrial nations such as Austria-Hungary and Italy before World War I. Russia had begun industrializing and transforming its rigid, petrified economic structure but remained overwhelmingly agricultural. By 1913, 70 percent of the population still worked in agriculture, which produced nearly two-thirds of the country's GDP.

Within the huge Russian Empire, regional differences in the level of industrialization were significant. The Ural and Donyec regions, as well as the Moscow and St. Petersburg areas, emerged as modern industrial islands in an ocean of agriculture and traditional economic practices. The Moscow region became the center of the Russian textile industry, whereas the St. Petersburg area was characterized by engineering. The Caucasus emerged as the center of the new oil-extraction industry.

The Western Territories

Poland, Finland, and the Baltic countries, the relatively newly occupied Western territories of the empire, emerged as special industrial centers in the economically backward empire. As a result of its more favorable historical and cultural legacy, this occupied and oppressed western rim of the empire became more successful at industrializing and reached a higher level of economic development than Russia itself.

Poland. After the third partition of Poland in the late eighteenth century, nearly two-thirds of the country became part of the Russian Empire. Other parts of the former Polish kingdom were incorporated into the Prussian, later German, and Hapsburg Empires. Poland profited from the legally guaranteed inner Polish trade, a free trade agreement between the Polish territories now belonging to three empires. So-called German Poland, with its center in Posnan/Posen, itself became well industrialized as a part of a successfully industrializing Germany. Russian Poland imported tax-free semifinished industrial products and spare parts from German Poland, finished processing, and then sold the finished products in the Russian market, which otherwise had surrounded itself with Europe's highest tariff barriers. The czarist government abolished internal tariffs between Russia and Russian Poland in 1851 and from the 1860s onward connected the area by railroad to St. Petersburg, Moscow, and the enormous Russian market. The relatively backward but huge Russian market was opened to Polish industrial products. Polish industry, until that time insignificant, gained momentum. In the first two decades after tariff unification, Polish industry increased its output three times and during the next two decades, nearly another four times. Behind Moscow and St. Petersburg, Poland emerged as the third-strongest industrial center of the Russian Empire. By 1910, 10,000 industrial firms in Russian Poland employed more than 400,000 workers and increased their output by more than eight times between 1877 and 1910. Poland produced 40 percent of the Empire's coal output, 23 percent of its steel, 15 percent of its iron, and 20 percent of its textile production. The per capita industrial output in Poland became twice as high as that of Russia itself. Lodz, a village with 800 inhabitants in the 1820s, rose as an industrial city, a so-called Polish Manchester, in which 240 textile firms were already in operation by the end of the 1880s and at the end of the century was home to more than 300,000 inhabitants. Before World War I, the textile industry produced 45 percent of the Polish industrial output, and food processing accounted for another 18 percent. Coal output nevertheless also became crucial, increasing seven times between the late 1870s and 1913. An engineering industry around Warsaw produced for agriculture and the railroads. The domestic market remained limited because of the relative backwardness of agriculture, which limited purchasing power. The driving force of industrialization of Poland was the virtually unlimited demand coming from the Russian market. The two leading industrial sectors, textiles and iron, sold 80 percent and 40 percent of their output, respectively, on the Russian market. Altogether, exports to Russia increased 500 times from the mid-1850s to 1910, and more than 60 percent of Polish industrial products were delivered to Russia.

Finland. Finland enjoyed an even higher status within the Russian Empire. The former frontier land of Sweden, occupied in the early eighteenth century by Russia, gained autonomy in the Russian Empire, increased its population fourfold in the nineteenth century, and became an exporter to the Russian market. The country, covered in forests, began cutting and then processing wood. Timber became the number one export item during the last third of the nineteenth century. Whereas in 1860, nearly all of wood exports consisted of firewood, by 1913, its share dropped to one-sixth. A Finnish pulp and paper industry emerged and processed the wood, increasing its production more than four times between 1885 and 1905. By 1913, nearly 40 percent of Finnish exports to Russia were paper products. Meanwhile, the country exported unprocessed wood to Western markets. In 1913, 60 percent of Finnish exports to the West was wood. Finland followed the Scandinavian industrialization pattern and introduced certain branches of food processing. Butter production and exports became significant, with exports amounting to half of Swedish production. The country's per capita income level before World War I was approximately 25 percent higher than Russia's.

Baltic States. Similar developments occurred in the Baltic countries, which became part of the empire in the eighteenth century. Industrialization was based on export to the Russian markets. From the mid-nineteenth century, Latvia built up an export industry based on timber and butter, selling 70 percent and 30 percent of their products abroad, respectively. The Russian market fueled the development of certain branches of engineering, asbestos and rubber industries in particular, which sold 90 percent of their products in Russia. The textile, shoes, and leather industries sold 70 percent of their output to Russia, and the glass and paper industries 60 percent. Although only 35 percent of industrial production, mostly from the food and consumer-goods industries, targeted domestic markets, approximately two-thirds of Latvian industrial output was sold in Russia. Latvia produced 28 percent of the rubber output of the Russian Empire, 13 percent of its wood processing, and 10 percent of its metal production. The per capita industrial output of Latvia and of the other Baltic countries reached nearly twice the per capita industrial output in Russia (74 rubles and 40 rubles, respectively). The Baltic countries, like Poland, had achieved a much higher level of industrialization than Russia itself.

None of the western territories of the Russian Empire, however, became industrialized. Poland, Finland, and the Baltic countries remained overwhelmingly agricultural, with nearly two-thirds of their populations working in that sector. Moreover, agriculture, except in Finland, remained obsolete, based mostly on subsistence farming. The level of industrialization, however, had about reached the average Central European standard, similar to Hungary.

Late Industrialization

Industrialization was accomplished only during the twentieth century, when a real takeoff was artificially triggered by the Soviet Union. After a severe but temporary decline in the early 1920s, a unique forced-industrialization project was realized under state tutelage, doubling the income level of the country during the 1930s. Two consecutive five-year plans industrialized the Soviet Union. Finland and the Baltic area, which became independent after 1917, also made some advances, but Poland, after having lost the Russian markets, suffered a setback. The breakthrough of industrialization in Poland and the Baltic region was accomplished only after World War II, after they had been reintegrated into the Soviet sphere, as a result of forced industrialization. Industrialization in the Soviet Union, the Baltic countries, and Poland was based on obsolete technology and an isolationist strategy of regional self-sufficiency, resulting in the perpetuation of economic backwardness. Finland emerged on a different road and gradually caught up with Western Europe.

FURTHER READING: Berend, Ivan T., and György Ránki. *The European Periphery and Industrialization 1780–1914.* Cambridge: Cambridge University Press, 1982; Gerschenkron, Alexander. "Agrarian Policies and Industrialization: Russia 1861–1917." In *Cambridge Economic History of Europe,* ed. Michael Postan, Donald Coleman, and Peter Mathias. Vol. 6/2. Cambridge: Cambridge University Press, 1965; Laue, T. H. *Sergei Witte and the Industrialization of Russia.* New York: Columbia University Press, 1969; Luxemburg, Rosa. *The Industrial Development of Poland.* New York: Campaigner Publications, 1977; Milward, Alan, and S. B. Saul. *The Development of the Economies of Continental Europe, 1850–1914.* London: Allen and Unwin, 1977; Trebilcock, Clive. *The Industrialization of the Continental Powers, 1780–1914.* London: Longman, 1981.

IVAN T. BEREND

S

Seaports

Seaports are concentrations of marine terminals and other waterfront facilities for the berthing and maintenance of seafaring ships and for the movement of passengers and/or cargoes between ships and land. Until recently, most seaports were integral parts of cities located along coasts or navigable rivers, with the waterfront facilities in close proximity to the port city's central business district (CBD). During the late twentieth century, however, technological developments led to the movement of most shipping operations to other locations and the abandonment of CBD waterfront operations. Cargo ships now dock at container terminals located on the outskirts of the city, and transoceanic jet travel has reduced passenger ship travel to vacation cruise lines operating from a handful of warm-weather seaports and a limited number of more northerly ports, such as New York City; Vancouver, British Columbia; Southampton, England; and Hamburg, Germany.

Early Seaports

During the centuries preceding the Industrial Revolution, there was relatively little change in the technology of seafaring ships and seaports. Almost all ships were wooden sailing ships, measuring 100 feet or less in length and powered by the wind, with a draft of a dozen or so feet.

There were numerous seaports, and almost every coastal or major riverine city had waterfront facilities for berthing of ships, including wharfs, piers, and lighterage facilities. The landside infrastructure also involved the roads that served the city and provided routes for transport of goods and people between the port's hinterlands to the waterfront facilities. Loading and unloading of ships were done almost entirely by human power, although movement of goods from the waterfront to other parts of port and hinterland could involve animal power.

Initial Technological Innovations

Three sets of technological innovations affected the development of seaports during the Industrial Revolution. The first set of innovations involved changes in water transport, particularly the development of metal **steamships**. The second set involved changes in land transport, with the invention of the **railroads** and, later, trucks and **automobiles**. The third set involved changes in the waterside facilities, whereby the transfers of passengers and cargo between ship and land were accomplished.

The development of the **steam engine** and the evolution of portable steam engines led to the invention of the railroad and the steamship, thereby revolutionizing waterborne and landside transportation. As these two modes of transport evolved, so did their interface, the seaport.

The evolution of the steamship led to the construction of larger ships with deeper drafts, carrying much larger amounts of cargo and passengers. By the end of the nineteenth century, the largest ships were nearly 1,000 feet long, and had drafts of 30 feet. This required the dredging of channels in many instances, for example, at New York City; Rotterdam, the Netherlands; Liverpool, England; and other major seaports. The development of larger ships, particularly giant passenger liners (which were viewed as symbols of national power among the industrialized nations), also required the construction of larger and longer berths.

The development of railroads, and the rapid growth of railroad traffic from the 1850s onward in the major industrial nations, also altered the development of seaports. They became the focus of national railroad networks, carrying increasing amounts of goods and passengers between the waterfront and the hinterland. The necessity of developing new railroad facilities to handle the waterfront traffic created extreme congestion in many of the seaport waterfronts. Demand for waterfront land also increased as a result of the need for larger warehouses to hold the increasing volume of cargoes carried in international trade.

The more frequent scheduling of ships required faster methods to load and unload them. One response was the construction of giant warehouses close to, and then actually on, the piers where ships were loaded and unloaded. This had the effect of lessening the number of piers at which traditional sailing ships could load and unload. The lengths of the ship's cross-spars and sails prevented sailing ships from getting close enough to the pier to load and unload cargoes.

Growth and Concentration of Seaports

The Industrial Revolution had the effect of concentrating most of the growing oceanic and coastal trade at a small number of very large seaports. Railroads were expensive to construct, and their builders could not serve every potential port, so they concentrated their networks on a few large coastal cities or riverfront cities with access to the sea. New York City, Boston, and Baltimore grew, whereas Richmond, Virginia, and Wilmington, North Carolina, declined. British shipping was focused in London, Liverpool, and Bristol; Dutch shipping focused in Rotterdam and Amsterdam; German shipping focused in Hamburg and Bremen. France had only a few good natural harbors to begin with: Marseilles and Le Havre. Japan after the **Meiji Restoration** limited its foreign shipping to Nagasaki, Osaka, and Kobe.

The development of larger ships also limited the number of potential seaports, because the construction of large piers and dredging of deeper channels required large expenditures that only major cities could finance. In addition, London and other seaports with large tide movements required the construction of enclosed docks to allow easy loading and unloading.

As ships became larger and larger, they needed more men to load and unload them. Some of the men were stevedores, with specialized skills that permitted rapid, safe, and efficient stowage of cargoes, whereas others, the longshoremen, usually were unskilled casual laborers who worked under the direction of the stevedores. During the twentieth century, the distinction between the two groups lessened. Strong movements emerged in the late nineteenth century to unionize dockworkers, and some rather bitter strikes erupted.

Waterfront workers usually were located in working-class neighborhoods near the waterfront, frequently given the name Sailor Town. These included London's Docklands (also known as the East End) and New York City's Hell's Kitchen.

Later Technological Innovations

A second set of technological innovations associated with the Second Industrial Revolution of the late nineteenth century (metallurgy, **petroleum industry**) also altered the pattern of seaport layout and operations. The new technologies led to shipping innovations involving the development of specialized ships. These handled only a single type of cargo, usually as specialized marine terminals located some distance away from the traditional CBD waterfront. The use of specialized ships and terminals allowed a much faster and efficient throughput of cargo at a lower per-unit cost than general ships and terminals.

The demand for massive amounts of coal during the First Industrial Revolution led to the development of specialized ships (colliers) that carried only coal and used specialized waterfront facilities for rapid loading and unloading of coal. These coal terminals required extensive acreage for temporary storage as well as numerous rail lines for large numbers of specialized coal cars. They usually were located on the outer edges of the seaports' traditional CBD waterfronts.

The Second Industrial Revolution saw the development of the **iron industry** (which required large amounts of iron ore) and the petroleum industry (which involved shipments of large volumes of crude and unrefined oil) in the 1870s and following decades. The continual demand for large amounts of shipments led to a further development of specialized ships and terminals designed to handle only one type of cargo. The first metal ore carriers and marine terminals were developed on the ports of the Great Lakes, handling eastbound shipments of ore to the foundries of Pennsylvania and Ohio.

The development of oil fields in the United States (and later Russia) was followed by a growing demand for kerosene and other petroleum products throughout the industrialized world. Shipments evolved from barrels carried on traditional ships to bulk shipments on specialized tankers, which could carry crude oil from the oil fields to refineries and also refined oil products from refineries to locations around the world. The first such was a tanker, the *Gluckauf*, operated by a subsidiary of the Standard Oil Corporation, which made its first transatlantic voyage in 1886.

The new bulk carriers evolved along with specialized terminals, which handled only a single cargo and had expensive, specialized equipment and required high investment costs but relatively few waterfront laborers. They also required lots of land, including nearby refining and storage facilities. They usually were located even farther from the traditional urban waterfront than coal terminals. The **Port of New York** oil terminals were located in New Jersey and Staten Island, rather than in Manhattan and Brooklyn.

The development of specialized ships and terminals designed to handle only a single type of cargo created a new distinction in the maritime industry, between bulk cargo (coal, ore, petroleum, etc.), and break-bulk cargo (everything else).

Development of Port Authorities

The growing size, cost, and complexity of waterfront operations led to the creation of a new type of government entity, the port authority. This had responsibility for overall planning and coordination and varying amounts of operational control over the waterfront facilities. Until the mid-1800s, few seaports had any type of specialized bureaucracy for the planning or operation of seaport facilities. Docks and piers were owned and operated by a combination of private interests and municipal government. During the late 1800s, Parliament authorized London and Liverpool to create a new type of government agency, with responsibility over waterfront operations. These were semiautonomous agencies that had the authority to float their own bonds for construction of new waterfront facilities.

The first U.S. port authority was the Port of New York Authority (now the Port Authority of New York and New Jersey), created jointly by the legislatures of New York and New Jersey under the authority of federal legislation. It was established in 1921 as a result of the bistate nature of the port and growing hostility on the part of New Jersey that its waterfront was being overshadowed by New York. The port authority concept was soon adopted by other U.S. seaports, and within a few years, the American Association of Port Authorities was founded. It functions as a central clearinghouse for port information and also plays a role in the dissemination of seaport technology.

Late-Twentieth-Century Urban Waterfront Abandonment

The second half of the twentieth century saw dramatic changes in the nature of seaports, due largely to technological innovations. The invention of the jet plane and the advent of transoceanic passenger jet service in the late 1950s put an end to passenger liners, except for the narrow category of cruise line services, which usually were based in temperate regions, such as Miami, Los Angeles and Long Beach, California.

The trend toward specialized ships and terminals that had begun with the development of bulk cargo ships and terminals in the late 1800s was paralleled a century later by the development of cargo containers for the transport of nonbulk cargoes. This involved almost all cargoes being packed in standardized containers, analogous to the van portion of a truck, which could be carried by ship, railroad, truck chassis, or barge.

Containerization required the construction and use of giant container terminals, frequently 100 acres to 500 acres in size, located outside the CBD waterfront and with access to major freeways. The trend was started in 1956, when trucking entrepreneur Malcom McLean began shipping cargo containers from Port Newark, New Jersey, to the Port of Houston, Texas. McLean chose Port Newark because of its proximity to the New Jersey Turnpike, which provided easy access to the Port of New York's hinterland. In 1958, the Matson Steamship Company began shipping cargo containers to Hawaii from Alameda (and later Oakland), California, which had better access to highways and railroads than the crowded CBD waterfront of San Francisco.

After a decade of using cargo containers on U.S. coastal routes, McLean (who owned the SeaLand Corporation) and Matson announced that they planned to offer container service on transatlantic and transpacific routes. This prompted virtually all the other major shipping lines in the United States and elsewhere to offer container service to their customers. These lines also began to move their shipping operations away from the traditional CBD waterfronts to new container terminals being constructed on the outskirts of major seaports. By the end of the 1970s, the traditional waterfronts at New York City, London, and many other seaports were abandoned and being planned for conversion to nonshipping uses.

FURTHER READING: Arnesen, Eric. *Waterfront Workers of New Orleans: Race, Class, and Politics, 1863–1923.* Urbana: University of Illinois Press, 1994; Breen, Ann, and Dick Rigby. *The New Waterfront.* London: Thames & Hudson, 1996; Broeze, Frank, ed. *Brides of the Sea: Port Cities of Asia from the 16th to 20th Centuries.* Honolulu: University of Hawai'i Press, 1989; Fischer, Lewis R., and Adrian Jarvis. *Harbours and Havens: Essays in Port History in Honor of Gordon Jackson.* St. John's, NF: International Maritime Economic History Association, 1999; Jackson, Gordon. *The History and Archaeology of Ports.* Tadworth, U.K.: World's Work, 1983; Marshall, Richard. *Waterfronts in Post-Industrial Cities.* New York: Spon Press, 2001; Palmer, Alan, and Peter Ackroyd. *The East End: Four Centuries of London Life.* New Brunswick, NJ: Rutgers University Press, 2000. WEB SITES: http://www.mun.ca/mhp/imeha.htm; http://www.portcities.org.uk/; http://www.southstseaport.org/.

STEPHEN G. MARSHALL

Sewing Machine

Sewing machines, mechanized devices that use thread to join pieces of fabric into garments or other articles, transformed the production of clothing in the United States, Europe, and other industrialized regions over the second half of the nineteenth century. A U.S. engineer, Isaac Merit Singer (1811–1875), adapted elements of existing sewing machines, patenting his model in 1851. Mass-produced and marketed internationally by 1853, the Singer sewing machine and its competitors rapidly rendered commercial hand sewing outdated.

The mechanization of manufacturing processes in the late eighteenth and early nineteenth centuries generated widespread interest in machine sewing. Designs for sewing machines were developed in 1755 by Karl Weisenthal in Germany, in 1790 by Thomas Saint in Britain, and in 1818 by John Adams Doge and John Knowles in the United States. Barthelemy Thimonnier, a French tailor, devised the first fully functional prototype in 1830. Thimonnier's machine, which used a foot treadle to move a curved needle to produce a chain stitch, was quickly adopted by the French army to produce uniforms. In 1831, two hundred tailors, participating in a wave of demonstrations resisting the mechanization of skilled crafts, set fire to his factory, destroying the machines.

In 1834, a U.S. inventor, Walter Hunt, developed a sewing machine that interlocked two threads through the layers of fabric. Stronger than the single-thread chain stitch, the lockstitch also was used by Elias Howe, who patented a machine in 1846. Synthesizing elements from Thimonnier's, Ward's, and Howe's machines, Singer produced a line of sewing machines for sale in 1853, priced at $100. Singer's company offered purchasers the option of paying for the expensive machines over the course of several years in one of the earliest corporate installment plans. By 1858, Singer and Company was selling 3,000 machines annually; a competitor, Wheeler and Wilson, produced even more machines through the 1850s and 1860s. Singer rapidly expanded into European markets, opening branch offices in Paris, Glasgow, Brazil, and Hamburg. By 1880, Singer had sold more than 500,000 machines worldwide and developed the first functional electric sewing machine, using an Edison motor.

For most home sewers, the sewing machine was an alloyed blessing, transforming what had been an arduous household task. For seamstresses and tailors, the machine had mixed consequences, as the French artisans had anticipated. It made stronger, smaller, and more even stitches than most hand sewers could achieve and was immeasurably more efficient than hand sewing, resulting in an enormous increase in productivity; however, machines remained prohibitively expensive for seamstresses and tailors. Large producers who could afford the outlay for many machines gained substantial advantage over individuals or smaller workshops: By dividing garment construction into

Early sewing machine by Elias Howe, ca. 1846. Science Museum/ Science & Society Picture Library.

piecework, manufacturers could raise output dramatically while reducing the need for skilled labor. Individual garment makers who purchased machines sometimes incurred debt that consumed their earnings; those who could not afford machines had to specialize or, increasingly, work for employers subcontracting garment production to sweatshops. By the turn of the twentieth century, factories and sweatshops that mass-produced clothing on electric sewing machines essentially had replaced the small-scale tailor as the source for everyday garments.

FURTHER READING: Brandon, Ruth. *A Capitalist Romance: Singer and the Sewing Machine.* Philadelphia: Lippincott, 1977; Godfrey, Frank P. *An International History of the Sewing Machine.* London: Robert Hale, 1982.

JANE WEISS

Shipbuilding

Shipbuilding is the construction of seagoing vessels for commercial or naval purposes at shipyards, specially designed facilities located on seacoasts or major rivers. The Industrial Revolution saw the evolution of such vessels from relatively small wooden sailing ships into large metal steamships. Changes in the size, design, and number of major ships caused the shipbuilding industry to develop the characteristics of other industrial manufacturing operations. The shipbuilding industry became dominated by a small number of large firms using mechanized methods of production, extensive use of fossil fuels, and the application of specialized scientific research and technological training.

Preindustrial Ships and Shipbuilding

During the two centuries before the Industrial Revolution, the technology involving ships and shipbuilding evolved very slowly. Virtually all major vessels were wooden sailing ships, rarely exceeding 200 feet in length and usually 100 feet or less. These carried crews of twenty to thirty men and approximately 100 tons of cargo (the equivalent of five or six contemporary cargo containers).

Sailing ships were constructed at numerous small shipyards scattered between the various seaports and river ports of the maritime states and their colonies. The shipyards were small-scale enterprises that usually employed fewer than one hundred shipwrights, woodworkers, and sailmakers. Power for sawing and other tasks was supplied by humans, animals, and, occasionally, water mills.

During the 1700s and early 1800s, most of Europe's ships were constructed at North American shipyards in the New England states and Canada's Maritime Provinces, which had ready access to large old-growth forests. The major British shipyards were located in southern England, around London, and at other sites on the Thames and its Medway River tributary. These had to rely upon lumber imported from Scandinavia and North America.

Technological Innovations

The Industrial Revolution led to two major changes in ship design: first, the application of the **steam engine** to provide ships' propulsion in place of wind, and, second, the substitution of metal (initially iron and later steel) for wood in the construction of the hull and other structures. Both changes had important consequences for the world's shipbuilding industry.

The use of steam engines for water transport had been successfully demonstrated by William Symington, Robert Fulton, and others in the early 1800s. The first such steam-propelled vessels were relatively small wooden steamboats, used on the rivers, lakes, and other sheltered waters of Britain and the United States. Construction of these early steamers required different materials and construction techniques than previous vessels. In addition to a portable steam engine, the steamboats also required enormous paddle wheels to convert the engine's output to propulsion power.

Shipyards constructing steamboats and, later, the larger oceangoing steamships needed to acquire and process different raw materials. They also needed to employ engineers and skilled labor with different technological expertise than needed for simple wooden sailing ships. The construction of steam engines required metal plates, pipes, and rivets as well as personnel skilled in boiler construction and other aspects of metalworking.

Additional amounts of metal and metalworking skills were needed after the introduction of metal hulls in the mid-1800s. Initially, wooden ships had their hulls covered with copper sheathing to reduce decay and increase resistance to collisions. Later, naval architects began to design ships with hulls constructed entirely of metal, starting with iron in the 1850s and then steel in the 1870s. The vulnerability of wooden hulls to the battering of waves had limited wooden sailing ships to a maximum length of 300 feet. The use of metal for ship construction removed this limit, and by the late 1800s, the largest steamships were nearly 1,000 feet long.

Steamships required the use of enormous amounts of coal, not only to constantly feed their engines after launching but also for their construction. The initial construction of ships' steam engines, and later the construction of ships made entirely of metal, required shipyards to construct and operate their own large steam engines for metal-fabrication processes such as rolling and stamping. In addition, as ships increased in size, larger and larger steam-powered cranes were needed to lift materials and workers to the upper levels of the ship's frame. As a result, shipyards became major consumers of coal as well as major users of energy-intensive materials such as iron and steel. These required preliminary, off-site consumption of large amounts of coal for the metals' mining, refining, and transportation to the shipyard.

The development of passenger liners also caused shipyards to acquire and use additional new materials and workers skilled in luxury-item work. Passengers in first-class cabins expected furnishings and other amenities similar to those provided by luxurious hotels. For example, the *Titanic* and its sister ship, the *Olympic,* each had electric lighting, several swimming pools and exercise gyms, intimate cafés, and a grand salon with an immense staircase.

Changes in Size and Number of Shipyards

Changes in ship technology, a demand for larger steamships, and the industrialization of the shipbuilding process led to changes in the size, number, and location of shipyards. As the nineteenth century progressed, the structure of the shipbuilding industry changed, with most activity becoming concentrated in a small number of large shipyards and shipbuilding firms. The construction of the first steamships marked the start of the industrialization of the shipbuilding industry. Steamships were more expensive to construct than sailing ships because they required steam engines, paddle wheels, and other additional mechanical apparatus to propel the ship. Shipyards needed to purchase additional materials as well as hire engineers and workmen with new technical expertise.

As steamships became larger and more complex, they also became much more expensive. The construction of large steamships required tremendous amounts of capital, raw material, and labor, which was beyond the capabilities of traditional small shipyards. Shipbuilders were required to raise larger amounts of capital for the construction of each new generation of steamships.

The trend accelerated with the introduction of metal ships. The construction of metal hulls, and then completely metal ships, further increased the cost of ship construction. In addition, shipping lines would continually place orders for larger ships, which could carry more revenue-producing cargo and passengers, in order to help amortize the cost of construction.

The *Savannah,* which in 1819 was the first steamer to cross the Atlantic (using a combination of steam-powered paddle wheels and sails), was 98 feet long, 28 feet wide, and 14 feet deep. The *Titanic,* which was constructed in the early 1900s, was 883 feet long, 92 feet wide, and 64 feet deep. The *Titanic* cost £1.5 million, or $7.5

million (the equivalent of $165 million in contemporary U.S. currency). Only a small number of giant corporate shipbuilding firms were able to raise the capital necessary to construct such giants.

Regional Distribution of Shipyards

Once wooden hulls were succeeded by metal hulls, the traditional lumber-based shipyards of the United States and Canada began losing business to British shipyards. A declining number of traditional shipyards would continue to construct wooden ships throughout the nineteenth century, and it was not until the 1870s that the number of metal ships constructed annually began to exceed the number of new wooden ships. The inherent limits upon the maximum size of wooden ships and the ever-increasing size of the largest metal ships, however, meant that by that time a much larger portion of the world's shipping was carried in metal steamships.

The rise of metal steamships caused the major determinants of successful shipyards to be: ready access to supplies of coal and iron, engineers with expertise in steam power and metalworking, and a cheap labor force. The once-great shipbuilding industry in North America drastically declined during the mid-1800s. Although the United States had large supplies of coal and iron, as well as engineers with expertise in steam technology, the nation's relatively high cost of labor put it at a relative disadvantage to Britain. After the **Civil War**, most U.S. shipyards closed. By the late 1800s, the only major U.S. shipyards were located in Pennsylvania and Delaware, along the Delaware River; at Newport News, Virginia; and at the Great Lakes.

The traditional British shipyards in southern England also lost much of their business because of their lack of access to coal and iron and the prosperous region's relatively high cost of labor. From the 1850s onward, the British (and world) shipbuilding industry was centered in Scotland and northern England. Sites along the Clyde, downriver from Glasgow, contained the largest concentration of shipyards. Other major shipyards were located on the Tyne River near Newcastle, the Tees River near Middleborough, and on the Mersey River near Liverpool and Birkenhead. Ireland lacked substantial coal and iron deposits, but it had a large, poverty-stricken population. The low cost of labor in Ireland compensated for the expense of transporting iron and coal across the Irish Channel, so several major shipyards were located in Belfast. The largest was Harland and Wolff, which constructed the *Titanic*.

During most of the nineteenth century, British shipyards constructed a majority of the world's steamships, just as British engineering firms constructed a majority of the world's railroads located outside of the United States. After the unification of Germany in the 1870s, however, the growth of German nationalism caused that nation's government to begin subsidizing German shipyards. The German Empire adopted a policy of encouraging the construction of ocean liners and naval warships equal to, or larger than, those of Britain. By the early 1900s, Hamburg was a major shipbuilding center, and two German ocean liners constructed there in 1914, the *Deutschland* and the *Imperator*, each more than 900 feet long, were the largest ships in the world at that time.

Growing nationalism also led to the development of modern shipyards in Japan, the only major Asian shipbuilding nation. The arrival of U.S. fleets (containing both sailing ships and steamships) under Commodore Matthew Perry in 1853 and 1854 forced that country to open its borders to international trade and also impressed upon many Japanese the urgent need to modernize their government and economy. After the 1868 **Meiji Restoration**, the Japanese government gave a high priority to the acquisition of steamships for commercial and naval use. The first Japanese steamships were purchased from foreign shipyards, and the government sent students to Europe to study engineering and to train in European shipyards. The government then developed large shipyards at Nagasaki, Hyogo, and Yokosuka for the construction of major steamships.

The first Japanese-built steamships were constructed according to plans purchased from European shipbuilders. By the late 1800s, Japan had acquired sufficient expertise to design and construct its own large steamships. The Japanese government sought to hasten Japanese shipping lines' transition to steam by enacting a law in 1885 that prohibited the construction of any large wooden sailing ships. During the mid-1890s, the Japanese government (following the example of the German government) began granting substantial subsidies to Japanese shipping lines that purchased Japanese-built steamships rather than ones constructed in foreign shipyards.

The Japanese government also directed Japanese shipyards to begin construction of modern naval warships designed along lines set by Britain and Germany. The Japanese destruction of the Russian fleet during the 1904–1905 Russo-Japanese War established Japan as a major power. After the end of **World War I** and the destruction of the German shipbuilding industry, Japan became the world's third-ranking nation in ship production and a major exporter of ships.

Institutional and Scientific Innovations

Another feature of shipbuilding in industrializing nations during the Industrial Revolution was its transformation from an unregulated industry using largely unwritten rule-of-thumb methods, to an industry subject to bureaucratic regulation and using the results of systematic research in science and engineering.

At the onset of the Industrial Revolution, shipbuilders in Europe and the United States were subject to minimal regulation. They were required only to register their ship's class and size with the government (for purposes of taxation) and, if they chose, with an insurance society. As ships increased in size and cargo capacity and as ships' ownership became increasingly separated from cargo ownership, insurance coverage became more important. Ships' customers and their insurance firms demanded more detailed information about the ships' construction and began setting minimum standards required of ships seeking to obtain cargo insurance. Britain led the way, with the standards set by Lloyd's Register of British and Foreign Shipping being made mandatory for all British ships. Other nations had their own similar bodies, including France's Bureau Veritas International Register of Shipping, Germany's Germanischer Lloyd, and the U.S. Record of American and Foreign Shipping.

After steamships began to specialize in passenger transport and the number of passenger liners began to increase in the mid-1800s, the government of Britain (and later other nations) began setting safety standards for passenger liners. In addition, the governments of Britain and other nations began setting standards for the seaworthiness of cargo ships in the late 1800s. The most important step was designed to prevent ships from sinking as a result of being overloaded with cargo. All ships using British ports were required to have a Plimsoll mark, indicating the waterline of a safely loaded ship, permanently painted on the ship's hull.

The shipbuilding industry also was affected by the use of systematic scientific research seeking to optimize ship design. In the early 1800s, John Scott Russell pioneered the science of hydrodynamics by studying wave-disturbance patterns and their impact on ships. The desire to optimize steamships' travel time and establish set dates for their arrivals caused later researchers to focus upon one central question: How much (engine) power was required for a ship to attain a desired speed? William Froude pioneered the method of using scaled ship models towed by precisely calibrated devices in experimental water tanks to measure water resistance and other frictional forces acting upon moving vessels.

The development of scientific information relevant to ship design and marine engineering was paralleled by the establishment of educational institutions to disseminate this information. Russell played an important role in the establishment of the Institution of Naval Architects in 1869, whose *Transactions* became the field's leading publication. Britain also established the Royal School of Naval Architecture and Marine Engineering (later the Royal Naval College) in 1864. The United States adopted naval engineering as an integral component of the curriculum at the U.S. Naval Academy at Annapolis, Maryland. France, Germany, and other seafaring nations also established government-funded institutions designed to conduct and disseminate the results of scientific research in hydrodynamics and naval engineering.

FURTHER READING: Chida, Tomohei, and Peter N. Davies. *The Japanese Shipping and Shipbuilding Industries: A History of their Modern Growth.* Atlantic Highlands, NJ: Athlone Press, 1990; Evans, David. *Building the Steam Navy: Dockyards, Technology and the Creation of the Victorian Battle Fleet 1830–1906.* Annapolis, MD: Naval Institute Press, 2004; Green, Rod. *Building the Titanic: An Epic Tale of the Creation of History's Most Famous Ocean Liner.* Pleasantville, NY: Readers Digest, 2005; Pollard, Sidney, and Paul Robinson. *The British Shipbuilding Industry, 1870–1914.* Cambridge, MA: Harvard University Press, 1979; Thiesen, William H. *Industrializing American Shipbuilding: The Transformation of Ship Design and Construction, 1820–1920.* Gainesville: University Press of Florida, 2006. WEB SITES: http://www.clydesite.co.uk/articles/; http://gdl.cdlr.strath.ac.uk/airgli/airgli0112.htm; http://www.geocities.com/naforts/ships/yards.html; http://www.mhi.co.jp/nsmw/indexe.html.

STEPHEN G. MARSHALL

Siemens, Ernst Werner von (1816–1892)

Ernst Werner von Siemens, known as Werner, was a Prussian electrical engineer who was instrumental in initiating a number of electrical industries in the nineteenth century. He and his family advanced the Second Industrial Revolution and laid the foundation for what is today a multibillion-dollar and multinational global conglomerate. Siemens founded the company named after him in Berlin in 1847 and used this platform to expand upon his inventions such as the electric dynamo and the world's first pointer telegraph. He became more than an inventor and engineer toiling in a workshop and emerged as an entrepreneur and industrialist, often credited with the founding of the electrical engineering discipline.

Siemens's early contribution to the field of communications was a telegraph featuring a needle that pointed to the correct letter as a result of transmitted electrical impulses. Siemens's design solved the problem of transmitting messages reliably over great distances with the first European electric telegraph link extending 500 miles from Berlin to Frankfurt am Main. He established the company Telegraphen-Bauanstalt von Siemens und Halske in his little workshop in 1847. Siemens contributed another major advance in telegraphy by suggesting the use of gutta-percha to insulate wire conductors in cable. Gutta-percha, a resin extracted from the *Isonandra gutta* tree in Malaya, was found suitable to insulate and moisture-proof cable. In 1850, Siemens & Halske linked Dover, England, and Calais, France, with the first major submarine cable.

Siemens advanced the field of electrical generation. In 1866, he discovered the principle of the dynamo, now called a generator, a device that converts mechanical energy into electrical energy without the use of permanent magnets. His moving-coil transducer extended Michael **Faraday**'s work by providing an alternative source of power to the battery. This discovery embraced the notion of self-excitation and allowed Siemens to produce energy conversions in an economical way. Siemens received a German patent for the dynamo in 1877.

Later, Siemens extended his work to the field of transportation. Participation at the 1879 Berlin Trade Fair saw the first demonstration of an electric railway. The locomotive was powered by electric energy supplied by a third rail in the middle of the track. The resultant three horsepower generated propelled the three-car train around a circular track at four miles per hour. Shortly thereafter, the first electric streetcar was made operational at Lichterfelde, near Berlin, in 1881; electric propulsion subsequently revolutionized urban mass transit.

Emperor Friedrich III ennobled him in 1888 as Werner von Siemens. He retired from his company at the age of 74 and died two years later in 1892. Due to the widespread recognition of the Siemens name and its association with *Elektrotechnik,* the German word for electrical engineering that Siemens coined, he became known as the father of electrical engineering.

Siemens's work spanned many fields of electrical innovation—communications, electrical generation, and transportation—during the Second Industrial Revolution. Many believe the impetus for this was the discovery and widespread acceptance of electricity during the late nineteenth century. Siemens was a major contributor to this advance. Consequently, in his honor, the Siemens name has been adopted as the international unit of electrical conductance. *See also* Electric Dynamo; Telegraphy.

FURTHER READING: Koslowsky, Robert. *A World Perspective through 21st Century Eyes: The Impact of Science on Society.* Victoria, BC: Trafford Publishing, 2004; Siemens AG. "Siemens History." Siemens AG Web Site. At http://w4.siemens.de/archiv/en/index.html.

ROBERT KARL KOSLOWSKY

Skyscrapers

Skyscraper is a term used to describe a building of great height, although it was originally used in a nautical context to describe the tall mast on a sailing ship. In an architectural context, however, the term dates from the 1880s when it was employed to explain the large vertical form of buildings in U.S. cities like Chicago and New York. Today, in the United States, the expression refers to edifices of 495 feet or more in height, suitable for residential or commercial use, and with a steel skeleton frame structure, a technological invention dating from the latter half of the nineteenth century. In past times, the term was used to describe buildings of much lower height, hence the definition can be subjective, used merely to describe a structure that presents an imposing appearance. Thus the term can be applied to any building that stands out in the local environment, just as the first tall buildings did in New York and Chicago in the 1880s and 1890s, even though they were lower than 495 feet in height.

The development of technology was fundamental to the evolution of skyscrapers. The invention of steel framing, pioneered by William Le Baron Jenney (1832–1907) in Chicago, for instance, was crucial in allowing building design to take on an increased vertical scale, but important, too, are technologies such as elevators to transport people quickly and safely from the ground floor to upper floors, the development of water pumps and central heating systems, plus the widespread adoption of steel, glass, and reinforced concrete within the construction process. Thus skyscrapers represent material manifestations of modern technology.

The reasons why buildings since the 1880s have taken on an increased vertical height are many. They include the high demand for centrally located land; the limited supply of available land; the high cost of urban real estate that makes it unaffordable to have wide, low buildings; and advances relating to construction and materials of strong resistance to tensile stress. Additional reasons included the desire of companies to locate their offices at the central core of cities so as to be accessible to labor pools, the practical needs of large companies with many departments for large amounts of space within the same building so as to operate effectively, and ego, the status associated with very tall buildings.

Although the history of skyscrapers has been dominated by the United States (before 1998, the tallest building in the world was located either in Chicago, the home of the world's first skyscrapers, or New York City), other cities presently are synonymous with skyscrapers. Among some of the earliest skyscrapers are, in New York, the New World Building (1890), MetLife Building (1909), and Woolworth Building (1913), though for many years, the Sears Tower, built in 1974 in Chicago, was the world's tallest. In the past few years, Asian cities like Hong Kong, Shanghai, Singapore, Kuala Lumpur, and Taipei—home of the world's tallest building, the 1,676-foot Taipei 101 Tower—have undertaken tall-building construction, and as such, skyscrapers in Asia represent displays by companies and societies that they, too, are technologically and economically advanced and able to compete economically and culturally with nations of the West.

FURTHER READING: Moudry, Roberta. *The American Skyscraper: Cultural Histories.* Cambridge: Cambridge University Press, 2005; Oxlade, Chris. *Skyscrapers: Uncovering Technology.* Tonawanda, NY: Firefly Books, 2006.

IAN MORLEY

Slavery

Slavery is a system in which one class of people is owned by and under the control of a dominant group. The process is both economic and social in nature because slaves cannot be self-sufficient and must rely on the controlling group for their basic needs. In return, they perform work that produces a value that is proportionally greater than the so-called compensation they receive; thus, in a market economy, the dominant group makes a profit from the labor of the slaves.

In the New World, prior to the Spanish conquests, slavery existed wherever there were warring factions, whether the political structure was tribal or highly stratified, such as in the Mesoamerican state formations. Native Americans in South America, the Mochica, documented the capture and slavery of their enemies in distinctive pottery. Often, after a number of years, slaves integrated into the culture and became full-fledged members of the capturing society.

In Europe, the slave trade originated in the fifteenth century in Portugal after two of Prince Henry the Navigator's captains explored Africa and discovered an opportunity to trade spices and precious metals for so-called heathens. With the pope's permission and the church's blessings, a slave trade was started. The first 1,000 Africans were brought to Portugal to work on large farms as their means to salvation. Sometimes, African warriors invaded villages and took prisoners to be traded with Europeans for weapons, fabric, or wine.

After Spain reached the Bahamas and the New World, indigenous people from the Caribbean, specifically those who did not convert to Christianity, were forced into slavery to build the churches and missions of the Spanish government. In the Greater Antilles, by 1500, Hispaniola, the island now shared by the Dominican Republic and Haiti, had grown to become the Spanish capital in America. Sugar plantations, a form of commercialized agriculture, were established but required large numbers of African slaves to work. In Latin America, large-scale mining operations were developed by the Spanish that also required slave workers. As large numbers of people were forced into the pristine areas of the New World, Old World diseases such as smallpox, measles, typhoid, influenza, and mumps came with them. In Brazil and the Caribbean, malaria and yellow fever ran rampant. Native Americans were rapidly exterminated, either from disease or execution for heresy, and it is estimated that the 25 million people in Mesoamerica at the time of the conquests were reduced to 1.5 million by 1650. Hence, more Africans were imported to work as slaves.

The English slave trade had been minimal until British colonies were established in the Caribbean, where sugar cane was grown. On the mainland, in the colonies established by England and France, Native Americans were used as slaves. Another group of people forced to work for wealthy landowners were immigrants from England or Ireland, poor whites, who were indentured servants, prisoners, or redemptioners (immigrants who had agreed to pay a ship's captain for their trip to America after they arrived). They were given a time frame to fulfill their contract and, if they did not comply, were sold as slaves to the highest bidder. As whites fulfilled their obligations to their sponsors, they were freed from their indentured status.

In 1663, the Company of Royal Adventurers was established for the sole purpose of slave trading, but it did not thrive and was replaced by a new company, the Royal African Company, that did. Between 1700 and 1740, 55,000 Africans were shipped to the Chesapeake area alone from Africa. By 1800, 10 million to 15 million Africans had been transported as slaves to the Americas. The morbidity and mortality on slave ships was so high that only one-third of those originally captured survived to be sold. Once in America, families were separated, never to see each other again. These people, weakened from the stresses of the voyage and rough handling, were forced into cages with Africans from other tribes, usually speaking mutually unintelligible languages. In this way, any solidarity or coalitions to protest were not possible. They were stripped naked and paraded like livestock for sale to the highest bidder.

Slavery probably would not have been so crucial to the economy of North America had it not been for the growth of the **cotton** industry in the eighteenth and nineteenth centuries, fueled by the intense demand from Great Britain. In 1790, 1,000 tons of cotton was being produced every year in the south. To accomplish that amount of work, 500,000 slaves were required. By 1860, 1 million tons of cotton was being produced by 4 million slaves. Georgia became the leading state in cotton production. Other crops such as rice, indigo, tobacco, and sugar cane required the labor of slaves as well. The tobacco industry started in Virginia and North Carolina then expanded into Missouri and Kentucky. At the start of the American **Civil War** (1861), 15,000 slaves worked in tobacco processing.

The continued growth of an industrial economy in North America created a need for factory workers, shipbuilders, fishermen, and various maritime occupations. Sometimes, slaves were trained to be apprentices or skilled in certain trades, and they achieved a certain modicum of autonomy, but nonetheless they remained slaves. Iron manufacturing in Richmond, Virginia, employed slaves for more than half of its labor force. Slaves were used in coal, gold, copper, lead, and salt mines, all dangerous and unhealthful activities. Although 80 percent of these industrial slaves were owned by entrepreneurs, others were rented.

Working conditions for factory slaves were harsher than for agricultural slaves. Rarely was their welfare considered, and as in Britain at the beginning of the Industrial Revolution, hours were long, machinery was treacherous, temperature conditions were extreme both indoors and out, and no laws for health or safety existed.

Although the original British colonies in the north had established slavery, the independent states officially abolished it, starting with Vermont in 1777, followed by Pennsylvania in 1780, Massachusetts and New Hampshire in 1783, Connecticut and Rhode Island in 1784, New York in 1799, and New Jersey in 1804, but it was not until much later that slavery actually ended in those states. The southern states were different. At the time of the Civil War, Alabama, Arkansas, Delaware, the District of Columbia, Florida, Georgia, Kentucky, Louisiana, Maryland, Mississippi, Missouri, North Carolina, South Carolina, Tennessee, Texas, and Virginia were slave states. Some states such as Missouri had both free and slave boundaries because of the Louisiana Purchase.

Slavery had a distinct economic advantage to the plantation owner because black slaves, purchased for their entire lives, cost the same amount of money as hiring a white servant for 10 years. Owning black slaves had another advantage: If a white escaped, his skin color made him invisible in a world populated by whites, but an African was doomed because his dark skin exposed him. The Fugitive Slave Act, passed in 1850, allowed slave owners to recapture slaves who ran away. When Dred Scott, a slave in the free area of Missouri, sued the Supreme Court for his freedom, he was denied that right because he was considered property, not a person. That 1857 Supreme Court decision stated that people of African descent were not and could not be citizens and therefore could not sue in any of the courts. Although Scott lived in free territory, that fact did not make him free, and the Missouri Compromise, which had been the reason that the state was split between slave and free, was declared unconstitutional.

In September 1862, President Abraham Lincoln issued the preliminary Emancipation Proclamation. In January 1863, it became official. "All persons held as slaves within any state or designated part of a state the people whereof shall then be in rebellion against the United States shall be then, thenceforward and forever free." Interestingly, it declared slaves free in the South in those areas fighting to secede from the union but made no provisions for slaves behind union lines. After emancipation, many slaves chose to participate in the Civil War despite the fact that they were paid less than the white troops.

Had it not been for the contributions the slaves made to the colonial settlements in the Caribbean and North and South America and the production of coffee, cotton, rum, sugar, and tobacco, capitalism in the Americas probably would never have achieved such a high level. The relationship between southern cotton growers and northern textile factories created an industry that depended on slavery for its survival. The per capita wealth that was generated in the southern states from slave-produced cotton would not be matched by either Mexico or India (two other cotton-producing countries) until 100 years after the Civil War ended.

FURTHER READING: Brace, Richard E. *The Making of the Modern World.* New York: Rineholt and Winston, 1961; Horton, James, and Lois Horton. *Slavery and the Making of America.* Oxford: Oxford University Press, 2005; Middleton, Richard. *Colonial America: A History, 1565–1776.* Victoria, BC: Blackwell, 2002; Miller, Randall M., and John David Smith, eds. *Dictionary of Afro-American Slavery.* New York: Greenwood Press, 1988; Olson, James S. *Encyclopedia of the Industrial Revolution in America.* New York: Greenwood Press, 2002; Scupin, Raymond, and Christopher Decorse. *Anthropology: A Global perspective.* 4th ed. Englewood Cliffs, NJ: Prentice Hall, 2001; Stearns, Peter N., and John H. Hinshaw. *The Industrial Revolution.* Santa Barbara, CA: ABC-Clio, 1996; Urdang, Laurence, ed. *The Timetables of American History.* New York: Touchstone, 1996; Williams, E. *Capitalism and Slavery.* Chapel Hill: University of North Carolina Press, [1944] 1994; Zinn, Howard. *A People's History of the United States.* New York: HarperCollins,1999.

LANA THOMPSON

Smith, Adam (1723–1790)

Adam Smith is generally credited as the first representative of the classical school of economics. He was born in Kirkaldy (near Edinburgh), Scotland, on June 5, 1723. Smith was a good student and attended Glasgow College before receiving a scholarship that permitted him to attend Oxford University. He studied at Oxford between 1740 and 1746 then gave occasional lectures in Scotland before being appointed professor of logic at Glasgow College in 1751. The following year, he was elected professor of moral philosophy. (There was no academic discipline called *economics* at that time; moral philosophy was what would now be considered social science. Smith covered natural philosophy, ethics, jurisprudence, politics, and economics.)

During his tenure at Glasgow, he wrote *The Theory of Moral Sentiments* (1759). He resigned in 1764 to become tutor to the young duke of Buccleugh, a post that also involved traveling in Europe with his charge. In the course of these travels, he met many of the leading European thinkers, in particular the French physiocrats François Quesnay and Anne Robert Jacques Turgot. (It is these French physiocrats to whom we owe the phrase, long associated with Adam Smith, of *laissez faire, laissez passer.*) Smith also spent part of this time working on his second major work, *The Wealth of Nations,* which was published in 1776 (the same year his friend the philosopher David Hume died). Smith's tutorship ended in 1776 with a lifetime pension.

He also was appointed commissioner of customs for Scotland in 1777, a post he held until his death in Edinburgh on July 17, 1790.

Adam Smith generally is considered to be the founder of the classical political economy tradition, and both followers and critics of this line of thinking start from this point. Writers had written on economic topics before Smith, but even when insightful, the topics were simply isolated ideas, rather than complete attempts to explain an economic system and how it worked. Simply put, before the advent of widespread market systems, there were few interesting economic questions to ask about what people did and why they did it; in a traditional economy such as a medieval feudal one, the answers were obvious. They were no longer obvious in a market economy, however, in which there seemed to be no clear coordinating mechanism holding society together.

What Smith (and the later classical economist David **Ricardo**) did was to bring order to economic thinking. Based on Smith's presentation in the *Wealth of Nations*, he was the first to describe the categories that ever since have been studied as the academic discipline of economics.

His influence on practical matters also was considerable. In much the same way that John Calvin, via the development of the Protestant ethic, had made merchants' money-making activities socially acceptable more than a century earlier, so Smith did the same for industrialists. Writing in the second half of the eighteenth century, before most of the major technological and institutional changes associated with the Industrial Revolution had taken place, he made industrialists' activities socially respectable. He did this by advocating that the private pursuit of profits was actually in the public interest. He was influential in providing theoretical justification for the removal of restrictions on foreign trade, policies that also contributed to the expansion of industry.

Smith never became as influential outside Britain, however, most likely because the conditions that led to the initial industrialization of Britain were not duplicated elsewhere. Smith was very much a product of his time and place, and it is possible to identify four major influences on his work. First was the general intellectual climate of the times, the eighteenth-century Enlightenment. Isaac Newton and other scientific thinkers had emphasized that human reasoning could uncover the laws governing the natural universe. Smith applied this concept of a natural order to human society, then the task was to find out what these laws were and to organize society so that it was in accordance with them.

The second influence came from his association with the physiocrats, who opposed mercantilist restrictions and wanted to remove barriers to trade. Where Smith differed from both the mercantilists and the physiocrats, however, was in his focus on manufacturing, rather than the exchange of an already-produced volume of output (mercantilists) or on the growth of agricultural output (physiocrats). By his time and in his country, Smith was aware that industrial activity was more than simply the conversion of a given amount of raw materials into a given amount of final goods; rather, it contained the potential for an expanding volume of material wealth because of the use of productive labor in the manufacturing process. Ultimately, wealth was the outcome of the labor of the people who produced it.

The third influence came from his instructor at Glasgow College, Francis Hutcheson. Hutcheson taught that people could find out what was ethically good, not through divine revelation but rather by discovering (and performing) those actions that would serve to benefit humans. Finally, the fourth influence came from his close friend David Hume, a natural-law philosopher, whose idea of harmony led Smith to the idea of an equilibrium, and equilibrium economics has been a standard concept in mainstream economics ever since.

When combined, Smith's two works together provide a coherent view of a capitalist society. It provides a call for an end to artificial restrictions that limit the potential for growth. Using the principle of organizing society according to its underlying natural laws implies a limited role for government, or laissez-faire. In such a society, government's role should be limited solely to providing defense against external aggression, administering justice (and preserving competition), and the building and maintenance of public works and institutions such as roads and schools.

From *The Theory of Moral Sentiments* came the ideas describing the components of the natural order of society. There are certain moral forces that provide checks and balances on each other; they are a desire for individual freedom balanced by a sense of what is socially right and proper, a need for work to create goods balanced by a need to exchange them, and self-interest balanced by altruism. When combined, these support a harmonious social order in which the common good is promoted even though each individual is acting to advance his own particular individual interests.

In *The Wealth of Nations* (whose complete title is *An Inquiry into the Nature and Causes of Wealth of the Wealth of Nations*), he is attempting to find a theory of economic growth. Smith's wealth is what we would now refer to as *national income,* or gross domestic product. Labor, Smith believed, is the source of all wealth, and it is the application of human ingenuity and skill to inanimate materials that produces wealth. The cause of an expansion of output is the division of labor. (Although acknowledging that more and better capital equipment also will increase output, Smith's primary focus on labor is probably more influenced by his particular time period.) The division of labor increases output because workers simply get better at doing a task if they have to perform only one task rather than many; they save time by not having to move from one task to another. Finally, by simplifying tasks to their individual components, it becomes easier to invent a machine to do it faster than a human.

Ironically, although Smith emphasized the labor of the members of society as the source of all wealth, it often seems as though he lost sight of the fact that it is humans who produce this labor. His treatment of labor as a commodity rather than a creative human activity, with labor to be purchased by the capitalist, is echoed in the nineteenth-century factories with their references to workers as (almost disembodied) *hands,* rather than sentient human beings. He did recognize, however, that the farther the division of labor was taken, the more it would simplify each task and make it boring and repetitive. This would reflect on the person doing the work, dulling their senses, and essentially dehumanizing the person.

Economic activity produces a harmony of interests as if an invisible hand channels all individual actions toward some social equilibrium. So although self-interest motivates people's actions, competition limits it. (Despite the fact that the concept of the invisible hand is always associated with Smith, it is only mentioned once in the 900-plus pages of *The Wealth of Nations*.) By identifying the principles underlying the working of the capitalist system and developing policies that will remove any barriers preventing the operation of these natural laws, the economy can achieve its growth potential. This justifies a laissez-faire approach. Hence, with the exceptions noted earlier, any government action that interferes with the ordinary business of commerce and industry is harmful. Any restrictions on trade such as prohibitions, excessive import duties, or restrictive trade treaties will limit industrial expansion and thus the nation's wealth. Thus, the appropriate regime is one of laissez-faire, competition, and free trade, the standard policy prescriptions of the classical economists and a message that was like music to the ears of the nation's industrialists. In practice, Smith was writing in a period in which the first steps toward dismantling trade restrictions were being taken and, with the exception of periods of warfare at the turn of the century, continued to contribute to the expansion of the British economy.

FURTHER READING: Oser, Jacob, and Stanley L. Brue. *The Evolution of Economic Thought.* 4th ed. New York: Harcourt, Brace, Jovanovich, 1988; Roll, Eric. *A History of Economic Thought.* 4th ed. London: Faber & Faber, 1973; Smith, Adam. *The Wealth of Nations.* Ed. Edwin Cannan. New York: Modern Library, 1994. Originally published 1776; Spiegel, Henry William. *The Growth of Economic Thought.* Rev. ed. Durham, NC: Duke University Press, 1983. WEB SITE: http://www.adamsmith.org (Adam Smith Institute).

CHRISTINE RIDER

Smoot-Hawley Tariff (1930)

The Smoot-Hawley Tariff, passed by the Congress of the United States in 1930, marked the end of any pretense of free trade and accelerated the onset of the **Great Depression** that affected the industrialized nations in the 1930s. The free-trade era of the nineteenth century, initiated by Great Britain's removal of mercantilist restrictions after 1815 and symbolized by the repeal of the **Corn Laws** in 1846, began to weaken in the last third of the century, under pressure from both farmers and industrialists in many nations. The so-called golden age of competitive capitalism of the mid-nineteenth century was accompanied by the continued expansion of industrialization and international trade, which intensified competition, and there was often a backlash against free trade, led by those adversely affected. This was so especially in those industries created or greatly expanded by industrialization.

With the improvements of transportation associated with the **railroads** and the steamships, it was feasible for the first time to trade relatively low-value goods in the international market. The opening of new agricultural areas—in the U.S. Midwest, the Ukraine, Hungary, and Australia, for example—meant that the European workforce had access to cheaper food imports. Although farmers in these new areas gained from access to these international markets, farmers in many European countries found the competition from low-cost imports damaging and began to demand protection from foreign competition. This protectionist sentiment began to be evident in the depressed conditions of the 1870s, and many countries, with the exception of Britain, which held fast to its free-trade principles, began to impose protectionist duties. In France, for example, imports of U.S. pork were banned in 1881, tariffs were imposed on imports of cereals in 1885, and a two-tier tariff structure was introduced in 1892, affecting both agricultural items (with the exception of raw cotton) and manufactured goods. Farmers in other countries also demanded protection from foreign competition, and, even though production costs would rise if cheap food were no longer imported, industrialists also saw an advantage for themselves if tariff barriers were raised.

Trade liberalization consequently slowed in depressed times as protectionist policies were put into place. Then came the outbreak of **World War I** in 1914, which ended any pretence of continuing normal trading patterns. The war's end revealed a dramatic shift in the global balance of economic power. The United States ended the war period as the world's largest economic power but, unlike Britain a century earlier, did not grasp the opportunity to influence the international economy, except in a rather negative way. The country also had emerged as a net creditor nation and had lent significant amounts to the European Allies to help pay for the war. For example, Britain had borrowed about $5 billion, and France had borrowed almost $4 billion. After the war, the United States insisted on full repayment of these war debts. Unfortunately, protectionist sentiment in the United States coupled with an isolationist tendency (as evidenced by Congress's refusal to ratify the treaty establishing the League of Nations) made it difficult for the European nations to earn the foreign exchange necessary to repay the debts, as various trade barriers were imposed limiting access to the large U.S. market.

All the industrialized nations found recovery after World War I difficult and tried to protect their own nation's economy by raising tariffs in the misguided expectation that this would help the domestic economy if foreign competition were kept at bay. In the United States, the Fordney-McCumber Tariff of 1922 increased import duties to an average 38 percent. Then came the stock market crash of October 1929, which led to pressure on the Congress to add further protection. Hence the passage in June 1930 of the Smoot-Hawley Tariff, which raised U.S. tariffs to historically high levels, an average of 52.8 percent.

Some of the explanation for its passage can be found in political reality. U.S. farmers had lost some of their markets once European farmers recovered after World War I, and the 1920s saw agricultural overproduction and falling commodity prices, leading to demands for help from farmers. Congress, whose members represent local interests rather than national ones, had the power under the Constitution to develop commercial policy, and it acceded to these pressures, although the vote in the Senate was extremely close: 44 votes in favor and 42 against. U.S. industrialists also joined the proprotectionist tide, fearing loss of their markets as European industry recovered. (Although international markets were never as important to U.S. manufacturers as they were to British ones, nevertheless they could not be ignored.) There were some industries that neither needed or wanted tariff protection. The U.S. automobile industry, for example, was rapidly becoming a world leader and argued strongly in favor of free trade and against passage, but the act actually placed a 10 percent duty on all imported automobiles anyway.

Once the new high tariffs were in place, U.S. trading partners retaliated with their own, beginning a series of so-called beggar-thy-neighbor policies in which each country tried to improve its own position at the expense of the others. The end result was predictable. Between 1929 and 1933, world trade fell to a third of its previous level, from $35 billion to $12 billion. U.S. exports to Europe alone fell from $2.3 billion in 1929 to $784 million in 1932, and its imports from Europe fell from $1.3 billion in 1929 to only $390 million in 1932.

Although this tariff did not cause the Great Depression, it did nothing to prevent the fall of output and employment levels and was an important reason for its continuance worldwide. Economists almost universally recognized this, as evidenced by the protest to Smoot-Hawley signed by 1,000 leaders in the field. This depressing effect occurs because international trade links countries' economies. One country's imports are another country's exports, and without the boost to demand and thus to domestic output and employment levels given by export production, there will be less demand (and less foreign exchange) for imported goods that provide a similar boost for the exporting trading partner. For the United States, the worst year of the Depression was 1933, although full recovery would have to wait for the wartime demand of World War II. Some recovery in trade began to be made in 1934, however, following passage of the Reciprocal Trade Agreements Act by Congress. This act transferred tariff-setting authority to the president (who presumably could act in the national interest), who was empowered to lower tariffs up to 50 percent from Smoot-Hawley levels in the event of a bilateral trade agreement being signed with another country. Before 1945, 27 such bilateral agreements were made, lowering tariffs to about the levels they were before Smoot-Hawley. This act marks the start of a preference for trade liberalization over protectionism, which definitely would characterize the period after World War II with its movement toward multilateral agreements.

FURTHER READING: Cohn, Theodore H. *Global Political Economy: Theory and Practices*. New York: Addison Wesley Longman, 2000; Eichengreen, Barry. "The Political Economy of the Smoot-Hawley Tariff." *Research in Economic History* 12 (1989), p. 1–43; Hacker, Louis M. *The United States since 1865*. 4th ed. New York: Appleton-Century-Crofts, 1949; Jones, Joseph M., Jr. *Tariff Retaliation: Repercussions of the Smoot-Hawley Bill*. Philadelphia: University of Pennsylvania Press, 1934; Kindleberger, Charles P. *The World in Depression, 1929–1939*. Berkeley and Los Angeles: University of California Press, 1973. WEB SITE: http://www.state.gov/r/pa/ho/time/id/17606.htm.

CHRISTINE RIDER

Socialism

Derived from the French word *socialisme*, socialism generally refers to a belief system that holds that material goods and their means of production (i.e., factories and other resources) should be owned and managed collectively by society rather than on an individual basis. Furthermore, the overall societal ethos should be an egalitarian or a communitarian one that does away with substantive wealth or income disparities and rigid class and status hierarchies.

Socialism usually is viewed as an alternative to market capitalism, with its market-determined salaries, rewards and resource allocation, and private ownership of the means of producing goods and services, as a way of organizing society. Socialists want to substitute a more communitarian ethos and social ownership of the means of production for the profit motive and selfishness that they see as characterizing capitalist societies. Although elements of socialist thought are found in virtually all societies, religions, and historical eras, currently socialism refers to the set of critiques emerging from the gross income and wealth disparities, abysmal working conditions, and social unrest and turmoil resulting from the rapid economic growth and social transformation caused by the Industrial Revolution in many European societies in the nineteenth and early twentieth centuries.

Broadly speaking, socialism may be subdivided into three distinct categories: utopian, revolutionary, and evolutionary.

Utopian Socialism

Essentially, utopian socialists held that humans could learn to be better human beings if they lived in a society that did not actively encourage undesirable traits. The hallmark of utopian socialism was the attempt to design a perfect society in which humanity would be allowed to develop in the best possible way. *Utopian socialist* was the derogatory term coined by Karl **Marx** (1818–1883) to describe those who, in his view, constructed elaborate social systems without first carefully analyzing how they might be achieved or sustained.

Although theorists such as the Comte de Saint-Simon (1760–1825) simply wrote about their perfect society, some of the utopian socialists actually attempted to put their ideals into practice. By far the best known of these practical utopianists were Robert **Owen** (1771–1858) in Britain and Charles **Fourier** (1772–1837) in France.

In an age of inhumane employers and dangerous and degrading working conditions, Owen, a successful Manchester textile mill owner, was known as a compassionate employer. In contrast to his contemporaries, Owen was content with a 5 percent return on his investment and actively promoted his workers' welfare. His philanthropic work won him a great number of admirers and considerable influence in Britain. In 1826, Owen sank most of his fortune into establishing New Harmony, Indiana, as the site of his ideal near-autarkic community. Money and religion were banned and work and child rearing done communally; New Harmony failed because it was hard to survive in its surrounding environment that was hostile to its beliefs and was dissolved within a few years. Owen returned to England nearly bankrupt and devoted the rest of his life to furthering communitarian and trade-union goals.

Fourier developed his idea of phalansteries, producer cooperatives, as an antidote to the intense competition seen in modern societies. He envisaged a system in which workers would live communally in one large building, take turns doing the most disliked jobs, be paid on the basis of work desirability, and strive to achieve self-sufficiency in all respects. Several attempts were made in the United States in the 1840s to create such worker communities, but most failed within their first few years.

Today, utopian socialism is found in such diverse examples as the early Israeli kibbutzim, agrarian cooperatives, and organizations in the United States such as the remarkably successful but very small East Wind commune in Missouri.

Revolutionary Socialism

Also rejecting modern society, but not willing to distance themselves from it, were the revolutionary socialists. Although this school is usually associated with Karl Marx (1818–1883) and Friedrich Engels (1820–1895) and their followers, revolutionary socialism predates them.

For instance, François Babeuf (1760–1797) was executed by the revolutionary French government for advocating an equal redistribution of all property and conspiring against the government. Pierre-Joseph Proudhon (1809–1865), best known for his assertion that "All property is theft," and Mikhail Bakunin (1814–1876) were both revolutionary anarchists who sought the violent destruction of all governments, laws, and restrictions on people. In the sense of maximizing individual liberty, they may be considered a strong influence on U.S. libertarianism. By the ending decades of the nineteenth century, several anarchist European trade unions, especially in France and Spain, favored syndicalism after the traditional state was abolished. Syndicalism, rule by trade unions, was a relatively short-lived movement, although the early days of the Russian Revolution of 1917, with workers' councils determining policy, did seem to imply a triumph of syndicalism.

The dominant strain of revolutionary socialism, however, is Marxian in origin and is based on the labor theory of value (LTV). First propounded by Adam **Smith** (1723–1790) and further refined by David **Ricardo** (1772–1823), the LTV essentially states that the true worth or inherent value of any material object is a function of the labor time that went into its production. This is in contrast to subjective value theory, which dominates neoclassical economics theory and holds that a good is worth only as much as someone is willing to pay for it.

Society, according to Marx, was divided into two main groups or classes: the **bourgeoisie**, who owned the means of production and hired workers, and the proletariat, who had to hire out their labor. The relationship between these groups is exploitative because the proletariat are not paid for the full value of their labor. In Marxian terms, surplus value is maximized by reducing compensated and increasing uncompensated labor time in order to increase the profit level.

A simple example might serve to better illustrate this: Suppose a worker is hired for one hour, paid $10, and produces goods worth $17.50. The compensated labor time is $10 and the uncompensated $7.50. This uncompensated labor, or surplus value, is what is commonly termed *profit*. The logic of capitalism holds that, if a capitalist firm is to survive, it must exploit its workers, maximize surplus value (profit), and reinvest to stay ahead of its competition.

According to Marx, capitalism contained an internal contradiction: It is to every capitalist's benefit to cut labor costs by reducing wages and replacing workers with machinery. If all capitalists do so, however, workers, who are the majority of the population, will not be able to purchase the goods being manufactured. Thus, declining sales and profit margins will bankrupt smaller firms and the economy comes to be dominated by a few giant firms, a stage Marx called monopoly capitalism. The system would lurch from crisis to crisis as unemployment grows and popular discontent rises.

At the same time, workers will attain class consciousness by realizing that their fundamental identity is not their ethnicity or religion, but that they all must sell their labor power in order to survive. This would increase the level of class struggle (the conflict between dominant and subordinate classes) in society.

Marx argued that class struggle was the driving force in human history and that it eventually produces a new system: So feudalism gives way to industrial capitalism, which gives way to socialism, and it, eventually, to **communism**. At these latter stages, exploitation would be minimized because the means of production would be socially owned. Marx wrote very little, however, on what exact form socialism or communism would take.

By the mid-nineteenth century, the growth of **urbanization**, factories, and the industrial labor force, along with the abysmal income distribution and average Western European worker's quality of life, seemed to bear out Marx. The success of the capitalist Industrial Revolution, it seemed, would carry its own seeds of destruction.

The political revolts that shook most of Europe in 1848 gave Marx and Engels hope that the socialist age had arrived. Their *Communist Manifesto* was written at the request of the German Communist League and laid out the revolutionaries' aims. By far the best known of their voluminous writings, the *Manifesto* ends with a stirring call to arms: "The proletarians have nothing to lose but their chains. They have a world to win. Workingmen of all countries, unite."

The *Manifesto,* inspiration to generations of revolutionaries worldwide, included some measures that strike many observers as quite reasonable: progressive income tax, free public schools, women's rights, and abolition of child labor. It also called for the abolition of private property and inheritance rights, state control over communication and transport, and, above all, the dictatorship of the proletariat. Although the 1848 revolts failed in most key respects, the *Communist Manifesto* established Marx as the leading socialist thinker of his time.

In 1864, Marx founded the First International as a forum for the propagation of socialist ideas. The brutal crushing, after only three months of existence, of the **Paris Commune** in 1871 by the new French government confirmed to Marx that the transition to socialism would be a bloody one. The Commune, the popular socialist government of Paris that emerged during the Franco-Prussian War, was for Marx and generations of Marxists after him a living example of what a progressive, reformist socialist government would look like and the dangers it would face.

Marx's analyses inspired successful revolutionaries such as Vladimir Ilyich Lenin (1870–1924), the creator of the Soviet Union, and Mao Zedong (1893–1976), the creator of the People's Republic of China, and unsuccessful ones such as Che Guevara (1928–1967) in Latin America and generations of intellectuals and students worldwide. Marxism-Leninism was the official ideology of the Soviet Union for much of the twentieth century (1917–1991) and of Eastern Europe in the post–World War II period. In addition, the Chinese and Russian governments supported some form of Marxism, such as Julius Nyerere's (1922–1999) Ujaama in Tanzania, in many Third World countries.

Revolutionary socialism was never as influential in the United States as it was in mainland Europe. In 1919, the moderate leadership of the Socialist Party of America, the third largest party in the country after the Democrats and the Republicans, expelled the revolutionary socialists rather than join the USSR-controlled Communist Third International (Comintern). The revolutionary socialist **Industrial Workers of the World** (IWW or the Wobblies) labor union continued a more revolutionary struggle until it was effectively destroyed by the U.S. government in 1917–1919 for opposing U.S. entry into World War I.

Marx's analysis of capitalism and its flaws has been severely criticized by many. Prominent among these are members of the Austrian School within economics, religious conservatives, evolutionary socialists, feminists, and a host of others. No doubt, however, Marx remains one of the great philosophers of the twentieth century, and his ideas still carry weight today.

Evolutionary Socialism

Socialists who disagree with Marx's characterization of capitalism and of the violent nature of the transition from capitalism to socialism fall under the broad rubric of evolutionary or democratic socialism. Marx paraphrased the famous socialist slogan "From each according to his abilities, to each according to his needs" from Louis Blanc (1811–1882), a French socialist politician who felt that democracy and the right to vote would allow for a peaceful transition to socialism.

The founder of what became Germany's largest political party, the Social Democratic Party (SDP), Ferdinand Lasalle (1825–1864) was originally a Communist imprisoned for his part in the failed 1848 revolt. After prison, he decided to forego revolution in favor of reform, as he felt that the trade unions could influence the government into making concessions. The leading force behind the SDP's strategy was Eduard Bernstein (1850–1932). He argued that, given the creation of an elected legislature, the Reichstag, by Chancellor Otto von Bismarck (1815–1898) in 1871 and the SDP's legalization in 1890, a peaceful transition to socialism was now possible. Bernstein's views gained strength within the rank and file of the SDP as Chancellor Bismarck already had implemented several major reforms, such as retirement, accidental injury, and health insurance benefits, that clearly benefited workers.

Coupled with his critiques of Marx's methodology, Bernstein's views, derogatorily termed *revisionism*, became very controversial within Marxist circles. The growing strength of the SDP and its domination by men such as Bernstein and the monarchist Friedrich Ebert (1871–1925; SDP secretary general in 1905 and chancellor and first president of Weimar Germany after World War I) confirmed the view of the more radical SDP members that it had abandoned revolutionary socialism. Many of the radicals joined revolutionary organizations such as the Spartacus League, whose violent suppression by the SDP-led government in 1919 marked the permanent break between it and revolutionary socialism. Although remaining firmly committed to the welfare state ideal, the SDP formally renounced all Marxist principles in 1959.

A second strain of evolutionary socialism was the British **Fabian Society**, founded in 1884, which provided substantial intellectual leadership for the British Labour Party. Several Labour prime ministers have been members of the Fabian Society, notably Clement Atlee (1883–1967), who nationalized public utilities and several large industrial firms and created the National Health Service during his 1945–1950 tenure, and Anthony Blair (born 1953). Although never a revolutionary party, it was only in 1995 that Labour formally renounced its more Marxist views (such as a commitment to nationalize the means of production). Labour is still committed to the social-welfare state, however, albeit to a lesser extent than is found in mainland Europe. Most of the Labour-initiated industry nationalizations (e.g., that of British Rail, British Steel, British Airways, etc.) were reversed in the 1980s by Margaret Thatcher's (born 1925) Conservative government.

In general, all Western European countries, to a greater or lesser extent, have seen the triumph of evolutionary socialism, as exemplified by the social-welfare state. In the United States, however, evolutionary socialism has had much less success. The closest that the United States had was the Socialist Party of America and Samuel **Gompers** (1850–1924), a labor-union organizer who founded what eventually became the **American Federation of Labor** (AF of L; later merged with the **Congress of Industrial Organizations**, AFL-CIO). Gompers eschewed political activism, however, and focused almost exclusively on better working conditions and higher wages for his union members; that is, skilled workers. The high point of the Socialist Party was in the 1920 elections when its presidential candidate, Eugene V. Debs (1855–1926), received almost a million votes, but it was never able to translate its popularity into effective legislation, and it declined rapidly over the next several years.

Conclusion

The violent transition from capitalism to socialism never took place in Europe or the United States, despite the grinding poverty, exploitation, and inhumane working conditions of much of the first several decades of the Industrial Revolution, because of the spread of democratic principles and practices in the second half of the nineteenth century. The power of democratically elected legislatures and the enlightened self-interest of conservative politicians such as Bismarck meant that the worst excesses of industrial capitalism were ameliorated, working conditions improved, and the masses given a voice in political and economic decision-making. This meant that evolutionary-socialist theorists could plausibly argue that peaceful change was not just possible but was actually taking place. *See also* Bourgeoisie; Chartism; Child Labor and Child Labor Laws; Communes; Communism; Factory Acts; Grand National Consolidated Trade Unions; Labor and the Industrial Revolution; London Working Men's Association; Luddites; Pauper Children; Revolution of 1848; Sweated Labor and Sweatshops; Syndicalism.

FURTHER READING: Busky, Donald F. *Communism in History and Theory: From Utopian Socialism to the Fall of the Soviet Union.* Westport, CT: Praeger, 2002; Desai, Meghnad. *Marx's Revenge: The Resurgence of Capitalism and the Death of Statist Socialism.* London: Verso, 2004; Maass, Alan. *The Case for Socialism.* Chicago: Haymarket Books, 2005; Tucker, Robert C., ed. *The Marx-Engels Reader.* New York: W. W. Norton, 1978. WEB SITES: http://home.vicnet.net. au/~dmcm/ (The Socialism Website); http://www.fordham.edu/halsall/mod/modsbook33. html (The Internet Modern History Sourcebook).

FEISAL KHAN

Spain, Industrial Revolution in

The advent of the Bourbon dynasty in Spain at the beginning of the eighteenth century brought a series of economic and administrative changes to a country still living with its eyes focused on the successes of the preceding Hapsburg Empire. In the second half of the eighteenth century, however, some theoreticians, including Cenon de Somodevilla, marques de la Ensenada (1702–1781); Pedro Rodriguez, count de Campomanes (1723–1803); and Gaspar Melchior de Jovellanos (1744–1811), were pointing to the clear need for changes such as the abolition of internal customs duties, free trade in grain (1765), free trade with America (1765 and 1778), protection for manufactures, the establishment of the San Carlos Bank (1782), and initial attempts to loosen property inheritance laws (disentailment) (1798).

This process was interrupted by the French Revolution. The following fifty years were marked by profound internal and international disputes that left the country in ruins. In addition, the independence of the Spanish colonies in the Americas (1810–1822) cut off trade flows, which upset the structure of the economy; the importance of Andalusia in the south continued to dwindle, whereas Catalonia and the Basque country in the north, the two main industrial areas, were thriving.

In 1797, 11.5 million people inhabited peninsular Spain. Of the active population, 65 percent worked in a stagnant primary sector, 13 percent were employed in the secondary sector, and 22 percent were in the tertiary sector. Modernization had to start with the liberalization of an agriculture plagued by obstacles to production and marketing and with the liberalization of the market in land. Hence, the legislative measures put forward by the liberals included the disentailment of Mendizabal, lands held by religious orders and the clergy. In 1836, the religious orders were dissolved except for those dedicated to education and the care of the sick; their lands by law could not be sold on the free market so were nationalized and sold by the state to a new rising **bourgeoisie**. In 1841, properties of the secular clergy were confiscated, with sales of these lands aimed at financing the war against the Carlists (1836–1839), who were supporters of Don Carlos, Ferdinand VII's younger brother, who claimed the throne from his niece, Isabella II.

In 1855, the disentailment of Madoz established the sale of state-owned lands plus land held by military orders, brotherhoods, the ex-Infante Don Carlos, and the municipalities, in hopes of financing construction of the railroad and the reduction of government debt. Much earlier, abolition of the manorial system (1812 and 1837), the disentailment of entailed estates (1841), the disappearance of the guilds *(gremios)* in 1813, the dissolution of the Mesta (association of sheep and cattle owners) in 1836, and new legislation on contracts and leases began the removal of elements blocking progress. Together, these measures redefined property rights and initiated the slow process of institutional modernization.

Spain in this period was torn by dynastic struggles and political instability, as exemplified by the fight over the succession to Ferdinand II, in which Don Carlos's claim to the throne was supported by the church and the great nobles, whereas Isabella's claim was supported by the army, the courts, and most of the middle class, who would stand to gain from liberalization.

Agricultural production increased slowly, and in the 1880s the area under cultivation rose from 26 million acres to 46.5 million acres, although per capita output did not increase. In 1860, agriculture was based on cereal crops, which accounted for 80 percent of output, almost half of it cultivated on a fallow land system. Even in 1900, agriculture was an underdeveloped sector that still occupied 66.3 percent of the active population, with such a low productivity that life expectancy was only 34.8 years. The structure of ownership also stood in the way of modernization. As recently as 1930, 78 percent of landholdings were only 2.5 acres in size, whereas 33 percent were at least 600 acres, and of these, about one-third were large estates *(latifundios)* of 1,200 acres or more. Such a pattern of agricultural holdings was fraught with explosive social consequences. A modern agricultural sector existed, however, cultivating grapes for wine or raisins, growing trees for (olive) oil, citrus fruits, dried fruit, and cork, located mainly in Mediterranean areas. From 1850 to 1950, agriculture's contribution to growth was 14.4 percent of gross domestic product (GDP).

Start of Industry

The first basic industry to be industrialized in Spain was textiles, which was concentrated in Catalonia and whose growth was financed by capital obtained from the thriving export trade in viticulture. The first modern cotton-textile-bleaching factory was opened in Barcelona in 1737, to be followed by spinning factories (1765) and the introduction of new technologies: the spinning jenny was first used in Spain in 1780, the water frame in 1791, and Crompton's mule in 1803. This modernization process utilized the **steam engine** in the manufacturing process (first by Bonaplata and Company in 1833) and subsequently captured the domestic market.

In the middle of the nineteenth century, the Catalonia-based textile industry was the world's fourth largest, processing up to 95 percent of all imported cotton. In 1900, the textile industry also accounted for 85 percent of the mechanical looms for wool, 66 percent for linen and hemp, and 96 percent for silk. Lack of cheap coal caused growth to slacken in the second half of the nineteenth century, however, which meant that factories had to be built on riverbanks to use hydraulic turbines.

The iron and steel industry also was affected by the lack of high-quality coal; Spain had several soft-coal mines in Asturias, León, Ciudad Real, and Córdoba, but the coal was of poor quality and expensive. The first blast furnace was built in 1832 in Marbella-Málaga, which used charcoal. Soon afterward, however, factories using coal appeared: in Asturias (Sociedad Metalúrgica Dura y Cía) and in the Basque Country (La Vizcaya, Altos Hornos y Fábricas de Hierro y Acero de Bilbao, La Iberia). Their output increased from 15,000 tons of ingots in 1856 to 54,000 tons in 1875—still lagging behind the industrialized countries, but the gap gradually was narrowed, thanks to the Bessemer converter and imported Welsh coal, in the last 30 years of the nineteenth century. In 1890, 280,000 tons of iron and steel were produced. The Basque Country was the primary center; after 1902, the Sociedad Anónima Altos Hornos Vizcaya dominated the Spanish iron and steel industry and attracted other activities and services such as shipping, insurance, chemical, and electrical companies, as well as banks and machinery producers, into the area.

Spain had other metals, such as copper and lead. The lead industry took off beginning in 1817, when the mines located in the Gador, Almagrera, and Cartagena Sierras started to be worked. Production represented 8.4 percent of exports in 1827 and 29 percent between 1860 and 1879, when it was overtaken by the United States, which became the world's largest exporter. Copper also was exported from the Mines de Cuivre de Huelva (established in 1835), which had been financed by French capital. Later, the demand for sulfuric acid by British industry was to have an impact on the Huelva pyrites. Two firms were dominant here, the Tharsis Sulfur and Copper Mines Limited (1866) and the Rio Tinto Company Limited (mid-1880s). The Mining Law of 1868 permitted the privatization of this industry, and with foreign capital and technology it burst into a cycle of headlong growth. Most of its production, between 87 percent and 96 percent, however, was exported. The industry contributed 34.9 percent of the growth of GDP between 1850 and 1950.

Trade evolved from a state of virtual autarchy to liberalization, starting in 1820, exactly as happened in the rest of Europe, but subsequently reverted to protectionism after the tariff of 1891 was imposed. During this period, the composition of trade changed. In 1827, the percentage value of the main exports was 17 percent olive oil, 16.6 percent wine, 9.6 percent wool, 7.4 percent lead, and brandy; whereas between 1890 and 1894, wine accounted for 23.1 percent, iron ore for 5.9 percent, lead 7 percent, copper ore and metal 5.1 percent, cotton textiles 4.7 percent, cork 3 percent, raisins 2.4 percent, oranges 2.1 percent, olive oil 2 percent, and footwear 1.7 percent. In 1827, the breakdown of imports showed textiles accounting for 55 percent, sugar for 9.5 percent, timber for 3.6 percent, and codfish for 3.5 percent. Later in the century, between 1890 and 1894, the main imports were raw cotton accounting for 9.1 percent, coal for 6.1 percent, wheat for 5.4 percent, timber for 4.8 percent, and tobacco for 3.9 percent. These changes show an increasing degree of openness (imports + exports/

GDP), from an initial low index of 7.8 around 1850, rising to 25.8 in 1896, then falling to 3 in 1942, and rising steadily up to the year 2000 when it was 57.1.

At the end of the eighteenth century, the Spanish treasury (Hacienda) was running a deficit, a situation that was further exacerbated by the loss of the American colonies and that persisted into the nineteenth century. This necessitated a fiscal reform that began in 1845 (Mon-Santillán) and turned into the great tax reform that lasted up to 1977. Nevertheless, a budgetary deficit continued. Hence, if the country wanted to modernize, it would be necessary to import foreign capital.

Traditionally, the Spanish financial system was geared to providing the state with funds. The Banco Nacional de San Carlos was first established in 1782 and managed to survive until 1829, when it became the Banco de San Fernando. During the same period, merchant bankers provided private credit. Gradually, during the1840s, the Banco de Barcelona and the Banco de Isabel II were founded, the latter merging with the San Fernando to become the Banco de España in 1856. That year, the Law on Banking and Credit Companies (Ley de Sociedades Bancarias y Crediticias) was passed, which regulated the creation of joint-stock companies, made possible the building of the railway, and led to a profusion of banks and credit companies, most of which failed in the 1866 crisis. Granting the Banco de España a monopoly on the issue of banknotes enabled the government to have access to an unconditional moneylender, thus generating a cyclically accumulating debt, but at the same time, the country enjoyed the benefits of a unified monetary market through its creation of a network of branch offices (1883). The twentieth century would see the birth of the Hispano-Americano bank (1901), the Vizcaya (1901), Español de Crédito (1902), and the Central (1919), a combination of commercial and investment banking that continued after the banking reform of 1962, when the Banco de España was nationalized.

In the middle of the nineteenth century, the transport situation left much to be desired, as physical conditions in the country and the sorry state of public finances had left the road network in a state of disrepair, creating a real bottleneck holding back the growth of the domestic market. For these reasons, it was essential to build the railway. The first track was laid between Barcelona and Mataró in 1848, but it was only after the passage of the General Railways Law that railroad building really took off, with the support of state funding. During the next decade, its construction centered on Madrid as the hub, and some 280 miles per year were built, although Spanish industrialization slowed because most of the construction material was imported. The import of foreign, mainly French, capital made it possible for it to be built quickly. The Crédito Mobiliario Español, Pereire Brothers, Sociedad Española Mercantil e Industrial (house of Rothschild), the General de Crédito Español company (Prots and Guilhou), together with two major railroad companies, the Compañía de los Ferrocarriles del Norte de España (Railroad Company of Northern Spain) and the Compañía de los Caminos de Hierro de Madrid a Zaragoza y Alicante (MZA Railway Company), were the major players. The railway system resulted in major social savings in the form of faster and cheaper transportation costs of up to 7 percent of GDP in 1878 and 20 percent in 1912. Between 1850 and 1950, the service sector contributed 47 percent of the growth of GDP.

Twentieth Century

In 1900, Spain's population reached 18.6 million, with 66.3 percent of the active population in the primary sector, 16 percent in the secondary, and 17.7 percent in the tertiary. Population growth plus the agricultural crisis at the end of the nineteenth century encouraged emigration to Algeria and later to Cuba and Argentina; more than 1.5 million emigrants left between 1905 and 1914. Another wave of emigration occurred in the 1960s and 1970s, mainly to France, Switzerland, and Germany.

Spain lost its colonies of Cuba, Puerto Rico, and the Philippines in 1898, resulting in a weakened international position. To recover losses, Spain attempted a process of internal regeneration and acquisition of new colonies in North Africa, which required a strong military presence in Morocco but also resulted in internal problems. Spain was neutral during **World War I** (1914–1918), but the country was split between the (leftist) pro-Allies and the (conservative) pro-Central Powers. Neutrality, however, made it possible to produce goods that had previously been imported as well as to benefit from external demand and to recover businesses owned by foreign capital.

The beginning of the twentieth century also saw the state assuming a protectionist stance in the growth process. Tariffs were increased in 1891, 1906, and 1922 to avoid foreign competition. State intervention in economic life was further accentuated during the dictatorship of Primo de Rivera (1923–1929), who used the state budget to reconstruct and modernize the naval fleet. Protective legislation also encouraged shipbuilding companies such as the Sociedad Española de Construcción Naval, Euskalduna, and the Unión Naval de Levante and the state arsenals in Cartagena and Ferrol. The aeronautics industry also got its start. Public works also received a boost: the railway and the road network, the extension of irrigation, and progress in electrifying the country. In 1927, the CAMPSA monopoly (petroleum) came into being. The decade 1920–1929 was a period of major economic growth, averaging 3.54 percent annually.

During the Second Republic (1931–1936), the most dynamic sectors of the Spanish economy—the production of wine, citrus fruits, olive oil, pyrites, and iron ore—were hard hit by the **Great Depression** of 1929–1939, although devaluation of the peseta improved competitiveness in foreign markets. The country's problems, however, as well as misguided actions by a state intent on defending a balanced budget, had a disastrous impact on economic activity. To ease social tensions, agrarian reform was enacted in 1932, but with limited effects.

After the Civil War, the new fascist-leaning government of Gen. Francisco Franco (1940–1975) intervened in the economy, creating the Instituto Nacional de Industria (INI) in 1941 to promote the setting up of state industries (including the national airline Iberia, the electric company Endesa, and automaker SEAT). The railways were nationalized under the Red Nacional de Ferrocarriles (RENFE). The state controlled prices and investment, prime commodities were rationed, and a black market sprang up; there was extreme poverty, and industrialization was halted. The annual growth rate of GDP between 1929 and 1952 slowed to 0.6 percent.

Starting in 1950, foreign relations began to return to normal, and Spain joined several international bodies, including the Food and Agriculture Organization (FAO) in 1950, the World Health Organization (WHO) in 1951, and UNESCO in 1952. Cooperation agreements were signed with the United States in 1953. In 1955, Spain entered the United Nations and in 1958 joined the International Monetary Fund. Within this framework, liberalization of the country took place, state control was reduced, ration cards disappeared, and free-market pricing was allowed. Industry developed and emigration increased. Because technology had to be imported, the balance of trade suffered, and inflation grew.

To resolve the problem of economic imbalance in the economy, the Stabilization Plan was implemented in 1959, its purpose to revamp and liberalize the economy, thus attracting foreign investment. Starting in 1964, a series of four-year development plans was initiated in order to promote growth. The economy took off with a vengeance, as did tourism, investment, and an inflow of foreign currency from emigrants.

Industry received such a powerful boost that in the 1950s and 1970s, its growth rate was higher than 7 percent, and in the 1960s higher than 11.2 percent. Metalworking activity was a generator of growth. ENSIDESA (Asturias), the producer of household appliances and electrical goods (white and brown lines), proliferated in the Basque Country-Navarra, Zaragoza, and Catalonia triangle; the SEAT (cars) and Barreiros (trucks) companies were founded, and Renault, Citroën, and Ford granted patents or manufactured vehicles. In 1975, Spain was the fourth largest shipbuilder in the world. Fertilizer production continued to be important, organic chemistry (perfumery, detergents, and plastic goods) became more relevant, and the pharmaceutical industry was boosted by the passage of the law requiring health insurance in 1941; many small pharmaceutical companies manufacturing antibiotics were formed, with three-quarters of pharmaceutical expenses underwritten by social security. It was at this time that Spain became a modern country, under the influence of its linkages within Europe.

The death of General Franco in 1975 led to a change of political system. The advent of democracy and the adoption of the constitution in 1978 paved the way for entry into the European Economic Community in 1986. During the years 1974–2000, the annual growth rate of GDP was 3.03 percent, the culmination of a process that had begun two centuries previously.

Why did the process of industrialization in Spain fail in the nineteenth century? Divergent views exist about who brought about industrialization, and how they did it, and two schools of thought exist in answer to this question. On the one hand, Catalan authors believe that the lack of consumption of (domestically produced) textiles by a backward Castilian agricultural sector and the lack of iron for building railroads were the reasons for the lack of industrialization. The other view, upheld by the Madrid school, blames the scanty output provided by businesses (Catalan for the most part), their low degree of mechanization, and their inability to mass-produce goods at economical prices for an impoverished domestic market.

Recent studies, nevertheless, give the lie to the idea that the nineteenth was a century of failure and the twentieth century one of success, pointing out that the process of growth was continuous between 1850 and 1950, with an annual growth rate of 1.34 percent of GDP, and it only speeded up during the second half of the twentieth century. Between 1950 and 1974, the rate of growth of GDP was 6.42 percent, and it was 3.03 percent between 1974 and 2000.

FURTHER READING: Carreras, Albert, and Xavier Tafunell. *Historia Económica de la España contemporánea*. Barcelona, Spain: Crítica, 2004; Carreras, Albert, and Xavier Tafunell, eds. *Estadísticas históricas de España, siglos 19 and 20*. 2nd rev. and exp. ed. 3 vols. Madrid, Spain: BBVA Foundation, 2005; Comín, Francisco, Mauro Hernandez, and Enrique Llopis eds. *Historia económica de España, siglos 10–20*. Barcelona, Spain: Crítica, 2002; Nadal, J. ed. *Atlas de la industrialización de España, 1750–2000* . Barcelona, Spain: Crítica. 2003; Prados de la Escosura, Leandro. *El progreso económico de España (1850–2000)*. Madrid, Spain: BBVA Foundation, 2003, 2005; Tortella Casares, Gabriel. *The Development of Modern Spain: An Economic History of the Nineteenth and Twentieth Centuries*. Cambridge, MA: Harvard University Press, 2000. WEB SITE: http://www.bde.es/informes/be/sroja/esthisteco.htm (Banco de España).

DONATO GÓMEZ-DÍAZ
Translated by V. H. PINCHES

Standard of Living and the Industrial Revolution

The question of whether the overall standard of living improves in those societies that go through an Industrial Revolution has been vigorously debated in the historical literature. Philosophically, the analysis begins with the relationship between standard of living and happiness. Insofar as standard of living is defined strictly in economic terms, there is little disagreement that the correlation with happiness is not strong. Descriptions such as "poor but happy" seem to support such a view. Much depends on the definitions used for *standard of living* and *happiness.* When the economic standard of living is defined primarily in terms of money, there seems to be considerable concern about whether money can buy happiness. In any case, the issue of happiness is highly normative, and economics alone cannot provide a complete answer.

Human history clearly shows a tendency to strive for a more satisfactory and satisfying material condition, however, as represented by the production and distribution of goods and services. Not only have societies striven to increase the quantity and quality of these goods and services but they also have sought to distribute this output broadly over the population. The limitations of tradition-based, low-technology economic arrangements are clear in this regard. It was not until the First Industrial Revolution that widespread improvement in the economic standard of living, regardless of definition, became a meaningful objective. The characteristics of this industrialization process are detailed elsewhere in this encyclopedia. Briefly stated, the process involves the mechanization of the production process, the utilization of inanimate energy, and the extension of technology over a wide range of industries. The industrialization process significantly multiplies the productivity of human labor and generates output far beyond the consumption capability of any one individual.

The specifics of each society's Industrial Revolution vary considerably, but the political entities that have undergone the process are characterized as countries that are developed, wealthy, or rich. Less than 25 percent of the world's population, however, which is more than 6.5 billion people, lives in countries that are substantially industrialized. Consequently, the role of industrialization in the improvement of the economic standard of living is not purely academic.

The transformation of production processes associated with an industrial revolution has spawned a literature on the assessment of working and living conditions that are collectively assumed to represent the standard of living. The origins of these assessments began in conjunction with the First Industrial Revolution in Britain. The presumption that the mechanization of British manufacturing could be anything other than beneficial to the workers was challenged. This challenge and the response to it established the framework for much of the subsequent research on the topic. Many well-known historians got involved with the issue and helped develop analytical tools that could be generalized well beyond the experience of Britain.

The Pessimistic Point of View

Those who believed that working and living conditions in Britain deteriorated as a result of the emerging industrialization process were deemed pessimists. They purportedly relied primarily on qualitative evidence in their assessment of the standard of living. The famed Blue Books, the reports of parliamentary commissions in the early nineteenth century, and a variety of anecdotal and descriptive observations were put forth to document the allegedly miserable and declining quality of life in industrializing Britain. Highlighted were the long hours of work at low wages with minimal employee amenities. The employment of women and children in the factories also was deemed inappropriate because of the dangers of industrial accidents and other occupational hazards that put life and limb at risk. Historians such as Barbara and John Hammond characterized the British factory workers as "industrial slaves."

Outside the factory, the pessimists pointed to the shoddy and expensive housing in crowded and unsanitary locations to which workers were relegated. Inadequate sewage and garbage disposal and lack of uncontaminated drinking water were other pieces of negative evidence on standard of living.

The British Parliament used this qualitative evidence to pass legislation on behalf of the workers. Political reformers took issue with the market-based, capitalist ideology that they claimed originated and condoned what they considered to be appalling working and living conditions. People like Robert **Owen** and Friedrich Engels sought no less than the adoption of a socialist political and economic paradigm.

The Optimistic Point of View

On the surface, if the conditions reported in the Blue Books and anecdotal accounts of living and working conditions were representative of what life would be like in any society that underwent an industrial revolution, there would be justifiable cause for great concern. If the industrialization process led unequivocally to deterioration in the material conditions of human existence, it would be understandable that the process would be something to be avoided or, at the very least, managed differently, if possible. Thus, several historians decided to look at the situation more systematically. When they did, they concluded that the pessimistic point of view did not hold up.

These historians recognized that the changes in working and living conditions brought about by the first industrialization process were traumatic. The shift from agriculture to manufacturing, from rural to urban living, from a domestic workplace to the centralized workplace of the factory, from a work cycle controlled by nature to one controlled by the clock and the speed of the machine, from an occupational status in which workers did not own the means of production or the output are just a few of the major changes that marked the first and most subsequent industrial revolutions. Nor did these historians deny that hours were long, compensation was low, fringe benefits were nonexistent, and residential conditions in factory towns were suboptimal.

Given these circumstances, it would seem that the case for a pessimistic assessment would be made stronger; however, the argument took a different tack. One consideration was that working and living conditions during an industrialization process have to be compared to what they were before and not to a normative view of what they should have been. Life in rural societies based on low-technology agriculture is quite onerous for peasant farmers and hardly the idealized existence often portrayed. This is why, from eighteenth-century Britain to twenty-first-century China, the shift away from a rural, agrarian lifestyle is consistently observed.

Another consideration is what other things might be going on in a country during its industrial transformation that might help explain what appear to be declining working and living conditions. Thomas Ashton showed how the Napoleonic Wars of the early nineteenth century created in Britain shortages of consumer goods that are typical of a war economy. Thus, in a dynamic society, countervailing forces may be at work that offset the effects of industrial transformation.

The first two considerations raise the question of when the observations relative to standard of living and the industrialization process are taken. The issue of timing complicates the identification and isolation of cause-and-effect relationships. The issue of timing was raised as to the First Industrial Revolution by many historians, including Arnold Toynbee, John Nef, John Clapham, and Walter Rostow. Some see an industrial revolution as a sharp break from past means of production, whereas others see it as a slow, evolutionary process stretching over many decades. The timing issue makes interperiod comparisons more difficult.

Another important consideration in the analysis of standard of living relates to its definition and measurement. This constitutes the major methodological difference between the pessimists and optimists. The latter rely heavily on quantitative evidence and reject the qualitative approach as lacking objectivity. Yet, the pessimists also began to use empirical approaches to challenge the statistical analysis and conclusions of the optimists. The debates between E. J. Hartwell and R. M. Hobsbawm are illustrative.

Quantitative Assessment of the Standard of Living

The major consideration was to develop data series that were considered to be representative of the standard of living. Among the early attempts in this direction was the development of time-series data relating to wages, cost of living, consumption, population growth, and mortality. Not surprisingly, much of this work suffered from data inadequacies.

In general, however, the historians using quantitative analysis came mostly to positive assessments of the standard of living during and after British industrialization. The longer the time horizon involved, the more likely that data sustained the hypothesis that industrialization significantly improved the overall standard of living of a country's population.

The counterarguments challenged the indicators selected as the surrogate for standard of living, pointed to the poor quality of the statistical data, considered alternative time frames for the analysis, and made other methodological and statistical criticisms. At the very least, these historians were able to establish that the improvement in the overall standard of living was not uniform over the length and breadth of a country's industrialization process. Though, for the most part, the challengers conceded that the long-run secular trend in standard of living was up, they showed that the trend was marked by fluctuations due to endogenous factors such as recessions and exogenous factors such as war. They also showed that not all categories of workers benefited equally nor did workers in all industries. For example, skilled workers did considerably better than the unskilled. Unemployed and underemployed labor often was underestimated in labor-force data. Female labor also did not fare very well. These and other critiques of the optimists helped put greater emphasis on the distribution of income as a major consideration in the assessment of living standard.

Assessing Quality of Life

In recent years, economists and historians have concentrated on real wages and real income per capita as the best indicators of standard of living. Though significant improvements have been made in the computation of these series, it should be noted that they are highly sensitive to the measurement of the price level changes that represent the cost of living. Studies by N.F.R. Crafts, Charles Hilliard Feinstein, and Peter Lindert and Jeffrey Williamson are notable in this research area. Although there is widespread agreement that industrial revolutions improve per capita standard of living as measured by real income, there is also widespread agreement that wages and income do not tell the whole story.

Increasingly, quality-of-life (QOL) issues such as health, nutrition, education, and environment have been receiving significant attention. As difficult as material indicators such as wages, income, and consumption have been to measure, these other variables are even more difficult to quantify and assess. The Human Development Index (HDI) is an attempt to address some of these concerns. The HDI incorporates longevity and knowledge along with income in an effort to provide a more comprehensive assessment of living standards. Other measures such as the Gender Development Index (GDI) and the Dasgupta and Weale (DW) Index try to add other QOL elements into the mix. The GDI tries to evaluate the male-female experience in society. The DW Index attempts to incorporate economic, health, educational, and political factors into a single indicator. Needless to say, attaining such comprehensiveness is fraught with numerous problems, including the assignment of weights to the various components.

Although there are concerns that an industrial revolution is not totally beneficial to all aspects of human existence, the material standard of living as measured by per capita income clearly improves substantially in those countries that undergo this transformation in the production process. This is most readily seen on a comparative basis as the Industrial Revolution diffuses over more of the globe. From Western Europe to North America to the Pacific Rim, those countries that have experienced an industrial revolution have a standard of living and associated quality of life substantially higher than those that continue to stagnate economically in traditional production arrangements. There may be justifiable concerns about intracountry income distribution, but these pale in comparison with the intercountry inequalities that characterize the gap between developed, developing, and underdeveloped nations. By some estimates, the per capita income differential between the poorest countries and the richest countries is on the order of 15 to 18 times. This is far from the approximate parity that existed before the First Industrial Revolution began in Britain at the end of the eighteenth century.

Given the billions of persons in the contemporary world that are subsisting on only a few dollars a day, the only hope for an improvement in living standards is for the continued diffusion of the Industrial Revolution, or evolution, as some might argue. The growth rate of world production has risen to 4 percent annually from less than 0.5 percent in the eighteenth century, so the potential of the diffusion process is great. Notwithstanding the fact that industrial transformation may be a traumatic change from traditional arrangements and may have some unfavorable short-term and long-term consequences, history has shown that an industrial revolution can provide a release from grinding poverty. History also provides a basis for reducing the steepness of the learning curve and making possible a more humane transition.

FURTHER READING: Crafts, N.F.R. "Some Dimensions of the 'Quality of Life' during the British Industrial Revolution." *Economic History Review* 50 (1997): 690–712; Lucas, Robert

E., Jr. "The Industrial Revolution, Past and Future." Annual report. Federal Reserve Bank of Minneapolis, 2003. At http://www.minneapolisfed.org; Mokyr, Joel. *The Economics of the Industrial Revolution.* Totawa, NJ: Rowman and Allanfield, 1985. Repr. Rowman and Littlefield, 1989; Mokyr, Joel. "Is There Still Life in the Pessimist Case: Consumption during the Industrial Revolution." *The Journal of Economic History* 48, no. 1 (March 1988): 69–92; Taylor, A. J. *The Standard of Living in Britain in the Industrial Revolution.* London: Routledge Kegan and Paul, 1975; Voth, Hans-Joachim. "Living Standards during the Industrial Revolution: An Economist's Guide." *AEA Papers and Proceedings* 93, no. 2, (May 2003): 221–26.

JOSEPH A. GIACALONE

Steam Engine

The steam engine is undoubtedly the major technological breakthrough associated with the First Industrial Revolution. The use of an inanimate, but controllable, energy source dramatically increased industrial productivity and thus gave rise to the huge expansion of output that has characterized industrial societies ever since the eighteenth century. In combination with major improvements in making iron—in particular, Henry Cort's puddling process—it permitted newly industrializing economies to overcome the previous constraints on the expansion of output. For the British economy in the early eighteenth century, these constraints were given by shortages of wood, which was used for constructing buildings, ships, and machines as well as providing fuel. Many significant scientific experiments had taken place in the previous century; because British society at this time was becoming more entrepreneurial, many of these experiments provided the rationale for practical applications. The results dramatically altered the technologies of several industries that would become the core of modern industrial economies. Most significantly, these changes were cumulative and irreversible.

Early Power Sources

In the eighteenth century, most British manufacturing was still small scale and handicraft based, and early innovations focused more on developing new markets (such as exports) or on new methods of organization (such as the shift to the factory system). The most important power sources were water, wind (windmills had been used in Europe since the twelfth century), animal, or human muscle power. The latter two are obviously subject to size limitations. Most important were water and wind power, but even here, the amount of power provided (typically, around 10 horsepower) was only compatible with a small production unit. Their main uses were to pump water (mines and canals), in textile mills, to operate bellows in iron foundries, and to grind grain, but in spite of improvements such as John Smeaton's overshot waterwheel (1752), neither was capable of providing a suitable energy base for a modern industrial economy. Production facilities had to be located near the power source, as power was not transferable. Neither wind nor water are consistently reliable and controllable power sources, and the lack of flexibility of location was a disadvantage.

The principle that steam could generate motion was not a particularly new idea, but as with so many other inventive ideas, for it to become a reality required the right combination of prerequisites. In the seventeenth century, efforts were being made to utilize steam to pump water out of mines. For example, in 1663, Edward Somerset, Marquis of Worcester, was granted a monopoly for a so-called water-commanding engine that pumped water up about 100 feet. Thomas Savery, a British army officer, either improved this engine or independently developed a similar machine that worked by condensing steam in a tank to create a vacuum that then caused a piston to move, working the pump. Savery's machine worked but was not very good at pumping water from mines, which led to continuing efforts to find a more efficient solution. These efforts also would help overcome the wood shortage by turning coal into the basic fuel source of the Industrial Revolution when it was used to heat water to produce steam.

The best known of these efforts was Thomas Newcomen's engine, more accurately called an atmospheric engine. Newcomen was an ironmonger who, in about 1708, used steam to move a piston in a cylinder; the piston was attached to a beam that provided motion. In Newcomen's engine, steam was injected into the cylinder from a boiler to move the piston up; the steam was then condensed by injecting cold water into the cylinder, producing a vacuum, which forced the piston down the cylinder. This engine worked, was more reliable than other early steam engines, and was used to pump water from mines in the 1720s. Several improvements were made to it over time. For example, automatic valves were added to control inflows, and safety valves were added to reduce the risk of the engine exploding if too high a pressure built up inside. It had a major drawback, however: It was fuel inefficient, because alternately heating and then cooling the cylinder to create a vacuum required large amounts of fuel, thus limiting its appeal for uses outside the coal fields. (Although it had drawbacks, some Newcomen engines were still in use in some old British mines in the first half of the twentieth century.)

Watt's Steam Engine

James **Watt**, a scientific instrument maker at the University of Glasgow, received a model of the Newcomen engine for repair and recognized the flaw in its design. In 1763–1764, he solved the problem by separating the condenser from the cylinder in which the piston moved. The air in the condenser was removed by an air pump that created a vacuum that drew in steam from the main cylinder, which remained hot throughout; this then reduced the engine's fuel consumption by up to 75 percent.

Watt's next problem was to get financial backing and to produce the engine on a commercial basis. He moved from Glasgow to Birmingham, a center of iron works, and in 1769 entered a partnership with Matthew **Boulton**, an established Birmingham manufacturer of hardware. In that year, Watt received a patent for his design ("A New Method of Lessening the Consumption of Steam and Fuel in Fire Engines"), and this, and later patents, dominated the production of steam engines until 1800 when they expired, permitting other engineers to enter the market with different designs. Further improvements to the Watt engine included the double-acting steam engine, which used steam pressure to move the piston in both directions (1782), the addition of a centrifugal governor that controlled the flow of steam, making the movement smoother (1788), and, a real breakthrough, adding a rotary action (1781). A link with the military production of guns and cannons, which also required cylinders, also was important here. For example, John Wilkinson developed a boring machine that could produce finer cylinders that in turn made efficient steam engines more efficient.

Up to this point, the piston action of steam engines limited its potential uses, but adding a rotary movement expanded these uses—steam now could power industrial machinery. Watt designed a so-called sun-and-planets gearing to convert perpendicular motion to a rotary motion. This was done by connecting the beam (moved by the piston) to a flywheel via the gearing, which in turn conveyed motion to production machinery. When used in factories, the engine moved a belt that passed through each floor of the factory and to which each machine was connected via another series of gearings. (Boulton and Watt built a double-acting rotative steam engine in 1788, which was used at Boulton's Soho factory to drive 43 metal polishing machines for the next 70 years.) By 1800, approximately 500 Boulton and Watt steam engines were in use throughout the world.

Nineteenth-Century Improvements

After Watt's patents expired in 1800, various innovations and advances were made that further extended the usefulness of steam power. Watt, fearing the dangers of explosion, hesitated to develop so-called strong steam (steam under high pressure), but others did. This advance made it possible to make smaller engines with greater power and then to make steam power mobile—in **railroads** and ships. For example, Richard Trevithick (1771–1833) was a Cornish engineer who built engines using steam under high pressure. One advantage of strong steam was that it could be compounded (reused), which made steam engines more fuel efficient, powerful, and cheaper to use. In addition, Trevithick's engines could be made small and compact, in contrast to the large size of Watt's engines. An early example of a compound engine was built in 1804 by Arthur Wolf, which could do the same amount of work as a Watt engine but used only half the fuel. In Trevithick's 1806 high-pressure engine, the piston movement was conveyed to connecting rods, one of which turned the engine's flywheel directly, and the other turned it via a crank, an action that made locomotion possible. Trevithick built a working-model locomotive as early as 1797 and made a full-size steam locomotive in 1803, but after losing money on this project, he left this line of work. He did, however, build a steam-powered locomotive in 1804 that was used to haul coal for the Penydarren Ironworks in South Wales.

Making steam power movable attracted the attention of many engineers. An early experiment was made by William Symington, a mining engineer who was commissioned by Edinburgh banker Patrick Miller to build a steam engine to power a boat in 1788. This engine had two single-acting cylinders with separate condensers driving two paddle shafts through a system of chains and ratchets. It worked, but Miller failed to interest James Watt in the project, and the experiments ended. In the United States, Robert Fulton propelled a riverboat, the *Clermont,* with a steam engine. Later developments would see ship construction and propulsion revolutionized by steam power.

On land, applying steam power to railroads continued. Using fixed tracks to move heavy and bulky items such as coal was not a new idea, but making the movement easier with steam locomotives instead of horse-drawn wagons was. The early ones were private, built by the coal mines' own engineers. In 1814, the first successful steam locomotive was built; by the middle of the nineteenth century, steam-powered railroads were beginning to revolutionize commercial land transport across the globe.

Many developments helped make this safer and cheaper. For example, in 1817, Marc Seguin in France introduced a tubular boiler, and in 1849, Eugene Bourdon's pressure gauge made control of high-pressure steam safer.

Continued developments in the design and construction of stationary steam engines expanded their potential industrial uses by increasing their power and flexibility while reducing their size. One innovator in this area was Henry Maudsley. Maudsley's table engine (1840) was an early, successful, self-contained steam engine for small factories, and his engines sold the world over. (Maudsley also helped the development of the machine-tool industry and revolutionized the construction of metal machines by increasing the accuracy by which they were made.) He also was instrumental in training many other engineers who would contribute to continuing innovation. For example, one of his protégés was James Nasmyth, notable for his steam hammer used to shape metal.

Impact of the Steam Engine

Without an inexpensive but powerful source of energy, industrialization would have taken much longer to take place. The development of steam power made the

Headly Mill steam engine, 1865. Cambridge Museum of Technology.

energy contained in coal exploitable, and this required the development of industrial materials strong enough to permit this exploitation: Steam power, coal, and iron thus became the backbone of industry until well into the late twentieth century. Even though steam power was not used in every single productive enterprise, its effects rippled throughout the economy. In Britain, even in the mid-nineteenth century, most firms were still small, but the competitive demands for modernization encouraged the trend to larger factories and larger machines powered by steam in most of the leading-edge industries. All parts of the economy benefited from the falling costs of transportation offered by the steam-powered railroads, especially for heavy, bulky items such as coal and other raw materials. Lower transportation costs meant that location decisions were more flexible: No longer would enterprises have to locate near their power source or near their raw-material sources or their markets. Falling input costs for items such as glass, bricks, and construction materials made possible by steam power encouraged new building designs; the glass-and-steel train termini associated with Victorian towns are examples. New activities became possible and within the financial reach of more groups of people than ever before, such as taking trips to coastal resorts, which in turn opened the possibility of new industries catering to leisure-time activities.

For Britain itself, the development of an industry devoted to building steam engines (early ones were usually built by engineers within the actual industry they were designed for) was a sign of the maturing of an industrial economy. Sales, including export sales of steam engines and other capital goods, not only turned Britain into the nineteenth-century so-called workshop of the world but also encouraged the industrialization of other countries, which would later become Britain's industrial competitors.

Steam remained the most important source of power until well into the twentieth century, before new technologies emerged to reduce its importance. In land transportation, the emergence of diesel engines and the internal combustion engine fuelled by gasoline, and consequently the development of road transportation, led to the decline of the railroads for moving both freight and people by the middle of the twentieth century. The development of electricity (although often generated by steam-powered turbines) led to an increased flexibility of location for industrial activity and finally gave a competitive edge to smaller enterprises; later in the twentieth century, it also provided power for the emergence of the totally new computer-manufacturing and computer-using industries based on the exploitation of knowledge.

FURTHER READING: Clough, Shepard B., and Richard T. Rapp. Chapter 14 "The Mechanization of Industry," p. 291–320. *European Economic History: The Economic Development of Western Civilization*. New York: McGraw-Hill, 1986; Deane, Phyllis. *The First Industrial Revolution*. Cambridge: Cambridge University Press, 1965; Stoneman, P. *The Economic Analysis of Technological Change*. Oxford: Oxford University Press, 1983. WEB SITE: http://www.sciencemuseum.org.uk.

CHRISTINE RIDER

Steamship

A steamship is a large seagoing vessel propelled partly or entirely by a wood- or coal-fueled **steam engine**. Steamships had better speed, reliability, and maneuverability than sailing ships but required a constant source of fuel and crew members with specialized engineering expertise. Merchant fleets and naval forces composed of steamships were a distinguishing characteristic of a major power and played important roles in the global spread of **international trade** and imperialism during the nineteenth century.

Steamships were a product and a facilitator of the Industrial Revolution. The invention of the steam engine was a prerequisite for the creation of the steamship, but, once created and improved, the steamship enhanced the growth and spread of the factory system and use of fossil fuels. Steamships provided a cheaper means of transporting raw cotton and other raw materials to the factories of the industrializing nations and of carrying their textiles and other manufactured goods back to the rest of the world. Steamships also carried food into Britain and other industrial nations whose populations were shifting from agriculture to the industrial sector. In addition, steamships carried bulk loads of fossil fuel from nations with coal deposits to nations that needed (and could afford to purchase) this prerequisite for their own industrialization.

Early Steamships

Prior to the invention of the steam engine, water transport relied upon wind and animal power. During the 1700s, various inventors attempted to apply the steam engine to water transport, but all attempts were unsuccessful until the invention of smaller, portable steam engines in the early 1800s. The Scot William Symington and the American Robert Fulton are credited with the first economically viable steamboats. The first steam-powered vessels were paddle-wheeled steamboats running in the sheltered waters of British and U.S. lakes, rivers, and canals.

The engines of the initial steamers were powered by wood, cut into five-foot lengths. Wood-fueled combustion, however, was difficult to control and caused dangerous burning embers to spew from ships' (and railroad engines') smokestacks. Coal soon proved to be a better fuel. Its combustion was more easily regulated and, pound for pound, provided more than twice as much heat as wood. The discovery and exploitation of large subterranean forests of coal deposits in Britain, the eastern United States, and the Ruhr in Germany provided a steady source of fossil fuel to replace diminishing forests of industrializing nations.

The application of steam engines to deep-sea vessels occurred in two stages. Initially, steam engines were installed in sailing ships that also retained traditional sails and rigging and were used only to supplement wind power. The first transoceanic steamship voyage was made by such a hybrid ship, the SS *Savannah,* between Savannah, Georgia, and Liverpool, England, in 1819. As steam-engine technology improved, and less coal was required for long voyages, shipbuilders started constructing large steamships that did not have any sails. The first transatlantic crossing by steamships relying exclusively on steam engines occurred in 1838, by two British ships traveling from Cork, Ireland, and Bristol, England, to New York City.

Later Innovations

Throughout the rest of the nineteenth century, technological innovations further increased steamships' speed, safety, and reliability. Engine efficiency was improved by advances in metallurgy and new boiler designs that safely allowed increased steam pressure. Another important step was the invention of multiple-chambered, compound steam engines that allowed boiler steam to be used several times before release. Between 1860 and 1890, the amount of coal required to produce one horsepower of energy was reduced from 5 pounds to 1.5 pounds. Ships' steam engines were eventually superseded in the twentieth century by the diesel engine, invented during the 1890s, which provided even greater power per pound of fossil fuel.

Another important innovation was the substitution of the screw propeller for the paddle wheel as the device to transform the steam engine's energy into propulsive power. The American Robert Stevens had invented an early ship propeller in 1804, but it was not until the 1830s that the propeller had sufficiently improved in efficiency to challenge the paddle wheel. During the 1830s and 1840s, many new steamships were equipped with both propellers and paddle wheels.

In 1845, the British Royal Navy conducted a series of tests with two almost identical steamships, the *Alecto* and the *Rattler*. Their only difference was that the *Alecto* had a paddle wheel and the *Rattler* had a screw propeller. The two ships first raced against each other, and the *Rattler* ran several knots faster than the *Alecto*. The next test had the two ships placed back to back, their sterns were connected by strong cables, and the captains started running their engines at full power. The *Rattler* easily overpowered the *Alecto* and began pulling it stern-forward at a rate of 1.5 knots. As a result of this maritime tug-of-war contest, virtually all steamships constructed after 1845 were equipped with screw propellers rather than paddle wheels.

Steamships also benefited from the introduction of metal construction techniques, initially using iron and later steel. At first, wooden hulls were covered with metal plating and only later made entirely of metal. Metal hulls were more durable than wood and provided ships with additional security in collisions with rocks and other ships as well as protection from cannon fire. Later, the entire ship's structure was constructed of metal. The impact of battering ocean waves upon wooden ships had limited their maximum length to 300 feet, but by the end of the nineteenth century, the lengths of the largest metal steamships approached 1,000 feet.

Advantages of Steamships over Sailing Ships

Steamships were more expensive to construct and to operate than sailing ships because they required an expensive steam engine and a constant supply of coal, sometimes referred to as bought wind. Steamships, however, could travel much faster and maneuver against (or in the absence of) wind as well as against strong tides and oceanic currents. Sailing ships required anywhere between 30 to 90 days to make a transatlantic crossing, depending upon the weather conditions and prevailing winds, but the first steamships reduced the trip time to two weeks. By the early 1900s, the fastest ocean liners could make the trip in less than a week.

Although steamships were more capital-intensive than sailing ships, they were less labor-intensive. The absence of sails and rigging meant that steamships needed a smaller crew, albeit one that contained personnel specially trained to operate and repair steam engines. The steamship's engine also could be used to power additional ship's devices, such as anchor winches and bilge pumps, which also reduced the number of crew required to run a ship.

In spite of their larger fixed and variable costs, the greater speed and maneuverability of steamships made them much more economically efficient than sailing ships for certain routes. Shipping lines' investment in steamships resulted in a much greater, faster, and more predictable throughput of ships' cargoes and passengers.

Steamships provided a much lower per-unit cost of delivery than sailing ships, and their economic efficiency increased with the application of other nautical inventions: the iron, and later steel, hull, the screw propeller, and the triple-expansion engine. The reduced per-unit costs of ocean transport led to large increases in the volume of shipping and the number of steamship as well as the specialization of different types of steamships.

Specialization of Steamships

Previously, most wooden sailing ships were undifferentiated general-purpose vessels that transported both cargoes and passengers. The only important distinction was between merchant ships and warships, with the latter carrying rows of cannons.

The continual decrease in cost of ocean transport resulting from the increased use and improvement of steamships caused a continual increase in the volume of cargo and number of passengers throughout the nineteenth century. The increase in passenger shipping led to the development of specialized passenger liners, which also carried high-profit fine cargoes and mails. The first dedicated passenger steamship with scheduled voyages was the *Great Britain,* which could carry 630 passengers and began transatlantic voyages in 1845.

The governments of industrializing nations considered having large and fast steamships a matter of national pride, and most provided subsidies for their construction and operation. The subsidies contained requirements that mandated the steamships be turned over to the government in time of war, for conversion to use as troop carriers or hospital ships.

By the end of the nineteenth century, the combination of commercial rivalry, national pride, and government subsidies resulted in the construction of passenger steamships approaching 1,000 feet in length, which could carry more than 3,000 passengers and crew. The largest passenger liners, such as the famous *Titanic* (which unfortunately sank after hitting an iceberg on April 14, 1912), provided the dozens of first-class cabin passengers with luxurious accommodations comparable to the finest hotels in London and New York. Smaller and less expensive second- and third-class cabins also were available for the few hundred middle-class passengers, whereas the poorer and more numerous steerage passengers experienced crowded conditions in communal quarters.

Another stage in steamship specialization involved the development of liner cargo ships, which transported only general cargoes on fixed schedules along established routes. The declining fleet of sailing ships became known as tramps, running on irregular routes without any fixed schedule. They also were relegated to carrying grain, coal, lumber, and other low-profit bulk cargoes until well into the twentieth century, at which time technical innovations had lowered the costs of steamships sufficiently to make these cargoes also profitable to carry.

One additional type of steam-powered vessel merits particular notice: the tugboat. These small boats equipped with very powerful engines became commonplace in every major port. They were used to maneuver the increasingly large passenger liners and cargo ships through the ports' busy harbor channels and into their narrow berths.

Global Spread of Steamships

The first deep-sea steamships traveled only on transatlantic routes, carrying passengers and high-profit cargoes between ports in nations with established coal supplies: the United States, on the one hand, and Britain and the nations of northwestern Europe, on the other hand. Initially, the other oceanic routes continued to be served almost exclusively by sailing ships, which did not require supplies of coal.

As steamship technology advanced, engines became smaller and more efficient, requiring less coal for their voyages, whereas the ships themselves became much larger. This increased the steamships' range of operations as well as the size of ships' revenue-generating cargo space. Every seaport did not have access to reliable supplies of coal, however, particularly those in Asia and South America. Many steamships thus would need to carry enough coal to use for their entire round-trip voyage or until they could reach a port where they could replenish their coal supply.

In the mid-1800s, Britain and other major seafaring nations began acquiring locations along the coasts of the Middle East and Far East (such as Steamer Point in Aden, Kowloon and Foochow in China) as well as small islands in the Indian and Pacific Oceans (such as the Seychelles and Pago Pago) to use as coaling stations. These enlarged the range of steamship travel by reducing the amount of coal the ships needed to carry for long-distance voyages.

By the mid-1800s, British steamships were on regular routes to South Africa and India, and in 1867 a U.S. line began the first scheduled transpacific steamer service, between San Francisco and Yokohama, Japan. The opening of the Suez Canal (a 180-mile ship canal cut through Egypt from the Mediterranean Sea to the Gulf of Suez and the Red Sea) in 1869 shortened the marine distance from Europe to the Far East by several thousand miles, further enlarging the range of steamships. By the late 1800s, steamships outnumbered sailing ships. The latter were used only on the longest routes (e.g., Britain to Australia or New York to Japan) and carried low-profit bulk cargoes, such as coal, sugar, jute, rice, and grain.

Steamships and Imperialism

Naval steamships, with their greater maneuverability and the power to travel against the wind and tides, had a tremendous military advantage over the wooden sailing ships of nonindustrialized nations and empires. British warships easily defeated wind-powered Chinese junks in the Opium Wars (1839–1842 and 1856–1860) and, together with victories in land battles, forced the Chinese Empire to make its first major concessions to foreign powers. The U.S. fleet of Commodore Matthew Perry's black ships that visited Japan in 1853 and 1854 and forced that nation to open its borders to international trade contained several steamships.

Construction of metal steam-powered warships became standard practice after the metal-hulled Russian fleet annihilated the Turkish fleet of wooden warships in the 1853 Battle of Sinope. During the American **Civil War**, the Confederates' ironclad *Virginia* (also sometimes known as the *Merrimack*) inflicted mortal damage upon enemy wooden warships until the Union's ironclad *Monitor* forced it to a stalemate.

The establishment of a global network of coaling stations not only facilitated international trade by extending the range of commercial steamships, it also facilitated the global expansion of the colonial powers by extending the range of steam-powered naval warships.

The overwhelming majority of steamships built during the nineteenth century were designed and constructed at shipyards in Britain, northwestern Europe, or the United States. The primary exception was steamship construction by Japan after the **Meiji Restoration** of 1868. Japan's new leaders recognized the crucial role of coal and steam engines for national power and gave a high priority to the creation of steam-powered merchant and naval fleets. Japan initially purchased foreign steamships. The first Japanese-owned steamship, the *Kanko Maru*, was built in the Netherlands, but subsequent steamships were purchased from Britain and France. Japan then established three nationally subsidized shipyards that initially constructed steamships using plans purchased from foreign shipbuilders. Later, the Japanese constructed steamships designed by Japanese naval architects and engineers trained at European schools and shipyards. Eventually, Japan began producing engineers and naval architects trained at Japanese institutions.

Subsequent Evolution of Ship Technology

During the 1890s, inventors developed other new engines for ship propulsion: the coal-powered **steam turbine**, the gasoline internal combustion engine, and the diesel engine. The first could obtain greater speed than traditional steam engines but soon was bypassed in favor of engines that relied upon petroleum-based fuels. Petroleum-based fuels (gasoline and diesel oil) proved superior to coal in almost every aspect. They were much easier to load and did not require labor-intensive shoveling into the boiler fire and the subsequent removal of ashes. In addition, pound for pound, petroleum took up half the storage space of coal and provided twice the motive power of coal.

The invention of the gasoline-powered internal combustion engine and its application to automobiles soon was followed by experiments with gasoline-powered engines for marine transport. The highly volatile nature of gasoline, however, made it unsuitable for large ships. Large gasoline-fueled engines needed a large amount of gasoline, and there was a constant danger of spontaneous combustion of gasoline fumes in half-filled tanks. There were no fire engines at sea, so a ship's gasoline-tank fire would be as deadly as a torpedo explosion. Marine gasoline engines became limited almost exclusively to small, recreational boats with small gas tanks.

The much heavier and less volatile, low-grade distilled petroleum by-products proved to be more useful fuel for marine propulsion. Rudolph Diesel invented an engine that used this fuel (soon named *diesel oil*) in engines that were initially used in automobiles and later in ships and boats. Large ships using diesel engines had four times the cruising range of steamships of a similar size using coal and did not require a worldwide network of coaling stations. After **World War I**, diesel-powered ships replaced coal-powered steamships on almost every shipping route.

FURTHER READING: Allington, Peter. *First Atlantic Liners: Seamanship in the Age of Paddlewheel, Sail and Screw.* London: Conway Maritime Press, 2003; Fox, Stephen. *Transatlantic: Samuel Cunard, Isambard Brunel, and the Great Atlantic Steamships.* New York: Harper, 2004; Greenhill, Basil. *The Advent of Steam: The Merchant Steamship before 1900.* Conway's History of the Ship Series. London: Chrysalis Books, 1993; Lambert, Andrew. *Steam, Steel and Shellfire: The Warship 1840–1905.* Conway's History of the Ship Series. London: Chrysalis Books, 1994. WEB SITES:

http://www.bryking.com/royreg/links.html; http://www.fathom.com/course/10701037/session2.html; The Steamship Historical Society of America at http://www.sshsa.org/.

STEPHEN G. MARSHALL

Steam Turbine

A steam turbine converts the heat of pressurized steam (produced by the combustion of fossil fuels or by nuclear fission) into rotational kinetic (mechanical) energy that is used to run electricity generators, propulsion systems, compressors, or pumps. Although the reciprocating motion of a **steam engine** had to be first converted into rotary motion in order to turn dynamos or power shafts, a steam turbine runs these assemblies directly. Two other key differences make steam turbines superior to steam engines: Because of their staged expansion of highly pressurized steam, turbines are inherently much more efficient, and their mass-to-power ratio is considerably lower.

The first modern steam turbine was designed in 1882 by the Swedish engineer Carl Gustaf Patrick de Laval (1845–1913). This impulse turbine extracted steam's kinetic energy by releasing it from trumpet-shaped nozzles on a rotor with appropriately angled blades. (An impulse turbine has rotor blades shaped in such a way that the force of the jets of fluid on the blades moves the wheel without a pressure drop occurring across the blades.) The inherently high rotational speeds and huge centrifugal forces of this arrangement made it impossible to build machines of large capacity, and even small units had to be run at reduced rates. Blades in Laval's turbine move solely by impulse: There is no drop of pressure as the steam passes the moving parts. In contrast, Charles Algernon Parsons (1854–1931), a mathematically trained engineer (Trinity College, Dublin and Cambridge), invented a very different machine that eventually became the world's most powerful and widely used prime mover. In his turbine, whose concept was based on theoretical thermodynamics, he avoided extreme velocities by dividing the fall in steam pressure into small fractional expansions over a large number of individual stages, similar to water in hydraulic turbines.

The design was patented in April 1884, and the first completed machine had a capacity of just 7.5 kilowatts, ran at 18,000 revolutions per minute, and its efficiency was quite low at 1.6 percent. Rapid improvements allowed for scaling up the design to 75 kilowatts (4,800 revolutions per minute, efficiency of about 5%) for the first commercial turbines installed at Forth Banks station in Newcastle-on-Tyne in January 1890. In 1889, Parsons lost the patent rights to his invention when he left Clarke, Chapman and Company and established his own company, C. A. Parsons and Company, but he recovered them in 1894 and began to produce large stationary units as well as turbines for ships. His first one-megawatt unit was installed in the Elberfeld station in Germany in 1899, a 5-megawatt turbine was added in 1907 in Newcastle-on-Tyne, and Parsons's largest pre–World War I machine was a 25-megawatt turboalternator installed in 1912 at the Fisk Street station of the Commonwealth Edison Company in Chicago; its overall efficiency was about 25 percent. These machines were far more powerful than the largest steam engines, yet their mass-to-power ratio (at only 10 grams per watt) was much lower!

Parsons's steam turbine axial flow generator, 1902. Science Museum/Science & Society Picture Library.

In the United States, George Westinghouse bought the rights to Parsons's machines in 1895, built its first turbine in 1897, and scaled up to 1.5 megawatt by 1900. In 1895, Charles Curtis (1860–1936) patented a new turbine concept, a hybrid of Laval's and Parsons's designs. His machines, made by the General Electric Company, reached capacities of up to nine megawatts and were used at many smaller U.S. plants. During Parsons's lifetime, steam turbines reached a maximum capacity of 200 megawatts (nearly 27,000 times more powerful than his first machine), and today the largest units installed in power plants rate nearly 1.5 gigawatts. Steam turbines in fossil-fuel-fired and nuclear stations now produce most of the world's electricity. The rotation of steam turbines that are directly coupled to electricity generators must match the system frequency (3,600 revolutions per minute for the standard 60-hertz network). The high speeds of turbines used for ship propulsion must be reduced by gearing to the required (much slower) rate of rotation.

Parsons also pioneered the use of the steam turbine for marine propulsion. By 1897, his experimental vessel *Turbinia* (40 tons, 100 feet long, driven by a single radial-flow turbine capable of 715 kilowatts) was the world's fastest vessel in the world (34.5 knots), and it outran the fastest British destroyers powered by compound steam engines. As a result, the Royal Navy equipped its ships (including the famous *Dreadnought*) with Parsons's direct-drive turbines, and so did the leading passenger shipping companies of the early twentieth century. Diesel engines or gas turbines now dominate freight and passenger shipping, but steam turbines propel the largest (nuclear-powered) aircraft carriers.

FURTHER READING: Parsons, Charles A. *The Steam Turbine*. Cambridge: Cambridge University Press, 1911; Parsons, Robert H. *The Development of Parsons Steam Turbine*. London: Constable, 1936; Termuehlen, Heinz. *100 Years of Power Plant Development*. New York: ASME Press, 2001.

VACLAV SMIL

Stephenson, George (1781–1848)

George Stephenson, the pioneer of railway development and builder of the first practical locomotive, was born on June 9, 1781, at Wylam, near Newcastle-upon-Tyne, England. He worked with his father in the Wylam colliery (coal mine) at the age of 14. Machinery had a special attraction for him, and he developed mechanical expertise through repairing watches. Stephenson noted the wagon way that ran from the Wylam colliery to the River Tyne, which had wooden tracks and horse-drawn wagons, and wondered whether steam power could be applied to it. So in 1804, he joined Matthew **Boulton** and James **Watt**'s steam-engine firm to gain experience. Two years later, he became a brakeman at the Killingworth Colliery, where he studied the mechanism of colliery engines while working at its West Moor pit. After being pro-

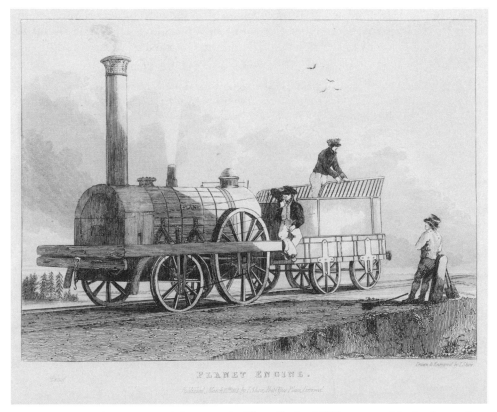

Designed by Robert Stephenson and Company, the "Planet Engine," 1831, was one of the first locomotives. Science Museum/Science & Society Picture Library.

moted to head engineer, Stephenson had a good knowledge of steam engines by this time, and in 1812 he started to build them himself.

Even with all the disadvantages of the time, when engines were made by hand, Stephenson completed his first locomotive, *Blutcher*, in 1814. It was tested on July 25 at the Collingwood Railway and ran at four miles per hour pulling eight wagons of 30 tons weight. He built a second, improved engine in 1815 and patented it. Over the next five years, he produced 16 engines at Killingworth. Then in 1821, he became the engineer of the Stockton and Darlington Railway, responsible for constructing a rail line joining the River Tees with the collieries of West Durham and Darlington. His son, Robert Stephenson (1803–1859), also was a respected civil engineer and followed his father in the locomotive business. In 1824, the father-son duo established the world's first locomotive construction company, headquartered in Newcastle, and built its first engine, the *Locomotion*. On September 27, Stephenson drove the *Locomotion* along the nine-mile Stockton and Darlington line in two hours. It pulled 36 wagons and reached a speed of 15 miles per hour in its final lap. The company's most famous locomotive was *Rocket*, which achieved a world record speed of 36 miles per hour at the Rainhill trials organized by the Liverpool and Manchester railway in 1829.

Stephenson had an insatiable desire to improve railway engines and tracks, and as chief engineer for railway companies, he advised on numerous projects and locomotive manufacture. The Stephenson gauge of 4 feet, 8.5 inches that he devised became the standard gauge for many railways around the globe (but not in the United States). Stephenson also invented an explosion-resistant safety lamp for miners in 1815. He established the Institution of Mechanical Engineers in 1847 and was its president. His activities were restricted after he contracted pleurisy, and he died on August 12, 1848, at Tapton House, near Chesterfield.

FURTHER READING: Brown, William H. *The History of the First Locomotives in America*. New York: D. Appleton, 1871; Rolt, L.T.C. *The Railway Revolution: George and Robert Stephenson*. New York: St. Martin's Press, 1962; Rowland, John. *Rocket to Fame*. London: Target, 1971; Smiles, Samuel. *The Life of George Stephenson and of His Son Robert Stephenson*. New York: Harper & Brothers, 1868. WEB SITE: http://www.britainexpress.com/History/bio/stephenson.htm.

PATIT PABAN MISHRA

Submarines

A submarine is a ship specially designed to travel and perform operations underwater, primarily for military purposes. It usually contains a crew, so it must have a complex life-support system that allows humans to survive and function safely without any direct contact with the atmosphere over extended periods of time.

The early Industrial Revolution saw the development of two new forms of transportation on land and water: the **railroads** and the **steamship**. Both were made possible by the development of the portable **steam engine**. The later stage of the Industrial Revolution saw the development of three other new methods of transportation for land, water, and air: **automobiles**, the submarine, and the airplane. These new methods of transportation took longer to evolve because they needed the development of more complex technologies, particularly the internal combustion engine for motive power. In addition, the development of the submarine also depended upon other new technologies associated with the Second Industrial Revolution: steel-based metallurgy for vessel structures that could withstand deep sea pressures and electrochemistry for massive batteries and oxygen-based life-support systems.

Early Subsurface Vessels

There have been recorded instances of devices permitting brief human travel underwater since the time of Alexander the Great's immersion in a leather bell (fourth century B.C.). During the sixteenth and seventeenth centuries, there were similar experiments with diving apparatus, which relied upon surface ships for movement and ascent. These devices paralleled the development of balloon travel, in which the device was a passive instrument of the air currents, and any directed movement was very limited. In addition, underwater travel also had an additional inherent problem of adequate oxygen supply. The initial models fell into two categories: passive, which relied upon a connected surface ship for its movement, and self-propelled, which relied upon human-powered propulsion devices.

Technological Innovations

The development of economically viable steamships in the early 1800s sparked further interest in underwater vessels, particularly after the development of metal hulls led to technological advances that could withstand water and water pressure better than hides, canvas, or wood.

Many of the innovations made in developing the steamship also were relevant to the development of the submarine: a fossil-fuel engine, screw propeller, and metal hull and internal superstructure. Other crucial technical components, however, required the later innovations associated with the Second Industrial Revolution of the late nineteenth century: an internal combustion diesel engine and chemical engineering advances associated with large-scale battery-powered engines and oxygen-recycling life-support systems.

During the U.S. **Civil War,** several Southern inventors developed prototypes using hand-cranked propellers. The most famous was the *H. L. Hunley,* developed by Horace Lawson Hunley, which had an explosive device mounted on a long pipe at the front of the vessel. On February 17, 1864, the submarine attacked and sank a Union warship blockading Charleston, South Carolina, but the attacker evidently also was injured by the blast and soon sank.

Popularization and Further Development

Shortly after the Civil War ended, the idea of submarine vessels achieved a place in popular thought as a result of two novels by Jules Verne, *Twenty Thousand Leagues under the Sea* (1869) and *The Mysterious Island* (1875). These involved a giant submarine, the *Nautilus,* run by Captain Nemo, a disgruntled Indian nobleman angry at the British for its rule over India. He used the *Nautilus* to attack the British navy, in hopes of weakening the British Empire. The submarine also was used for scientific exploration and the collection of deep-sea marine life.

Verne's predictions began to come to life during the 1870s and 1880s through the work of John Holland, an Irish American inventor. He initially started his work on behalf of the Irish Republican Brotherhood, which wanted to use submarines to attack British warships. After developing small versions of the first working submarine, however, Holland apparently became interested in exploiting the commercial aspects of his invention. He wanted to consider marketing his invention to any navy, rather than limiting its use to Irish insurgents. In 1883, these disagreements over basic strategy between Holland and his backers led to the latters' confiscation of the *Fenian Ram,* one of Holland's early prototypes. Holland's backers had a ship tow the submarine to a berth in Connecticut but then discovered none of them were able to operate the submarine.

During the 1890s, Holland finally developed the dual-engine method of propulsion that became the dominant design for almost all subsequent submarines. The submarine was equipped with two engines. An internal combustion engine was used for surface movement and to charge massive electrochemical batteries; the second engine was powered by these batteries, which ran the electric motor that was used for underwater movement as well as the vessel's life-support system.

Holland organized the Motor Torpedo Boat Company to build and market his invention and began entering them in competitions sponsored by various naval powers. The process of development was very expensive, and Holland's financial ability did not match his inventive skills. He soon had to merge his company with the Electric Boat Company (now a subsidiary of General Dynamics) in a deal that ceded control of his patent rights.

Disputes between Holland and the new company led to his eventual departure, and he was left without control of the patents he had developed. The Electric Boat Company later sold the first submarines to the United States and soon afterward to the British navy and to other naval forces. Holland died in poverty in 1914, shortly before the outbreak of **World War I** and the first extensive use of his invention.

Submarines during and after World War I

During World War I, Germany relied upon the submarine (*Unterseeboot,* or U-boat) as a counterforce to Britain's large fleet of naval warships. The first submarine sinking of a British ship occurred on September 5, 1914, shortly after the war started. The British navy began a naval blockade to deprive the enemy of food and war materials, and the Germans responded by torpedoing ships carrying materials to Britain and France. German sinking of the British ship *Lusitania* was a factor that prompted U.S. involvement in World War I.

Alternative Uses

Hunley, Holland, and most other inventors focused upon the military functions of the submarine, particularly its role in attacking and sinking traditional warships and, later, civilian cargo ships and passenger liners. Another line of development of submersible vessels focused upon nonmilitary uses, however, including scientific exploration and salvage work. The main inventor in this line was another American, Simon Lake, who constructed the *Argonaut* and several successors in the 1890s and later. His initial model had wheels and traveled on the beds of rivers and other shallow waters. Such devices had a limited market, however, and Lake, too, began to focus upon naval submarines, particularly for European navies and, after World War I, for the United States.

After the end of World War I, several firms and research organizations began developing submarines (called submersibles), which were designed to perform scientific research. August Piccard started the trend with launching of an untethered bathyscaphe in 1948. The most famous and versatile submersible is the *Alvin,* operating out of Woods Hole, Massachusetts.

FURTHER READING: Keegan, John. *The Price of Admiralty: The Evolution of Naval Warfare.* New York: Penguin, 1990; Lambert, Andrew. *Steam, Steel and Shellfire: The Warship 1840–1905.* Conway's History of the Ship Series. Annapolis, MD: Naval Institute Press, 1994; Morris, Richard K. *John P. Holland, 1841–1914: Inventor of the Modern Submarine.* Columbia: University of South Carolina Press, 1998; Parrish, Thomas D. *The Submarine: A History.* New York: Penguin, 2005; Poluhowich, John J. *Argonaut: The Submarine Legacy of Simon Lake.* College Station: Texas A&M University Press, 1999; Ragan, Mark K. *Submarine Warfare in the Civil War.* Cambridge, MA: Da Capo Press, 2003; Tall, Jeffrey. *Submarines and Deep-Sea Vehicles.* San Diego, CA: Thunder Bay Press, 2002. WEB SITES: http://www.chinfo.navy.mil http://inventors. about.com/library/inventors/blsubmarine.htm; http://www.sonic.net/~books/new.html; http://www.vectorsite.net/twsub1.html.

STEPHEN G. MARSHALL

Sweated Labor and Sweatshops

Sweated labor, a term that came into common use in the 1840s, refers to manufacturing subcontracted by a middleman known as a sweater for production in small slop shops or sweatshops or as piecework in workers' homes instead of large factories. Industrialization, the shift from small-scale artisanal work to mechanized mass production, could not eliminate the need for manufacturing processes that could be completed more efficiently by human hands. Subcontracting was cost-effective for large-scale manufacturers when producing relatively small, portable items involving handwork, because it relieved manufacturers of the need to construct and maintain factories while still keeping the corporate structure of owners, managers, and workers. In contrast to the traditional guild system in which a craftsman progressed from apprentice through journeyman to master craftsman, the sweating system kept laborers permanently dependent on the sweaters, subcontractors who provided workers with orders and materials. As in a factory, the individual sweatshop worker repeatedly performed only one step in a longer process. Many industries relied on sweated labor in the nineteenth and twentieth centuries to produce large quantities of commodities, including artificial flowers, cigars, paper boxes, shoes, toys, housewares, and saddlery, but the sweating system was most strongly identified with the garment trade.

Clothing

Sewing long had been recognized as difficult, unremunerative work, especially plain sewing, the production of relatively simple items such as shirts or bed sheets as opposed to the tailoring of more sophisticated articles. In 1843, evangelical novelist Charlotte Elizabeth Tonna dramatized the plight of seamstresses in her novella *Milliners and Dressmakers,* in which the health of the young heroine is shattered by drudgery in a stifling and poorly lit workroom. In the same year, poet Thomas Hood published the ballad *The Song of the Shirt,* depicting an exhausted and starving woman who sits in a garret "plying her needle and thread." Hood's bitter refrain, "Stitch! Stitch! Stitch! In poverty, hunger and dirt," resonated powerfully with the British and U.S. public, spurring investigations by journalists, including the crusader Henry Mayhew (1812–1887). Mayhew's reports detailing the slop trade appeared in 1849 in a London newspaper, the

Morning Chronicle, as installments in a comprehensive study of "Labour and the Poor" in England. Mayhew decried the horrendous conditions in the slop shops, describing seven or more people sewing in rooms measuring only 8 feet by 10 feet. Receiving one to six shillings for every dozen shirts they completed, whole families often sewed for 14 or more hours a day, seven days a week, to cover their most minimal living expenses. Mayhew also deplored the economic impact that the slop trade had on so-called honorable tailors, reporting that between 1844 and 1849 the number of honorable masters—traditional master tailors assisted by apprentices and journeymen—had declined by more than 15 percent, whereas the number of sweaters and their employees had more than doubled as traditional tailors found themselves unable to compete with the low prices and high profit margins of the sweating system.

Hood's poems, Tonna's novels, and subsequent pamphlets and novels by popular author Charles Kingsley (1819–1875) transformed the poor seamstress into a cultural icon who appeared as a figure of pathos in dozens of Victorian literary and artistic works. Despite some consternation occasioned by Mayhew's findings, the use of sweated labor grew steadily over the second half of the nineteenth century.

The first mass-produced and distributed **sewing machine** dramatically accelerated the sewing process. With the advent of relatively lightweight, movable sewing machines, clothing production could be truly mechanized outside of the confines of a factory. Sweaters acted as assembly lines, relaying the materials to workers as each stage of the process was completed. To produce shirts, for example, cutters would cut the material, using shears and patterns also provided by the sweaters; basters would join the pieces with temporary hand stitching; machinists sewed the shirt's seams, often on machines rented from the sweaters; hemmers or fellers finished the shirt's raw edges; buttonholers would finish the buttonholes by hand or machine; buttoners, who were often small children, sewed on the buttons by hand.

Accounts abounded of the desperate poverty and appalling living and working conditions spawned by the sweating system. Repeating a single process over and over, a machinist might process 12 to 18 shirts per day, at rates that could be as low as one shilling (about 20 cents) per dozen. Nor were other specialties more rewarding; a journalist in 1882 described a mother and daughter who finished the edges of 2,880 buttonholes on shirt collars to earn 10 shillings one week. To survive on such low pay, workers toiled for up to 18 hours a day in overcrowded tenement kitchens or in tiny, unventilated workrooms. Similar conditions existed in industrial areas throughout Western Europe and the Americas. "Stitch, stitch, stitch, from early morn till weary eve—this is the fate of thousands of girls in the great metropolis," George Ellington wrote in 1869 in *Women of New York* (p. 589). "The occupation of the seamstress," he continued, "is a sad example of the struggle going on around us for existence; and it is about the most uninteresting and wearying species of toil that could well be imagined."

Other Industries

Although the garment industry epitomized the sweating system, other industries also relied on piecework. Straw hats long had been mass-produced in workers' residences, where each worker or group of workers completed a single step of construction: plaiters braided the straw, stitchers coiled and sewed the long braids, and steamers blocked the hats into the desired shapes. Similarly, leather shoes and harnesses were distributed to workers to complete each stage as piecework. As immigration to Britain and the United States surged in the late nineteenth century, desperate new arrivals provided large labor pools, with the various ethnic groups becoming associated with particular industries. In New York City, southern Italian immigrants found work making artificial flowers by binding or gluing precut cloth petals provided by a manufacturer onto ready-made stems. Other immigrants rolled cigars using tobacco and molds provided by subcontractors or folded and labeled pasteboard boxes. Families turned their tenement apartments into workshops in which children as young as four or five could contribute labor long after legislation prohibited the employment of small children in factories.

The boundaries of the sweating system sometimes were difficult to define: Although the phrase *sweated labor* referred specifically to work subcontracted to domestic settings or small workshops, sweatshops and formal factories overlapped in many respects. Factory work itself often could be dangerous, exhausting, and poorly paid, with uncompensated overtime and harsh working conditions: The 500 operatives employed at the notorious Triangle Shirtwaist Factory in New York City, where 146 workers died in a fire in 1911, enjoyed few advantages over pieceworkers in tenements. Factory operatives did not have to pay for heating or lighting the factory out of their own pockets, however, as home workers did. Working conditions in factories drew more attention from journalists and politicians, in part because factories dominated urban landscapes, and tiny and temporary workshops in tenement districts were hidden from public sight. Most significantly, factory workers who worked together in one location as a group recognized the benefits of organizing to protest their lot and make demands of employers and lawmakers. Among factory workers, membership in labor unions surged in the 1890s, but pieceworkers who rarely compared notes with or even saw other pieceworkers could not organize as easily. Moreover, sweatshops were almost impossible to regulate effectively through legislation. In 1893, Massachusetts enacted laws requiring garments made in domestic or tenement-house workshops to bear identifying labels, but the labels did not have discernable effects on demand for the products. In Britain, the Trade Boards Act of 1909 applied minimum wage standards to the sweated trades. The Fair Labor Standards Act enacted by Congress in the United States in 1938 set minimum wages for workers engaged in interstate commerce, including workers producing goods for sale; an amendment of the Act in 1949 required employers to ensure that workers paid by the piece earned at least the equivalent of the hourly minimum wage for the time that they worked. Another strategy was the enforcement of zoning laws limiting commercial activities in residences and of building codes prohibiting overcrowding and requiring adequate ventilation and unimpeded access to exits.

Nonetheless, illegal sweatshops continue today in defiance of the laws. Moreover, many industries have responded by outsourcing, relocating manufacturing through subcontractors in developing countries where safety regulations, minimum wage requirements, and limits on working hours or child labor are less stringent. Piecework and sweatshops remain a substantial element of the international economy, employing hundreds of thousands of workers in developed nations and millions in developing countries.

FURTHER READING: Bender, Daniel E., and Richard A. Greenwald, eds. *Sweatshop USA: The American Sweatshop in Historical and Global Perspective.* New York: Routledge, 2003; Blythell, Duncan. *The Sweated Trades: Outwork in Nineteenth Century Britain.* New York: St. Martin's Press, 1978; Ellington, George. *Women of New York.* New York: Arno Press, [1869] 1972; Hapke, Laura. *Sweatshop: The History of an American Idea.* New Brunswick, NJ: Rutgers University Press,

2004; Schmiechen, James A. *Sweated Industries and Sweated Labor: The London Garment Trades, 1860–1914*. Urbana: University of Illinois Press, 1984.

JANE WEISS

Sweatshops

See Sweated Labor and Sweatshops

Syndicalism

The French word *syndicalisme* means "trade unionism," and the international syndicalist movement took its name from the French—where the movement was then strongest—at the beginning of the twentieth century. Syndicalism had become the dominant tendency in the fractured French labor movement in the 1890s, and the Confédération Générale du Travail (CGT) remained at least nominally syndicalist until the outbreak of **World War I** plunged the movement into a crisis from which it never truly recovered.

The movement was hardly confined to France, however. Similar ideas were percolating in workers' movements around the world. In the United States, proponents of the Chicago Idea espoused similar principles in the 1880s and were influential especially in that city's labor movement before its most prominent proponents were hanged as the Haymarket martyrs.

Emerging out of workers' resistance to the Second Industrial Revolution, syndicalism briefly rivaled socialism in the radical workers' movement. Syndicalism was strongest in the Americas and Europe, but Australia, China, Japan, and South Africa also had significant syndicalist tendencies. Although popular treatments credit George Sorel with the creation of syndicalism, the movement predates him by many years and emerged out of a long tradition of anarchist and mutualist thought.

Syndicalism both emerged from practical workers' struggles and placed these struggles at the heart of its vision. For the syndicalist, means and ends come together in a revolutionary unionism that simultaneously struggles for better immediate conditions on the job and seeks to be the instrument through which workers ultimately supplant capitalist control of industry and replace it with workers' self-managed production. Syndicalism's organizational form is the revolutionary union, its methods direct action and the general strike, its objective the overthrow of capitalism and its replacement by workers' control both of the job and of the larger economy. Given its roots in the anarchist tradition, syndicalists have not surprisingly placed great emphasis on creating democratic structures for their unions, relying upon rank-and-file initiative rather than bureaucratic structures or a cadre of paid staff. At its peak, in 1936, the Spanish Confederación Nacional del Trabajo (CNT) prided itself on having only one paid secretary to administer a union of more than 1 million members.

Its focus on the job often enabled syndicalists to overcome deep political divisions in the workers' movement. Although many syndicalists were explicitly antiparliamentary and syndicalist ideology left little room for the state, syndicalist organizations typically stressed their independence from political parties while welcoming radical workers of all stripes. Anarchists, socialists of various tendencies, and workers with no fixed ideology looking for an organization prepared to do battle with the employers for control of the workplace all could come together in a common organization. The early CGT may have been headed by veteran anarchists, but its ranks also included many members of France's contending socialist parties as well as pure and simple trade unionists. Among the founders of the **Industrial Workers of the World** (IWW) were the leaders of both of the U.S. socialist parties, along with anarchists and many veteran unionists. Independent socialists played a central role in the founding of Swedish Sveriges Arbetares Centralorganisation (SAC). In many countries, syndicalism brought together workers tired of seeing their immediate concerns subordinated to party interests; in countries with substantial disenfranchised immigrant populations, such as Argentina or the United States, it also provided a forum for those immigrant workers to pursue their broader political concerns.

A deeply practical movement, syndicalism adopted different structural approaches in response to local conditions. Faced with strong unions closely tied to the Social Democratic Party, German syndicalists focused their efforts on building factory committees that struggled over immediate grievances and abhorred larger bureaucratic structures. France's movement was a hybrid of national trade unions with locally based chambers of labor that focused on broader social concerns and built solidarity for local struggles. Canadian, Spanish, and Swedish syndicalists favored a One Big Union approach based on local general unions, although the SAC eventually grafted industrial union structures (perhaps borrowed from the IWW) onto its local federations. The IWW (which never officially defined itself as syndicalist, although its Chilean section affiliated to the syndicalist International Workers Association) responded to the fragmented craft unionism that dominated U.S. labor by attempting to build strong industrial unions based on industrial branches that federated locally into industrial district councils and internationally into industrial union administrations.

Syndicalists differed in their approach to other unions as well. France's syndicalists, who held positions of great influence in the CGT from its inception, urged radicals to work within existing unions to revolutionize them. German and U.S. syndicalists rejected this approach, finding that the established labor movement in their countries offered little scope for such activity. Mexican workers turned to syndicalism in a context of social upheaval and government-dominated unions but ultimately succumbed to the joint force of co-optation and brutal repression.

Syndicalism always considered itself an intensely practical movement. The CGT's emphasis on direct action (more colorfully described as sabotage) emerged in a context of economic upheaval and political weakness, enabling the syndicalists to mount effective struggles for improved conditions within the workplace (and thus be relatively safe from bayonets and police). The general strike enabled workers to project their power directly (and to unite in common action, even if they belonged to disparate organizations), rather than working through political parties and other structures the syndicalists had learned to distrust. Until the movement shattered under the pressure of the outbreak of World War I and the international labor movement's failure to act to halt it, syndicalism offered a program around which many organized workers could unite on a daily basis, even if its broader revolutionary aspirations were more controversial.

Although the movement's main focus was on workplace organizing, syndicalists also engaged in expansive agitational activity, including the publication of daily newspapers in Argentina, Spain, Sweden, and the United States (the latter two continued daily publication into the 1950s); educational and cultural programs; and antimilitarist campaigns. Even these more cultural and political activities were rooted in syndicalists' belief—borne out by a long history of armed suppression of strikes—that the state's military forces and control of education posed a major obstacle to their objectives. Syndicalists also gave serious attention to the structure of the new society they envisioned, conducting empirical studies of industry in several countries, and adopting organizational plans for the postrevolutionary period that were radically decentralist, democratic, and egalitarian.

The movement declined in the 1920s as a result of repression, co-optation of many unions into collaborative labor relations regimes, and the attraction of the successful Russian Revolution for many militants. The anarcho-syndicalist CNT played a central role in putting down a fascist uprising in much of Spain in 1936, however, and quickly brought large sectors of the economy under workers' control in the months that followed. The Spanish Civil War briefly reenergized the movement around the world before the triumph of fascism crushed the CNT (the German and Italian movements already had been crushed), and military dictatorships suppressed syndicalist movements throughout Latin America. Although the U.S. IWW survived, if as a much smaller union, only in Sweden did syndicalism still have a significant organizational presence in the 1940s.

Although syndicalism ultimately was eclipsed by the twin rise of the social-welfare state and communism, it played a central role in the labor movement, both directly and through the spread of its methods to workers in competing unions. Today, syndicalism survives in the International Workers Association (IWA) and its affiliates (many of them rebuilt in the aftermath of World War II), in the IWW, and in a loose network of independent syndicalist unions based in France, Spain, and Sweden. Although the movement has experienced growth in recent years in response to the decline of the social-welfare state and an increasingly casual workforce, syndicalism remains marginalized, struggling to develop effective strategies through which a militant minority can project industrial power in a world dominated by global corporations.

FURTHER READING: Caulfield, Norman. *Mexican Workers and the State: From the Porfiriato to NAFTA.* Fort Worth: Texas Christian University Press, 1998; Linden, Marcel van der, and Wayne Thorpe, eds. *Revolutionary Syndicalism: An International Perspective.* Aldershot, U.K.: Scolar Press, 1990; Mitchell, Barbara. *The Practical Revolutionaries: A New Interpretation of the French Anarchosyndicalists.* Westport, CT: Greenwood, 1987; Peirats, Jose. *The CNT in the Spanish Revolution.* London: Meltzer Press, 2002; Rocker, Rudolf. *Anarchosyndicalism.* London: Martin Secker and Warburg, 1938. At http://www.spunk.org/library/writers/rocker/sp001495/rocker_as1.html; Thorpe, Wayne. *"The Workers Themselves": Revolutionary Syndicalism and International Labour, 1913–1923.* Dordrecht, Netherlands: Springer, 1989; Thompson, Fred, and Jon Bekken. *The IWW: Its First 100 Years.* Cincinnati, OH: Industrial Workers of the World, 2006. WEB SITES: http://www.anarchosyndicalism.net/index.php (Anarcho-Syndicalism 101); http://www.syndicalist.org (Anarcho-Syndicalist Review).

JON BEKKEN

	T

Tariff Policy

Tariff policy refers to a government's approach to the taxation of imported goods to raise revenue for domestic spending and/or to raise the price of imported goods to protect domestic producers of similar goods. Here, *imported goods* refer to goods produced outside a country's borders and used for internal consumption. The tax itself most often is called a *tariff, import duty,* or *customs duty.* Although the importance of the tariff as a policy tool diminished significantly in the second half of the twentieth century, it was widely used in the United States and Europe during their periods of industrial development.

The two most commonly used tariffs are the ad valorem tariff and the specific tariff. The ad valorem tariff is a percentage rate that is multiplied by the assessed value of imported goods to determine the tax payment. The tax generally is paid by the importer who brings the foreign goods into his or her domestic market. As a hypothetical example, consider a U.S. importer of wine who purchases 10 bottles of French wine for sale in the United States. If the wine is worth the equivalent of $1,000, and the ad valorem tariff imposed by the United States is 10 percent, then the importer would owe $1,000 x 0.10 = $100 to the U.S. government. (This payment is in addition to the $1,000 the importer must pay for the wine.) In contrast, a specific tariff is a tax paid on each unit of the good imported. Returning to the hypothetical wine importer, if the tariff is a specific duty, say $10 per bottle, then the importer would pay 10 x $10 = $100 to the U.S. government. Finally, a tariff that combines both ad valorem and specific duties to a single imported good is called a compound tariff.

The Revenue Tariff

Today, most industrialized countries rely on personal, business, and property taxes to finance government spending. Prior to the shift toward these types of taxes, however, the tariff was one of the primary sources of national revenue. In the United States, the tariff accounted for more than 90 percent of federal revenues at the end of the eighteenth century and remained a significant revenue source into the first two decades of the twentieth century. In fact, one of the first bills passed by the U.S. Congress and signed by President George Washington was the Tariff Act of 1789—the first national U.S. tariff act. The 1789 act largely reflected the country's immediate need for federal revenues following its independence from Britain.

By the 1920s, however, revenue from the tariff began to decline substantially as the United States shifted toward alternative taxes. By the early 1940s, U.S. tariff revenue accounted for less than 5 percent of all federal revenues. With the public's acceptance of alternative taxes and a more favorable attitude toward international trade following World War II, the tariff is no longer an important tool for raising revenues. As a revenue source, most contemporary economists dislike the tariff because, in addition to reducing consumer choice and restricting competition in the domestic market, its burden tends to fall most heavily on low-income consumers.

The Protective Tariff

During the period of industrial development in Europe and the United States, the tariff also frequently was used to provide protection to domestic producers. This meant raising tariff levels beyond those needed to generate sufficient revenue for government spending. Tariffs set at this level often are called *protective tariffs*, and the individuals or groups supporting protective tariffs often are called *protectionists* or *mercantilists*. In the case of the United States, tariff legislation subsequent to the Tariff Act of 1789 increasingly was supported or opposed based on the degree to which the legislation protected domestic producers from international competition.

Tariffs offer domestic producers protection because they raise the price of competing imports. The higher import prices increase the domestic consumption of similar domestic goods and give domestic producers room to increase prices. As a result, the call for protective tariffs by domestic producers was often the result of foreign products selling at prices below what domestic producers could profitably sell their own products. Consider again the hypothetical example of the U.S. wine importer. Assume that, due to pressure from the U.S. wine industry, the U.S. government levies a 50 percent ad valorem tariff on all foreign-made wine because the average price of a bottle of foreign wine is less than for which domestic wine can be profitably sold. The imposition of a 50 percent tariff on foreign wine means the importer's costs increase by 50 percent: Wine worth $1,000 actually costs the importer $1,500. In order to cover the original cost of the wine plus the tariff, the importer will have to charge a higher price in the domestic market. Because all importers of wine must pay the tariff, the average price of foreign wine will rise; this will reduce the quantity of foreign wine demanded by domestic consumers while increasing the quantity demanded of domestically produced wine. Domestic producers of wine will respond by increasing the production of wine and, market conditions permitting, also will increase the average price of their wine to a level just below the tariff-inflated price of imported wine.

U.S. and European protectionists typically justified their position by focusing on infant industries, national security concerns, the welfare of domestic labor, and the impacts of economic downturns. The infant-industry argument rests on the idea that when a country starts to industrialize, its industries will need help to compete against more established foreign industries. National security concerns rest on the

disruptions created by the War of 1812 between the United States and Britain. In the years following the end of war, however, trade between the United States and Europe gradually recovered to the point at which imported woolen textiles were placing U.S. manufactures under serious competitive pressures.

By the late 1820s, the U.S. textile industry began agitating for higher tariffs on imported woolen textiles. Given the relative youth of the U.S. manufacturers compared to their European counterparts and the importance of woolen textiles for clothing and blankets, the infant industry and national security arguments were suggested as rationales for higher tariffs. Unfortunately, by the time the 1828 act was approved, it also included higher tariffs for products only loosely associated with infant industries or national security. In addition, the 1828 tariff granted higher tariffs on imported raw wool. As noted previously, this meant the effective tariff on woolen textiles was lower than expected. Making matters worse, the woolen tariffs created by the 1828 act were somewhat complicated in their design and, therefore, were difficult to apply consistently when calculating import duties. Commentary from the time period suggests that this complexity, coupled with the desire of importers to avoid the high tariffs, encouraged various forms of tax evasion before or at the time the duties were computed.

Later Tariffs

The 1828 act also pushed the South's agitation over the protective tariff to a new high. By 1832, South Carolina, a slave state, was threatening to halt the collection of import duties on goods coming in through the state's ports. At the height of the crisis, the U.S. Senate was considering a bill that would authorize President Andrew Jackson to use force to compel South Carolina to adhere to the legislated duties. Although the use of force was avoided by the Tariff Act of 1833, which called for the gradual reduction of most tariffs to a flat 20 percent ad valorem rate by the early 1840s, the political rift caused by the 1828 act would continue right up to the Civil War.

The Tariff Act of 1833 stayed in force for nearly ten years before being reversed by the Tariff Act of 1842. The 1842 act represented the last significant tariff increase until a few months before the start of the Civil War in 1861. The legislative support for the 1842 act came from the recently formed Whig Party. In defending its position on the tariff, the Whigs' 1844 platform stated that it supported protectionist tariffs for the dual purpose of collecting revenue and protecting the country's free (nonslave) labor. The Whig emphasis on industrial labor likely reflected the realization that (1) the infant industry argument could no longer be reasonably applied to key U.S. industrial sectors in the 1840s and (2) the country's industrial expansion since the early 1800s meant that the manufacturing sector had become a significant employer of free labor in many parts of the country. From the 1840s until the early 1930s, the call to protect domestic labor, sincere or not, would remain a key rallying point for U.S. protectionists, especially during economic downturns. In this respect, support for the 1842 act likely was enhanced by a prolonged national recession that started in 1839.

Similarly, the **Smoot-Hawley Tariff** Act of 1930 represented the last significant U.S. experiment with a highly protectionist tariff policy, late in its industrial era. Although the act's origins precede the start of the **Great Depression**, it gained addi-

idea that during wartime, a country cannot rely on foreign sources for strategic products; therefore, domestic industries providing these products need to be protected. Concerns for the welfare of domestic labor rest on the wage and employment impacts of competing with foreign producers that may have the advantage of cheaper labor and, therefore, the ability to dominate the domestic market at the expense of domestic labor. Finally, because economic downturns mean rising unemployment and lower profits, high tariffs, it is argued, can offer temporary relief to the extent that they can reduce import competition. Although these arguments often were effective in obtaining high tariffs into the early twentieth century, in practice, the tariffs' impacts proved to be less than ideal. As a result, the tariff's popularity was waning by the end of the 1930s.

Historically, one of protectionism's main problems was retaliation by a country's trading partners. If a country's protective tariffs are met with high, retaliatory tariffs from its trading partners, then their benefits are significantly reduced in the form of lower exports. In addition, because protective tariffs typically were not restricted to infant industries or those linked to national security, the internal benefits of the tariff also were reduced. This reduction came in the form of higher prices for important consumer goods and intermediate goods (goods used in the production process) and, in the case of the United States, an exacerbation of existing internal political tensions.

As noted previously, the higher prices on consumer goods fell most heavily on the poor and, in some cases, encouraged smuggling and other forms of tax evasion. The problem of higher costs for intermediate goods can be demonstrated by returning to the wine example. In addition to the 50 percent wine tariff, assume domestic producers of wine bottles also are successful in obtaining a high tariff on foreign-made bottles. In this case, the wine tariff's benefits are significantly reduced because wine's effective tariff—the legislated tariff adjusted for the tariffs on intermediate goods—can be much lower than the intended legislated tariff.

Finally, protectionist tariffs were a major source of friction between the North and South leading up to the U.S. **Civil War**. The South was dependent on exports of raw cotton, especially to Europe. Therefore, the South worried that U.S. protective tariffs on imported textiles would reduce overseas demand for its raw cotton. In one scenario, U.S. protective textile tariffs might reduce the production of foreign cotton textiles by more than the additional domestic production created by the textile tariffs. In another scenario, the South's European trading partners might impose retaliatory tariffs, including tariffs on raw cotton, in response to U.S. tariffs on Europe's manufactured goods. In addition to these concerns, however, the South also resented U.S. protective tariffs because it raised the price of manufactured goods used in the production of cotton, thereby reducing the profitability of Southern agriculture. Likewise, because manufacturing was concentrated in the North, whatever benefits the tariff produced also were concentrated in the North.

Tariff of Abominations

The controversy surrounding the U.S. Tariff Act of 1828 provides an illustrative example of some of the problems with the protective tariff. This act, also known as the Tariff of Abominations, was passed largely in response to the economic problems confronting the woolen textile industry in the 1820s. As an infant industry, U.S. woolen manufactures and growers had benefited substantially from the trade

tional legislative support in response to rising unemployment following the 1929 stock market crash; however, its employment benefits, if any, were largely negated when important trading partners, most notably Canada, retaliated with higher tariffs on U.S. products.

Following the end of World War II, the protectionist tariffs of developed countries dramatically declined through a series of multilateral agreements known as the General Agreement on Tariffs and Trade (GATT). The first GATT treaty was completed in 1947 and represented a sharp departure from the more unilateral protectionist policies of the previous two centuries. The GATT's underlying premise, based on the economics of specialization, is that **international trade** free of high tariffs will generate more economic growth than the former protectionist strategies.

FURTHER READING: Pincus, Jonathan J. *Pressure Groups and Politics in Antebellum Tariffs.* New York: Columbia University Press, 1977; Taussig, Frank W. *Free Trade, the Tariff, and Reciprocity.* Repr. New York: Macmillan, 1927; Taussig, Frank W. *Some Aspects of the Tariff Question.* 3rd ed. Clifton, NJ: Augustus M. Kelley, 1972; NJ: Augustus M: Augustus M. *Tariff History of the United States.* 5th ed. New York: G. P. Putnam's Sons, 1910; Teich, Mikulas, and Roy Porter, eds. *The Industrial Revolution in National Context.* Cambridge: Cambridge University Press, 1996; Zeiler, Thomas W. *Free Trade, Free World: The Advent of GATT.* Chapel Hill: University of North Carolina Press, 1999. WEB SITES: http://www.usitc.gov/tata/hts/index.htm (Current Harmonized Tariff Schedule of the United States); http://docsonline.wto.org/gen_browseDetail.asp?preprog=3 (Legal Texts of the World Trade Organization).

GRANT D. FORSYTH

Taylor, Frederick (1856–1915)

Frederick Winslow Taylor, the pioneer of scientific business management, was born on March 20, 1856, in Germantown, Pennsylvania, to a wealthy and educated family of Philadelphia Quakers. He was schooled at Philips Academy in Exeter and was admitted to Harvard University but did not attend due to problems with his eyesight. In 1873, he became an industrial apprentice in a factory, and in his spare time, he studied engineering, and was awarded a degree from Stevens Institute of Technology in 1883. In 1878, he joined the Midvale Steel Company, eventually becoming its chief engineer, before joining the Manufacturing Investment Company as general manager in 1890. He also worked for the Bethlehem Steel Works and was consultant engineer for various other companies.

Taylor wanted to use his workers as efficiently as the machines were used, and he also wanted to measure industrial productivity. To these ends, he devised a system based on time and motion studies that split each job into its component parts. The supervisor timed each step and hand movement of the workers using a stopwatch, and then the components would be rearranged into the most efficient combination, which then would be taught to the workers. (Time and motion studies using a stopwatch in the civil service was banned in 1912.) Taylor became famous after this procedure was used at Bethlehem Steel, when the number of workers shoveling coal was reduced from 500 to 140 without any decrease in output. He gave importance to both trained management and innovative workers, believing that each needed the other. He concluded that labor unions were unnecessary and that workers should cooperate with management. He was forced to leave Bethlehem Steel in 1901, however, when he tried to revamp management.

Taylor wrote a book, *Shop Management* (1903), but his industrial philosophy was best spelled out in his most famous work, *The Principles of Scientific Management,* published in 1911, which introduced the term *scientific management*. His stress on "the one best way" paved the way for efficient practice, in which the most suitable method would complete a task in the least amount of time.

Taylor was dismayed by the loss of output due to inefficiency in the United States, which could be remedied by adopting systematic management. He emphasized the need for competent men, starting at the top of a company all the way down to the lowest levels. A man would be competent after proper training; for him, so-called captains of industry were not born but made. His theory aimed for "maximum prosperity for the employer" along with "maximum prosperity for each employee," and using his measurement systems would establish unambiguous wage rates for each job, avoiding differences based on subjective factors. He also was convinced of the fact that some people were incompetent, greedy, and prone to crime, resulting in systematic inefficiency, but with scientific management, this would be only a temporary problem. Taylor believed strongly that application of the principles underlying this system would make the world a better place in which to live.

The impact of this early management guru was tremendous. Although sometimes referred to in a pejorative way, Taylorism was responsible for changing the new industrial world of the twentieth century.

FURTHER READING: Haber, Samuel. *Efficiency and Uplift: Scientific Management in the Progressive Era 1890–1920.* Chicago: University of Chicago Press, 1964; Kakar, Sudhir. *Frederick Taylor: A Study in Personality and Innovation.* Boston: Heffernan Press, 1970; Kanigel, Robert. *The One Best Way: Frederick Winslow Taylor and the Enigma of Efficiency.* New York: Viking Press, 1997; Nelson, Daniel. *Frederick W. Taylor and the Rise of Scientific Management.* Madison: University of Wisconsin Press, 1980; Taylor, Frederick W. *The Principles of Scientific Management.* New York: Harper Bros., 1911; Wrege, Charles D., and Ronald G. Greenwood. *Frederick W. Taylor: The Father of Scientific Management: Myth and Reality.* Burr Ridge, IL: Irwin Professional, 1991.

PATIT PABAN MISHRA

Technical Advances

There are some questions among historians about the beginning and end of the Industrial Revolution; the widest period, 1700–1950, will be used in this essay. The extraordinary nature, variety, and rapidity of technical advances remain the period's most obvious, as well as most enduring, hallmarks. Much like natural evolution, technical innovation proceeds both by slow, incremental transformations as well as by relatively sudden changes. By the eighteenth century, slow, incremental advances had improved the performance of most of the manufacturing, construction, and transportation techniques that were in use since antiquity. Some of these gains were marginal; others were substantial. For example, by 1750, the largest European waterwheels had capacities of more than 5 kilowatts, much more powerful than their late Roman predecessors, and at 5–10 kilowatts per unit, the power of large, self-regulating Dutch windmills was more than ten times greater than that of rather primitive, heavy, early medieval post mills.

In contrast to these incremental gains, the technical advances brought by the Industrial Revolution were exceptional, as they accomplished in a matter of a few generations far more than did the cumulative gains during civilization's entire preceding history. Another remarkable characteristic of the period is that no major activity was left behind: The progress of individual economic sectors was not, necessarily, concurrent, and the gains were uneven, but when the second phase of the Industrial Revolution (the great spurt that encompassed the two pre–**World War I** generations) ended, there was no productive enterprise whose fundamentals had not been radically reshaped and whose performance was not (often astonishingly) enhanced by extensive and rapid technical advances.

Moreover, this unprecedented linking of innovations created entirely new industries. A dozen or so key examples must include electricity generation, electric lighting and appliances, oil and gas drilling, oil refining, internal combustion engines, cars and airplanes, mass production of steel, aluminum smelting, inorganic fertilizers, syntheses of organic chemicals ranging from dyes to pharmaceuticals, and pulp-based paper. It also produced new means of transport—**railroads**, **steamships**, bicycles, cars, trucks and buses, commercial aviation—and of communication— the telegraph, telephones, wireless broadcasts, postcards—as well as new ways of retailing—department stores, mail-order shopping. In addition, these innovations created enough free time and purchasing power for new entertainment and leisure activities: Besides such obvious examples as photography and cinema, the list ranges from recreational mountaineering to the modern Olympic Games.

These unprecedented changes and gains resulted from many fundamental breaks with past practices, and the scope of innovations and the pace of their commercial diffusion were possible only because of the extent and efficiency of feedbacks between basic science, applied engineering, large-scale production, and new burgeoning markets. The early phases of this grand transformation rested, as did all the previous advances, on experience, experimental adjustments, and empirical tinkering, but later innovations were increasingly driven by new scientific precepts: For the first time in human history, engineering became an applied science, as deep theoretical understanding often preceded the construction of new machines or the design of new processes and syntheses. At least two additional attributes characterized these technical transformations: Often, astonishingly short periods elapsed between the patenting of an invention and its commercial success, and a rapid rate of subsequent improvements led to the speedy maturation and refinement of many techniques.

Given these realities, any encyclopedia entry covering this historic singularity easily could become just a listing of remarkable inventions and innovations, with hardly any room for noting their unique attributes and assessing their revolutionary nature and lasting impact. Instead, let us concentrate on only four classes of fundamental technical innovations, those that underpin the progress of all other specific endeavors. First, no human activity, hence no economic endeavor, is possible without the conversion of energy. Hence, the epochal energy transition, the substitution of biomass (neither fossil nor nuclear) fuels by the fossil energies of coals and hydrocarbons, was the most fundamental accomplishment of the Industrial Revolution. All previous civilizations were directly solar. All industrial (and postindustrial) societies have been energized overwhelmingly by fossil fuel, somewhat complemented by primary, that is hydro and nuclear, electricity.

Second, the consequences of this grand transition were greatly increased by the invention and commercialization of new mechanical prime movers. These were the **steam engine**, **steam turbine**, internal combustion engine using Otto and Diesel cycles, and gas turbines; their large-scale deployment eventually eliminated the need for draft animals, displaced virtually all hard manual labor (as humans ceased to be prime movers and became controllers of increasingly greater energy flows), and released labor from the fields to the cities. They also provided inexpensive, flexible, and yet precise means for providing energy to countless industrial operations and opened up new, seemingly magical, ways of long-distance transportation.

Third, the period saw an impressively rapid sequence of inventing an entirely new energy system of electricity generation, transmission, and conversion to light, heat, and motion as well as new means of telecommunication and information processing; in many ways, this has been the period's most far-reaching, most revolutionary legacy. Fourth, all of these advances were either predicated on or aided by mass production of inexpensive iron and its conversion into many kinds of steel: Only the Industrial Revolution has allowed us to live in what is truly the iron (or more accurately steel) age. The epoch's inventions include many ingenious processes for producing new materials, ranging from previously unavailable aluminum to synthetic plastics, but steel provides not only the structural and infrastructural foundations of industrial civilization (skeletons of buildings, reinforcing bars in concrete, most of the mass in vehicles, ships, drilling rigs, transmission towers, and pipelines) but also its tools, ranging from cutlery and surgical scalpels to metal-cutting tools, and the means for processing and producing other key materials, whether it occurs in crude oil refineries or via chemical syntheses.

Epochal Energy Transitions

In the most fundamental energy terms, the Industrial Revolution can be defined as the transition from biomass to fossil fuels, first to coal and then to oil and gas. Preindustrial societies drew their food, feed, heat, and mechanical power from sources that were either almost immediate transformations of solar radiation in the form of flowing water and wind or harnessed in the form of accumulated biomass and metabolic conversions. These conversions may have taken just a few months (such as in crops harvested for food, feed, and fuel) or a few years (draft animals, human muscles, shrubs, young trees) or a few decades (mature trees) of growth before becoming usable. In some countries, fossil fuels had been known since antiquity and used locally in very limited amounts, but their combustion never amounted to more than a negligible share of overall energy supply.

Transition to fossil fuels was highly country-specific. Britain accomplished the switch before 1800, coal was dominant in Germany and France by 1850, the United States began deriving more than half of its primary energy from it by 1884, and the best estimates show that the global use of fossil fuels surpassed that of biomass energies during the 1890s. This transition took place in Russia only during the 1910s, however, and China and India, the world's two most populous countries, accomplished the transition only after World War II. Fossil fuels are formed through slow but profound changes of accumulated biomass under pressure and heat, and their ages (with the exception of young peats and the poorest lignites) range from many millions to hundreds of millions of years.

A useful analogy with money flows is to see the preindustrial societies as relying on instantaneous or minimally delayed and constantly replenished solar income, whereas industrial civilization has been withdrawing accumulated solar capital at rates that will exhaust it—not physically, but in terms of economically viable recovery—in a tiny fraction of the time that was needed to create it. In the early decades of the Industrial Revolution, no one understood how large the earth's deposits of fossil fuels were but eventually came to realize that their stores could energize a high-energy civilization for only hundreds, rather than thousands, of years. Although the extraction and combustion of coal had obvious local environmental impacts (destroying natural land cover, polluting water and air), it was only during the twentieth century when we came to realize not only the serious large-scale regional effects arising from the combustion of coal and oil (respiratory disease, acid rain) but also the fact that the emissions of carbon dioxide will be a key factor in an unprecedented episode of anthropogenic global warming.

This inherently unsustainable and environmentally damaging dependence on fossil fuels provided the industrial societies with energy sources that, unlike solar radiation, are highly concentrated and easy to store and transport, and liquids and gases are particularly flexible and convenient to use. The most obvious advantage of fossil fuels is their relatively high energy density. Liquid fuels contain 42–44 megajoules (a joule is a measure of energy) per kilogram, and good-quality coal contains 25–29 megajoules per kilogram, compared to about 15 megajoules per kilogram for straw and 17–19 megajoules per kilogram for air-dry wood. Without the high energy density of refined liquid fuels, road transport using gasoline and a heavier diesel fuel for passenger cars and trucks and aviation using gasoline for propeller-driven airplanes and kerosene for jets would not be possible. Charcoal, with 29 megajoules per kilogram, is as good as hard coal, but its traditional production (requiring up to 10 units of wood per unit of charcoal) was extremely wasteful and consumed large areas of forests. For example, during the mid-eighteenth century, even a small English blast furnace with an attached forge needed about 2,000 hectares (a circle with the radius of about 2.5 kilometers, or 1.5 miles, equivalent to about 4,942 acres) of hardwoods for its charcoal annually, assuming a 5 : 1 wood : charcoal ratio. Charcoal-based smelting, and other energy-intensive industrial activities, was thus inherently restricted to relatively small and dispersed units.

The other obvious attribute of fossil fuels is the extraordinarily high power density of their extraction. The just-noted eighteenth-century English blast furnace and forge acquired its charcoal with a power density of only 0.4 watt per square meter. In contrast, a coal mine tapping just two one-meter coal seams of good coking coal would extract the fuel with power density of about 2,500 watts per square meter, and a single, small eighteenth-century colliery producing 10,000 tons of fuel annually could fuel five blast furnaces. Coal thus opened the way to an unprecedented concentration of industrial production, to economies of scale and high urban manufacturing and residential densities. The third key advantage of fossil fuels is their flexibility, the attribute that is particularly obvious in the case of hydrocarbons that can energize both stationary uses (fuel oil and natural gas for heating and electricity generation) and mobile applications (liquids for all modes of transportation). These fuels can be inexpensively and very safely transported by pipelines and ships and are also excellent feedstocks for chemical syntheses that range from nitrogenous fertilizers to a large array of plastics.

Harnessing fossil fuels elevated both the national aggregates and per capita energy use to unprecedented levels, and the gains are even greater when historical comparisons are done in terms of actually delivered energy services (heat, light, motion) rather than in terms of primary energy use. This difference was due to continuing technical advances that improved typical efficiencies of virtually all principal energy conversions. The difference has been most impressive for artificial lighting:

candles converted less than 0.01 percent of chemical energy in wax to light; Thomas **Edison**'s first short-lived carbon filaments turned 0.2 percent of electricity into light; before **World War I**, tungsten filament light bulbs were about 1 percent efficient; and by the 1930s, low-pressure sodium lamps (with their characteristic yellow light used for outdoor illumination) approached 10 percent efficiency.

The affordable abundance of more efficiently used fossil energy transformed every productive sector of the industrial economy. Field machines (the first practical tractors were introduced before 1910), synthetic fertilizers (the Haber-Bosch process made mass-produced nitrogen fertilizers available by 1913), and herbicides and pesticides (both introduced commercially during the 1940s) displaced animate labor and organic recycling in farming. Mechanization eliminated heavy exertion in the extraction of mineral resources and in every kind of manufacturing, often to the extent that the term has entirely lost its logical foundation as it ushered in the era of mass production and released labor from industries to services.

Some of these productivity multiples were stunning: Although a craftsman (and a helper) producing mouth-blown glass bottles could finish a dozen pieces per hour, by 1907, Michael Owens's bottle-making machine, supervised by a single worker, produced 2,500 bottles every hour. New prime movers revolutionized transportation, and new forms of communication and information processing had an even more profound effect on the service sector that evolved to create most of the new wealth in all affluent countries. In turn, these advances changed the structure and dynamics of industrial societies.

First and foremost, they raised **food** availability far above subsistence needs and assured the provision of adequate health care; these were the two key factors behind the steady increases in average life expectancy. They produced the worldwide trend toward increasing **urbanization**, and the cities have provided unprecedented occupational and intellectual opportunities. On the negative side, large-scale combustion of fossil fuels has been imposing significant environmental burdens on the biosphere. By far the most worrisome has been the rising level of carbon dioxide (CO_2) produced by the combustion of fossil fuels and also by land-use changes, mainly deforestation: It has been the single largest contributor to the gradual warming of our climate due to human activity. Before 1850, atmospheric CO_2 concentration was about 270 parts per million; by 1950, it rose to nearly 320 parts per million and surpassed 380 parts per million in 2005.

Development of new industries to extract, transport, process, and convert coal and hydrocarbons required a myriad of technical advances as these endeavors evolved rapidly from small-scale, low-volume practices to mass production and worldwide trade. Key improvements in underground coal extraction included the replacement of pickaxes and shovels, first by handheld pneumatic hammers and then, beginning after World War I, by mechanized cutters and loaders. Surface mining benefited from larger machines to remove overburden (the material on top of the coal seam) and from bigger excavators to mine the exposed coal seams. Until the end of the nineteenth century, drilling for oil and gas relied solely on cable-tool rigs. These were improved versions of ancient Chinese percussion drilling that first was used during the early Han Dynasty more than 2,000 years ago, but improved because they were powered by steam engines rather than by human muscles.

The first modern rotary rig was worked at the Corsicana field in Texas in 1895, but the technique spread only after World War I. Rotary drilling improved with the invention of a superior conical bit by Howard R. Hughes in 1907. His company went on to develop many modifications and improvements of the basic design, including the now-standard diamond-covered tricone bit. Another improvement came with the efficient cementing of wells, done by companies such as Erle P. Halliburton's, who started his well-cementing company in Oklahoma in 1919. Automatic well logging also improved drilling: Conrad Schlumberger proposed the use of electrical measurements in order to map subsurface rock bodies in 1912. These were both key advances, and the two eponymous companies still dominate worldwide in their respective fields.

Faster operation and increased drilling depth (the record rose from about a mile before World War I to 2.8 miles by the late 1930s and 3.7 miles a decade later) led to a spate of major new discoveries. In the United States, 64 giant oil fields were discovered between 1900 and 1924, but 147 such fields were added during the subsequent 25 years. The largest pre-1950 finds included the first giant oil fields in Iraq (Kirkuk in 1927), Saudi Arabia (Abqaiq in 1940 and al-Ghawar, the world's largest oil field, in 1948), Kuwait (al-Burqan, the second largest field, in 1938), and Venezuela. Crude oil refining was transformed first by the introduction of thermal cracking (William Burton in 1913), which increased the gasoline yield, and then, during the late 1930s and the early 1940s, by catalytic cracking. Seamless steel pipes, made possible by the piece-rolling process invented by Reinhard and Max Mannesmann in 1885, revolutionized the production of pipelines needed to carry oil and gas. The ocean transport of oil expanded with the increasing size of tankers, which grew from less than 2,000 tons capacity before 1890 to nearly 20,000 deadweight tons by 1945.

New Prime Movers

Dominant prime movers determine the productivity of a civilization and its tempo of life. The choice of preindustrial prime movers was limited, and their capacities were inherently restricted. The sustainable power of animate prime movers, human and animal muscles, has not changed for millennia, ranging mostly from 50–100 watts for steady exertions by humans and 100–600 watts for inefficiently harnessed and often poorly fed draft and pack animals. Only larger, well-fed horse breeds, with good collar harnesses and iron horseshoes (common only after 1700), could sustain one horsepower (equivalent to 745 watts). As already noted, the capacities of the largest preindustrial waterwheels and windmills were substantially above the ratings of their early medieval counterparts, but their absolute power remained low. The only other common prime movers were wind-filled sails, increasingly efficient on larger oceangoing ships but always readily becalmed by the absence of wind.

The steam engine changed all of this, first, between 1700 and 1780, only slowly, then, after 1820, much more rapidly. This machine remains the quintessential icon of the Industrial Revolution, but if it had remained the only new prime mover, then the scope of industrialization would be much more restricted and its environmental impact would be much more pronounced. The main reason for this is the engine's inherently limited efficiency and capacity. Before 1720, Thomas Newcomen's pioneering designs, which were used to pump water from increasingly deep English coal pits, had capacities of less than 4 kilowatts (about 5 horsepower) and converted at best just 0.7 percent of coal into useful mechanical energy. This inefficiency limited exploitation of only those coal mines with a ready fuel supply.

John Smeaton's designs roughly doubled the Newcomen engine's efficiency, and James **Watt**'s invention of a separate condenser (first patented in 1769) and other improvements raised the typical efficiency to about 4 percent by 1800, but the average power of engines made by Matthew **Boulton** and Watt's company was only about 20 kilowatts. Only the advent of high-pressure machines during the first decades of the nineteenth century by Richard Trevithick in the United Kingdom and Oliver Evans in the United States made the engine efficient enough and light enough to be used in railways. (Watt himself did not favor the high-pressure engine and, in fact, actively hindered its development.) The inherently high mass/power ratio of steam engines was not a major concern for their use on ships.

The transportation revolution accomplished by railways and steamships was both swift—with the 1830s being the pioneering decade and 1850s the time of maturation—and profound: horse-drawn coaches covered less than 6 miles per hour, heavy-goods wagons less than 3 miles per hour, but the fastest locomotives reached speeds in excess of 60 miles per hour by 1850 and railway speeds above 30 miles per hour were common. Even with favorable winds, an eastbound transatlantic crossing on a sailing ship took 17 to 20 days; by 1900, the steamships cut it to less than 6 days.

Gradual improvements raised the maximum efficiencies of the largest (larger than one megawatt) stationary steam engines to more than 15 percent by 1900, and they were installed to turn dynamos of new electricity-generating plants. At the same time, small steam engines were used to power some of the fastest vehicles of the first automobile generation. In 1902, Leon Serpollet's beak-shaped racer broke the speed record by traveling one kilometer (0.6 mile) in 29.8 seconds (the equivalent of 75 miles per hour), and Francis and Freelan Stanley's steam car set a new world speed record for the fastest mile (127.6 miles per hour) in 1906. But these temporary successes could not change an inevitable trend. Large steam engines were too bulky, too massive, and too inefficient compared to the rapidly improving designs of **steam turbines**, and the future of car transport was with inherently much lighter and more efficient internal combustion engines; by 1910, the era of steam engines was essentially over.

The invention of the steam turbine by Charles Parsons actually exemplifies the unprecedented technical advances of the Industrial Revolution much better than the better-known history of the steam engine. Parsons invented the machine because theoretical thermodynamics told him that it could be done. He improved it rapidly and made it into an unrivaled high-power stationary prime mover in less than two decades after its patent in 1884. Early designs had a small capacity and were much less efficient than the best steam engines, but just before World War I, the largest machines rated 25 megawatts and converted some 75 percent of steam's energy into rotary motion; a century later, steam turbines continue to dominate thermal (both fossil and nuclear) generation of electricity.

The rise of steam turbines was paralleled by the introduction and rapid improvement of two kinds of internal combustion engines: the gasoline-fueled Otto-cycle machine that eventually came to power most of the world's automobiles and propeller-driven airplanes and Rudolf Diesel's engine that captured heavy-duty markets first before gaining a major segment of the passenger-car market. Nicolaus Otto introduced an innovative design of a stationary, coal-gas-powered engine with a distinct four-stroke cycle in 1877, and less than a decade later, independent designs by Karl Benz and by Gottlieb Daimler and Wilhelm Maybach used the four-stroke cycle in light gasoline-fueled engines suitable for mobile applications.

The first cars were just motorized carriages with engines mounted under high-perched seats, with wooden wheels of unequal radius, and with dangerous cranks and stiff steering rods. In 1891, a radical redesign by Emile Levassor moved the engine from under the seats and placed it in front of the driver, a shift that put the crankshaft parallel with the car's principal axis (rather than parallel with the axles), made it possible to install larger, more powerful engines, and led to the design of a protective, later also aerodynamic, hood. Technical maturation was then rapid, and by 1900, the Mercedes 35 became essentially the first modern car.

Because of their artisanal production, however—car making had its roots in traditional carriage making as well as in the new business of bicycle construction—automobiles remained broadly unaffordable until Henry **Ford**'s introduction in 1901 of an efficient assembly line. These produced just a few versions of a single car, the Model T, of which about 15 million were sold before the model was discontinued in 1927. Notable automotive improvements of the first half of the twentieth century included electric starters in 1911 to replace the hand crank, replacement of open bodies by closed structures and wood frames by sheet steel, solid metal wheels, four-wheel brakes, and pneumatic balloon tires during the 1920s. Other developments included independent front-wheel suspension for a smoother ride, power brakes, front-wheel drive, more efficient transmissions, and air conditioning during the 1930s, and radial tires and automatic transmission during the 1940s.

All pre–World War I engines worked with compression ratios no higher than 4.3 to avoid violent knocking caused by a spontaneous ignition of the fuel-air mixture that produces a pressure wave moving in the direction opposite to that of the spreading ignition flame. Compression ratios began to rise to modern levels (8–10) only after Thomas Midgley identified tetraethyl lead in 1921 as the best gasoline additive to prevent knocking and after leaded gasoline was introduced in 1923. It was discontinued starting in the 1970s because of the health and environmental impact of the heavy metal.

Diesel's designs were based, much like Parsons's, on theoretical considerations. His dreams of designing an ideal prime mover remained unrealized, but his new engine ignited the injected fuel without sparking by using high compression ratios (15–20) and was much more efficient than the Otto-cycle machines; by 1911, the thermal efficiency of the best diesel engines was 41 percent compared to 14 percent to 17 percent for the more commonly deployed automotive Otto engines. Given the engine's inherently higher mass/power ratio, its first applications were in stationary uses (pumps, oil drills) and in heavy transport (locomotives, ships). Finally in 1927, Robert Bosch's high-precision injection pump opened the way for the widespread adoption of diesel engines in road vehicles: Trucks came first, introduced before World War II, followed by passenger cars, and in Europe nearly half of them are now diesels.

Only two new prime movers have been introduced since World War I: gas turbines and rockets. The first practical gas turbines were designed independently during the 1930s by Frank Whittle in Britain and by Hans Pabst von Ohain in Germany, and the first jet-powered planes saw action during the closing months of World War II. Postwar developments led to a profusion of military jet fighter and bomber designs as well as to the introduction of commercial jet planes. Robert H. Goddard tested the world's first liquid-propelled (oxygen and gasoline) rocket in 1926 in the United States, but the most important pioneering development took place in

Germany after Walter Dornberger recruited Wernher von Braun to work on the Wehrmacht's military rockets in 1932. Ten years later, they began testing the V-2 missile that in 1944 and 1945 killed about 2,500 Londoners. In a well-known case of expertise transfer, virtually the entire von Braun team was brought to the United States in 1945, where they formed the core of the effort that eventually sent the first men to the moon.

Electricity

Unlike steam engines, in which commercial adoption (Newcomen, John Smeaton, Watt, 1710s–1790s) preceded the formulation of thermodynamic theory (Sadi Carnot, 1820s; Rudolf Clausius, 1850s), electricity was a subject of considerable experimental and theoretical interest for decades before its large-scale industrial applications. Key milestones included Alessandro Volta's battery (1800), Hans Christian Ørsted's recognition of the magnetic effect of electric currents (1819), and André Marie Ampère's concept of a complete circuit. The most important one was Michael **Faraday**'s discovery of the induction of electric current in a moving magnetic field in 1831, which eventually led to three classes of machines that make

Replica of Charles Babbage's (1791–1871) difference engine, an early computer. Science Museum/ Science & Society Picture Library.

it possible to produce and transmit electricity and to convert it into mechanical energy: to turbogenerators, transformers, and electric motors.

Shortly after Faraday's fundamental discovery came the invention of the telegraph that by the 1860s had evolved into the first intercontinental method of wired communication, even if powered by batteries. By the late 1870s, however, there was still no commercially viable generation of electricity, no electric lights, and no practical means of converting electricity into motion. All of this changed during the 1880s when the key (and enduring) elements of the entire system of electricity generation, transmission, and industrial, commercial, and household uses were created completely (or nearly so) de novo in the course of a single decade. Bold conceptual thinking and the uncommon perseverance of Thomas A. Edison had a key role in these advances; other prominent participants included Nikola **Tesla** (the inventor of the induction motor in 1888), William Stanley (who introduced prototypes of modern transformers starting in 1885), George Westinghouse (whose company pioneered alternating-current transmission whose adoption was initially, and zealously, opposed by Edison), and, as already noted, Charles Parsons.

Coal-fired and steam-engine-powered commercial electricity generation as conceived by Edison began in 1881 in London and New York, and lighting was its first market. A practical carbon-filament electric light bulb for indoor illumination was first demonstrated in 1879–1880 by Edison and by Joseph Swan in Britain. This type of bulb was perfected during the subsequent two decades, only to be supplanted after 1900 by more efficient and more durable incandescent metallic filaments (osmium, then tungsten); the first fluorescent lights were patented in 1927 and became widely available during the 1930s. Introduction of transformers, beginning with imperfect designs after 1882 and progressing to essentially modern devices after 1885, made it possible to transmit electricity with limited losses at high voltages over increasingly longer distances. Efficient induction motors converted electricity into mechanical energy, and electricity also was used in electrochemical processes (most notably to produce aluminum) and in electric arc furnaces, in which it was mainly used to produce steel from scrap metal.

The progress of electrification was initially slow, with urban household uses limited only to a few low-power light bulbs and with rural areas remaining beyond the reach of high-voltage lines. Even in the United States, only 10 percent of all households were connected to a public electricity supply by 1910, but virtually all urban residents had access by the late 1920s, although rural electrification was not completed until after 1950. The first household appliances appeared between 1890 and 1910 (irons, toasters, washing machines) but became common possessions only after World War I. Refrigerators diffused widely only during the 1930s, after Midgley introduced inexpensive and efficient chlorofluorocarbon coolants, which were discontinued after 1987 because of their destruction of stratospheric ozone.

Once electricity became available, the economic and social transformations brought by its use were so profound because no other kind of energy affords such an instant and effortless access to consumers. To any homemaker used to the practices of the pre-electrical era, this form of energy was truly liberating as it gradually eliminated a large number of daily chores, including such heavy, tiresome tasks as drawing and hauling water, washing and wringing clothes by hand, ironing them with heavy wedges of hot metal, and lifting heavy rugs onto clotheslines to be pounded manually with carpet beaters. In contrast to the relatively slow diffusion of household appliances, manufacturing saw a rapid displacement of centralized power drives (with central shafts and transmission belts powered by a steam engine) by individual electric motors.

This was a much more revolutionary step than the previous prime mover transition that saw waterwheels replaced by steam engines in factories. That substitution did not change the basic mode of distributing mechanical energy, as factory ceilings continued to be clogged by complex arrangements of iron or steel line shafts that were connected by pulleys and belts to parallel countershafts, which, in turn, were belted to individual machines. With this arrangement, a prime mover outage or an accident at any point along the line of power distribution, such as a cracked shaft or just a slipped belt, caused the whole assembly to stop. Also, even if many of the machines were not needed, the entire shaft assemblies still had to be running.

Individual electric motors changed modern manufacturing by establishing a pattern of production that will be dominant for as long as electric motors remain by far the most important prime movers in modern industrial production. Their rapid adoption is demonstrated by reliable U.S. data: total mechanical power in the country's manufacturing sector roughly quadrupled between 1899 and 1929, but the capacity of electric motors grew nearly sixtyfold and reached more than 82 percent of the total available power compared to less than 5 percent at the end of the nineteenth century. An important additional benefit was that factory ceilings, uncluttered by transmission lines, could now be equipped with adequate lighting. On the railways, electricity supplanted inefficient, polluting steam engines; on farms, electricity did away with the primitive threshing of grains, milking of cows by hand, and laborious preparation of feed by manual chopping or grinding or with pitchforking of hay into lofts. Electric pumps eliminated slow and laborious water-raising powered by people and animals.

No other form of energy can equal electricity's flexibility: It can be converted to light, heat, motion, and chemical potential, and hence it has been used extensively in every principal energy-consuming sector except commercial flight. Besides this all-encompassing versatility, electricity is also a perfectly clean, as well as a silent, source of energy at the point of consumption, and its delivery can be easily and precisely adjusted in order to provide the desirable speed and accurate control for flexible industrial production. Electricity can be converted without virtually any losses to useful heat, and large electric motors can transform more than 95 percent of it into mechanical energy. It also can generate temperatures higher than combustion of any fossil fuel, and once the requisite wiring is in place, any new converters can be just added and plugged in. Electricity also powers a still expanding assortment of electronic devices; the first of these were based on vacuum tubes invented before World War I.

Iron and Steel

Charcoal-based smelting of pig (cast) iron, an alloy composed of roughly 95 percent iron, 4 percent carbon, and traces of other elements, in small blast furnaces was the norm in preindustrial Europe. Coke—a nearly pure carbon prepared by driving off nearly all volatile matter from suitable bituminous coals by heating them in the absence of air—was first produced in England before the mid-seventeenth century, but Abraham **Darby** succeeded in producing pig iron with coke only in 1709. His process offered a virtually unlimited supply of a superior metallurgical fuel, but it was initially wasteful and costly. It became the norm only after 1750 in

Britain, whereas pig iron production in both the United States and Russia remained largely charcoal-based until the last decades of the nineteenth century.

Coke could support heavier loads of iron ore and limestone than charcoal, leading to increased sizes of blast furnaces: Their heights rose from about 30 feet before 1800 to about 80 feet by 1840, and their maximum daily output of hot metal shot up from less than 3 tons per day in 1750 to 100 tons per day by 1850 and to nearly 300 tons per day by 1900. They also became more efficient users of coke thanks to the use of hot blast (patented by James Neilson in 1828) and to the recovery and reuse of hot gases escaping from the furnace's previously open top. As a result, global smelting of pig iron rose from less than 400,000 tons in 1800 to 5 million tons in 1850 and to nearly 80 million tons by 1913.

The metal is good in compression (cast iron makes excellent posts) but its high carbon content makes it weak in tension and, hence, unsuitable for beams, rails, or tools. Only its transformation into steel—a collective name for alloys with less than 1 percent carbon but often with the addition of other metals, such as nickel, vanadium, or chromium, which impart special properties—makes the metal suitable for many more demanding commercial uses. Preindustrial societies produced limited amounts of steel primarily by a process of cementation; that is, by adding a desired amount of carbon to practically carbon-free wrought iron. The alloy remained in restricted supply even after Benjamin Huntsman (1704–1776) began producing his crucible cast steel by carburizing wrought iron during the late 1740s, and it was used only for such specialized applications as razors, cutlery, watch springs, and metal-cutting tools. The first process of large-scale steelmaking was introduced independently and concurrently by Henry Bessemer in England and by William Kelly in the United States in 1856–1857.

In the **Bessemer process**, molten pig iron was poured into a large pear-shaped tilting converter lined with siliceous (acid) refractory material, and the subsequent blasting of cold air decarburized the molten metal and drove off impurities. The blowing lasted usually 15 to 30 minutes per batch, and because enough heat was generated by the oxidation of impurities, there was no need for an external source of energy to preheat the blown air. By 1861, Bessemer steel was being rolled into rails in a number of mills around England, and it was first produced in the United States in 1864. The process became common, however, only after it was discovered how to remove phosphorus from pig iron in order to be able to use many iron ores that contain the element. The solution was found in 1879 by Sidney Gilchrist Thomas and Percy Carlyle Gilchrist, who introduced a basic material into the furnace's lining, so that its reaction with the acidic phosphorus oxides present in the liquid iron could be removed as slag.

By 1890, nearly two-thirds of all European steel was smelted by the basic (as opposed to the acid) Bessemer process, and Bessemer steel output peaked in British and U.S. mills at about 80 percent and 86 percent of the total, respectively. Its use then began to decline rapidly as a new invention, the open-hearth furnace (OHF), proved to be an epoch-making innovation that produced most of the world's steel for more than two-thirds of the twentieth century. Its inventor, William (Carl Wilhelm) Siemens, combined a well-known technique of open-hearth smelting of iron with the heat economy of a regenerative furnace, in which much of the heat generated by fuel combustion did not escape as hot gas through a chimney but was absorbed in a regenerator, a chamber stacked with a honeycomb mass of bricks.

As soon as the bricks were sufficiently heated, the hot gases were diverted into another regenerating chamber, and the air required for combustion was preheated by passing through the first chamber. After its temperature declined to a predetermined level, the air flow was reversed, and this alternating operation guaranteed the maximum recovery of waste heat. This energy-conserving innovation (the fuel savings amounted to as much as 70%) was patented in 1861 and was first used at a glassworks in Birmingham. By 1867, Siemens was satisfied that the high temperatures (up to 1,700° C, 3,000° F) generated by this process would easily remove any impurities from mixtures of wrought iron scrap and cast iron charged into the furnace.

The OHF became known as the Siemens-Martin furnace, because French metallurgist Emile Martin filed definitive patents in 1865, and a year later the two inventors agreed to share the rights. Unlike the Bessemer converter, OHFs usually needed half a day to finish the purification of the metal. They began to spread in Europe during the early 1880s, and in the United States, the share of OHF steelmaking rose rapidly to nearly 75 percent of the total output by 1914; it continued to increase until after World War II. Areas of the largest OHFs grew from about 320 square feet during the late 1890s to more than 860 square feet during World War II, and heat sizes rose from just over 40 tons to 200 tons.

Yet another smelting innovation that became one of the mainstays of twentieth-century steelmaking was an electric arc furnace. William Siemens built the first experimental units, and Paul Héroult deployed the process commercially for the first time in 1902 in order to produce high-quality steel from scrap metal. The furnace operates on the same principle as the arc light, but on a much larger scale. The current passing between two large carbon electrodes in its roof melts the scrap, and the metal is produced in batches. Iron ore may also be added, as well as materials to absorb impurities.

The revolution in steelmaking is reflected in global production totals. Worldwide steel output was less than 100,000 tons a year before 1850; it reached 500,000 tons in 1870, 28 million tons by 1900, and 200 million tons by 1950. As steel production techniques improved, larger amounts of pig iron were converted into a greater variety of the increasingly ubiquitous alloy. Before 1860, less than 1 percent of the world's pig iron was turned into steel, by 1900 the share was nearly 75 percent, and before World War I it was virtually 100 percent. Steel became and—despite the impressively rising production of aluminum and, later, the large-scale synthesis of plastics—remains by far the most important material of the modern world, another lasting legacy of the Industrial Revolution.

FURTHER READING: Jacob, Margaret C. *Scientific Culture and the Making of the Industrial Revolution.* New York: Oxford University Press, 1997; King, Steven, and Geoffrey Timmins. *Making Sense of the Industrial Revolution.* Manchester, U.K.: Manchester University Press, 2001; Mokyr, Joel. *The Gifts of Athena: Historical Origins of the Knowledge Economy.* Princeton, NJ: Princeton University Press, 2002; Smil, Vaclav. *Creating the 20th Century: Technical Innovations of 1867–1914 and Their Lasting Impact.* New York: Oxford University Press, 2005.

VACLAV SMIL

Telecommunications

The word *telecommunication* was first used by Edouard Estaunié (1862–1942) in his *Traité pratique de télécommunication electrique,* published in 1904. Composed of the

Greek *(tele),* meaning "distant," and the Latin *communicatio,* meaning "connection," the term, in the literal sense of the word, denotes the conveyance of information over a great distance, a distance that cannot be covered by face-to-face communication. In the narrower sense of the word, however, only such means of communication qualify as telecommunication that dematerialize the transmitted information. Thus, homing pigeons or postal mail services are considered transport systems rather than telecommunications, even though they convey information over a great distance.

Early telecommunication systems have made use of acoustic (e.g., drums) and optical (e.g., smoke signals, beacons) means of transmission. Most of these techniques, however, suffered from severe limitations of range or practicability when transmitting more complex information. Thus, more modern definitions of telecommunication usually exclude such preelectric means of negotiating distance and apply solely to techniques of transmitting, emitting, or receiving information via electric, electromagnetic, or optical (i.e., fiber-optic/laser) systems. Here, we will widen this definition to accommodate the optical telegraph as well. Although information was transmitted visually, the optical telegraph first established a tight communication network to convey reasonably complex messages. It is, thus, the direct forerunner of electric **telegraphy.**

Telecommunication transmission systems principally use two different types of vehicle: In line transmission, the information is sent and received via lines and cables (either made from conducting material or, today, from optical fiber), whereas in radio transmission, the information is converted in electromagnetic waves and conveyed wirelessly. Both forms depend on the availability of electricity, either directly as the signal carrier or to produce the electromagnetic waves or optical impulses that carry the information.

The Optical Telegraph

From the beginning, the emergence of the centralized state was accompanied by the need to convey messages quickly over great distances. The administration and defense of more remote regions depended on the rapid and reliable transmission of information between the center and the periphery. Well into the eighteenth century, horse relay systems and—to a more limited extent—homing pigeons were the fastest means to send complex information over a great distance. Communication systems based on smoke signals, beacons, or acoustic signs were capable only of submitting simple messages with a prearranged scope of content. They were not sophisticated enough to satisfy the communication demand of a modern administration, let alone the emerging banking and business sector.

The earliest systems of telecommunications were usually reserved for exclusive government use (similar to the early postal services). There was already an emerging commercial demand for telecommunication, but, primarily for strategic reasons, many European governments safeguarded their monopoly and would not open their infrastructure for commercial use. Thus, private telecommunications systems for commercial use were built in Britain and Germany early in the nineteenth century even before the advent of the electric telegraph. Those commercial optical telegraph lines catered mainly to the merchant and banking community. A similar venture in France failed in 1832, and subsequent aspirations were outlawed by the French government in 1837.

Although the functioning of the optical telegraph rested on the improvements achieved in telescope building in the mid-eighteenth century, the electric telegraph depended on the mastery of electricity. An understanding of the properties of electricity, the provision of steady electricity supply, and the discovery of electromagnetism were all prerequisites for the successful utilization of electric power in telecommunications.

When experiments with electricity were still in their infancy, and neither electric current nor electromagnetic waves were available as means of information transmission, enhanced visual communication seemed the fastest and most flexible way to convey messages over a great distance. The invention of the optical telegraph is usually credited to the Frenchman Claude Chappe (1763–1805). An optical telegraph consisted of a chain of relay stations, each equipped with signaling machinery mounted on the roof. With the help of telescopes, which had been considerably improved during the eighteenth century, and an elaborate code system, the relay stations could encode and decode messages and pass them to the next station. The first line working successfully was opened between Paris and Lille in 1794. During the next decades, the French government established an impressive network of optical telegraphs connecting the regional centers to Paris.

In Britain, the first privately run optical signaling line had been established between London and Newmarket around 1760. After the establishment of the optical telegraph in France, British engineers in the Royal Navy learned from and adapted the Chappe system. A line from London to Portsmouth was opened in 1796, and one from London to Plymouth followed in 1805. Instead of Chappe's machinery that used signaling arms, the Admiralty system employed signaling shutters.

Strategic and administrative considerations had spurred the development of the optical telegraph. In France, the young republic was confronted with new administrative challenges, whereas Britain feared a French invasion via the English Channel. The routes of the earliest lines reflect these considerations, and use of the lines was reserved exclusively for administrative and military purposes in both France and Britain. Answering to the existing private demand for the commercial transmission of messages, a commercial optical telegraph line was opened between Liverpool and Holyhead in 1827, and another line from Hull to Spurn Head followed in 1839. In France, a private stockholder-funded line between Paris and Rouen had been opened in 1831, but it was financially unsuccessful and closed only a year later. To safeguard the government monopoly on telegraph communication, the French government prohibited the further establishment of private lines in 1837. In the same year, the first commercial optical telegraph line in Germany connected Hamburg with Cuxhaven.

The demand for commercial telegraph communication illustrates the social and economic change in Britain and, later, in Germany brought about by the Industrial Revolution. The emerging modern banking and stock market system promised large profits to the best informed. Success in trade and industrial production depended on information exchange. In short, the Industrial Revolution made knowledge and information a highly valuable commodity. We can, however, only speculate as to whether a commercial optical telegraph network would have emerged to cover Europe had not the advent of the electric telegraph rendered any such notions obsolete. Maintenance of the optical lines was expensive, whereas throughput was still low. Thus, the rates charged for the transmission of messages were extremely high and the cost-value ratio was not particularly favorable to the private customer. Therefore, public demand beyond the highest echelons of commerce might well have been limited.

Electric Telegraphy: The Beginnings

Before the installation of the optical telegraph line, sending a message from Portsmouth to London by horse relay system took about five hours; now, a simple message could reach London in a matter of several minutes, using 22 relay stations in the process. Although most lines proved strategically useful, the optical telegraph suffered from a number of disadvantages: First, its usability depended on clear sight and, thus, on weather conditions; second, daylight was necessary to convey messages; third, the maintenance and working of the lines was labor- and cost-intensive; and fourth, the throughput rate was low. Thus, the search for a more reliable and less expensive telecommunication system continued, and much work went into the design of better code systems to be used in optical telegraphy. The discovery of certain qualities of electricity, however, soon opened a new promising field of investigation.

The discovery of electromagnetism (generally attributed to the Danish physicist and chemist Hans Christian Ørsted in 1820 but probably already observed about twenty years earlier) provided a practicable way to determine whether an electric current was, at any given moment, applied to a conductor. If it was, a magnetic needle would be deflected by the electromagnetic field. Early systems of electric message transmission usually were not able to negotiate longer measures of wire (i.e., longer distances). A better understanding of electrical resistance was necessary to improve early telegraph designs and make them practicable for long-distance transmissions. Technical breakthroughs were achieved almost simultaneously in Britain and the United States. In Britain, the Cooke-Wheatstone needle telegraph (designed by William Fothergill Cooke and Professor Charles Wheatstone) was first successfully installed between the London and Birmingham Railway stations at Euston and Camden Town in 1837. Although the telegraph worked satisfactorily, adoption of the scheme was rejected by the railway company and the machinery dismantled. Two years later, however, the Cooke-Wheatstone telegraph was permanently employed along the Great Western Railway tracks between the Paddington and West Drayton stations. In the United States, Samuel Morse also had demonstrated the potential of his electric telegraph in 1837. In 1843, Congress commissioned the construction of an experimental line between Washington, DC, and Baltimore, Maryland. Running along the tracks of the Ohio and Baltimore Railroad, the line went into operation in 1844.

Electric Telegraphy: Overland and Underwater

Although error-prone at first, electromagnetic telegraphy soon proved to be superior to its optical counterpart. Constant improvements in wire insulation, encoding-decoding, and throughput rates made electric telegraphy more reliable, faster, and—last, but not least—available at more favorable prices. Both in the United States and Britain, a telegraph network soon emerged and expanded mostly along the railway lines or, at times, along roads and canals. The expansion of the telegraph network rested on private enterprise in both countries and gained initial momentum from early competition and commercial demand. Cooperation with the railway companies was of mutual benefit, as the telegraph depended on the railways' right-of-way and the railroads, in turn, needed a fast means of communication to coordinate their trains and schedules. Per-mile expansion of the electric telegraph was quickest in the vast territories of the United States. By 1852, only six years after Morse's pioneer line had gone into operation, more than 23,000 miles of telegraph wire had been strung. The more compact Britain was traversed by 8,800 miles of telegraph lines in 1855, and London soon emerged as the communication center of the country. The pace of telegraph expansion was much slower, however, in Continental Europe. The first French telegraph line was inaugurated in 1845 but opened to public use only in 1850. In Prussia and in Austria, the first experimental lines were constructed in 1846, but neither government granted public access to their telegraph lines until 1849.

After problems with insulation and resistibility had been solved, a submarine telegraph cable was laid across the English Channel and successfully connected Britain and France in 1851. Two years later, another submarine cable connected Dover with Ostend, and Portpatrick (Scotland) with Donaghadee (Ireland). By 1858, the British telegraph network was directly connected to the telegraph systems of France, Holland, Germany, Austria, and Russia. In the same year, a second attempt to lay a transatlantic cable succeeded, and a direct connection between Ireland and Newfoundland was established. The cable failed after three weeks, however, and the first reliable transatlantic connection was not made until 1866. By that time, cables also connected Sweden and Denmark; Italy, Corsica, Sardinia, and Algeria; Malta and Egypt; and India and Ceylon. After a failed attempt to directly connect Britain and India in 1859 via the so-called Red Sea cable, the construction of the Persian Gulf cable in 1864 linked the Ottoman, Persian, and Indian landline networks. A direct connection between Bombay and Suez (via Aden) was finished in 1870. Both the landline and submarine telegraph networks expanded at a fast pace during the remainder of the nineteenth century. In 1893, 445,082 miles of telegraph lines had been constructed in Europe, 341,282 in the United States, and 79,883 in Asia. Additionally, 160,933 miles of submarine telegraph cable had been laid.

Until 1901–1902, all submarine cables had been constructed by private enterprise. The laying of the transpacific cable between British Columbia, Australia, and New Zealand in these years marked the first government involvement. The governments of the United States, Canada, Australia, New Zealand, and Britain cooperated to close the last remaining gap in the telegraph network that now truly spanned the globe. Landline telegraphy, however, had been nationalized in Britain in 1870 and had come under the sole authority of the General Post Office.

The Telephone: Voice over Wire

Telephone communication is based on the transformation of sound into electric impulses. In 1861, the German autodidact inventor Philip Reis presented a crude version of a device that did exactly that; however, he failed to attract any public attention. Several years later, his *telephon* was brought to the notice of Alexander Graham **Bell**, a scientist experimenting with telegraphy in his workshop in Boston, Massachusetts. Bell improved the apparatus and applied for a patent in 1876. The first permanent telephone line was constructed a year later. Initially, telephony suffered from several technical weaknesses and extraordinarily high maintenance costs and was not believed to be capable of replacing telegraphy. Thus, after losing a patent suit, the undisputed U.S. market leader in telegraphy, Western Union, withdrew completely from the provision of telephone services in 1879 and left the field to the patent-owning Bell Telephone Company. Then, thanks to technological improvements and the initiative of this quasi-monopolist company, the telephone network expanded at a steady pace in the United States. In 1880, there were 47,900 telephones in operation in the entire country; by 1900, the number had increased to 1,355,000. After further technological improvements and the expiration of the Bell patent in 1896, the expansion of telephone services gained real momentum in the first decade of the twentieth century. By 1910, the number of telephones in the United States had risen to 7.6 million.

The development of the telephone network in Europe gathered speed at that time as well, and in 1910 there were almost 3 million telephones on the entire continent. Initially, however, the new technology had been received with reservations and skepticism, although Bell had personally promoted his invention in Britain and France. In both these countries, telephone services were declared to fall under the state monopoly of telegraphy in 1889, a decision that greatly slowed the expansion of the new technology. Expansion was quickest in Germany, where Bell had failed to register his patent, and where Ernst Werner von **Siemens** became the main producer of telephones. The German state also enjoyed a monopoly in the provision of telephone services but did much to establish a tight network open to public access. In 1880, there were only 1,900 telephones in all of Europe. The number had increased to about 800,000 10 years later. In 1910, however, Germany alone had more than 1 million telephones, and Great Britain came second with 649,000 connections.

Wireless: Riding the Waves

The electric telegraph and the telephone were major improvements over optical telegraph technology and rendered dematerialized telecommunications independent from line-of-sight connections. Wires had to be laid and maintained, however, and only such regions or installations could be connected that were accessible by submarine cable or overland lines. Only the utilization of electromagnetic waves for wireless telegraph transmission in the 1890s finally brought an end to telegraphy's dependence on wire transmissions. Since the middle of the nineteenth century, many renowned scientists such as Heinrich **Hertz** or Nicola **Tesla** had experimented with electromagnetic waves and radio transmission. Some of them even managed to transmit signals but failed to publicly establish the new technology.

This honor fell to the Italian Guglielmo Marconi (1874–1937), who not only improved the hitherto known radio transmission techniques but also had sufficient financial backing to market his invention. Marconi entered into negotiations with the British General Post Office (GPO) but, after having declined the GPO's parsimonious offer, founded his own company. Marconi realized that the prime opportunity for wireless telegraphy lay in shipping: Obviously, ships could not be reached by wired telegraphy and still relied on flag signaling. The advent of heavy and fast ironclad steamships—which needed much more maneuvering room and, thus, kept great distances between each other when traveling in convoys—intensified the communications problem on the seas. Marconi took advantage of that and entered into an exclusive contract with Lloyd's of London in 1901, which stated that every ship insured by Lloyd's had to be equipped with Marconi radio material. Furthermore, Marconi's strictly enforced policy of nonintercommunication denied wireless communication with any non-Marconi apparatus except in case of an emergency. Although Marconi's monopoly ended in the wake of the second international radiotelegraphy conference in Berlin in 1906, the company had secured a considerable head start in seaborne wireless telegraphy, mainly against its German competitors Slaby-Arco and Telefunken. Marconi also proposed the establishment of a co-called imperial chain of terrestrial radio stations in 1911 that would reach around the entire globe and would soften the cable companies' monopoly in intercontinental communication. The chain, however, was only realized when **World War I** impressively demonstrated the vulnerability of submarine cable communications and the necessity of an alternative means of communication in times of upheaval.

FURTHER READING: Headrick, Daniel R. *The Invisible Weapon: Telecommunications and International Politics, 1851–1945.* Oxford: Oxford University Press, 1991; Headrick, Daniel R. *When Information Came of Age: Technologies of Knowledge in the Age of Reason and Revolution, 1700–1850.* Oxford: Oxford University Press, 2000; Hills, Jill. *The Struggle for Control of Global Communication: The Formative Century.* Urbana: University of Illinois Press, 2002; Hugill, Peter J. *Global Communications since 1844: Geopolitics and Technology.* Baltimore: Johns Hopkins University Press, 1999; Huurdeman, Anton A. *The Worldwide History of Telecommunications.* Hoboken, NJ: Wiley, 2003; Kieve, Jeffrey. *The Electric Telegraph: A Social and Economic History.* Newton Abbot, U.K.: David & Charles, 1973; Standage, Tom. *The Victorian Internet: The Remarkable Story of the Telegraph and the Nineteenth Century's On-line Pioneers.* New York: Berkley Books, 1999; Winston, Brian. *Media Technology and Society: A History: From the Telegraph to the Internet.* London: Routledge, 1998.

ROLAND WENZLHUEMER

Telegraphy

The word *telegraph* comes from the French *télégraphe,* meaning "far writer," a term coined by Claude Chappe (1763–1805) for the invention of a system to transmit messages or information to a distant locale. French Emperor Napoleon I was a believer in the technology that allowed him to monitor his expanding empire.

European Telegraphy

Chappe invented and popularized the optical telegraph in France. He dabbled with the notion of an electrical telegraph, but the lack of a reliable power source steered his decision for developing a rapid communication system to the mechanical semaphore. This technology solution required operators to manipulate boards fastened to an outside pole that could be seen miles away. Wooden arm movements and the opening and closing of shutters transmitted message content. Each unique position corresponded to a different letter, word, or phrase. Chappe's optical telegraph gained greater acceptance after his death. It spread across Europe with about 1,000 telegraph towers operating in the early nineteenth century. This early mechanical Internet of sorts presaged the imminent electrical Internet of Morse fame and the computer Internet of the twentieth century. The very success of Chappe's system assured its ultimate demise as new technology and better designs with greater speed and reliability would surpass its capability.

Partners and combatants William F. Cooke (1806–1879) and Sir Charles Wheatstone (1802–1875), a Michael **Faraday** protégé, patented an electric telegraph system in 1837. Their initial design featured six needles used to point at letters on a message board. In their most advanced telegraph, only two needles were needed to move and select letters on a diagonal grid as technology and coding improvements were made.

Concurrent with the work of Cooke and Wheatstone in England, Ernst Werner von **Siemens** (1816–1892) of Prussia contributed to the field of communications with a telegraph featuring a needle that pointed to the correct letter as a result of transmitted electrical impulses. Siemens's design solved the problem of transmitting messages reliably over great distances, with the first European electric telegraph link extending 500 miles from Berlin to Frankfurt am Main. His scheme was competitive to contemporary optical telegraphs then in widespread use in Europe and an alternative to the eventual domination of electrically produced dots and dashes of Morse code.

U.S. Telegraphy

Samuel Finley Breese Morse (1791–1872), the painter-become-inventor, was a master of assembly. He envisioned both a simple telegraph design coupled with a binary coding system of dots and dashes; these Morse code designs became worldwide standards. Morse listened, learned, and then proceeded to sort out and simplify telegraphy for almost any operator. He overcame the complexity of Wheatstone's message board and the isolation of Siemens's needle system in the German states and dominated the marketplace. Morse built on Joseph Henry's electromagnets, Wheatstone's telegraph pole and relay, Carl Steinheil's earth return implementation, William Grove's sealed and improved wet-cell battery, and the talents of two colleagues: Alfred Vail, who built the telegraph key and sounder, and Professor Leonard Gale, who provided scientific knowledge.

Morse advanced the telegraph's system of encoding and decoding messages over long distances in the 1830s, building on the use of electrical impulses sent over iron wires to transmit messages. In 1842, Morse demonstrated the telegraph between two committee rooms in the U.S. Capitol. With intensive lobbying, Congress passed a $30,000 appropriations bill in 1843 to build the first telegraph line from Baltimore, Maryland, to Washington, DC, a distance of 37 miles. Morse was named superintendent of telegraphs and was responsible for overseeing its construction, which was completed in 1844; Morse invited prominent people to the May 24 formal opening. The first message sent was the biblical quotation "What hath God wrought!" After this, acceptance was rapid as thousands of miles of telegraph cable were strung along railway lines all across North America. The word *telegram* entered the lexicon in 1852, and more than 200 million telegraph messages were sent annually at the height of its popularity.

Telegraph lines were placed along planned railway rights-of-way, even as the new tracks were being laid. This urgency was heightened by the value of dispatching trains using the telegraph. Efficient, instantaneous communications enabled by telegraphic dispatching easily quadrupled the traffic-carrying capacity of the single-

TABLE 1 Extent of Telegraph Infrastructure, 1852

Country	Miles of telegraph wire	Comment
United States	23,000	20 telegraph companies in operation
United Kingdom	>2,200	Predominantly Cooke-Wheatstone
Prussia	>1,400	Use of Siemens's needle system
Austria	>1,000	Use of Siemens's needle system
Canada	>900	Morse system deployed
France	>700	Optical telegraphs still in use
Australia	0	First line installed in 1854

Source: Various.

track railroad. Trains could be sent on their way by telegram, even before others arrived. Businesses recognized the productivity gains telegrams afforded in sending money orders, contracts for review, and newspaper stories filed by field reporters, to name a few.

From the ideas of the 1830s to wide-scale global deployment in the 1850s, the growth of electric telegraphy was explosive. By 1852, the amount of telegraph wire exceeded 1,000 miles in many countries, as shown in Table 1.

The next two decades saw the global mileage of telegraph wire swell to 650,000 miles. The innovation of using gutta-percha (a rubberlike gum produced from the latex of various Southeast Asian trees) to prevent water damage to telegraph wires, first used by the Siemens and Halske Company, saw the proliferation of underwater cables, with 30,000 miles of telegraph wire put in place. The first submarine cable linked Dover, England, and Calais, France, in 1850, laid by Siemens's company. The telegraph began humanity's quest for global connectedness, at least on the physical level, through the medium of wire and moving electrons. The 1870s found 20,000 towns and villages around the world able to send and receive telegrams. By 1856, 35,000 miles of telegraph line in the United States delivered more than 17 million messages, generating $7 million in revenue for U.S. telegraph companies.

Christopher Sholes (1819–1890) was spurred to develop a typewriter in 1867 for use by telegraph operators. **Typewriters** increased the speed and accuracy of message reproduction. Productivity gains achieved by the typewriter led operators to use a common set of abbreviations. Using this Phillips Code, top-notch operators dealt with 20,000 words per shift. Electronic shorthand, such as *Scotus* for "Supreme Court of the United States," developed in the 1870s is reminiscent of today's Internet shorthand used in instant messaging, such as *LOL* for "laughing out loud," which started in the 1990s. The need for secrecy for many transmitted messages demanded both the senders and receivers adopt codes. For example, classified material sent between the various atomic bomb development sites working on the Manhattan Project in the early 1940s employed code words and phrases. The technical term *isotope of uranium* became *igloo of urchin* when used in a message sent across the telegraph network.

Wherever telegraph offices were established along U.S. railway lines, tremendous social and economic benefits emerged. Telegraph technology was instrumental in standardizing time zones across the breadth of North America, critical for revolutionizing how trains were dispatched and for enabling instant transmission of news and stock market activity. The telegram found people at home, at work, and aboard railway trains. Its ability to speed communications drove people's actions; this in itself was revolutionary. Just like the revolution of the printing press, which delivered books for the reflection of ideas and subsequent implementation, telegraphy used the speed of light to send telegrams for instant absorption and immediate action. Telegraphy became big business and invaded all walks of life. It reigned for more than 150 years, but eventually all good things must come to an end. The last telegram was sent by Western Union on January 27, 2006, its technology replaced by fax machines using telephone lines, e-mail over the computer-driven Internet, and text messaging leveraging new wireless networks.

Telegraphy and the Industrial Revolution

Prior to the advent of electricity and the emergence of the electrical telegraph, the steam-powered Industrial Revolution made people more productive using machine power in ways that everyone understood. The harnessing of electric power to provide for instantaneous communication using the telegraph was revolutionary. In a world accustomed to the pace of a walking messenger or a galloping horse of Pony Express fame or a sailing ship delivering mail, the new ability for anyone to immediately reach someone else anywhere in the world was almost beyond human comprehension. The rise of telegraphy at the dawn of electric communication and the rapidly evolving science of electricity triggered what many call the Second Industrial Revolution. During this period, from 1870 to 1930, the electric telegraph played a defining role. In fact, Morse's telegraph system transformed journalism, transportation, industry, government and military operations, and the very pace of daily life. The telegraph system was the defining step in ushering in the communications explosion of the twentieth century.

FURTHER READING: Davis, L. J. *Fleet Fire: Thomas Edison and the Pioneers of the Electric Revolution.* New York: Arcade, 2003; Koslowsky, Robert. *A World Perspective through 21st Century Eyes.* Victoria, BC: Trafford Publishing, 2004; Oslin, George P. *The Story of Telecommunications.* Macon, GA: Mercer University Press, 1992 (the author is the creator of the singing telegram); Silverman, Kenneth. *Lightning Man: The Accursed Life of Samuel F. B. Morse.* New York: Alfred A. Knopf, 2003.

ROBERT KARL KOSLOWSKY

Temperance Movement

Throughout the nineteenth century, a movement developed among those who sought to eradicate the negative effects of alcoholic beverages on individuals and society. It was known as the temperance movement, and a belief in the destructiveness of alcohol found outlet in a loose association of organizations beginning in the 1820s and culminating in the United States in 1919 with the ratification of the Eighteenth Amendment to the Constitution (Prohibition).

Temperance organizations in the United States began just after the turn of the century, in Saratoga, New York, in 1808, and then spread through New England. By the 1830s, local chapters of temperance organizations numbered in the thousands. In Ireland in 1829, the Ulster Temperance Society commenced, forming the first significant European organization in opposition to alcohol. The movement spread from Ireland to the rest of Britain, then across the English Channel. In 1832, seven English workers signed a pact against the use of liquor. Their influence spread, and three years later the British Association for the Promotion of Temperance began. On the Continent, temperance organizations gained influence in the Scandinavian countries by the late 1830s.

The scope of temperance organizations evolved as time went on. At first, the focus was far more personal, with members of different groups pledging not to drink alcohol. As the 1830s became the 1840s, however, groups began refusing alcohol to others. Finally, advocacy of an alcohol-free society and laws to make that society possible became the temperance goal. Advocates wanted social reform, as did many others in the new industrial society. Activists from all sides of the political spectrum took up causes from temperance to slavery to the dispossessed as apprehension at the rapid rate of industrial progress led to a perception that laws for social control could thwart potential problems. One of the most common early tactics, however, was the temperance pledge. Local and national organizations in the United States and Britain encouraged citizens to sign prefabricated pledges promising to abstain from alcohol. Signing was far easier than abstaining, however, and the pledges were often used as publicity tools for politicians or protective fronts for drinkers.

The temperance movement gained momentum as the Industrial Revolution gained momentum. The world was shrinking. The 1830s and 1840s witnessed the massive growth of the railroad industry. Later in the century, the internal combustion engine and the automobile further speeded travel. Organized postal service led to decreased prices, and in the 1870s, Alexander Graham **Bell** invented what would become the telephone. As communication between areas became swifter, those areas also became far more centralized. **Urbanization** and industrialization brought people together but paradoxically divided them into different classes. As the exponential growth of cities led to a vast increase in slums and tenements for growing numbers of blue-collar workers, the rich got richer, and the poor got poorer. Long hours, low wages, and poor (often dangerous) working conditions led to higher crime rates and a growing problem among the lower classes with alcohol abuse.

As the crusade for abstinence from alcohol picked up steam, many different groups and individuals took part, some affiliated with organized temperance societies and others on an individual basis. In Britain, artist George Cruikshank authored a series of books on the dangers of alcohol, including *The Bottle* in 1847 and *The Drunkard's Children* in 1848. His illustrations, along with those of William Hogarth, depicted the bleak life available to those who imbibed. Theobald Matthew, a Catholic priest, led thousands in Ireland to the temperance cause. In the United States, the crusading Carrie Nation often took violent measures in saloons across the country in an effort to persuade Americans of the dangers of liquor. Various religious groups became involved as well. In Britain, Quakers, Baptists, and Congregationalists actively advocated temperance. They were not the only ones, however. In Europe and the United States, abstinence from alcohol often was portrayed as a measure of Protestant decency, a counter to the Catholic vulgarity of drink. Catholics, however, also were ardent temperance advocates in many parts of Britain and the United

States; groups such as the Pennsylvania Catholic Total Abstinence Society preached temperance as a religious duty.

Probably the most notable group of temperance advocates, however, were women—particularly U.S. women. In addition to Nation, Susan B. Anthony and Frances Willard also took stands against alcohol. Though originally a male-dominated endeavor, temperance slowly came under the purview of women as the nineteenth century progressed. In the United States, women first entered the public sphere in significant numbers when they were employed in the Sanitary Commission during the **Civil War**. The leadership lessons learned would serve them well in later attempts to eradicate alcohol. In 1874 in Cleveland, Ohio, the Woman's Christian Temperance Union (WCTU) was founded, followed in 1895 by the Anti-Saloon League. Male drunkenness, which produced the bulk of temperance grievances, was considered a particular problem for their female counterparts due to the social system in place. Men were perceived as the breadwinners—an age-old custom only reinforced by the Industrial Revolution—and in a system in which women were financially dependent on men, they took a special interest in the problem. Additionally, in an age in which women were lauded as paragons of domesticity, temperance offered many a route to the public sphere that otherwise may have been withheld from them.

Perhaps the most significant mass movement of temperance advocacy (other than established organizations such as the WCTU) was the Woman's Crusade. Throughout 1873 and 1874, U.S. women engaged in nonviolent direct action against liquor distillers, transporters, and retailers through petitions, demonstrations, and prayer vigils. The organizational success of these women led to state and local legislation as the groups sought aid from the religious community. Many women (and, for that matter, men) used the temperance movement as a springboard into the suffrage movement. Many temperance advocates also were abolitionists, and the various reform movements often were cast in similar lights. Though freedom from slavery and the right to vote seem like measures of social freedom, and the restriction of liquor traffic seems like a measure of social control, reformers of the era of the Industrial Revolution thought very differently. Demon rum constituted its own form of slavery, and devils and hellish landscapes often were incorporated into illustrations and literature about the problems with alcohol abuse. Abstinence, in this view, was another form of freedom: freedom to succeed in the new industrial age.

Industrialists of the day understandably sought to convince their employees of that freedom to succeed. Their motives, however, were different. As the divide between rich and poor grew, employers sought to control their employees through tactics such as liquor laws. A safe workforce was in their best interest, and sober employees were far more productive than drunken ones. Healthy employees also were more productive than those who were sick, and the potential damage of alcohol on the physical body was emphasized almost as often as its spiritual counterpart. Benjamin Rush, in 1784, became one of the first significant advocates of temperance in a newspaper editorial titled "An Inquiry into the Effects of Spirituous Liquors on the Human Body and the Mind." He later published the "Inquiry" in book form, eventually selling more than 170,000 copies. The body and spirit were not wholly disconnected, however, and Rush's "Inquiry" included a so-called moral thermometer that gauged the negative effect of spirits on every aspect of the drinker, no matter where in the world he did his drinking.

The WCTU gained an international membership in the early 1880s, leading to the formation of the World Woman's Christian Temperance Union in 1883. The ability of the WCTU to develop into a global entity was indicative of the time, reflecting the smaller world created by the better communications of the Industrial Revolution. The Order of the Good Templars, founded in New York in 1851, had an international membership. Later, in 1909, the International Prohibition Confederation began in London. Formed from an international conference on prohibition, the confederation's membership included representatives from Europe, the United States, Canada, Australia, India, and various nations in both Africa and South America. Eliza Daniel Stewart, a leader in the Woman's Crusade of the 1870s, used her success to publicize a speaking tour that took her across the United States and, in 1876, to Britain, where her enthusiasm led to the British Woman's Temperance Association.

The country of Stewart's birth had been actively engaged in the temperance debate for almost a hundred years at the time of her trip to Britain. The American Temperance Society had more than 1 million members before the Civil War. In 1851, Maine prohibited alcohol sales and consumption, making it the first dry state, and though the temperance movement ultimately abated, its legacy remained. As citizens in Europe and the United States adapted to the changing society, cultural apprehension somewhat dissipated, and U.S. prohibition officially was repealed by the Twenty-first Amendment in 1933. Individual counties across the United States, however, still retain the legacy of the temperance movement by banning the sale of alcohol, creating dry counties. Most of them are located in rural areas, as those in the country attempt to reclaim what those in the burgeoning cities of the Industrial Revolution never could.

FURTHER READING: Bordin, Ruth. *Frances Willard: A Biography.* Chapel Hill: University of North Carolina Press, 1986; Bordin, Ruth. *Women and Temperance: The Quest for Power and Liberty, 1873–1900.* Philadelphia: Temple University Press, 1981; Harvey, Bonnie Carman. *Carry A. Nation: Saloon Smasher and Prohibitionist.* Berkeley Heights, NJ: Enslow, 2002; Lambert, W. R. *Drink and Sobriety in Victorian Wales, 1820–1895.* Cardiff: University of Wales Press, 1983; Shiman, Lilian Lewis. *Crusade against Drink in Victorian England.* New York: St. Martin's Press, 1988; Tyrrell, Ian R. *Sobering Up: From Temperance to Prohibition in Antebellum America, 1800–1860.* Westport, CT: Greenwood Press, 1979. WEB SITE: http://www.wctu.org/ (Woman's Christian Temperance Union).

THOMAS AIELLO

Terminology and Language

The Industrial Revolution permeated written and spoken language at every level of society. New terms, coined to name and describe inventions, processes, institutions, and concepts, flooded the discourse of industrializing societies. Moreover, the increased mobility and literacy resulting from industrialization had subtle but profound effects on language.

Large-scale, mechanized industry demanded a new vocabulary to denote and describe its paraphernalia and conditions. Words that had been obscure, such as *factory* or *manufacture,* came into common use as the structures themselves became commonplace in the landscape. Some words already in use changed meaning to refer to new objects or processes. For example, *mill,* which originally denoted a device or structure for grinding grain into flour, came to refer to a large building housing machinery powered through a series of gears, whether for sawing wood or weaving textiles; *cable,* originally applied to a heavy rope, was adopted metaphorically to the wires that transmitted telegrams and eventually used for the messages, or cables. Scientific innovation demanded new terms, often adapting Greek or Latin roots, coining words such as *potassium* (1807), *protein* (1844), and *calorie* (1866). New devices, such as **railroads** (1773) and **steamships** (1819), were coined from English roots, and *gasometer* (1808), *photograph* (1839), and *telegram* (1867) invoked classical sources. Names of popular commercial products, such as *margarine* (1836), *gasoline* (1869), and *aspirin* (1899), rapidly entered the general lexicon with the help of colorful and ubiquitous advertising campaigns.

Physical mobility changed language through loanwords from languages all over the world, the fruit of exploration and colonialism. *Parka* (1780) entered English from Inuit languages, *chutney* (1813) and *pappadum* from Hindi. With the help of steamships and railroads, middle-class businessmen and their families were likelier to move between European and other non-English-speaking nations, adopting loan words like *menu* (1837) and *camisole* (1866) from French, *graffiti* (1851) from Italian, and *hamburger* (1889) from German. Business and recreational travel, whether international or regional, also had an impact on the way people conceived of their own language. Although it hardly diluted the wide range of regional variations in spoken language, exposure to new places or visitors to their own localities acquainted people with unfamiliar dialects or accents and created the realization that one's familiar speech patterns were particular rather than universal. Social mobility had its own impact on speech; aspirants had more opportunities to hear and imitate the dialects of wealthy and privileged classes. The desire to manifest refinement encouraged the emergence of euphemisms, such as *water-closet* (1842) or *commode* (1851) to allude politely to a container for body wastes.

Until the nineteenth century, most people had little or no acquaintance with written forms of their own language; even among the small portion of the population who could read, written media, including books, periodicals, and letters, were scarce and precious except for an elite few. Over the course of the century, however, rising literacy rates and much cheaper publications and postage rates extended printed matter into most people's lives. Familiarity not only with letters but also with so-called book language, received grammar and formal vocabulary, was evidence of aspirations to gentility, whereas literacy, and the information gained through written texts, proved a powerful tool for upward mobility.

FURTHER READING: Bailey, Richard W. *Nineteenth-Century English.* Ann Arbor: University of Michigan Press, 1996; Cmiel, Kenneth. *Democratic Eloquence: The Fight over Popular Speech in Nineteenth-Century America.* New York: Morrow, 1990.

JANE WEISS

Terms of Trade

Terms of trade refers to the relative prices of imports and exports and contributes to a measure of how much (or how little) a country gains from trade. It takes into account both the relative quantities of goods and services being traded as well as the exchange rate, the value of one country's currency unit expressed in terms of another's.

The first part of this statement refers to the *commodity terms of trade.* What this means is that if a given quantity of a country's exports can be exchanged for a larger quantity of what it imports, the commodity terms of trade are said to have moved in its favor. Put another way, this means that a given amount of effort to produce items for export can acquire a relatively larger bundle of items available for consumption, increasing the country's **standard of living**, other things being equal. Correspondingly, if a country's commodity terms of trade move against it, then a smaller quantity of imports can be obtained for that given amount of effort to produce items for export, and the standard of living falls.

With very few exceptions, countries do not directly swap their goods with each other. Importers must pay the foreign producers in their own currency, which means that the terms on which currency units can be exchanged, the exchange rate, also will influence the outcome. If, from one country's standpoint, its exchange rate falls (its currency value depreciates or loses value), this means that one of its currency units will exchange for fewer of its trading partners' currency units, which makes buying imported goods more expensive but makes its exports relatively cheaper to buyers in other parts of the world. Conversely, if a country's exchange rate has risen, its currency is now worth more when converted into another currency, so for a given monetary outlay, its importers can acquire a larger volume of foreign-made goods, but its exporters now find that their products are relatively more expensive to foreign buyers, so its sales fall, other things being equal. (Because these changes can affect a country's balance of trade, both the commodity terms of trade and the exchange rate can be influenced by direct policy measures.)

In the absence of policy, the commodity terms of trade are influenced by worldwide changes in supply-and-demand conditions. Improvements on the supply side, such as the adoption of new technologies and improved machinery, which lower costs of production, tend to reduce output prices, causing the terms of trade to move against the supplying country. Rising demands due to rising income levels tend to raise prices, causing an improvement. Whether a country's total trade position deteriorates or improves depends on offsetting changes, such as changes in the volume and composition of trade. In the nineteenth century, the expansion of industrial production and the increase in the numbers of industrializing countries tended to result in the terms of trade moving against them relative to the suppliers of agricultural goods and raw materials (which are called primary products because they have not yet been processed). Because it is relatively harder to increase the output of these goods than of manufactured goods (economists would say that their supply is relatively inelastic), the countries producing them gained, relatively speaking. As transportation costs fell later in the century, however, due to the impact of steam power, railroad building, and faster oceangoing steamships, the costs of transporting food and bulky commodities fell, reversing this trend. Also, increased investment in mines and commercial agriculture improved the production conditions of these items, further putting downward pressure on their prices. In addition, rising income levels and overall population growth increased the demand for manufactured items at a faster rate than for primary products, so the net result was that the terms of trade tended to move in favor of the industrial countries.

Throughout the nineteenth and twentieth centuries, however, the terms of trade for any individual country have varied as the underlying forces influencing them have varied. In addition, as previously noted, deliberate policy measures, trade treaties, and international agreements can influence trade patterns and flows.

FURTHER READING: Kreinin, Mordechai E. *International Economics: A Policy Approach.* Orlando, FL: Dryden Press, 1998.

CHRISTINE RIDER

Tesla, Nikola (1856–1943)

Nikola Tesla was a key contributor to the global spread of electricity, which enabled the Second Industrial Revolution and raised the quality of life for a great portion of humanity. His ability to visualize operational inventions and then subsequently implement them led to a synthesis of electrical theory with electrical engineering. Tesla's seminal invention, the alternating current (AC) motor that took advantage of rotating magnetic fields, was the foundation for an electrical system that would generate and distribute electrical power over great distances. Thomas **Edison**'s approach to electricity favored a direct current (DC) generation with distribution limited to about a mile from a noisy generating plant, and suitable only for lighting. Tesla understood the problems with Edison's approach and fought to introduce AC implementation so that electrical power could be transmitted over hundreds of miles. In addition to lighting, AC could be used for powering residential appliances and industrial machinery.

During his lifetime, Tesla viewed the delivery of AC to the world as his altruistic mission. He achieved this without the objective of amassing personal wealth. Tesla instinctively knew that a cost-effective AC motor would liberate most workers from the struggles of manual labor. He was proved right with the proliferation of household appliances and factory retrofits of **steam engines** and mechanical belts with electric motors.

In the early 1880s, electric lighting was an expensive novelty that few could afford. The rejection of Tesla's lighting proposal by the Zagreb, Croatia, city council in 1892 was one factor behind his immigration to the United States. (In 2006, the Croatian capital city's council recognized this past error and delivered a posthumous apology by unveiling a statue of Tesla to mark the 150th anniversary of the inventor's birth.) Tesla's development of AC in the United States proved to be the most cost-effective technology solution. Its reach not only embraced smaller cities and rural populations but also enabled the general population to enjoy the benefits of electric power. As President George W. Bush said in May 2006, "Nikola Tesla is a proof that real greatness surpasses national borders and differences" (Reply to Croatian President Stjepan Mesic's message to President Bush informing him of events marking Tesla's 150th anniversary).

Tesla leveraged AC technology to harness the water of Niagara Falls for the Niagara Mohawk Power Company in 1894. This installation set the foundation upon which all electrical power systems throughout the world are built. Tesla insisted on the use of 60 cycles per second AC to maximize operating efficiency—the system that is still in use today.

Electrification is considered the greatest achievement of the twentieth century, according to the National Academy of Engineering, and Tesla was a major contributor in making this happen. Tesla's many other contributions include wireless **telegraphy** (for which he had priority over Guglielmo Marconi), fluorescent and neon lighting, the fundamental development of robotics using remote radio control, radar basics, and the fluid diode (a pump without moving parts). Even though Tesla invented **radio** and is recognized as its patent holder, Marconi developed broadcast radio for commercial advantage. Tesla's most spectacular invention was the Tesla coil to produce high frequencies in his experiments. It led to the emergence of broadcasting antennae for point-to-multipoint communication and automobile ignition systems. Tesla made the cover of *Time* magazine on July 20, 1931, and he is one of two Americans to have an electrical unit named after him, the tesla, to quantify magnetic flux density.

FURTHER READING: Jonnes, Jill. *Empires of Light: Edison, Tesla, Westinghouse, and the Race to Electrify the World.* New York: Random House, 2003; Seifer, Marc. *Wizard: The Life and Times of Nikola Tesla—Biography of a Genius.* Secaucus, NJ: Birch Lane Press, 1996.

ROBERT KARL KOSLOWSKY

Transportation

See Ocean Transportation

Tristan, Flora (1803–1844)

Flora Tristan, a French writer, argued in 1843 in *The Workers' Union* for an international alliance of men and women workers, whether skilled or unskilled. Her work emerged from utopian socialist and feminist responses to the nineteenth-century dual revolutions: the French and Industrial Revolutions. Tristan joined those seeking to solve new problems of poverty and workers' alienation from economic, political, and social power in an age of democratic reforms.

She was born Flore Céleste Thérèse Henriette Tristan y Moscoso, the daughter of a Peruvian nobleman, Don Mariano Tristan y Moscoso and Anne-Pierre Laisnay, a French émigré during the French Revolution. The Napoleonic Civil Code required all marriages to be registered with civil authorities, but her parents, who had married in a religious ceremony in Bilbao, Spain, never legalized their union. Forced from their Parisian home after her father's death in 1807, neither mother nor daughter was recognized as legal heirs to the family property or income. Apprenticed at 15 to the engraver André Chazal, whom she married in 1821, Tristan became trapped in an abusive marriage. Unable to divorce, she separated from Chazal in 1828 and traveled to Peru. Although her Peruvian uncle, Pio Tristan, did not legitimate his brother's heir, he did give Tristan a living allowance.

The young writer entered the Parisian world of writers and social activists, meeting such utopian reformers as Charles **Fourier**, followers of Henri Saint-Simon, Charles Blanc, Victor Considérant, and, later, the English socialist, Robert **Owen**. Tristan encountered other women writers, such as Eugénie Niboyet, also influenced by the utopian socialists and their efforts to create utopian communities to counteract the economic and social ills of the Industrial Revolution. Additionally, both Saint-Simonians and Fourierists linked working-class emancipation to female emancipation.

Such connections influenced Tristan's socialist and feminist ideals. *Flora Tristan's London Journal* (1840) provided a social critique of the working and living conditions of the urban poor and working classes. She paid particular attention to women's conditions, critiquing legal and social institutions that denied them an adequate education, employment opportunities, and decent wages.

Tristan did not find a publisher for her most radical and influential work, *The Workers' Union*. She spent the last years of her life soliciting funds for its publication, giving speeches in France to the working classes. The workers of Lyon financed publication of the third edition. Although her ideas for universal unionization and the right to work were well received, she encountered resistance among working-class men and women for the equal inclusion and payment of women. *The Workers' Union* predated Karl **Marx** and Friedrich Engels's *Communist Manifesto* (1848), yet her work was largely forgotten after the 1848 revolutions. Workers in 1848 did commemorate Tristan with a monument in Bordeaux, the city where she died while working for the emancipation of all workers. *See also* Communism; France, Industrial Revolution in; Revolution of 1848; Socialism.

FURTHER READING: Beik, Doris, and Paul Beik, trans. and eds. *Flora Tristan: Utopian Feminist.* Bloomington: Indiana University Press, 1993; Rice-DeFosse, Mary. "Flora Tristan (1803–1844)." In *French Women Writers: A Bio-Bibliographical Source Book,* ed. Eva Martin Sartori and Dorothy Wynne Zimmerman. New York: Greenwood Press, 1991; Sivert, Eileen Boyd. "Flora Tristan: The Joining of Essay, Journal, Autobiography." In *The Politics of the Essay: Feminist Perspectives,* ed. Ruth-Ellen Boetcher Joeres and Elizabeth Mittman. Bloomington: Indiana University Press, 1993.

LAURA TALAMANTE

Trust-Busting

Trust-busting is the purposeful dissolving of corporate trusts set in place to stifle competitive forces in various industries for the financial gain of those organizing the trust. Trust-busting actions in the United States are taken principally by the federal government to ensure continued competition and innovation in industries threatened by monopoly.

Around 1877, the term *trust* began to be used to refer to an organization designed to reduce competition through various acts of dominance and mutual agreement, which were meant to lead to financial gains for the trust partners. At that time, the inherently territorial nature of **railroads** in particular lent plausibility to the design of new approaches to how markets could be protected from competitive pressures. These obvious territorial advantages underpinned early ideas of trust formation and were easily extended to sectors in which commodities were produced. Other exclusionary possibilities soon emerged.

The French mathematician Antoine Augustin Cournot (1801–1877) worked out the first rigorous economic theories of monopoly in 1838, but the frontier expansion of industrial firms, particularly railroads, soon developed its own practical approaches to how to squeeze out competitors and raise profits.

Wealth was concentrated in the hands of relatively few people in the late nineteenth century, with a peak at around 1900, when perhaps 45 percent of all wealth in the United States was held by the wealthiest 1 percent of the population. This concentration enabled relatively few participants to close off industries through manipulating the tools of power politics and mutual agreement. It also led to a positive feedback loop as the wealthy continued to close off prospects to outsiders by using the social connections of urban society to further consolidate their gains for relatively few participants. The resulting monopolies often were made up with many different corporate faces—remnants of the predecessor firms—but they were effectively subsumed under the governance of one trust arrangement, usually structured by commodity (agriculture and manufactured goods) or region (transportation; in particular, railroads).

Without competitive forces to fragment industries and encourage innovation, trusts threatened to create what amounted to an essentially feudal society, as indicated by the coining of the term *robber barons* for the leaders of these trusts. It fell to government to preserve market forces by engaging in trust-busting.

No single figure is more associated with trust-busting than President Theodore Roosevelt (1858–1919) the 26th president of the United States (1901–1909). Vice President Roosevelt succeeded President William McKinley, who had been assassinated by an anarchist in 1901. The social strife of labor versus capital thus had reached into the White House and reminded Roosevelt, a reflective writer and student of great leaders, that government would need to be the force to ensure balance in U.S. society. In many respects, Roosevelt's embracing of an active government set in force the height of the **Progressive Era**.

Although the Republican Party to which Roosevelt was then loyal was considered a probusiness party, Roosevelt had a history of progressive use of the administration and the courts to address social issues. An example of this activism was his championing of the formation of the Department of Commerce and Labor in 1903, which later would be split into two cabinet-level administrative departments of the U.S. government. At the same time, Roosevelt began to use the tools of the presidency to shatter trusts.

No single tool for trust-busting was more important than the Sherman Antitrust Act, which was first passed into law in 1890. The Sherman Antitrust Act was the first federal law to limit commercial combinations in restraint of trade. Notably, it also served as a vehicle for government antiunion efforts. The act was the basis for Roosevelt's executive prosecution of trusts that gave rise to the term *trust-busting*. Roosevelt himself rejected the term as inappropriate. His view was not one based on antibusiness sentiment, but he was rather committed to the notion that business needed regulation by the government to maintain appropriate balances in society.

The case of the Northern Securities Company, a trust of railroads centered in the northwestern United States formed in 1901, was perhaps the most notable application of the Sherman Antitrust Act by President Roosevelt's administration. That trust had been organized by John Pierpont **Morgan,** E. H. Harriman, and James J. Hill, among others, out of railroads stretching from Chicago to Seattle. The Supreme Court ruled in 1904 (by the narrow margin of 5–4) that the trust must be dissolved. It was a notable victory for President Roosevelt and encouraged continued trust-busting in other administrations such as William Howard Taft's actions against the Standard Oil Trust of John D. **Rockefeller**, who also was a principal in the Northern Securities Company. In general, trust-busting played out in the actions of federal government lawyers suing corporations. More than forty such actions were brought in the Roosevelt administration alone.

In several respects, the concept of trust-busting continues under various pieces of federal legislation and court actions related to fair trade. The dissolution of the Bell telephone companies (facing challenges from 1974 to 1981, with actual divestiture occurring in 1984) and antitrust litigation against Microsoft (started by the Federal Trade Commission in 1992, taken over by the Department of Justice in 1993, and divestiture ordered in 2000 but appealed by Microsoft) are but two high-profile examples of recent government action. Other examples of alleged trusts outside the reach of national regulation include the Organization of Petroleum Exporting Countries (OPEC).

FURTHER READING: Gellhorn, E., W. E. Kovacic, and S. Calkins. *Antitrust Law and Economics in a Nutshell.* 5th ed. Minneapolis, MN: West, 2004; Machlup, F. *The Political Economy of Monopoly: Business, Labor, and Government Policies.* Baltimore: Johns Hopkins University Press, 1952; Roosevelt, Theodore. *Theodore Roosevelt: An Autobiography.* New York: Scribner, 1913.

RYAN L. LANHAM

Tull, Jethro (1674–1741)

Born in Berkshire, England, in 1674, Jethro Tull was a pioneer in agricultural methods and technology that helped improve agricultural productivity as a prelude to the First Industrial Revolution. Despite a desire to study law and pursue a political career, poor health and financial problems caused him to reluctantly go into farming with his father. He became extremely dissatisfied with the low-productivity, hand methods used by farm labor of the time. This led him to investigate farming methods with the objective of developing machinery to replace the inefficient and inconsistent manual methods. He was determined to raise crop yields.

His major achievement was the invention of a mechanical seed drill in 1701. This machine facilitated the planting of seeds in uniform rows, replacing the traditional method of planting seeds by broadcasting them by hand, a practice that wasted a lot of seed. The seed drill also planted with sufficient spacing between rows, making it easier to control weeds. Weed control was crucial to keeping the grain seeds from being crowded out and starved of the necessary plant nutrients. He subsequently invented a horse-drawn hoe for the removal of the weeds.

Though Tull's seed drill was neither the first nor immediately successful, he perfected it based on observations he made in several years of European travels. His ideas on farming methods and machines were published in a 1731 volume entitled *The New Horse Hoeing Husbandry.* At the time, Tull's methods were quite controversial but were ultimately accepted and made a significant contribution to Britain's eighteenth-century agricultural revolution, which resulted in dramatic increases in labor productivity and in farm output. Tull died in Berkshire on February 21, 1741.

FURTHER READING: Overton, Mark. *Agricultural Revolution in England: The Transformation of the Agrarian Economy 1500–1850.* Cambridge: Cambridge University Press, 1996. WEB SITE: http://www.bbc.co.uk/history/historic_figures/tull_jethro.shtml; http://www.berkshirehistory.com/bios/jtull.html.

JOSEPH A. GIACALONE

Typewriters

The success of the typewriter in the late nineteenth century was the result of decades of inventive and technical efforts. Typewriters changed the commercial world by increasing the efficiency of business and introducing women into the office as trained typists.

The concept of a writing machine is found in an English patent assigned to Henry Mill in 1714, but the first typewriter known to have worked was constructed in 1808 by the Italian Pellegrino Turri. Later in the nineteenth century, writing machines were proposed by dozens of inventors in Europe and the United States. A few designs were manufactured in small numbers in the 1850s, and the precisely engineered Writing Ball was produced in 1870 by Pastor Malling Hansen of Denmark. Far more influential was the Sholes and Glidden Type Writer (1873), primarily invented by Christopher L. Sholes of Milwaukee, Wisconsin, and produced by the Remington Arms Company, which had made advances in metallurgy and manufacturing during the U.S. **Civil War**. The Sholes and Glidden introduced the term *typewriter* and the QWERTY keyboard, apparently designed to minimize the jamming of type bars at the printing point. Despite various more ergonomic schemes, QWERTY remains standard for most Western keyboards today.

Initially seen as an expensive curiosity, the typewriter gained acceptance in the 1880s as a tool of business and government, usually operated by a new class of clerical workers: women. The Remington (successor to the Sholes and Glidden) faced

Caligraph, 1880, the second typewriter on the American market. Richard Polt.

competition from makes such as Caligraph, Crandall, and Hammond. The Remington and Caligraph were understroke or so-called blind writers, requiring users to lift the carriage in order to see their work; the Crandall and Hammond provided relatively visible writing and offered interchangeable type elements in various styles.

Scores of companies entered the market in the 1890s, hoping to profit from the demand for typewriters while avoiding infringing on each other's patents. Designs ranged from $100 office machines to $1 index typewriters (the user must select a character on an index and then perform another action to print that character). Franz X. Wagner's visible Underwood (1895) eventually was imitated by most manufacturers. Although the U.S. typewriter industry led the way, manufacture also arose in Germany, England, and other European countries.

Typewriter production employed advanced technology and new materials. It was common for a keyboard typewriter to contain 2,000 precisely manufactured and adjusted parts. Aluminum was used to reduce weight; vulcanite (an early plastic made of hardened rubber) was used in type elements. The concept of an electric typewriter appeared in 1854, and a partially electrified version of Hansen's Writing Ball was produced. Various electric typewriters were marketed in the first half of the twentieth century, but they were not widely accepted until the 1950s.

FURTHER READING: Adler, Michael. *The Writing Machine: A History of the Typewriter.* London: George Allen & Unwin, 1973; Davies, Margery W. *Woman's Place Is at the Typewriter: Office Work and Office Workers 1870–1930.* Philadelphia: Temple University Press, 1982; Hoke, Donald. *Ingenious Yankees: The Rise of the American System of Manufactures in the Private Sector.* New York: Columbia University Press, 1990. WEB SITE: http://staff.xu.edu/~polt/typewriters/index.html.

RICHARD POLT

U

United Kingdom

See Britain, Industrial Revolution in

United States Civil War

See Civil War, American (1861–1865)

United States, Industrial Revolution in

The United States became the richest country in history in the late nineteenth century, and for a century and more it has remained so, in consequence of the Industrial Revolution. The advances in machine production, transportation, and communications at the center of that revolution, themselves a consequence of ongoing technological innovation, fueled not only a revolution in the market economy but also a complex, sometimes rapid-fire, series of social, cultural, and demographic changes that transformed the United States. The United States is a very different place today than it was in 1800, when the Industrial Revolution was just gaining a foothold. It was then a horse-and-buggy nation, in which, so the census of 1800 reported, more than 75 percent of men worked full-time in agriculture. By the early twenty-first century, however, less than 2 percent of the population work crop fields, and cars, jets, and rockets—along with instantaneous communication by telephone and computer—have replaced the horse and buggy in a broad-ranging (and increasingly globalizing) consumer culture.

Since the advent of the Industrial Revolution, the U.S. economy has, on average, grown about 1.7 percent per year. That seemingly small per annum growth rate can be deceiving, for, compounded over the course of two centuries, it has meant unheralded economic growth: a 25-fold increase in income, as economist Jeffery Sachs has observed, from around $1,200 per capita in 1820 to about $30,000 per person in 2004 (in 1990 dollars). By comparison, in the 800 years prior to the Industrial Revolution's beginnings in eighteenth-century Britain, real income in Western Europe may have tripled—whereas, in the 1,000 years from the first to the tenth centuries A.D., global living standards were essentially flat. In 1800, the United States was about four times richer than the poorest places on the planet; by 2000, it was more than twenty times richer, per capita, than the world's most impoverished regions.

Beginnings

Historians sometimes describe the Industrial Revolution as having occurred in successive waves: The first, beginning in mid-eighteenth-century Britain, was characterized by development of the **steam engine**, the coal industry, and large textile and iron manufacturers. A second wave, with a taking-off point following the U.S. **Civil War** (1861–1865) and continuing into the early twentieth century, was characterized by extensive industrialization, rapid **urbanization**, and mass immigration. A third wave was characterized by technological advances in the internal combustion engine, electricity (and the appliances it makes possible), and the chemical industry. These advances included the introduction of aspirin, early plastics, and a process for fixing nitrogen, developed in the 1910s by two German scientists, that, when used as a fertilizer, greatly increased agricultural yields and helped feed much of the planet. This third wave saw a globalizing economy dominated by Europe and, as the twentieth century progressed, increasingly by the United States. A fourth wave of the Industrial Revolution, characterized by atomic power, jet propulsion, computers, the worldwide Web, the rise of service industries, and ever-increasing globalization, is, some argue, the latest wave.

The Industrial Revolution transformed the United States, but it began in eighteenth-century Britain with technological advances—particularly with James **Watt**'s improved steam engine design (Watt's 1769 patent built on earlier, less efficient, models developed by Thomas Savery and Thomas Newcomen)—the increased use of fossil-fuels, and the birth of the modern industrial factory system in Richard Arkwright's **cotton** textile mills of the 1770s and 1780s. Arkwright's entrepreneurial genius combined his own 1769 invention of the water frame with other eighteenth-century advances in textile production, including John Kay's 1733 patent of the flying shuttle, James Hargreaves's 1764 spinning jenny, and other mechanical cloth-making improvements in his English mills. Although these and other ingenious inventions lay at the technological heart of the Industrial Revolution, that revolution was also a consequence of the legal and cultural framework in which it arose. By the mid-1700s, the medieval system of feudal vassalage had given way to the rights of the freeborn Englishman, including, increasingly, the legal right to hold and exchange property privately, on a contractual basis. The legal right to private property, together with the Puritan ethic with its "insistence on the value of time, the condemnation and abhorrence of pleasure and diversion ... [that] constituted in effect an imposition of the criterion of efficiency on every activity," as historian David Landes has written, were important. These factors combined with an Enlightenment culture increasingly enamored of science and its application and a banking and commercial system accommodating the entrepreneurial spirit were essential parts of the web of society and culture that nurtured the Industrial Revolution in Britain.

The United States began as a British colonial outpost, its British settlers sharing the heritage of comparative liberties, private property rights, Protestant work ethic, the rule of law, and an appreciation of science and entrepreneurship (even as they and their fellow non-British settlers adapted these inheritances uniquely in each of the 13 colonies' disparate climates, terrains, polities, and economies). After independence, and the subsequent ratification of the U.S. Constitution in 1788, the United States remained closely tied by trade, language, and cultural tradition to the British, and it was through these links and through technology transfer—including industrial espionage—that the Industrial Revolution found its starting point in the United States. It is important to note, too, that for all of the remarkable changes the United States underwent (and continues to undergo) in consequence of the Industrial Revolution, that the core element of its government, the U.S. Constitution, has not been fundamentally changed. Though amended to end slavery and to expand suffrage to include, first, African American men with ratification of the Fifteenth Amendment in 1870 and then votes for women with the Nineteenth Amendment in 1920, the federal system of governance in the United States, including its balance between states' rights and federal powers and its mixed polity of executive, legislative, and judiciary branches, checks and balances, and its guarantee of minority rights, has not been changed by the Industrial Revolution. In fact, the freedoms that this system has afforded have contributed importantly to shaping the Industrial Revolution in the United States.

Alexander Hamilton, the nation's first secretary of the treasury, set out, as historian Darren Staloff has noted, a "blueprint for a national policy of rapid industrialization" in his 1791 *Report on Manufactures*. Against those like Thomas Jefferson who saw the future of the United States in farming, Hamilton was obdurate. Manufactures—industry and commerce—not agriculture alone, was the future. And Watt's steam engine, as Hamilton wrote in the *Report*, had a central role in newly emergent industry, for, by "substituting the Agency of fire and water," it had "prodigiously lessened the necessity for manual labor." Though Hamilton's program of federal subsidies to aid industry and commerce as outlined in the 1791 *Report* was not adopted, his vision that the future of the United States lay in commerce and industry proved prescient. As Staloff sums it, "Hamilton's vision was simply too bold and aggressive for the rural nation. Early U.S. industrial development would occur at a more leisurely pace, one prompted by the growth of domestic demand rather than federal policy."

Manufactures

Industrialization in the United States began, in part, by importing British and European technology. Many of the Industrial Revolution's early technological advances and business methods were brought to the United States by immigrants practiced in their use. The best known of these immigrants was Samuel Slater, who, after years of experience working his way from apprentice to supervisor in Richard Arkwright's cotton mills in Britain, was able to replicate the machinery and production processes of those mills, following his arrival in the United States in 1789. In 1793, he established the first successful cotton-spinning mill in the United States at Pawtucket, Rhode Island (under the auspices of the firm of Almy and Brown). Slater had left Britain disguised as an agricultural worker because the emigration of cotton-mill workers was illegal, precisely because they might take with them the much-valued knowledge of the industry that was rapidly making Britain the workshop of the world.

In 1798, Slater formed Samuel Slater and Company and built a number of mills in New England that made him rich. Alexander Hamilton, in his 1791 *Report on Manufactures*, had noted the importance of women and children as potential factory laborers: "It is worthy of particular remark, that, in general, women and Children are rendered more useful and the latter more early useful by manufacturing establishments, than they would otherwise be." And it was to children, women, and then entire families that Slater turned. Employing children from orphanages and others who were wards of their communities, and subsequently contracting with men for their wives' and their children's labor, Slater offered comparatively decent wages and the opportunity for schooling within the context of a strict, patriarchal system of management.

Following Slater's success, the Harvard College graduate and Boston merchant Francis Cabot Lowell visited several textile mills on a trip to Britain in the early 1810s and, upon his return, founded, together with Nathan Appleton, the Boston Manufacturing Company, establishing in 1814 a large cotton mill at Waltham, Massachusetts. The firm employed young women from farming families and offered them an opportunity, in their hours outside work in the mill, to attend lectures, join clubs, and socialize. Integrating the spinning and weaving processes in the Waltham facilities proved an economic success partly because the Jeffersonian embargo and the subsequent War of 1812 cut economic ties with Britain: No longer able to acquire British goods, consumers turned to U.S.-made products.

Beginning in the early1820s, the Boston Manufacturing Company constructed a massive textile factory complex on the banks of the Merrimack River, at Lowell, Massachusetts, employing hundreds of girls and young women from rural New England who lived in company-supplied dorms and stayed, on average, in Lowell's employ for about three years. The profitability of the textile mills drew competitors, and with increased competition came a scenario often to be repeated in other competitive nineteenth- and twentieth-century industries: To remain profitable, owners sped up work, extended hours, and cut wages. By the mid-1830s the so-called Lowell girls were protesting the speedups and cuts with meetings, processions, and strikes; in 1844, a group of women formed the Lowell Female Labor Reform Association, the first organization of women workers in the United States. By the late 1840s, however, Irish immigrants, escaping the Irish potato famine, along with Canadian and other immigrants, flooded into the Massachusetts mills.

Free and Slave Labor

The early Industrial Revolution in the United States was rooted not only in the entrepreneurial and inventive spirit of northern capitalists and inventors' new technologies but also in the labor of women, children, and men in northern factories and by the labor of those Americans held in the brutal bondage of southern **slavery**. Slave labor supplied the cotton mills with the raw cotton. In 1793, the same year that Slater opened his mill at Pawtucket, an enterprising young Massachusetts-born Yale graduate, Eli Whitney, having traveled to Georgia to work as a tutor, invented the cotton gin to separate the sticky seeds of the short-staple cotton plant from the surrounding cotton fiber. Not only did this make many white plantation owners rich, it also contributed, as historian Steven Deyle has observed, to the proliferation of the domestic slave trade and the continuation of slavery for another seven decades as cotton production grew from less than 1,000 tons in 1790 to more than 1.2 million tons in 1860, and the slave population increased from 700,000 to more than 4 million. By 1860, the value of slaves in the five cotton states of South Carolina, Georgia, Alabama, Louisiana, and Mississippi totaled more than $1.5 billion and constituted 45.8 percent of those states' wealth. The value of all slaves, around $3 billion in 1860, was, as Deyle notes, second only to land as the nation's most valuable investment. Indeed, the profits generated by the labor of enslaved African Americans in the first half of the nineteenth century—principally by way of cotton sold to British and northern textile mills—fueled the growth of the nation's market economy as slave masters poured their profits into purchases of northern-made factory goods.

Five years after his invention of the cotton gin, Eli Whitney opened a gun-making factory outside New Haven, Connecticut, pioneering coordinate-assembly production of standardized, interchangeable parts in a process that would come to be called the *American system,* a system subsequently developed by Samuel Colt in gun making, Cyrus McCormick in building reapers, and Isaac Singer in making sewing machines.

Interrelated Advances

The Industrial Revolution was fueled by a cascade of interrelated advances: The steam engine created a demand for more coal, iron, and better metalworking. The use of steam engines as water pumps meant that flooded mines could run deeper. In turn, more coal and iron, the most important fuel and metal of the early Industrial Revolution, was available for use in steam engines. The U.S. inventor Robert Fulton used steam power in his development of the first economically practical steamboat, the *Clermont,* on the Hudson River in 1807. Three years earlier, in Britain, Richard Trevithick had contrived to use iron, coal, and steam to build the first practical railroad locomotive, soon adapted and improved in the United States. A canal craze followed. The **Erie Canal** opened in 1825, and with local, state, and federal subsidies, others soon followed, continuing into the 1840s. Next came a **railroad** boom. By 1828, the first commercial railroad in the United States, the Baltimore and Ohio, was in operation; by 1840, there were 9,021 miles of track in the United States; in 1869, the transcontinental railroad was completed; by 1910, a quarter-million miles of track crisscrossed the country, subsidized by state and federal land grants. The transportation revolution of steamboats and locomotives enhanced the fluidity of nineteenth-century trade, as cars and trucks would do in the twentieth century: More goods, from more distant markets, could be transported more quickly than previously imaginable. In 1830, it took three weeks to travel from Chicago to Manhattan; by 1857, the same trip, now possible by rail, took two days. Farmers from the Midwest could ship their crops to the nation's growing urban-industrial centers with ease. Livestock slaughtered in Chicago was sold in East Coast markets. Goods from northeastern factories were shipped across the country. Growing markets meant growing demand and the birth of the modern consumer culture. Demand in turn fueled the building of more factories, spurred invention, and boosted industrial employment, all of which furthered demand. Almost 11 million Americans fled the countryside to move into cities between 1870 and 1920. To accommodate this growing population of urban workers, some cities rose vertically, a growth made possible by the iron (and later steel) that framed **sky-scrapers** and by the U.S. inventor Elisha Otis's 1857 elevator. By 1902, the 22-story Flatiron Building had been completed in Manhattan, a decade later it was eclipsed by the 59 story Woolworth Building.

In 1844, combining many earlier inventions in the field, Samuel F. B. Morse demonstrated the power of **telegraphy** by sending a message, "What hath God wrought," over telegraph lines from Washington, DC, to Baltimore, Maryland; 22 years later, in 1866, completion of a transatlantic cable enabled telegraphic communication between the United States and Europe.

Urban Industrial Centers, Large and Small

The second wave of the Industrial Revolution, beginning at the Civil War's end and carrying on into the early twentieth century, was a time of dynamic and expansive economic growth. Until 1880, most Americans worked on farms, but that year's census found, for the first time, a majority working in nonagricultural employment. The household and small-shop artisanal manufacturing that characterized colonial and early nineteenth-century production gave way increasingly to work in large shops, mills, and factories. By 1913, half of the industrial workforce labored in companies of more than 250 workers. In the years after 1865, with investment capital from Europe (especially Britain) aiding growth, the so-called visible hand of new managerial methods, federal tariff policy, and technological advances all improved productivity: By 1913, the United States was turning out a third of the world's industrial output.

New England, the Mid-Atlantic states, and the Midwest were the areas of greatest industrial capacity, whereas the South lagged behind. Indeed, one of the strengths of U.S. capitalism, as historian Walter Licht writes, was its regional and local diversity. Pennsylvania, the leading industrial state throughout the nineteenth century, was home not only to Philadelphia (the nation's second largest industrial city until Chicago overtook it in the 1900s) but also to other centers of industrial output, among them Harrisburg (iron and steel), Reading (machine shops and textiles), and Altoona (railroad equipment repair). Pittsburgh, Pennsylvania, was an international icon of industrialization: By 1900, it turned out a sixth of the nation's steel, the smoke from its mills darkening the skies and covering the city in a film of ash and soot. In Delaware, the city of Wilmington, headquarters for the DuPont corporation, was a leader in the chemical industry. In New Jersey, Trenton became known for its ironworks, Paterson for silk. In Connecticut, Bridgeport built machine tools, rifles, and ammunition casings; Waterbury was known for its brass works. New York City, with a population of 3.4 million in 1900—only 737,477 of whom were native, the rest immigrants and their children—was a city of extremes: home to many of the nation's growing corporations and the millionaires who owned them and also to many of the country's worst sweatshops. In Upstate New York, Schenectady, a major locomotive works, became home to General Electric in the early twentieth century; Utica was a center of steam-powered garment manufacturing; at Rome they made copper wire; in Rochester, a city of mills and machine shops, George Eastman established the Kodak camera company. In Ohio (where 60 percent of the workers were employed in manufacturing as early as 1880), the pattern was repeated as the state's largest cities, Cleveland and Cincinnati, known best for oil refining and the soap industry, respectively, were joined by midsize cities: Akron was best known for rubber; Canton for watches; Youngstown for steel; Toledo for wagons, glass, and steel; Dayton for office machinery and railroad cars. In Michigan, Detroit, by the early twentieth century, had become the automobile capital of the world; Grand Rapids was known for lumber and furniture manufacturing. In Illinois, Chicago dominated. There they made locomotives and train cars, manufactured iron, brewed beer, ground flour, and packed meat. Minneapolis, Minnesota, was a grain-storage and grain-processing city. Davenport, Iowa, made farm machines. Other cities, including Boston, Baltimore, and St. Louis—with growing contributions from the cities of the West Coast as the twentieth century progressed—contributed importantly to the nation's productive capacity with a broad range of goods.

In industrial terms, the South lagged behind. In 1860, the South had 36 percent of the nation's population but only 15 percent of its industrial manufacturing capacity. Although most enslaved Americans, as historian Walter Licht notes, worked in agriculture, there was a thriving industrial slavery in the antebellum South with some 150,000 to 200,000 of the nation's 4 million slaves working in manufacturing, including tobacco-processing plants, cotton mills, sugar refineries, lumber mills, on railroads, and in construction. The years following the Civil War saw the New South continue to lag behind northern advances as sharecropping replaced slavery in the fields and the hilly Piedmont region of Alabama, Georgia, South and North Carolina, and Virginia became home to cotton mills. By 1900, the South's per capita income was only half that of the rest of the nation, and, beginning in **World War I**, hundreds of thousands of African Americans and poor whites fled northward to better-paying industrial jobs.

Immigrant Labor Force

Millions of Europeans poured into the urban industrial centers of the Northeast, and, until passage of the Chinese Exclusion Act of 1882, tens of thousands of Asians immigrated to the West Coast to take advantage of new jobs in the industrializing economy. As the Industrial Revolution advanced during the course of the nineteenth century, immigration grew. Between 1820 and 1930, around 60 percent of the world's immigrants came to the United States. Indeed, in the 50-year period from 1870 to 1920, 25 million people immigrated into the United States. Many to "take advantage of the greater wages paid for industrial labor in this country," as the 1911 U.S. Immigration Commission noted. Irish and German immigrants began arriving in large numbers in the 1840s: the Irish fleeing the potato famine, the Germans escaping in the aftermath of the failed **Revolutions of 1848**. In the decades following 1880, large numbers of emigrants from southern and eastern Europe followed. In 1800, the U.S. population had been 5.3 million, half of whom were British immigrants and a fifth African American slaves. A century later, in 1900, the population was 77 million, in 45 states, a diverse population including African Americans, Irish, Germans, British, Italians, Poles, Mexicans, Japanese, Chinese, and Native Americans. Increasing **urbanization**—the growth of cities, large and small—was yet another demographic consequence of the Industrial Revolution. The United States had been predominantly a rural nation from its founding, but the census of 1920 revealed that, for the first time, more people lived in cities—large and small—than in the countryside.

The Spur of Science and Technology

The late nineteenth and early twentieth centuries was a time of great scientific and technological advancement—principally by Europeans, but contributed to importantly by Americans—which included Charles Darwin's *Origin of Species* (1859), Wilhelm Roentgen's discovery of X-rays (1895), J. J. Thomson's discovery of the electron (1897), Max Planck's quantum theory of matter (1900), Albert Einstein's special theory of relativity (1905) and theory of general relativity (1915), and Ernest Rutherford's 1911 theory of the atom. Inventions were transforming everyday life, including U.S. inventor Elias Howe's **sewing machine** of 1846, Philo Remington's typewriter of 1874, Alexander Graham **Bell**'s telephone (1876), the Croatian-born U.S. citizen Nikola **Tesla**'s alternating-current motor, Guglielmo Marconi's radio (its first transatlantic message made in 1901), Ohio bicycle shop owners Orville and Wilbur Wright's airplane in 1903, U.S. inventor Lee De Forest's triode vacuum in 1906, and Henry **Ford**'s 1908 Model T automobile. In 1913, Ford lowered costs and increased productivity with the application of the assembly line to automotive manufacturing. The number of inventions that poured from Ohio-born inventor Thomas Alva **Edison**'s research facilities at Menlo Park and Orange, New Jersey, were no less impressive: the improved incandescent light bulb, phonograph, motion picture camera, and a direct-current electric generator, with which, in 1882, he brought electricity to lower Manhattan. In medicine, Marie and Pierre Curie developed X-ray technology, and between 1897 and 1910, viruses were identified, blood groups classified, the whooping cough bacillus isolated, a vaccine for typhoid discovered, and tests for diphtheria, syphilis, and tuberculosis developed.

Kitchens, parlors, streets, and skies were not what they had been. By the second decade of the twentieth century, more than 7 million telephones were in use in the United States, and electric toasters, washing machines, and rudimentary plastics were introduced to the marketplace. The Industrial Revolution's cascade of invention and productivity boosted health, increased longevity, improved the everyday lives of millions, and offered new leisure-time entertainment, including broadcast radio's growing popularity in the 1920s and television's rise in the two decades following World War II. Although it was time of social mobility, geographic mobility, and changing gender roles, the era of the Industrial Revolution also was a time of anxiety and uncertainty.

The Industrial Revolution transformed work: In 1860, the industrial workforce numbered 1.5 million; by 1900, it numbered 5.9 million. Instead of lives in sync with the seasons and a farmer's sowing, harvesting, milking, and mending, factory workers became so-called hands catering to seasonless, never-tiring machines. Adam **Smith** had written eloquently about the advantages of the division of labor for increasing productivity in his 1776 *The Wealth of Nations*. Using the example of a "very trifling labour," Smith described how a single, unskilled worker could make between 1 and 20 pins per day, but by breaking down the process of pin making into 18 distinct operations—"one man draws out the wire, another straights it, a third cuts it, a fourth points it," and so on—18 workers might turn out 48,000 pins in a day. Such division of labor, however, could make work mind-numbingly repetitive as workers performed tasks rather than made complete products. For many, long hours of industrial labor—often 12 or more per day—meant that "the factory," as historian David Landes writes, "was a new kind of prison; the clock a new kind of jailer."

A Capitalist Market Economy

Capitalism was the economic system of the Industrial Revolution, and it led, as Adam Smith wrote, to the wealth of nations. With capitalism's competitive market economy, people's self-love—their greed and selfishness—will, if allowed to function in a competitive market, lead to economic growth. It is not, as Smith put it, from the benevolence of the butcher or the baker that we expect our dinner, but rather from their self-love and our own: "He will be more likely to prevail if he can interest their self-love in his favour, and show them that it is for their own advantage to do for him what he requires of them.... Give me that which I want, and you shall have this which you want." As individual butchers or bakers seek to maximize their profits, however, they will—where competition prevails—find themselves in a marketplace of other butchers and bakers, and as each tries to entice customers into their shop to buy their wares, they will tend to drive prices down and quality up and, along the way, invent improved efficiencies for delivering the best goods to their customers. Disciplined hard work and innovation tend to be rewarded in the capitalist marketplace. Not intending the benefit of others, it was (and is), as Smith put it, as if there were an invisible hand guiding the economy onward and upward, for, as each person selfishly seeks to maximize his or her own profit, all boats rise. Of course, some boats rise more than others; indeed, one consequence of the capitalist system in the United States (as elsewhere) is the inequitable distribution of wealth. in 2001, for example, the richest fifth of the U.S. population received half the income, the same amount as the remaining four-fifths, and the bottom fifth received only 3.5 percent of the total. Owners and employees could find themselves at loggerheads; as capitalists (owners) sought to maximize their own profits, they frequently did so by keeping workers' wages, especially those of the unskilled, low. It was (and remains) a systemic problem of competitive markets. For example, in the garment industry around the turn of the twentieth century, with sewing and cutting done by hand in an unregulated marketplace, bosses, if they wished to remain profitable, found they had to drive their workers' wages down so as to offer cheaper prices than their competitors. Overhead was cut by getting rid of the costs of rent for a factory or workshop; workers could do much of the cutting and sewing at home, often in the cramped, poorly lighted quarters of tenements. Paying workers by the piece—piecework—was another way to cut costs. For workers in such circumstances, the consequence of a lack of laws to regulate industrial capitalism's dynamism was **sweated labor and sweatshops** and paltry economic gain. Workers might blame bosses, and bosses were sometimes culpable, but the logic of the marketplace often was the real culprit.

Government Regulation

Reform-minded social scientists pointed out that government regulation could bring a semblance of rationality and humanity to capitalist markets, and laws regulating wages, hours, and working conditions became a cause in the late nineteenth century and thereafter. If, as with workers' compensation laws in the 1910s, all employers in a state had to fight for profits in a marketplace in which they all were required to pay into a workers' compensation system, then none would be penalized because all would add the costs of workers' compensation to the price of their product. Just how much to regulate the economic markets was bitterly contested, however, and when the first federal child labor laws were passed by Congress in the 1910s, the U.S. Supreme Court struck them down as unconstitutional. The Supreme Court did uphold the constitutionality of a state's right to regulate women's hours of work (*Muller v. Oregon* in 1908), but a New York law regulating the hours of labor for men in the private sector was held unconstitutional in 1905 (*Lochner v. New York*). Not until the 1938 Fair Labor Standards Act were federal child labor, minimum wage (25 cents), and maximum hours (the 8-hour day and 40-hour week) laws enacted.

In the late nineteenth century, workers increasingly formed or tried to form unions to slow the downward pressure on their wages, and their employers sought to regularize the downward pressure on profits that resulted from competition by developing pools and trusts (whereby firms in the same industry that appeared to be in competition with each other were actually in collusion, sharing the same director or same groups of corporate board members in interlocking directorates). Alongside creation of trusts and pools, another method business owners hit upon to mitigate competitive pressures on prices and profits was to merge firms in the same industry. Between 1897 and 1904, about 4,000 firms merged to form larger corporations; among those formed were U.S. Steel and Standard Oil. The financier John Pierpont **Morgan** crafted U.S. Steel, the first billion-dollar corporation, by merging eight major (and a few minor) steel corporations, including, most famously, Andrew **Carnegie**'s vast, vertically integrated, steelworks in western Pennsylvania. John D. **Rockefeller** organized Standard Oil of Ohio initially as an oil-refining business and, through clandestine deals and price fixing, controlled between 90 percent and 95 percent of the nation's oil-refining capacity by the mid-1870s. Congress sought to ensure the competitive markets essential to capitalism by outlawing monopolies and trusts with the Sherman Anti-Trust Act of 1890.

With the Industrial Revolution came wealth unheralded in human history but also, for some of the men, women, and children who worked in its mines, mills, and factories, hardship, disease, and death. From the late nineteenth century and into the twentieth century, thousands of workers were killed or injured annually, including railroad workers in rolling stock accidents and mine and mill workers who contracted black or brown lung from inhaling black coal dust or brown cotton dust. The federal Occupational Safety and Health Administration (OSHA) was established in 1970.

The path of economic advancement in the Industrial Revolution in the United States was not smoothly upward but was characterized by business cycles of growth and recession and, on occasion—as in the period from 1873 to 1897 and from 1929 to 1939—by economic downturns so sharp that they have been called Great Depressions. Years of economic recession include 1837, 1857, 1873, 1907, 1918–1921, 1973, 1979, and 2001.

Labor Organizing

The medieval guilds of skilled workers—carpenters, bricklayers, printers, shoemakers, and the like—carried over into the workmen's organizations of colonial America and the early republic. By 1866, the National Labor Union (NLU) had formed, bringing skilled workers together with unskilled workers and farmers to promote the eight-hour workday as well as immigration restriction. They hoped that restricting the flow of immigrants would, by lowering supply, increase wages, but the NLU was never large and collapsed in 1872. The Knights of Labor, formed in 1869, invited both skilled and unskilled workers to join its ranks and for a short time claimed almost 750,000 members, but it declined rapidly after 1886.

Organizing unskilled workers proved difficult because an ever-increasing number of newly arrived immigrants were willing to work for long hours at low wages. Strikes became commonplace and sometimes violent: More than a hundred people were killed during the mass strike in the railroad industry in 1877. Alternatives to the capitalist system were sometimes promoted, including anarcho-**syndicalism** and **socialism**, which proposed that the nation's workers who created the nation's wealth by their labor in factories, mines, and mills might control the means of production, distribution, and exchange. Not until the **American Federation of Labor** (AF of L), founded in 1886, did organized labor find some measure of longer-term success. As an umbrella organization of skilled-workers' craft unions, the AF of L's so-called pure-and-simple trades unionism seeking better pay, shorter hours, and safer working conditions found support. Its membership was almost exclusively white, male skilled workers. By 1910, 10.2 percent of nonagricultural workers were unionized. By the mid-1950s, union membership in the United States reached its historical peak when about a third of U.S. workers were union members. Union membership declined in subsequent years.

Industrialized Warfare: Mass Death and Destruction

The same Industrial Revolution that transformed what had been a world of work by human and animal muscle into one powered by fossil fuels, steam engines, internal combustion engines, and, later, electrical motors and atomic energy saw that the American system of standardized parts and continuous-process manufacturing that churned out material goods with astonishing rapidity and abundance was bitterly cruel in war. Modern war brought industrial efficiency to death and destruction. The results were horrifying: about 630,000 dead in the U.S. Civil War, some 20 million dead worldwide in World War I, and 55 million dead in World War II. With warfare industrialized, battlefield braveries of hand-to-hand combat increasingly gave way to the industrial efficiencies of death at a distance in which the courageous and cowardly, innocent civilian and fighting soldier killed indifferently. In World War I, death at a distance came by machine gun, poison gas, artillery shell, biplane, tank, or submarine; in World War II, mass death arrived by long-distance bomber, aircraft carrier and battleship, atomic bomb, and factory-style death camps. In war, industrial efficiencies had pitiable consequences.

A Postindustrial Age?

In the course of the second half of the twentieth century, the relative importance of industrial work in the United States declined, as many machine-intensive industrial jobs moved overseas to developing countries. By 2002, manufacturing, mining, and construction supplied fewer than a fifth of U.S. jobs, whereas the service sector—including those who worked in stores, financial institutions, medical services, entertainment, and education—had grown to about 64 percent.

FURTHER READING: Chandler, Alfred D., Jr. *The Visible Hand: The Managerial Revolution in American Business.* Cambridge, MA: Harvard University Press, 1977; Deyle, Steven. *Carry Me Back: The Domestic Slave Trade in American Life.* New York: Oxford University Press, 2005; Landes, David S. *The Unbound Prometheus: Technological Change and Industrial Development in Western Europe from 1750 to the Present.* New York: Cambridge University Press, 1969; Licht, Walter. *Industrializing America: The Nineteenth Century.* Baltimore: Johns Hopkins University Press, 1995; Ransom, Roger L., and Richard Sutch. "Capitalism without Capital: The Burden of Slavery and the Impact of Emancipation." *Agricultural History* 62, no. 3 (Summer 1988); Ransom, Roger L., and Richard Sutch. *One Kind of Freedom: The Economic Consequences of Emancipation.* New York: Cambridge University Press, 1977; Sachs, Jeffrey D. *The End of Poverty: Economic Possibilities for Our Time.* New York: Penguin Press, 2005; Smith, Adam. *An Inquiry into the Nature and Causes of the Wealth of Nations.* Chicago: University of Chicago Press, 1976; Staloff, Darren. *Hamilton, Adams, Jefferson: The Politics of Enlightenment and the American Founding.* New York: Hill and Wang, 2005; U.S. Bureau of the Census. *Historical Statistics ... Colonial Times to 1970.* Washington, DC: U.S. Government Printing Office, 1975; Walton, Gary M., and Hugh Rockoff. *History of the American Economy.* 10th ed. Mason, OH: Thomson/South-Western, 2005.

JOHN L. RECCHIUTI

Urbanization

Urbanization refers to the enlarged degree of urban development within a given geographical area, such as a region or country, and often is regarded incorrectly as being the same as urban growth, which more precisely relates to the rate at which an urban population or urban area increases in a given period relative to its own size at the start of that period. In particular, urbanization is concerned with two distinctive urban features: first, an increased urban proportion during a given time relative to its size at the start of the defined chronological period, such as a year or decade; second, the term *urbanization* can be employed to describe the proportion of total population or area in urban localities such as towns and cities.

Britain was the world's first urbanized society: By about 1851, more than half its population lived in an urban area, and its level of urbanization is measured every 10 years, a process dating from 1801 when the first national census was undertaken. Today, just as at different times in the past, there are different levels of urbanization between continents and between countries within continents. Europe and North America have high levels of urbanization, levels that are higher than in Africa and Asia, where a great many people still reside in rural locations. Yet when comparing the rate of urban growth, places such as Asia are experiencing far higher degrees of urban growth than regions like Europe or North America, which not only urbanized much earlier but currently have much lower rates of rural-to-urban migration—an influential factor upon urbanization. Nowadays, countries like Bangladesh, China, India, Indonesia, Nigeria, and Pakistan are experiencing high levels of urbanization when compared to, for example, European nations, partly due to the fact that many African, Asian, and Latin American countries did not industrialize on a wide scale until the second half of the twentieth century and also because many rural dwellers are migrating to urban places, which are perceived as places of greater wealth, that offer greater possibilities for survival and betterment than rural environments.

Regardless of the localized causes of urbanization, its effects can be extremely problematic. These effects, which are discussed more fully later, are economic, social, ecological/environmental, and psychological in nature and are exacerbated by issues such as large numbers of migrants with low education and/or job skill levels coming into cities, an inadequate housing supply, and underdeveloped administrative policies for urban management.

A major global influence on urbanization in recent centuries has been industrialization, a process of industrial development coupled with social and economic change that transforms societies from an agrarian to an industrial (manufacturing) base, centering on the factory system, a phenomenon that has to some extent influenced the majority of nations of the world in one form or another. Beginning with what is known as the Industrial Revolution—that is, the application of power-driven machinery to the process of manufacturing, a process starting in Britain in the late-1700s—industrial growth has led to radical changes in most societies across the world. Outcomes of the Industrial Revolution include the rise of manufacture, the decline of the significance of agrarian labor and output, and the rise of per capita income accompanied by much societal transition. Changes that have occurred can be associated with demography, transportation, cultural rules and behavior, and methods of thought, for instance, and include:

- A dramatic rise in national populations, a result of changing birth and death rates.
- A change in the composition of the urban hierarchy. Those places previously found at the top of the preindustrial hierarchy are commonly swept aside after industrial development begins by places located near to raw materials and natural resources and ports—places that provide **economies of scale** for the industrial capitalist machine.
- A more rapid rate of urban growth for existing towns and cities and the enlarged influence of these settlements over the hinterlands. Ultimately, this leads to a given society shifting from a rural to an urban base. In turn, this has led to fundamentally different urban dynamics, which initially may include environmental degradation as workers and migrants reside in hastily built, poor-quality, small-size (and overcrowded) unsanitary dwellings often situated close to sources of possible employment, most typically factories.
- The growth of new social classes and the erosion of the traditional social organizations. Previously, preindustrial urbanization was assisted by factors such as the role of local elites, an agricultural surplus, availability of adequate water supplies, good soil, and favorable climate; with industrialization, however, issues affecting urbanization now include concept of profit, a nation's ability to import and export goods, and the need for labor supplies within the factory system.
- Increases in per capita income and the nation's overall wealth and a growing gap between the poorest and most wealthy groups. The accumulation of finance and capital within growing urban places also can stimulate new industries, such as service-based business and banking.
- Developments in transportation such as the train and automobile and the infrastructure of communication.

The Effects of Industrialization and Urbanization

Industrial growth, regardless of location, was, and still is, accompanied by urbanization, and its effects have been felt worldwide. Historically, these effects first spread from British regions like the West Midlands across Western Europe and into North America; however, the dates at which different countries industrialized and urbanized in Europe differed due to the influence of local circumstances. France, for instance, was not subject to a marked change in urbanization until possibly 60 to 70 years after Britain, and as already noted, in many parts of the world, countries did not begin to industrialize until the twentieth century. In China, for example, industrialization and economic and urban development did not start in earnest until the change of political policies relating to the economy at the end of the 1970s, and today China exists as an important modern example of how urban growth can be used as a motor for national economic development. Significantly, however, as industrialization has been accompanied by urbanization, it also has made it possible to deal with the resulting economic, social, and environmental problems that also have emerged with industrial change and rapid urban growth, such as the creation of sewerage and clean water systems.

The effects of urbanization can be dramatic and have a major impact on the way people live in urban places. In Britain, the increase in urban growth and urbanization had profound effects, most noticeably on the environment and people's quality of life when the process of rapid urbanization began in the eighteenth century. By the early decades of the nineteenth century, there were major changes in the economic, political, social, and aesthetic values of Britain as a consequence of this rapid industrial and urban growth. These, in turn, were reflected in the changing appearance and form of urban land. Urbanization affected not only the building industry but also overwhelmed administrative practices, which previously had safeguarded the urban environment, as overcrowding, poverty, inadequate sanitation, dirt, and disease demonstrated. These problems were in no way uncommon but now increased in significance. As a consequence, the British had to develop new mechanisms for dealing with urban quality-of-life issues, and this resulted in the development of a new system of government to be applied at the local level in the mid-1830s. These new approaches marked a change in the understanding of the association between social and economic growth and the urban environment. Despite such comprehension, the wage structure and the working classes' capacity to participate in the housing market had to be suppressed so as to support economic prosperity, the basic cultural gift created by the Industrial Revolution. Slum housing was therefore an unfortunate, yet inevitable, consequence of Victorian culture and its economy. Significantly in this context, the dynamics of any public intervention to improve urban conditions had to do so without encroaching upon society's apparatus for creating and maintaining its wealth.

Much change in British housing occurred due to urbanization. To capitalize on the rush of migrants coming into towns and cities to work in factories, speculative builders hastily erected low-quality houses where worker families would reside. Significantly, too, these houses usually were packed together in high-density fashion, often close to the location of local factories, in the form of back-to-back or blind-back terraced houses, which exacerbated any existing social tensions and environmental problems, particularly because of the presence of particular ethnic groups in the poorest districts who had little option but to live in the cheapest and, therefore, worst houses because of discrimination. Existing housing and even new housing frequently degenerated in the context of deteriorating social and environmental conditions, and often the worst buildings were large houses that were subdivided into numerous units of accommodation once the previous owners fled to the suburbs to escape increasingly deteriorating urban conditions. Disease often was rife in such districts due to a lack of sewers, toilets, and a clean supply of water for drinking and washing. Any water needed would be gathered from local rivers or from water pumps located nearby, but its quality was far from perfect as drinking water because it contained various waste materials from people, animals, and industry. Consequently, epidemics of water-borne diseases such as cholera and diphtheria occurred periodically and had the potential to kill thousands of urban dwellers in any given large-size settlement. As already emphasized, problems such as overcrowding, poverty, pollution, inadequate sanitation, poor housing amenities, a lack of clean water, dirt, and disease were by no means new problems in Britain, but what urban growth had done was elevate these problems to a scale never witnessed before. Such problems also are being experienced in many parts of the world today due to the high level of urbanization.

In Britain by the early decades of the nineteenth century, politicians realized that the problems endured by the laboring classes in towns and cities would not resolve themselves without major assistance. Inspired by medical practitioners, British politicians by the 1840s created a system of environmental management based on removing noxious matter and providing light and air around new, privately built houses to ensure the good health of urban dwellers. Most significantly and for the first time, the move to make the environment healthier gave as a right something that was once a privilege for the rich: good health. For the upper echelons of urban society, wealth provided the choice of living in spacious suburban developments or the option of moving completely out of polluted, industrial settlements to healthful rural situations or even spa towns like Brighton and Bath. These towns, to meet the needs of their new, wealthy residents, developed new streets, some with fashionable crescent and circus layouts, consisting of buildings often in classical styles. For the working classes, however, daily life was a constant fight against not only social problems like the low wage economy, poverty, and unemployment but also environmental issues like pollution, dirt, and disease. Another burden in the toil of daily life and survival for laboring people was the increased cost of urban land, an urban characteristic that had a major influence on the poor as it affected, when coupled with low incomes, their ability to compete for better accommodation in the housing market. Despite government intervention at the central and local levels to eliminate problems that predominantly affected the laboring population as a result of their inability to compete with commerce, transport, and industry in the market for urban land, life for most working people in Britain was harsh throughout the nineteenth century. In addition, despite huge steps being made in terms of urban management as a result of the growth of problems created by urbanization, intervention by municipal authorities often was hesitant and limited, and for much of the nineteenth century the only apparent alternative to speculative urban development was provided by a small number of model communities, established either by utopians or by philanthropic and paternalistic industrialists like Robert **Owen**. Communities such as New Lanark, Saltaire, Port Sunlight, and Bournville, created at different times in the nineteenth century, were nonetheless important to the British model of living, for they encouraged community development and gave clear examples to the developing housing reform movement, which by the late nineteenth century was evolving into the formative town planning and garden city movement, the physical manifestation of that concept being Letchworth Garden City (after 1904).

Many of the effects of urbanization worldwide not only take root quickly but also are extremely difficult to tackle once problems arise, and governments universally reacted only slowly to new social problems. To refer again to the factory towns of Britain, the unique pressure created by the combination of the cumulative volume of rapidly expanding urban populations, the immaturity of local governments, and the rise of speculative building all too frequently led to the erection by jerry-builders of literally thousands of swiftly built, congested, unsanitary dwellings thrown up with little thought to health or living considerations. Despite government intervention in the form of new housing rules, houses for the working classes continued to be built to minimal standards, and despite new rules promoting some kind of improvement, housing still degraded all too rapidly as the pressure put upon the environment by people and their living habits were too great for the administrative system to cope with. Even in places where urban development was not so rapid, such as factory settlements built in New England, it was still common for environmental and housing conditions to degrade over time. As noted already, environmental degradation could result where the administrative machinery was not adequate enough to deal with the environmental issues put to it and/or when the problems were of such a large scale they rendered any regulation of environmental matters useless. Ecological effects also can arise with urbanization, including air pollution (particularly from industry), waste disposal, water pollution, the increased consumption of water, the loss of flora and fauna, and disruption to local ecosystems both on land

Drawing of Swainson Birley cotton mill, Lancashire, England, 1834. Science Museum/Science & Society Picture Library.

and in local bodies of water (rivers, estuaries, lakes, or the sea) close to industry and housing.

Since the onset of industrialization, many changes to global society have occurred. One effect, urbanization, has led to, for instance, new lifestyles for people residing in cities. Urban dwellers live not only in different buildings now when compared to the past, but the growth of urban places simultaneously has created new urban lifestyles and mentalities. Urbanization has led to increased levels of cosmopolitanism, overturned traditional urban land-use patterns, and led to radical increases in the cost of centrally located land. In addition, transport developments like the **railroads** and urban mass transit systems have had a major influence on where people can live as they have broken down the preindustrial spatial relation between urban space, walking ability, and time available to get from one place to another. Many people now commute from the suburbs to the urban center on a daily basis, and the growth of cheap worker tickets, initiated in Britain in the 1880s, has meant that working-class suburbs also have developed, increasing the urban sprawl of a city and its impact upon its hinterland.

FURTHER READING: Cherry, Gordon E. *Urban Change and Planning.* Henley-on-Thames, U.K.: G. T. Fouls, 1972; Creese, Walter L. *The Search for Environment.* London: Yale University Press, 1996; Dyos, H. J., and Wolff, M. *The Victorian City: Images and Reality.* 2 vols. London: Routledge and Kegan Paul, 1976; Flint, Corrin, and Flint, David. *Urbanisation: Changing Environments.* New York: Collins Educational, 2001; Meakin, B. *Model Factories and Villages.* London: Unwin, 1905; Schmal, Henk, and Schmal, Wolfgang. *Patterns of European Urbanisation since 1500.* London: Croom Helm, 1981; Tarn, John N. *Five Percent Philanthropy.* Cambridge: Cambridge University Press, 1973; Wirth, Louis. "Urbanism as a Way of Life." *American Journal of Sociology* 44 (1938): 1–24.

IAN MORLEY

Urban Transportation

Preindustrial communities were typically small in both population and land area. Work and home were close together—farms are the obvious example—so the question of the journey to work was not significant. People walked when they needed to get somewhere, although the wealthy could ride horses or use horse-drawn carriages, but with the possible exception of taking goods to market, distances were short. There were exceptions, such as the traveling merchants of medieval times. Some of the larger cities on rivers, such as London or Paris, saw the development of commercial riverboats rowed by boatmen. For the majority of the population, however, walking was sufficient.

All this changed with industrialization. Cities grew larger; population densities increased. As this trend continued, the need grew for some provision of efficient mass transport in cities, considered vital for the continuation of urban growth and, thus, economic prosperity. With an improved ability to move people around larger cities faster than before, the general environment for economic activity would be enhanced. In order to accomplish this required the setting up of a system in which regularly scheduled passenger services operated on a predetermined route, using shared vehicles. The first such systems were privately owned and operated but, increasingly, came into public ownership because of their importance to the urban infrastructure. The vehicles used for mass transportation would supplement privately owned carriages or commercial for-hire taxi services that provided flexible door-to-door service for individuals.

At first, public transportation was provided by horse-drawn buses. Over time, as city populations and population densities increased, cities began to consider moving people underground on underground railways. The first of these were steam-powered, which had obvious limitations. The development of electricity as a reliable power source, however, permitted a much more effective way of providing underground mass transit as well as overland transportation. Because a continuous supply of electricity could be provided through rails or overhead wires, electric traction permitted the operation of large passenger vehicles, in contrast to its use for powering individual passenger cars. (The drawback of electricity as a power source for these was the lack of continuous provision: Batteries in which electricity could be stored were too large, and using a smaller battery required frequent stops for recharging.)

In surface transportation, horse-drawn buses were replaced, first by steam-powered or electrically powered ones and then, early in the twentieth century, by (gasoline or diesel) internal combustion engine motor buses. Although originally intended to speed up movement within an overcrowded city, the speculative extension of bus or rail lines outside the immediate city core permitted the suburbanization of the nineteenth-century city.

Roads and Buses

The largest cities experienced the problems of how to move large numbers of people around the city first. The solutions generally were in the form of short-stage horse-drawn coaches operated by private entrepreneurs or for-hire horse-drawn taxicabs. Wealthier residents had their own private carriages.

London's experience was typical. By the beginning of the nineteenth century, London had become an international financial center, the country's largest port, an industrial center (although manufacturing mainly was in small workshops rather than in large factories), and was the location of the center of government. Its population was about 1 million by 1800, increasing to 1.5 million by 1821, and to 1.75 million by 1831. As businesses expanded, they frequently took over the most central sites; those residents who could afford to move did so, but the poorer sections of the city, whose inhabitants could not afford to move, became increasingly overcrowded and congested.

Privately operated horse-drawn coaches had been operating since the 1760s to and from the villages just outside central London. More operators appeared as the city grew in population, and by the 1820s, about a fifth of all the stage coaches licensed in the country, about 600, operated in the London area. Their design made them unsuitable for extended travel on city streets, however, and they were expensive (horses were expensive to look after, and license fees and mileage duties increased their operating costs), thus putting them out of reach of most working people. (Horses also added to the unsavory conditions in city streets, giving rise to the occupation of street crossing sweeper!)

A better design—simply a box on wheels that was easy to get into and out of—had been pioneered in Paris, where in 1828, 100 of these so-called city coaches had been granted permission to operate in congested central Paris. This design was adapted by a London coach builder, George Shillibeer, to carry 20 passengers pulled by

Model of Shillibeer's omnibus, 1829. Science Museum/Science & Society Picture Library.

three horses. The first, known as Shillibeer's omnibus, started operations in July 1829, running into the financial center. Shillibeer added more, and the market also was entered by rivals operating smaller omnibuses holding 12 passengers.

The costs of operating omnibuses in London fell as the mileage duty was reduced. The number of passengers who could be carried increased with the addition of lengthwise seats on the top—the first double-decker buses. Similar horse-drawn buses operated in all major cities. In the United States, the first ones were used in New York City in 1829 and in Philadelphia in 1831. Some cities, including London and New York, improved the comfort of the ride by laying iron rails in the streets, flush with the surface (to avoid disrupting other traffic), which made the journey in these horse-drawn buses much smoother.

Steam Power

Steam engines had been adapted for use by riverboats early in the nineteenth century, and most major cities saw them in use. The problem with adapting the **steam engine** to land transport was the size: Early steam engines were too heavy for ordinary roads and required specially built tracks for street railway use. London's first such steam-powered street railway opened in 1836.

A later alternative to street-level steam railways were cable-hauled systems. With these, a continuous-loop cable was laid just under the road surface, turned by a large steam engine located in a central powerhouse. Each carriage attached itself to the cable and was hauled along its route as the cable moved. London's first such cable rail line opened in 1841; in the United States, 23 cities operated cable systems in 1890, but soon after, they were replaced by electric traction systems, except in San Francisco, where cable cars proved more suitable than electric traction for the hilly terrain.

Going Underground. Even providing mass transportation systems still created enormous road congestion, especially as cities grew larger. In the second half of the nineteenth century, attention began to turn to solving this problem. New York City adapted the steam railway to the city by putting it above street level on an elevated track (the el), opening its first elevated line in 1876. An alternative was to go underground. The first underground passenger railway, 3.5 miles in length, opened in London in 1863. It was not at first a true, completely closed underground system, as the steam locomotives had to periodically vent built-up steam in one of the cuttings that existed along the tracks. As the system expanded, ventilation remained a problem, partly solved by the changeover to electric traction at the end of the century. Once deep-level lines were built, ventilation fans were a necessity.

Electrification. The first application of electricity to urban mass transit was in Richmond, Virginia, in 1888, using power from overhead lines. In London, the electrification of tramways developed slowly, with the first being opened in 1901, but speeded up with the decision to electrify the former horse tramways in the center

Construction of the Metropolitan Underground line, London, 1867. Science Museum/Science & Society Picture Library.

of the city in 1903. The first application of electricity underground in 1890 was not successful, as the line was too small and underpowered, but ones built by private entrepreneurs after 1900 were more successful once technology had developed sufficiently to enable larger trains to be powered by electricity.

The impact of electrification, both underground and on the surface, was great. It was much cleaner than horses and quieter than steam, although the generation of electricity contributed to a different type of pollution, as did the later changeover to liquid fuels. Fast, improved access to the center of the city permitted residential growth outside, following the new lines. Above ground, the shift to gasoline- or diesel-powered buses, replacing earlier electric battery or steam buses, began in earnest after 1890. These buses were cheaper to operate than horse-drawn ones and could carry more passengers: In London in 1911, only 13 percent of all passenger vehicles were still horse-drawn, a share falling to 6 percent by 1913. (At this time, however, a majority of goods vehicles were still drawn by horses.)

In Continental Europe, the Paris Metro opened its first line in 1900, although plans to build an underground rail system there dated back to 1845. Its carriages were made of wood and offered both first- and second-class carriages, a two-class system that remained in place until 1991. The Berlin U-Bahn opened its first line in 1902.

The building of underground systems was slower in the United States. The first was a short line in Boston, opened in 1897, and the first in New York City was opened in 1904. Both these systems were initially built by private interests. In the United States, public transit systems reached a peak passenger load of 17.2 million in 1926 but then began losing riders due to competition from private automobiles.

FURTHER READING: Barker, Theo. *Moving Millions: A Pictorial History of London Transport.* London: London Transport Museum, 1990; Post, Robert C. *Urban Mass Transit.* Westport, CT: Greenwood Press, 2006; Trench, Richard, and Ellis Hillman. *London under London: A Subterranean Guide.* London: John Murray, 1993. WEB SITE: http://eh.net/encyclopedia/article/schrag.mass.transit.us (by Zachary M. Schrag).

CHRISTINE RIDER

W

Waltham-Lowell System

The Waltham-Lowell system was a system of **cotton** textile manufacturing in which all of the steps needed to turn bales of raw cotton into finished bolts of fabric took place within a single facility. Originating in Waltham, Massachusetts, in 1815, the bale-to-bolt system was realized in the specially constructed town of Lowell, Massachusetts, and the Lowell system consequently came to refer to the comprehensive arrangements designed by the manufacturing corporations for housing, governing, entertaining, and educating the workforce. With its towering "mile of mills" bordering the Merrimack and Concord Rivers and powered by their waters, Lowell epitomized the nineteenth-century industrial city.

In the Boston suburb of Waltham in 1815, the scion of a wealthy Boston family of merchants, Francis Cabot Lowell, supervised the construction of the first textile mill in the United States in which the entire textile production process was integrated within one mill and mechanized using water power. While traveling in Great Britain from 1810 to 1812, Lowell had observed both the power looms in the factories of Manchester and the sordid slums that surrounded the mills. With capital provided by Lowell, his brother-in-law Patrick Tracy Jackson, and Nathan Appleton, the Boston Manufacturing Company rapidly expanded to three mills in Waltham, using all of the available water power afforded by the Charles River to produce coarse cotton cloth.

After Lowell's death in 1817, the Boston Associates, owners of the Boston Manufacturing Company, selected the small rural town of East Chelmsford, 30 miles from Boston, for expansion. The site's advantages included the Pawtucket Falls, rapids over which the Merrimack River dropped more than 30 feet over less than a mile, and the mile-and-a-half-long Pawtucket Canal, which had been dug in 1796 to allow boats to bypass the falls through a series of locks. Although the Pawtucket Canal as a transportation artery had been quickly superseded by another canal just upstream, the investors saw the potential of the Pawtucket Canal as an energy source for the full range of spinning and weaving machinery.

Construction of the planned city began in 1822, comprising additional canals, locks, mills, machine shops, housing for workers and managers, streets, markets, and a church. The first Lowell textile factory, the Merrimack Manufacturing Company Mill, opened in 1823, producing printed calico fabric. Its success inspired immediate imitation. Ten more large mill complexes—the Hamilton, Appleton, Lowell, Middlesex, Tremont, Suffolk, Lawrence, Boott, Massachusetts, and Prescott Mills—opened in Lowell before 1850. The Boston Associates also expanded in other New England cities, including Chicopee and Lawrence in Massachusetts and Manchester, Vermont; other developers followed their lead throughout the northeastern United States.

Mills using the Waltham-Lowell system mechanized and integrated the full range of steps required to produce woven textiles out of cotton. Falling water turned several wooden overshot waterwheels. Each waterwheel turned a shaft that was connected by the crown gearing to a flywheel, whose larger dimensions helped compensate for small irregularities in water flow. Through a leather belt, the flywheel turned a rod running the length of a single floor of the factory, powering the machines on that floor via another series of leather belts. By midcentury, overshot waterwheels had been replaced by more efficient underwater turbines, powering still larger mills with a greater number of machines. Water power mechanized nearly every step of production of cotton fabric: picking, or processing the ginned cotton fibers into a thick, flat mat, or lap; carding, in which the fibers of the lap were straightened and aligned; drawing, in which the straightened fibers were stretched and combined; roving, in which the fibers were twisted and lengthened into longer threads; and spinning, twisting the threads into yarns onto bobbins. At this stage, the bobbins of yarn for colored textiles were manually dyed in vats, dried, and dressed with starch and sizing before being carried in bins to the floors with power looms for weaving. More machines were used for finishing, during which decorative patterns were printed onto calicoes, and white fabrics were bleached. The final steps were pressing, winding, and cutting the finished fabric into bolts for sale.

The architecture that housed such varied processes and powerful machines was a startling new presence. The buildings had to be large enough to accommodate dozens of carding machines, spinning wheels, and looms; they also needed to be of sufficient solid construction to withstand the vibration of the machinery. Enormous, monumental structures of brick and stone, far larger than any buildings that most workers had ever seen, lined the banks of the rivers and canals. Successive generations of mills grew still more imposing to permit the simultaneous production of a wide range of patterns and textures, with all processes remaining vertically integrated, each stage occupying a different floor under a shared roof.

The Mill City and the Mill Workers

The vertically integrated, bale-to-bolt concept of the Lowell system, however, went far beyond the mechanical processes of manufacturing to include management of the workforce inside and outside of the factories. Francis Cabot Lowell's original conception for his mills represented a radical departure from the conditions he had witnessed in Manchester, England, where whole families labored in the mills, forming a permanent impoverished working class. Lowell and the Boston Associates intended to avoid excessive exploitation of laborers, maintaining their dignity and upward mobility, while nonetheless keeping labor costs low. To these ends, the Boston Associates recruited a workforce composed of women between the ages of 15 and 25 from farms in the immediate region and from northern New England. Although women received only half the wages of male mill hands, they regarded themselves as middle class, literate, and articulate. The mill girls, as they came to be known, typically worked in the mills for periods of months or years, leaving to marry, to return to their farming communities, to migrate to the West, or to pursue other occupations. The corporation accommodated and underscored their middle-class identity, constructing comfortable boarding houses to house the workers and matrons in respectable, quasi-familial settings; wholesome meals were eaten in the boardinghouses rather than in public restaurants. To allay fears regarding the dubious propriety of allowing unmarried girls to go off to distant cities to work, the Lowell mills instituted rigid standards for behavior and morality on and off the job, setting evening curfews, requiring Sabbath observance and church attendance, and forbidding drinking, smoking, gambling, profanity, and so-called light conduct, or dalliance with the opposite sex. In fact, the corporation's rules and requirements intruded into almost every corner of the workers' lives, regulating each hour of the workday with bells that loomed over the city in each factory's bell towers. The clanging woke the workers before dawn and rang in and rang out for the morning working hours, the half-hour dinner at midday, and the evening, 12 to 14 hours after the working day had begun.

The corporation's provisions for workers, however, went beyond bare subsistence and minimal respectability. Although their work was repetitive and regimented, mill girls were able to exercise some decision-making in matters such as their work clothing, their positions at the machines, and the arrangement of their workplace environment. They also were permitted to decorate some areas of the mills with flowering plants. Some boardinghouses were furnished with pianos for musical entertainment in the evenings. In the city, the corporation and other organizations provided a remarkable range of educational and recreational activities, including lectures and musical performances. Speakers in the Lyceum Lecture series, sponsored by the Society for the Diffusion of Useful Knowledge, included Horace Greeley, Ralph Waldo Emerson, Robert Owen, and Horace Mann; mill girls crowded the hall and took notes assiduously. Foreign-language lessons, Mutual Self-Improvement Clubs, and literary societies flourished. Lowell also boasted several subscription circulating libraries providing the latest fiction by Sir Walter Scott and Edward George Bulwer-Lytton. Mill girls enthusiastically embraced the opportunity to earn their own incomes, live independently of their families, and especially partake of the unprecedented cultural and social riches the town afforded. Letters from employees to friends and relations back home advanced educational advantages as much as wages as reason to follow the writers to Lowell.

The most dramatic manifestation of the zeal for self-improvement emerged in 1840, when Abel C. Thomas, the minister of the Universalist church of Lowell, produced a magazine, the *Lowell Offering,* featuring pieces written by the mill girls. In 1841, the publisher of the corporation's official newspaper, William Schouler, produced the *Operatives' Magazine,* edited by two mill girls, Abba A. Goddard and Lydia S. Hall. The two periodicals merged as an enlarged *Lowell Offering* in 1842, now edited by two women who had worked in Lowell's mills since the early 1830s, Harriet F. Farley and Harriott Curtis. With contents comprising original poetry, short fiction, memoirs, and editorials, the *Offering* was an immediate success, winning accolades from literary luminaries such as Harriet Martineau and George Sand for its literary quality and the democratic ideals it embodied. A typical issue of the *Offering* might include a romance set among nobility in an exotic Italian location, a sentimental meditation on "Mother" or "First Love," a fictionalized but highly realistic story dramatizing relationships between boardinghouse roommates or workplace companions, a moral sermon, a comic or solemn verse, or an editorial demanding improvements in working conditions. After the *Offering* ceased publication in 1845, several of its authors went on to literary careers.

Their sense of dignity, the relative homogeneity of the workforce, and the intimacy of their boardinghouse quarters inspired solidarity among the young women, encouraging them to organize for more substantive concessions from mill owners. In response to reductions in pay, mill hands went on strike in 1834, without success; in 1836, 2,000 workers successfully protested increased room and board charges. Operatives organized the Lowell Female Labor Reform Union and addressed assemblies in favor of woman suffrage. Through protests, turnouts, and petitions, workers asserted their independence and right to self-determination, even though mill owners punished insubordinate workers through blacklists that effectively barred them from subsequent mill employment at Lowell or elsewhere.

The hardships of factory work barely were mitigated by cultural amenities and protests. Although workers constantly lobbied to reduce the workday from the 14 hours that were standard, neither the mill owners nor the state legislature were inclined to make such an important concession, and the 10-hour workday was not legislated until 1874. The long hours of repetitive tasks resulted in stress injuries, sometimes crippling. The lamplight required during winter months presented a deadly fire hazard in proximity to highly flammable cotton. The rotating drums, belts, and interlocking gears that powered the machinery of the Waltham-Lowell system also posed a constant danger. Workers suffered crushed and severed limbs and scalping when skirts, fingers, or hair got caught in the gears. The dense concentration of machinery produced deafening noise and constant, bone-jarring vibration. Most damaging of all was the cotton lint and dust that filled the air in factories, whose windows were sealed to maintain a high level of humidity and avoid damage to the fragile textiles and machinery. Workers inhaling cotton fibers in the unventilated factories had high rates of byssinosis, asthma, tuberculosis, and other respiratory diseases; up to 70 percent of the hands at the early mills eventually died of such diseases.

A Changing Workforce

Working conditions and morale deteriorated by the 1850s in mills across the northeastern United States. The utopian aspirations and paternalism of the Boston Associates did not withstand the promise of increased profits through the use of cheaper and less well-organized immigrant labor. The first influx of immigrant labor was provided by Irish refugees fleeing poverty and starvation in the late 1840s. Penniless and desperate immigrants were far less inclined to press for first-rate working or living conditions than New England Yankees who had recourse to family networks and a range of alternative occupations open to them. The Irish workers' willingness to accept lower wages antagonized their Yankee comrades, exacerbating anti-Irish and anti-Catholic bigotry. Because Irish immigrants frequently arrived as families, the corporation's regulated boardinghouses were abandoned in favor of apartments that soon became slums. By 1860, more than 60 percent of the workforce in the large New England mill towns consisted of immigrants, about half Irish. In the years before the Civil War, hoping to cut labor costs to offset potential losses, mill owners actively solicited French Canadian emigrants from impoverished areas in rural Quebec, creating so-called Little Canadas in mill towns throughout New England. Other ethnic groups followed. Italian, Russian, Austro-Hungarian, European Jewish, Greek, Polish, Portuguese, and Syrian communities subsequently contributed to the international mix. At the turn of the century, however, the workers—now almost entirely immigrants—organized and fought for safer factories and shorter working hours. In January 1912, more than 10,000 workers in Lawrence, Massachusetts, embarked on a strike that closed the factories there for two months to protest wage cuts. Lowell's workers followed suit in a general strike that galvanized the diverse workforce and won similar concessions.

Decline of the New England Mills

The New England textile industry did not survive the twentieth century. In the years following World War II, many mills were acquired by conglomerates involved in a variety of industries in different regions. The new generation of owners was reluctant to invest in the technological advances that would make factories viable or in the safety improvements to retain New England workers; federal tax codes made it more profitable to liquidate older factories than to install updated technology and attract the well-trained workers needed to service it. Textile companies transferred operations to southern states, where wage scales and production costs were lower and safety regulations more lax. In the 1980s and 1990s, the search for cheap labor and few restrictions took the textile mills still farther, to China and other rapidly developing nations. Although the factories in developing countries seldom integrate all aspects of manufacture in the manner of the Waltham-Lowell system, they do continue to use actual equipment from the first generations of Lowell mills.

In 1978, the Lowell National Historical Park was established to preserve and communicate industrial and labor history through museums, archives, libraries, and the city itself. The Boott Cotton Mills are now a museum chronicling the development of Lowell and the New England textile industry; facing the mills, the Patrick J. Mogon Cultural Center reconstructs an 1840s boardinghouse and offers exhibits depicting the evolving culture of the mill workers. Other mills have been converted to study centers, luxury apartments, offices for a variety of businesses, and studios; one factory continues to manufacture high-tech textiles.

FURTHER READING: Division of Publications, National Park Service. *Lowell: The Story of an Industrial City*. Washington, DC: U.S. Department of the Interior, 1992; Dublin, Thomas. *Women at Work: The Transformation of Work and Community in Lowell, Massachusetts, 1826–1600*. New York: Columbia University Press, 1979; Eisler, Benita. *The Lowell Offering: Writings by New England Mill Women, 1840–1845*. New York: Norton, 1997; Gross, Laurence F. *The Course of Industrial Decline: The Boott Cotton Mills of Lowell, Massachusetts, 1835–1955*. Baltimore: Johns Hopkins University Press, 1993; Moran, William. *The Belles of New England: The Women of the Textile Mills and the Families Whose Wealth They Wove*. New York: St. Martin's Press, 2002; National Park Service. *Lowell National Historical Park*. Available at http://www.nps.gov/lowe/; Robinson, Harriet Hanson. *Loom and Spindle; or, Life among the Early Mill Girls*. New York:

Thomas Y. Crowell, 1998; Zonderman, David A. *Aspirations and Anxieties: New England Workers and the Mechanized Factory System, 1815–1850.* New York: Oxford University Press, 1992.

JANE WEISS

Watt, James (1736–1819)

James Watt, whose work helped perfect the **steam engine**, was born in Greenock, Scotland, on January 19, 1736. Both his father and grandfather were instrument makers and experts at repairing work connected with shipping. Young Watt showed an early aptitude for scientific investigation. After finishing his education, he went to the University of Glasgow and established an instrument-making business in 1757. A man of exceptional mechanical skills, Watt was very versatile. He became a well-respected engineer, working on improving harbors and deepening rivers; he also surveyed various canal routes. In the 1760s, Watt turned his attention toward steam engines. While repairing a Newcomen steam engine in 1763, he discovered that separating the condensation and steam chambers would save energy and cut the heat loss in the cylinder. Six years later, he patented this efficient steam engine.

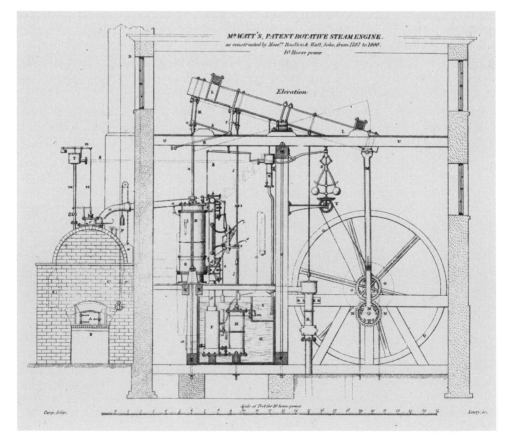

Technical drawing of a Watt Rotative Steam Engine, 1787. Science Museum/Science & Society Picture Library.

In 1774, Watt entered into partnership with the British manufacturer Matthew **Boulton** (1728–1809) in Birmingham, which combined Watt's inventive spirit with Boulton's manufacturing genius. The result was the production of a steam engine with a rotary motion. The condensing steam engine became operative in 1776 and was further improved with the installation of automatic speed governors in 1778. The firm of Boulton, Watt & Sons produced 50 complete engines between 1794 and the end of century, after having previously assembled components before Watt's patent ended. The modernized Soho factory continued manufacturing steam engines until the mid-nineteenth century.

Watt also devised a means for calculating the power of engines by comparing it with horsepower (hp). One horsepower was equivalent to a horse lifting a 150-pound weight by four feet in one second and is still used as a unit for measuring the power of an engine. (The electrical unit of power, equivalent to 1/746 of one horsepower, is called a *watt* in his honor.) Watt also developed an attachment used in telescopes and a copying process for documents. His steam engines became the basis for the later development of locomotives. After retiring from his firm, he devoted his life toward research, conducting extensive tours and studying nature. He died on August 19, 1819, in his home at Heathfield.

FURTHER READING: Carnegie, Andrew. *James Watt.* New York: Doubleday, Page, 1905; Hills, Richard L. *Power from Steam: A History of the Stationary Steam Engine.* Cambridge: Cambridge University Press, 1993; Marsden, Ben. *Watt's perfect engine: Steam and the Age of Invention.* New York: Columbia University Press, 2002; Marshall, Thomas H. *James Watt.* Ianfield, Edinburgh, Scotland: Leonard Parsons, 1925; Roll, Eric. *An Early Experiment in Industrial Organisation: Being a History of the Firm of Boulton & Watt, 1775–1805.* New York: A. M. Kelley, 1968.

PATIT PABAN MISHRA

Wealth and Poverty in the Industrial Revolution

The Industrial Revolution was a period of economic and social transition from a mostly agricultural economy and society to an urban society typified by capital-intensive, industrial production. Along with the changes in methods of production, the Industrial Revolution brought about changes in the institutions that determined wealth and poverty. Furthermore, in response to these social and economic changes, there was a corresponding change in how wealth and poverty were defined and understood. Thus, both the theory and the reality of wealth and poverty underwent significant change.

Wealth and poverty are socially constructed terms and realities, in that both their definitions (i.e., what society labels as *wealth* and *poverty*) and their manifestations (how reality fits the socially determined definitions) are socially created. Neither wealth nor poverty is natural categories or phenomena that exist independent of society; their existence and significance come from society. Thus, when we say that wealth and poverty changed during the Industrial Revolution, we mean more than just that the numbers of wealthy and poor people changed. There also was a change in the factors that cause people to be wealthy or poor, and more significantly, there was a change in the underlying ideas of what is wealth and what is poverty. Unlike the debate over changes in the standard of living during the Industrial Revolution—which is mostly a quantitative debate—the significant changes in these definitions of wealth and poverty are more qualitative and conceptual. This qualitative change, along with the absence of reliable data, complicates any attempt to demonstrate empirically changes in actual levels of wealth and poverty.

The Ideas of Wealth and Poverty

Before the Industrial Revolution, the definition of wealth was based on the idea of abundance, and it was mostly understood in communal terms (the wealth of nations). After the Industrial Revolution, the definition of wealth was based on the idea of scarcity and was understood in almost exclusively individualistic terms. The difference reflects the economic and social changes brought about by the Industrial Revolution.

The different views of wealth (which have corresponding differing views of poverty) are not merely the result of adopting a positive or negative approach to understanding wealth, for it gets to the heart of how wealth is created. Right before the Industrial Revolution, Adam Smith defined the wealth of a nation as "the annual produce of the land and labour of the society" (Smith, 1976, p. 12). Smith based his understanding of wealth in terms of material sufficiency and abundance, and he defined wealth in terms of society as a whole. This is very different from the earlier mercantilist view in which wealth was an abundance of gold and silver. Smith noted instead that money did not have value in itself; rather, its value rested in what it could buy. This abundance conception of wealth also determined how poverty was understood. Poverty was seen as the absence of sufficiency and abundance, and its remedy, that is, how poverty can be reduced, was to increase abundance production. "Every man is rich or poor according to the degree in which he can afford to enjoy the necessaries, conveniences, and amusements of human life" (Smith, 1976, p. 47). For him, the primary economic goal was to increase production so that the standard of living for all would increase and for all to share in society's abundance. To quote Smith: "No society can surely be flourishing and happy, of which the far greater part of the members are poor and miserable. It is but equity, besides, that they who feed, cloath and lodge the whole body of the people, should have a share of the produce of their own labour as to be themselves tolerably well fed, clothed and lodged" (Smith, 1976, p. 96).

By the 1870s, a new definition of wealth emerged based on the concept of scarcity, with the individual as the central unit of analysis. Léon Walras (in 1874) stated early in his *Elements of Pure Economics* that: "[B]y social wealth I mean all things, material or immaterial (it does not matter which in the context), that are scarce, that is to say, on the one hand, useful to us and, on the other hand, only available to us in limited quantity" (Walras, 1954, p. 65). This scarcity view of wealth came to dominate economic thinking: "Wealth is not such for economic purposes, unless it is scarce and transferable" (Bagehot, 1880, p. 132); "Wealth is not wealth because of its substantial qualities. It is wealth because it is scarce" (Robbins, 1932, p. 47).

As wealth was no longer directly related to the production of goods and services, it was no longer connected with improving the well-being of the whole population, especially the lot of the poor. Writing in Austria in the 1870s, Karl Menger (the founder of the Austrian school of economics) gave the clearest expression of this new approach: "[I]f there were a society where all goods were available in amounts exceeding the requirements for them [that is a society of abundance], there would be no ... 'wealth'" (Menger, 1976, pp. 109–10). Menger then noted that wealth for the individual is different from wealth for the community. "The problem," he wrote, "arises from the fact that a continuous increase in the amount of economic goods available to economizing individuals would necessarily cause these goods to lose their economic character, and in the way cause the components of wealth to suffer a diminution. Hence we have a 'queer contradiction' that a continuous increase of the objects of wealth would have caused, as a necessary final consequence, a diminution of wealth" (Menger, 1976, pp. 109–10). The change in the idea of wealth leads to a change in what economists call wealth and in how wealth is measured. Thus, until the early nineteenth century, wealth was understood and measured in communal terms. The classical economists talked about the wealth of the country, its overall level of output, and their central concern was how it was distributed. For the neoclassical economists after 1870, wealth consisted of the assets that an individual owned, and their value was based on the return these assets earned.

The change in how wealth was understood led to changes in how poverty was understood. For most observers, the term *poor* was almost completely synonymous with *worker.* Someone was poor because he had no visible means of support other than his labor. Distinctions often were made between the working poor and paupers (those in need of support or charity), who either did not work because they could not due to old age, sickness, or disability, and those who did not work due to some character flaw. Often it was argued that systems of poor relief encouraged idleness and thus were a contributing factor to the causes of poverty. In any case, most agreed that poverty was a social problem that the state had to address in some manner.

Furthermore, before the Industrial Revolution, there was a clear understanding that the existence of poverty was a necessary condition for the existence of wealth, though it was rarely stated as boldly as Bernard Mandeville's argument against educating poor children, as there would then be a shortage of low paid workers which would make manufacturing less profitable. Even Adam Smith noted that "For one very rich man, there must be at least five hundred poor, and the affluence of the few supposes the indigence of the many" (Smith, 1976, p. 710).

Adam Smith presented the optimistic view that economic growth could generate a sufficient increase in output that could lift the working poor out of poverty and offer attractive inducements for the idle poor to work. Furthermore, he noted that much wealth was generated by the laws and regulations of the mercantilist economic policy and that these laws created wealth at the expense of the poor. Smith felt that the elimination of such barriers to competition would lead to a type of wealth creation that would benefit the poor. Such optimism was lost when Thomas Malthus (1798) presented his population principle, which argued that poverty was the natural result of the tendency of human populations to increase whenever there is an increase in food supply, thus preventing an increase in standards of living. This pessimism was supported by David Ricardo's "iron law of wages," put forward in 1817, which, for similar reasons, argued the impossibility of a long-term increase in real wages. That the rise of free markets did not decrease poverty—and in fact it increased it—in England led John Stuart Mill, in 1848, to view the problem of poverty as one exasperated by what today we would call a *culture of poverty,* and he recommended that the state regulate the actions of the poor so as to force them to make better decisions. Mill also saw population growth as a major factor contributing to poverty and recommended exporting the poor to underpopulated areas such as the colonies.

Karl Marx, writing in 1860s, also saw poverty a social problem, yet for him poverty was based on the exploitation of workers. Marx's economic analysis was not particularly new, as the idea that wealth and poverty were two sides of the same coin was implicit (and often explicit) in the previous 200 years of economic analysis, yet what Marx added was the indignation that this exploitation was unjust. For Marx, wealth and poverty were caused by private ownership of the means of production, and thus the way to reduce this income and wealth inequality was to socialize such property.

The problem of poverty ceased to be an important topic for economics after the marginal utility revolution in economic theory in the 1870s. By the end of the Industrial Revolution, economic science had moved away from social categories like the poor, with economists instead preferring to carry out their analyses in exclusively individualistic terms. Viewing poverty in these terms meant looking for the individual characteristics that caused someone to be poor, which meant blaming the poor for their poverty. This approach also meant that just as the poor have earned their poverty, the wealthy had earned their wealth. For economists, the issue of wealth and poverty ceased to be a social or ethical issue. When poverty was rediscovered in the 1880s, it was mostly by sociologists and other social scientists or economists outside of the mainstream tradition. Poverty had become a social or cultural condition but not an economic issue.

The Changing Reality of Wealth and Poverty

This change in the idea of wealth reflected the change in the reality of wealth. The Industrial Revolution fundamentally changed the nature of the economic problem. Before the Industrial Revolution, the main economic problem societies faced was how to produce enough goods and services to meet their needs. The increase in production caused by the application of science to production made meeting a society's basic needs a relatively easy task. Yet the economic value of the owners' productive assets that produce goods and services required scarcity; that is, demand being greater than supply. In order for these assets to maintain their value, scarcity had to be created. This was accomplished via efforts to increase demand beyond wants, thus conspicuous consumption became an important feature of the economy, coupled with efforts to reduce production though competition-reducing industrial combinations.

This was paralleled by a change in the conception and reality of poverty. The Industrial Revolution led to the individualization of poverty, just as it led to the individualization of wealth. Although the roots for the individualization of wealth and poverty can be found before the Industrial Revolution in the Reformation, it is the changes brought about during the Industrial Revolution, and partly as a result of the economic changes created by the Industrial Revolution, that allowed for the full flowering and acceptance of an individual-based perspective. Before the emergence of fully marketized societies, individual poverty was a rare phenomenon (Polanyi, 1944). If the community had enough, then the individual members of the community had enough. If one person was excluded from the economic life of the community it was because that person was not considered part of the community. Poverty was based on a lack of abundance; that is, production was insufficient to meet basic needs. What the Industrial Revolution created were wealthy societies with large populations of poor people. This was a new phenomenon.

The change in the conceptions of wealth and poverty corresponds with the seemingly contradictory rise in both wealth and poverty during the Industrial Revolution, especially through its earliest phases, 1800 to the 1840s. The Industrial Revolution in England saw both a dramatic increase in wealth and an increase in poverty. The increase in wealth, generated by a rise in profits, led to the prominence of profit income as the source of wealth. Before the Industrial Revolution, wealth was based mostly on ownership of land or on a person's social status, with commercial wealth becoming more important after the beginning of the seventeenth century. According to Gregory King's estimate, income from enterprise in 1688 accounted for under 15 percent of aggregate income. After the Industrial Revolution, wealth from industry and money came to dominate. This is seen in Leone Levi's estimate in 1884 that 51.4 percent of England's national income was in the form of profit and interest income (Hobson, 1905, p. 3).

The rise in poverty was due to a fall in real wages for workers, which also was a contributing factor in the rise in wealth. Increases in economic output, with falling wages and without the dramatic fall in prices that would later take place, meant that all the benefits of this rise in economic activity went to the propertied classes: landlords and capitalists. Contributing to the decline in real wages were economic and institutional factors. The late eighteenth and early nineteenth centuries saw a rapid increase in the supply of workers, due to increasing population, urbanization, and the increase in the number of women and children entering the manufacturing labor market. This oversupply of workers pushed wages down, whereas rising prices, caused by increases in population and by war, reduced the purchasing power of wages, thus causing a significant fall in real wages.

Changes in labor-market institutions further lowered the economic status of workers. In the late eighteenth century, so-called exchange entitlements were an important part of workers' income. These "entitlements came from employers, gleaning after harvest, foraging on commons and woods, Church, charity, poor law, friends, and neighbours" (Daunton, 1995, p. 423). Exchange entitlements were based on the idea that workers were partners in production, a more social view of property that goes back to the Middle Ages. Property rights became more exclusive (individualistic), and entitlements started to be viewed as embezzlement and theft.

In England, the standard of living for workers started to improve after the end of the Combination Act in 1824 (although a weaker version of it was passed the next year), the repeal of the Corn Laws in 1840s (which promoted a reduction in the cost of living), and after the passage of the Factory Acts, which were designed to improve working conditions and shorten the workday. The Combination Act was part of a series of laws and regulations designed to keep workers' wages low. As James Rogers notes in his classic *Six Centuries of Work and Wages* (1884), "For nearly five centuries law after law had been passed under which the workman's wages had been regulated, for the reputed advantages of their employers.... For more than two centuries the law was a complete failure. For nearly three ... it was a complete success. Now it was entirely natural for the workmen to believe that what they had gained [the repeal of the Combination Act] at last was a boon, since their employers had so long and so successfully deprived them of its use" (Rogers, 1884, p. 508). Although the complete legalization of unions in England did not occur until 1871, the new institutional environment helped promote the move from falling real wages to moderately rising real wages and eventually to rising standards of living.

Slow economic growth also contributed to the delay in the benefits of the Industrial Revolution trickling down to the working classes and the poor. Although many industries experienced dramatic expansion during the early phases, it is

TABLE 1   Economic Growth in Western Europe, 1000–1913 (Annual Average Compound Growth Rates)

	GDP	Per capita
1000–1500	0.30	0.13
1500–1829	0.41	0.15
1820–1870	1.65	0.95
1870–1913	2.10	1.32

Source: Maddison 1995, 126.

only after 1870 that we see the level of economic growth we typically associate with industrialization.

It was only in the second half of the nineteenth century that we see the high levels of investment in fixed capital and the increases in labor productivity that allow for significant increases in output and, coupled with institutional changes, the eventual rise in incomes and standards of living. Thus, the rise in wealth in the first part of the Industrial Revolution was partially a redistribution from the lower classes and partially due to increased economic output, whereas the increase in wealth in the later phases of the Industrial Revolution was due to increases in output, and both workers' and capitalists' incomes were generally increasing.

Conclusion

Changes in wealth and poverty, which is to say the economic status of the wealthy and the poor, always are due to a combination of economic and noneconomic factors. Economic outcomes are the result of tradition (the activities of past generations), command (dictates from a central authority, laws, and regulations), and markets (the interaction of the forces of supply and demand). Most of the debates on changes in standards of living and real wages during the Industrial Revolution concentrate exclusively on markets. Although market forces are often important, changes in social institutions (tradition) and laws and regulations (command) play a significant role in the economic status of the wealthy and the poor.

Of course, the level of economic output is an important determinant of the level of wealth and poverty: The larger the size of the economic pie, the more there is to go around for all. How the economic pie is distributed, however, is only partially determined by economic factors. More important are the social and political institutions that determine the rules of the game for how the economic pie is sliced. This was best noted by John Stuart Mill in 1848: "[T]he Distribution of wealth ... is a matter of human institutions solely.... [I]n the social state, in every state except total solitude, any [distribution] ... can only take place by the consent of society, or rather of those who dispose of its active forces.... The distribution of wealth, therefore, depends on the laws and customs of society. The rules by which it is determined are what the opinions and feelings of the ruling portion of the community make them, and are very different in different ages and countries; and might be still more different, if mankind so chooses" (Mill, 1987, p. 200–1).

The history of the effects of changing human institutions and attitudes on wealth and poverty starts well before the Industrial Revolution. Economic historian James Rogers (1884, p. 522) noted that for nearly three centuries, up until the reign of Henry VIII, "the condition of the English labourer was that of plenty and hope," yet within a century of his reign their status had fallen to "so low a level as to make the workman practically helpless, and that the lowest point was reached just about the outbreak of the great war between King and Parliament." Following the Restoration, the standard of living of workers gradually improved up until the middle of the eighteenth century ("though still far below the level of the fifteenth") when "it began to sink again, and the workman experienced the direst misery during the great continental war." This roller coaster of standards of living of workers was due to a combination of changes in social institutions and attitudes (many brought about by the Reformation) and economic factors. Of particular importance were the Elizabethan Poor Laws, which reflected a political idea of dividing the poor into deserving and nondeserving, a new theology of individualism and its reduced responsibility for helping the poor, and the theft of the Catholic Church's property and suppression of its institutions (monasteries, hospitals, and other poor-relief organizations) that existed for the benefit of the poor. State institutions to help the poor became more institutions of social control.

Although the rise of individualism and the decline in social responsibility for the poor can be traced back to the sixteenth century, it took the dramatic social and economic changes brought about by the Industrial Revolution to lead to the full development of the individualization of wealth and poverty, both in theory and in reality. The Industrial Revolution brought about not only machine production but also a market attitude that encouraged the replacing of traditional social institutions with market mechanisms. For workers, this is the reality of a market-determined wage. Improvements in the standard of living for the poor came about from a reaction to this individualization and the establishment of countervailing power for workers. Thus, real significant progress in standards of living and the status of the poor following the Industrial Revolution were mostly due to the development of the welfare state and trade unions, whereas partial credit is due to Keynesian demand management policies that kept the level of output high.

FURTHER READING: Alford, Helen, Charles M. A. Clark, Steve Cortright, and Michael Naughton, eds. *Rediscovering Abundance: Interdisciplinary Essays on Wealth, Income and Their Distribution in the Catholic Social Tradition.* South Bend, IN: University of Notre Dame Press, 2005; Bagehot, Walter. *Economic Studies.* London: Longmans, Green, 1880; Clark, John Bates. *The Philosophy of Wealth.* Boston: Ginn, 1888; Deane, Phyllis. *The First Industrial Revolution.* 2nd ed. Cambridge: Cambridge University Press, 1979; Daunton, Martin J. *Progress and Poverty: An Economic and Social History of Britain 1700–1850.* Oxford: Oxford University Press, 1995; Himmelfarb, Gertrude. *The Idea of Poverty: England in the Early Industrial Age.* New York: Vintage Books, 1985; Hobson, John. *Problems of Poverty.* London: Methuen, 1905; Maddison, Angus. *Monitoring the World Economy, 1820–1992.* Paris: Organization for Economic Co-operation and Development, 1995; Malthus, Thomas Robert. *An Essay on the Principles of Population, as It Affects the Future Improvement of Society with Remarks on the Speculations of Mr. Godwin, M. Condorcet, and Other Writers.* London: J. Johnson, 1798; Menger, Carl. *Principles of Economics.* Trans. James Dingwall and Bert F.

Hoselitz. New York: New York University Press, [1871] 1976; Mill, John Stuart. *Principles of Political Economy.* [1848] 1987; Polanyi, Karl. *The Great Transformation,* Boston: Beacon Press, 1944; Ricardo, David. *On the Principles of Political Economy and Taxation.* London: John Murray, 1817; Robbins, Lionel. *An Essay on the Nature and Significance of Economic Science.* London: Macmillan, 1932; Rogers, James E. T. *Six Centuries of Work and Wages.* New York: G. P. Putnam's Sons, 1884; Smith, Adam. *An Enquiry into the Nature and Causes of the Wealth of Nations.* Oxford: Oxford University Press, [1776] 1976; Walras, Léon. *Elements of Pure Economics.* New York: Augustus M. Kelly, 1954.

CHARLES M. A. CLARK

Wedgwood, Josiah (1730–1795)

Josiah Wedgwood was born into a family of British potters that had been potters since the seventeenth century. He continued this tradition but added an innovative and inventive attitude to the design and manufacture of pottery. Wedgwood also was known as a political reformer.

Early experience as a potter was interrupted by smallpox, which prevented him from physically working as a potter, and led him to focus on research and experimentation rather than actual practical work. After business partnerships with other potters, he opened his own works where he produced both decorative wares and durable domestic pottery, which found a ready market in the growing middle classes of the time. This domestic pottery was called Queens Ware, after Queen Charlotte appointed Wedgwood as Queen's Potter to provide dinnerware for the royal household in 1762. (Other royal patrons included Empress Catherine II of Russia, who bought a 925-piece service.)

Wedgwood's decorative items included stoneware in various colors that were produced by adding different metal oxides, a result of his experiments. He invented the pyrometer to measure the high temperatures in the firing ovens and was elected a fellow of the Royal Society in 1783; he also was an active member of the Lunar Society, another scientific society of the period, which operated in the Midlands. (It was called that because members met every month when the moon was full; a necessity before adequate street lighting was available.) Wedgwood's new factory was called Etruria, and it incorporated many innovations in pottery making, still a technologically backward, craft-based industry at the time. He applied the division of labor by having workers specialize in one of the four main aspects of the potter's tasks—mixing, shaping, firing, and glazing—and it was the first pottery to install a steam engine in 1782. As an enlightened employer, he also provided decent housing for his workers.

Wedgwood also saw the importance of transportation to modern enterprises, especially breakables such as pottery, and was one of the backers of the Trent and Mersey Canal, completed in 1777. This canal reduced the cost of transporting clay to Etruria and finished goods to Liverpool for export.

As a political reformer, he favored annual parliaments and universal male suffrage. He also helped found the Society for the Abolition of the Slave Trade in 1781, and the reproduction of the society's seal became a fashion item. Wedgwood died in 1795.

FURTHER READING: Kelly, Alison. *The Story of Wedgwood,* London: Faber & Faber, 1975; Mankowitz, Wolf. *Wedgwood.* London: Batsford, 1953; Meteyard, Eliza. *The Life of Josiah Wedgwood.* London: Hurst & Blackett, 1865. Reprinted 1970.

CHRISTINE RIDER

Working-Class Protest Movements

Periods of social upheaval in human history, if not caused by warfare or external aggression, often are the result of political change lagging behind economic change. In Britain in the late eighteenth and early nineteenth centuries, remarkable economic changes were occurring as a result of the Industrial Revolution, including industrialization, **urbanization,** and economic relationships. The political structure remained relatively unchanged, however, reflecting the agrarian past of the country. Hence it is hardly surprising that the imbalance between the economy and the polity should lead to the growth of new political movements and demands for a greater share in the country's governance by the disenfranchised.

The Peterloo Massacre in 1819 was one of the most violent incidents in this struggle for workers' rights during a period when all preconceived notions of employment and individual rights were being turned upside down by the changes induced by the Industrial Revolution. The struggle for suffrage independent of property ownership in Great Britain was neither easy nor a short-term effort. At the beginning of the nineteenth century, the right to vote was limited and overwhelmingly controlled by the landed aristocracy. The rise of a manufacturing-based capitalist class, with limited access to the traditional political establishment, and the growth of an industrial working class meant that the majority of the population in Britain was disenfranchised. As such, they had no formal mechanism by which to pursue their economic and political goals and their rights as Englishmen.

In these circumstances, antipathy arose between the landed aristocracy and the burgeoning industrial capitalist and middle classes and between the working classes and the landed aristocracy and capitalists. This situation generated political support and sympathy between the disenfranchised classes that otherwise shared little in terms of their political and economic needs and objectives. The creation of cross-class movements arose to ensure the extension of the franchise as a means of furthering political and economic agendas.

As the size of the industrial working class grew, however, the interests of the workers and the capitalists became more and more divergent. Some workers began to form associations with other workers in the same trade to bargain for higher wages and benefits, although it was the skilled craftsmen who set up most of the lasting associations of working-class men during the period of 1750–1850. Workers united for several reasons: to protect themselves from exploitation, to maintain their living standards and distinctiveness, to attempt to increase their wages, and to provide a fund for unemployment and sickness benefits. Unfortunately, the unskilled workforce had very little to bargain with in the attempt to gain higher wages; for the most part, they were illiterate and did not earn high enough wages to set aside funds to protect themselves from the ravages of unemployment or sickness. They also lacked political representation to push for legislative solutions. The high prices accompanying the Napoleonic Wars and the resulting trade embargo caused severe distress for the working class; as early as 1795, Norfolk laborers agreed to organize a petition drive for higher wages. The embryonic workers' movement situated in the Corresponding Societies, however, was crushed by the Corresponding Societies Act of 1799 that made national associations with related branches illegal and by the **Combination Acts** (1800) outlawing all trade-union organizations. These laws provided for summary trial and conviction of workers threatening any form of collective action. They were used primarily against unskilled workers, leaving them unable to strike for higher wages as such action was now defined as a subversive act. Although the Correspondence Societies of the skilled workers were now formally illegal and could not bargain for higher wages or better conditions, they still were able to provide their members with unemployment insurance and sickness benefits.

Given that the unskilled members of the workforce were unable to set up lasting trade societies, they had little protection against unemployment and sickness. This made them vulnerable to changes in the prices of the items necessary for daily living and to the whims of the market in terms of their level of wages. The introduction of machinery leading to the loss of some types of labor, no limits to the length of the working day, and the lower levels of wages offered to unskilled workers became the focus of the ire of the working class. Working-class response was of a spontaneous nature and did not rely on coordinated action and tactics. Their primary response to an overly exploitative capitalist was called the *collective bargaining riot*. These machine-breaking riots were a familiar feature of the early stages of the Industrial Revolution and were directed not only at the machines replacing them in production but also at all of the property of the capitalists, such as raw materials, finished commodities, and buildings. A sustained form of this illegal action, Luddism, was active primarily in the period from 1811 to 1813. The eighteenth and early nineteenth centuries were punctuated by riots brought about by rising prices of wage goods, tolls, new machinery, enclosures, press gangs, and so forth. Riots occurred as early as the 1760s and 1770 (e.g., Wilkes Agitation) and continued in the Gordon Riots (1780) and the mobbing of the king (1795 and 1820).

Repression

Primarily under the control of the landed aristocracy, the government attempted to destroy this burgeoning working-class movement. From 1760 to 1810, the number of offences punishable by death increased by 63 and included petty theft, destroying machinery, breaking down fences when commons were enclosed, and the destruction of commodities. One in every three sentenced to death for these crimes actually was executed; most of those executed were for so-called economic crimes. Those whose execution was commuted were transported to Australia and the other prison colonies of Britain. Because there was not a police force at the time, the military often were called in to break up these riots. Results varied, however, when the presence of the military was requested. Independently of the mob, the military often created its own destruction, and an attack on the riot by the military had serious political ramifications.

It is essential to note that these riots were spontaneous in nature, and participants were not members of organizations that had goals and strategies; these people were responding to their situation with the only weapon they had available. These riots were not part of a sustained movement as a tactic used for a common end. The working classes did not have an ideology around which to unite, just their dissatisfaction with their situation, and they had no acceptable form of release for their anger. Champions of the working class at the time included Henry Hunt and William Cobbett; however, they did not have a sufficient understanding of the economic system or the organizational skills to unite these disparate people.

The rise in spontaneous working-class activity provoked additional measures, and the rights of habeas corpus were suspended in 1794, enabling imprisonment without judicial orders and detention without charges. Many strikes occurred in the early years of the nineteenth century in the textile districts, followed by trials of participants because of the illegality of strikes under the Combination Acts and a wave of repression against workers. Textile workers became convinced that strikes were futile without political change requiring parliamentary representation. This led to the issue of parliamentary reform; demonstrations and meetings pressuring for reform were held throughout industrial districts.

One of these meetings was in Manchester in 1819 and resulted in the Peterloo Massacre. Following a charge by the military in an attempt to arrest Henry Hunt at a peaceable political demonstration, 11 people were killed and hundreds injured. This massacre at Peterloo led to further demonstrations, severe criticism against those directly and indirectly responsible, and resulted in divisions among the landed aristocracy. The authorities' response to the unrest on the part of the working, middle, and capitalist classes led to the enactment of what is known as the Six Acts, which were intended to restrict public meetings and demonstrations. The acts enabled judges to pass more severe penalties, strengthened libel and sedition laws, allowed magistrates to search houses and confiscate weapons, restricted the right of public meeting, and imposed a stamp tax designed to prevent people from reading newspapers published by the radicals, such as the *Gorgon*, the *Black Dwarf*, and Cobbett's *Register*, by increasing their prices.

With the support of working-class leaders and movements, the industrial capitalists and middle classes obtained the franchise—provided they met the property qualifications—with the Reform Act of 1832. This reform, however, did nothing to ensure the franchise for those without property, like the working classes. In fact, the manner in which the reform was structured led to the loss of the limited representation that the working class had in agricultural districts. The organization of workers into movements, such as the cooperative movement or the National Union of the Working Classes, did not develop seriously until the 1820s and 1830s. Attempts to organize trade unions for unskilled workers did not begin until after the repeal of the Combination Acts in 1824. The organization of workers into a general political movement for parliamentary democratization did not come until the Chartist period (1838–1848). Universal male suffrage independent of property qualifications in Britain was not achieved until 1918, and universal suffrage was finally enacted in 1928 when women gained the right to vote.

The Peterloo Massacre did not directly influence the Industrial Revolution, but it could be seen as one of the worst outcomes of the changes in society brought about by it. Given the reaction to an armed attack upon a peaceful demonstration of workers merely demanding the right to vote led to some reticence on the part of the political authorities (local and national) to violently attack peaceful demonstrations, however, and such force was only rarely applied in future years. As the century wore on, better organizations to serve the interests of the working classes appeared, and more institutions to promote the spread of democratic ideas and practices began to be developed. Thus it became easier to express public opposition, which obviously affected the nature of public discourse.

FURTHER READING: Cole, G.D.H. *A Short History of the British Working Class Movement 1789–1848.* Vol. 1. London: George Allen and Unwin and Labour Publishing, 1927; Halevy, Elie. *A History of the English People in the Nineteenth Century: England in 1815.* Vol. 1. London: Ernest

Benn, 1960; Thompson, E. P. *The Making of the English Working Class.* New York: Vintage, 1966.

SUSAN PASHKOFF

World War I (1914–1918)

Economic warfare was of the utmost importance during World War I, the first modern, or total, war. The ability of each belligerent to disrupt the enemy's economy became as crucial for victory as success on the battlefield. When quick victory proved illusory in fall 1914, the strategies of economic warfare on both sides became more elaborate and brutal.

Due to a common view, politicians and generals in Europe shared short-war illusions prior to 1914. But popular conceptions in summer 1914 should not be mistaken for expert opinion. Many generals believed that the next war between the European Great Powers would be long, exhausting, and even indecisive. Modern weapons would bring the battle lines to a stalemate by making massed infantry attacks deadly for the attacker. The adoption of general conscription among the leading European states (with the exception of Britain) created abundant reserves on which a long war could feed. Third, the division of Europe into two hostile alliance systems meant that even a victory over one power would not itself end the war.

Therefore, the economic strength of the two alliance blocs, the Central Powers (mainly Germany, Austria-Hungary, and Turkey) and the Allies (Britain, France, Russia, and later the United States and Italy), became as important as their military power in pursuing victory. Economic warfare involved the strategic goal of disrupting the enemy's economy and severing its financial strength. By doing this, the enemy's ability to conduct military operations was impaired. Reducing supplies of all kinds that reached enemy forces became integral to the strategies of the two coalitions. The goal was to starve enemy populations and enfeeble their industrial production. Material privation could foster domestic pressures on enemy governments and weaken their internal cohesion. Contrary to expectations of a future war of attrition, economic preparations for war, necessary for extended fighting, received little consideration before the war. Only by the end of 1914, after five months of fighting and after hopes for a quick victory had vanished, did civilian and military leaders begin to plan for a lengthy struggle. The war had begun as a clash of twentieth-century technology with nineteenth-century military tactics. Both alliances developed very different strategies due to their different endowment with human and matériel resources. Britain, France, and Russia had a combined national income 60 percent greater than that of the Central Powers.

From the very start of the war, Britain, using her naval superiority, tried to interrupt Germany's maritime trade. Germany reacted with an attempt to maintain or even increase her trade with neighboring neutral countries, especially Holland and the Scandinavian states. Allied diplomatic and economic efforts, however, forced the neutrals to curtail their trade with the Central Powers, but the exchange of goods never vanished completely. Germany and Austria-Hungary increasingly were denied imports of agrarian products, raw materials, and machinery. Much more than naval strength was vital to the blockade's effectiveness. The government in London, the center of Allied blockade policy, refined the legal basis of the blockade through broad contraband lists of nontradable items, ensuring the completeness of interdiction. All these measures did little to impair the fighting efficiency of the German army (although the picture is somewhat different with the Austrian armed forces). Some of the explanation was due to the fact that Germany and Austria-Hungary consisted of one continuous geographic area, facilitating the movement of goods and matériel, and making the area much less dependent on imports, as Britain was. The blockade did have far-reaching social, psychological, and political impacts on the Central Powers, however; for example, prices inflated because of scarcities, which caused numerous food riots after 1916.

The most important component of the Central Powers' conduct of economic warfare was to ensure adequate food and raw material supplies. The wealth of conquered territories like Belgium and Romania supplemented Germany's and Austria-Hungary's own resources. Germany, the dominant power (as the Hapsburg monarchy played only an insignificant role in influencing strategy), was anxious to disrupt the enemy economies, especially Britain's. Besides maintaining trade across the Atlantic, the Allies also had to ensure adequate supplies for Russia, thus permitting the czar to maintain his armies against the Central Powers on the Eastern Front. German submarines were the most important means to cut off Allied maritime supply routes, and submarines were quickly recognized as a real, frightening weapon of war. In 1914, German submarines had sunk both military and merchant ships, but following the May 7, 1915, sinking of the liner *Lusitania*, and President Woodrow Wilson's protests to Germany on the resulting loss of U.S. lives, Germany promised to leave passenger ships alone, fearing U.S. entry into the war on the side of the Allies. By late 1916, however, when it seemed as though Germany was winning and hoping to defeat the Allies before the United States could enter the war, unrestricted U-boat warfare commenced again in February 1917. The subsequent entry of the United States into the war strengthened the Allies' resources. Initially, U.S. policy concerning the belligerents' economic warfare had been based on the demand for freedom of the seas. Even before entry, however, U.S. supplies and loans had flowed to Britain and France, with a large portion of this aid transferred to Russia. From Germany's perspective, the United States, although nominally neutral until April 1917, acted like a covert belligerent. The U.S. economy profited from allied orders and had become dependent on the war itself and on an ultimate Allied victory; taking into account enormous Allied debts to U.S. creditors, the United States could not afford to countenance an Allied defeat.

War Economy and New Technologies

The first major crisis of the war was one of production: shell shortages were widespread among all armies by winter 1914–1915 because the rate of fire exceeded the rate of production. The pressure to overcome this shortage required a fundamental reorientation of industrial production from peacetime to wartime conditions. Three specific areas received the highest priority: raw materials, labor, and the availability of plant. As early as August 1914, Germany established a raw-materials office for the centralized allocation of raw materials. Though the office remained under the guidance of the War Ministry, Germany, like all the other industrially advanced belligerents, relied on businessmen to staff the various war agencies. Even Russia, with its underdeveloped industry, created a central war-industries committee, and by 1916 the economy had grown more than 20 percent over 1913. The reverse happened in Austria-Hungary, where the state's supervisory apparatus was fragmented

The French Nieuport fighter plane. Dan Patterson.

by internal disputes. Production indexes fell dramatically in 1917 and collapsed in 1918. For Britain, with her maritime links intact, shortages of raw materials were of much less importance, but even there, a Ministry of Munitions was set up in June 1915.

Industry needed to replace the workers called up by the military. All belligerent governments were faced with the problem of labor shortages, and all were determined to curb the power of the trade unions, particularly with respect to the right to strike. France and other countries established the notion of military workers: men released from the military for work in war production. The use of unskilled labor in automated processes also was some compensation for the loss of skilled workers to the military. With the absence of men in military service, women were forced into the workforce in unprecedented numbers.

The third problem, the lack of plant, resulted from the inability of peacetime economies to sustain the level of plant that wartime orders demanded. Businessmen also were hesitant to make large investments in new plant, fearing excessive capacity at the war's end. Thus, it was the task of the newly erected war production agencies to increase the output of those arms manufacturers already in existence. The production of simple weaponry was entrusted to businesses with no background in arms production. Oddly, even trench warfare helped because it promoted the old technologies of siege warfare, none of them sophisticated. Production procedures were simplified, even if the consequence was a decline in quality. For example, during the battle of the Somme in 1916, 30 percent of the shells fired by British guns proved to be duds. Not until after that year would the defects inherent in the rapid expansion of production be overcome.

When production figures for standard military weapons had increased sufficiently, the major belligerents attempted to overcome the stalemate of trench warfare by using new technologies, the aim being to complement, or even to substitute for, manpower. One example was Britain's development of the tank, which returned mechanized warfare to the battlefield. Although the tank was intended to help provide machine gun or heavy weapon support for advancing troops, the first ones in the field were slow, underpowered, and mechanically unreliable, and senior commanders were extremely skeptical about their use. Development on them continued, however, and by summer 1917 this experiment finally proved its worth as protection against enemy weapons.

Light automatic weapons also were introduced, combining the firepower of the machine gun with the portability of the rifle. In 1914, two machine guns per battalion were standard across all armies; in summer 1918, each British battalion carried 30 light machine guns, 8 light trench mortars, and 16 rifle grenades. Other developments included the production of sophisticated heavy artillery, as well as chemical warfare using poison gas, and aerial bombardment. Uses of **aviation** included reconnaissance and close air support. Aircraft for strategic bombing were created by the Germans and the British, although the former used zeppelins (a type of dirigible) to this end as well. By the end of 1917, the major armies had modernized significantly and were making use of such technology as wireless communication, armored cars, tanks, and tactical aircraft. The infantry was reorganized so that 100-man companies were no longer the main unit of maneuver, in favor of the squad of 10 or so men.

The implementation of these new methods of warfare depended partly on the release of skilled workers from the military. The predominant issue in resource mobilization was to get the right balance between manpower and machinery: If new weapons could substitute for soldiers, labor could be released from the military to produce more of those munitions. Industrialized war demanded a policy that was comprehensive in its acknowledgment of the needs of the military, industry, and labor. All belligerents curtailed their civilian production in favor of the armament industries, thereby neglecting private consumption, one of the most important sources of civilian morale in the hinterland.

In Germany, the war industries increased the number of their workers by 44 percent during the war years, whereas the figure fell by 40 percent for the peacetime branch of the economy. The Allies with their enormous resources, however, succeeded in coordinating the purchase, distribution, and transport of foodstuffs and goods between themselves and their colonies. The needs of the military, business, and workers were interlinked and indivisible; if one sector failed or showed shortcomings, the other sectors were affected. Thus, the raw-material shortages among the Central Powers had far-reaching consequences, most evident in transportation. Coal production in Germany and Austria-Hungary fell in 1917–1918, partly for lack of labor and partly because of sustained underinvestment in rolling stock and rail track. The expansion of territory through conquest and the denial of maritime transport increased the burden the railways had to bear. Toward the end of the war, the insufficient production of coal only could be partly transported: The movement of coal depended on the railways, but they themselves were consuming the coal that was needed. Literally speaking, the Central Powers' war machine had come to a halt.

Economic Policy and Results of the War

Between 1914 and 1918, gross domestic product (GDP) increased for Britain, Italy, and the United States but decreased in France and Russia and in the main Central Powers. The decline in GDP in Austria-Hungary, Russia, France, and the Ottoman Empire reached between 30 percent to 40 percent. The Index of Industrial Production in Germany fell from 100 (1913 = 100) to only 57 in 1918. The only parts of all the economies that profited from the war were those that inaugurated new production methods and new products and that enlarged investment.

All nations saw the government's share of GDP increase, surpassing 70 percent in Germany (it was 17 percent in 1910) and reaching 48 percent in Britain (compared with 13 percent in 1910). One of the most dramatic effects was the expansion of governmental powers and responsibilities in Britain, France, and the United States, where in order to harness all the power of their societies new government ministries were created, new taxes levied, and laws enacted, all designed to bolster the war effort. To pay for purchases in the United States, Britain and France borrowed heavily on Wall Street. The war also strained the abilities of the formerly large and bureaucratized governments in Austria-Hungary and Germany, but here, however, these long-term effects were clouded by these countries' defeat. Germany spent the most money to conduct the war, $47 billion, Britain spent $44 billion, the United States spent $36 billion, France spent $28 billion, Russia spent $16 billion, and Austria-Hungary spent $13 billion.

World War I is perhaps the prime example of the wastefulness of war. Although one can point to individual examples of bravery or to impressive new technologies—such as the airplane—that would have a positive impact on future lives, wars are costly. The cost in lost manpower was tremendous, which would have an impact on postwar economic recovery and on the future of countries such as France. Out of a total in all countries of more than 67 million mobilized for the war effort, more than 8.5 million lost their lives, a further 21 million were wounded, and nearly 8 million were missing. Although some states went to war to try to maintain their power, this war was not the answer. The Russian Empire was reborn as the beginning of the Communist experiment in statehood. The Austro-Hungarian and the Ottoman Empires were divided, and the German Empire collapsed. Even the peace treaties, signed at Paris in 1919, were less the closing point of the war than a preliminary to a new one.

FURTHER READING: Broadberry, Stephen, and Mark Harrison, eds. *The Economics of World War I*. Cambridge: Cambridge University Press, 2005; Burk, Kathleen. *Britain, America and the Sinews of War, 1914–1918*. London: Allen & Unwin, 1988; Burk, Kathleen, ed. *War and the State: The Transformation of British Government 1914–1919*. London: Allen & Unwin, 1982; Feldman, Gerald D. *Army, Industry, and Labor in Germany 1914–1918*. Princeton, NJ: Princeton University Press, 1966; Godfrey, John F. *Capitalism at War: Industrial Policy and Bureaucracy in France, 1914–1918*. New York: Berg, 1987; Osborne, Eric. *Britain's Economic Blockade of Germany, 1914–1919*. London: Frank Cass, 2004; Siegelbaum, Lewis H. *The Politics of Industrial Mobilization in Russia, 1914–1917*. New York: St. Martin's Press, 1983.

MARTIN MOLL

Z

Zaibatsu

Japanese for "money/financial clique," the *zaibatsu* were the great industrial houses that dominated the Japanese economy after the **Meiji Restoration** (1868) until their official dissolution following World War II. Although functionally similar to Western industrial/financial trusts, the *zaibatsu* usually were tightly controlled by a single-family group and not publicly held firms. All *zaibatsu* owned a bank and a myriad of other industrial concerns, such as airplane and automobile manufacturing, breweries, chemicals, textile mills, trading companies, and so on.

A house bank allowed the *zaibatsu* access to cheap loans and working capital for their operations and so helped them overcome the shortage of finance capital that slows economic growth in poor countries with underdeveloped banking systems. Because many *zaibatsu*s were vertically integrated, most aspects of the production process, from raw material supply to marketing, were conducted within the firm. This ensured them of assured supplies and stable sales/marketing relationships. In addition, the diversified nature of *zaibatsu* enterprises allowed them to benefit from growth in dynamic—and weather downturns in slow—sectors of the economy. Their close ties with the Japanese government effectively suppressed labor unions, thereby ensuring a cheap and compliant labor force. The *zaibatsu* were thus able to reduce the high level of market uncertainty found in most developing economies and contribute to Japan's overall rapid economic progress and development.

Although *zaibatsu* usually are thought of as a post-Meiji creation, when the Japanese government was encouraging giant oligopolies as a route to rapid economic development, some long predate it. For example, of the four great *zaibatsu*—Mitsui, Mitsubishi, Sumitomo, and Yasuda—that effectively controlled the Japanese economy in the 1930s, Mitsui and Sumitomo both were founded in the seventeenth century. In addition to these four, more than a dozen smaller *zaibatsu* also existed, including Kawasaki, Nakajima, Nissan, and Suzuki, that were important in Japan's continued economic growth and industrial development.

Their close ties with the Japanese government meant that the *zaibatsu* were instrumental in the often brutal Japanese exploitation of its colonies, Taiwan and Korea, and played a significant role in the decision to occupy Chinese Manchuria for its mineral resources. Following the Japanese defeat in World War II, the Allied Occupation Authority proceeded to reshape Japan economically, politically, and socially, and among its reforms was the formal dissolution of the *zaibatsu* in 1946. The start of the U.S.-Soviet Cold War, however, convinced U.S. policy makers that an economically prosperous Japan was needed to counter the perceived Communist threat. The *zaibatsu* were allowed to reform themselves as *keiretsu* (consortium), a group of companies usually loosely centered around a bank and with cross-shareholding and interconnected directorships.

During the heyday of the *zaibatsu*, 1867–1945, the Japanese economy grew rapidly in size, technical sophistication, and output composition, shifting from a predominantly agricultural to a manufacturing economy. Although it still lagged behind its main Western competitors, Japan was clearly becoming a world industrial power. The *zaibatsu* were key in the start of this transition and their successor *keiretsu* finished it. *See also* Japan, Industrial revolution in; Meiji Restoration.

FURTHER READING: Okita, Saburo. *Zaibatsu: The Rise and Fall of Family Enterprise Groups in Japan*. Tokyo: University of Tokyo Press, 1992; Tatsuno, Sheridan. *Created in Japan: From Imitators to World Class Innovators*. New York: HarperCollins, 1991.

FEISAL KHAN

PRIMARY DOCUMENTS

1. Excerpts from Sir Isaac Newton's *Mathematical Principles of Natural Philosophy* (Great Britain, 1687)

The scientific revolution of the seventeenth century encouraged a greater curiosity about the natural world than had occurred before in Europe. The rise of science, practical investigation, and an emphasis on rationalism does much to explain the flowering of scientific advances and technological discoveries that helped advance the Industrial Revolution. Isaac Newton (1642–1727) was the English scientist who perhaps more than any one else influenced the progress of science for the next two centuries. Newton himself developed the fundamentals of calculus, the principles of gravitation, and synthesized earlier work in astrophysics by Johannes Kepler and Galileo Galilei on planetary motion with activity on the surface of the earth.

Previously, submission to religious authority had prevented significant investigation of the natural world and the laws of nature; once scientists (experimental philosophers) were free to uncover these laws, science flourished. Newton's interests ranged widely—astronomy, hydrodynamics, optics, mathematics, kinetics—and probably his greatest achievement was to provide principles that resulted in the development of the scientific method, which could be applied not only to physics but also to economics, political science, history, psychology, and other areas of intellectual life. (The scientific method, in brief, refers to the process by which a phenomenon is observed then a theory is developed that can be tested by further observation and experimentation by others to check the validity of the theory.)

What also helped the advance of science at this time was the development of many new instruments that made accurate measurement possible or that led to new types of experimentation. Some examples include improvements in the telescope and the microscope, the barometer, the air pump, the mercury thermometer, and the Leyden jar. The following excerpt from Newton's work illustrates several principles: cause and effect, that gravitation affects all heavenly bodies, and the importance of rejecting unsubstantiated conjecture.

NEWTON'S RULES OF REASONING IN PHILOSOPHY

Rule I

We are to admit no more causes of natural things than such as are both true and sufficient to explain their appearances.

To this purpose the philosophers say that Nature does nothing in vain, and more is in vain when less will serve; for Nature is pleased with simplicity, and affects not the pomp of superfluous causes.

Rule II

Therefore to the same natural effects we must, as far as possible, assign the same causes.

As respiration in a man and in a beast; the descent of stones in Europe and in America; the light of our culinary fire and of the sun; the reflection of light on the earth, and in the planets.

Rule III

The qualities of bodies, which admit neither intension nor remission of degrees, and which are found to belong to all bodies within the reach of our experiments, are to be esteemed the universal qualities of all bodies whatsoever.

For since the qualities of bodies are only known to us by experiments, we are to hold for universal all such as universally agree with experiments, and such as are not liable to diminution can never be quite taken away. We are certainly not to relinquish the evidence of experiments for the sake of dreams and vain fictions of our own devising; nor are we to recede from the analogy of Nature, which uses to be simple, and always consonant to itself. We no other way know the extension of bodies than by our senses, nor do these reach it in all bodies; but because we perceive extension in all that are sensible, therefore we ascribe it universally to all others also. That abundance of bodies are hard, we learn by experience; and because the hardness of the whole arises from the hardness of the parts, we therefore justly infer the hardness of the undivided particles not only of the bodies we feel but of all others. That all bodies are impenetrable, we gather not from reason, but from sensation. The bodies which we handle we find impenetrable, and thence conclude impenetrability to be an universal property of all bodies whatsoever. That all bodies are moveable, and endowed with certain powers (which we call the vires inertiae) of persevering in their motion, or in their rest, we only infer the like properties observed in the bodies which we have seen. The extension, hardness, impenetrability, mobility, and vires inertiae of the whole, result from the extension, hardness, impenetrability, mobility and vires inertiae of the parts; and thence we conclude the least particles of all bodies to be also all extended, and hard, and impenetrable, and moveable, and endowed with their proper vires inertiae. And this is the foundation of all philosophy. Moreover, that the divided but contiguous particles of bodies may be separated from one another, is a matter of observation; and, in the particles that remain undivided, our minds are able to distinguish yet lesser parts, as is mathematically demonstrated. But whether the parts so distinguished, and not yet divided, may, by the powers of Nature, be actually divided and separated from one another, we cannot certainly determine. Yet, had we the proof of but one experiment that any undivided particles, in breaking a hard and solid body, suffered a division, we might by virtue of this rule conclude that the undivided particles may be divided and actually separated to infinity.

Lastly, if it universally appears, by experiments and astronomical observations, that all bodies about the earth gravitate towards the earth, and that in proportion of the quantity of matter which they severally contain; that the moon likewise, according to the quantity of its matter, gravitates towards the earth; that, on the other hand, our sea gravitates towards the earth; that, on the other hand, our sea gravitates towards the moon; and all the planets mutually one towards another; and the comets in like manner towards the sun; we must, in consequence of this rule, universally allow that all bodies whatsoever are endowed with a principle of mutual gravitation. For the argument from the appearances concludes with more force for the universal gravitation of all bodies than for their impenetrability; of which, among those in the celestial regions, we have no experiments, nor any manner of observation. Not that I affirm gravity to be essential to bodies: by their vis infita I mean nothing but their vis inertiae. This is immutable. Their gravity is diminished as they recede from the earth.

Rule IV

In experimental philosophy we are to look upon propositions collected by general induction from phaenomena as accurately or very nearly true, notwithstanding any contrary hypotheses that may be imagined, till such time as other phaenomena occur, by which they may either be made more accurate, or liable to exceptions.

This rule must follow, that the argument of induction may not be evaded by hypotheses.

Source: Isaac Newton, *The Mathematical Principles of Natural Philosophy*, 2 vols. (London, 1803), vol. 2, 160–62.

2. Excerpts from *The Wealth of Nations* by Adam Smith (Great Britain, 1776)

Adam Smith wrote *The Wealth of Nations* (published in 1776 and revised in 1784) as an effort to explore why some nations are wealthy and others not. In contrast to the prevailing idea of the mercantilists, who believed that treasure (in the form of gold and silver) was wealth, Smith redefined wealth as what we would now refer to as gross domestic product, the annual output of a nation. The most important factor in creating this wealth was labor because labor had the ability to create more wealth than was required for its upkeep. This wealth-creating potential was assisted by machinery (capital) and by the division of labor. Because of the time at which Smith wrote, he spent more time focusing on the ability of the division of labor to produce more output than on the contribution of mechanization. Smith also opposed mercantilist restrictions on trade that hindered the ability of a nation to sell abroad what it was able to produce more cheaply than its trading partners and acquire from them what could not easily be made at home. The introduction discusses wealth and how it is created.

The annual labour of every nation is the fund which originally supplies it with all the necessaries and conveniences of life which it annually consumes, and which consist always either in the immediate produce of that labour, or in what is purchased with that produce from other nations.

According therefore, as this produce, or what is purchased with it, bears a greater or smaller proportion to the number of those who are to consume it, the nation will be better or worse supplied with all the necessaries and conveniences for which it has occasion.

But this proportion must in every nation be regulated by two different circumstances; first, by the skill, dexterity, and judgment with which its labour is generally applied; and, secondly, by the proportion between the number of those who are employed in useful labour, and that of those who are not so employed. Whatever be the soil, climate, or extent of territory of any particular nation, the abundance or scantiness of its annual supply must, in that particular situation, depend upon those two circumstances.

The abundance or scantiness of this supply too seems to depend more upon the former of those two circumstances than upon the latter (xxiii–xxiv).

Smith departs from the mercantilist idea of wealth as the value of treasure—gold and silver—to the more modern idea of wealth as the amount of goods a nation can produce.

This change will have implications for policy: Instead of simply accumulating bullion, or exploiting colonial possessions for their bullion, and trying to prevent its export, policy should be directed to encouraging trade by encouraging the production of exportable goods.

The greater part of the writers who have collected the money prices of things in ancient times, seem to have considered the low money price of corn, and of goods in general, or, in other words, the high value of gold and silver, as a proof, not only of the scarcity of those metals, but of the poverty and barbarism of the country…. This notion is connected with the system of political œconomy which represents national wealth as consisting in the abundance, and national poverty in the scarcity, of gold and silver; … the high value of the precious metals can be no proof of the poverty or barbarism of any particular country…. It is a proof only of the barrenness of the mines which happened at that time to supply the commercial world…. In China, a country much richer than any part of Europe, the value of the precious metals is much higher than in any part of Europe. As the wealth of Europe, indeed, has increased greatly since the discovery of the mines of America, so the value of gold and silver has gradually diminished. This diminution of their value, however, has not been owing to the increase of the real wealth of Europe, of the annual produce of its land and labour, but to the accidental discovery of more abundant mines than any that were known before. The increase of the quantity of gold and silver in Europe, and the increase of its manufactures and agriculture, are two events which, though they have happened nearly about the same time, yet have arisen from very different causes, and have scarce any natural connection with one another. The one has arisen from a mere accident.... The other from the fall of the feudal system, and from the establishment of a government which afforded to industry the only encouragement which it requires, some tolerable security that it shall enjoy the fruits of its own labour (273–74).

In chapter 1, he expands at length on the division of labor to show how much more productive workers can be when they specialize in particular tasks rather than making the entire product from start to finish. This exposition uses the famous example of the pin factory to make the point.

The greatest improvement in the productive powers of labour, and the greater part of the skill, dexterity, and judgment with which it is any where directed, or applied, seem to have been the effects of the division of labour.

The effects of the division of labour, in the general business of society, will be more easily understood, by considering in what manner it operates in some particular manufactures. It is commonly supposed to be carried furthest in some very trifling ones; not perhaps that it really is carried further in them than in others of more importance: but in those trifling manufactures which are destined to supply the small wants of but a small number of people, the whole number of workmen must necessarily be small; and those employed in every different branch of the work can often be collected into the same workhouse, and placed at once under the view of the spectator. In those great manufactures, on the contrary, which are destined to supply the great wants of a great body of the people, every different branch of the work employs so great a number of workmen, that it is impossible to collect them all into the same workhouse. We can seldom see more, at one time, than those employed in one single branch. Though in such manufactures, therefore, the work may really be divided into a much greater number of parts, than in those of a more trifling nature, the division is not near so obvious, and has accordingly been much less observed.

To take an example, therefore, from a very trifling manufacture; but one in which the division of labour has been very often taken notice of, the trade of the pin-maker; a workman not educated to this business (which the division of labour has rendered a distinct trade), nor acquainted with the use of the machinery employed in it (to the invention of which the same division of labour has probably given occasion), could scarce, perhaps, with his utmost industry, make one pin in a day, and certainly could not make twenty. But in the way in which this business is now carried on, not only the whole work is a peculiar trade, but it is divided into a number of branches, of which the greater part are likewise peculiar trades. One man draws out the wire, another straights it, a third cuts it, a fourth points it, a fifth grinds it at the top for receiving the head; to make the head requires two or three distinct operations; to put it on, is a peculiar business, to whiten the pins is another; it is even a trade by itself to put them into the paper; and the important business of making a pin is, in this manner, divided into about eighteen distinct operations, which, in some manufactories, are all performed by distinct hands, though in others the same man will sometimes perform two or three of them. I have seen a small manufactory of this kind where ten men only were employed, and where some of them consequently performed two or three distinct operations. But though they were very poor, and therefore but indifferently accommodated with the necessary machinery, they could, when they exerted themselves, make among them about twelve pounds of pins in a day. There are in a pound upwards of four thousand pins of a middling size. Those ten persons, therefore, could make among them upwards of forty-eight thousand pins in a day. Each person, therefore, making a tenth part of forty-eight thousand pins, might be considered as making four thousand eight hundred pins in a day. But if they had all wrought separately and independently, and without any of them having been educated to this peculiar business, they certainly could not each of them have made twenty, perhaps not one pin in a day; that is, certainly, not the two hundred and fortieth, perhaps not the four thousand eight hundredth part of what they are at present capable of performing, in consequence of a proper division and combination of their different operations. In every other art and manufacture, the effects of the division of labour are similar to what they are in this very trifling one; though, in many of them, the labour can neither be so much subdivided, nor reduced to so great a simplicity of operation. The division of labour, however, so far as it can be introduced, occasions, in every art, a proportionable increase of the productive powers of labour (3–5).

> In answer to the question about the origin of the division of labor, Smith believes that it is related to the principle of self interest, which makes an individual act so as to improve his situation in life. The motivating principle of self-interest subsequently has become part of the basic framework of mainstream economic analysis. But Smith believed that it would not lead to an anarchist society because people's actions also are subject to many checks and balances that modify pure greed and that result in a socially desirable outcome.

This division of labour, from which so many advantages are derived, is not originally the effect of any human wisdom, which foresees and intends that general opulence to which it gives occasion. It is the necessary, though very slow and gradual, consequence of a certain propensity in human nature which has in view no such extensive utility; the propensity to truck, barter, and exchange one thing for another.

Whether this propensity be one of those original principles in human nature, of which no further account can be given; or whether, as seems more probable, it be the necessary consequence of the faculties of reason and speech, it belongs not to our present subject to enquire. It is common to all men, and to be found in no other race of animals, which seem to know neither this nor any other species of contracts....

Man has almost constant occasion for the help of his brethren, and it is in vain for him to expect it from their benevolence only. He will be more likely to prevail if he can interest their self-love in his favour, and shew them that it is for their own advantage to do for him what he requires of them. Whoever offers to another a bargain of any kind, proposes to do this. Give me that which I want, and you shall have this which you want, is the meaning of every such offer; and it is in this manner that we obtain from one another the far greater part of those good offices which we stand in need of . It is not from the benevolence of the butcher, the brewer, or the baker, that we expect our dinner, but from their regard to their own interest (14–15).

. . .

But the annual revenue of every society is always precisely equal to the exchangeable value of the whole annual produce of its industry, or rather is precisely the same thing with that exchangeable value. As every individual, therefore, endeavours as much as he can both to employ his capital in the support of domestic industry, and so to direct that industry that its produce may be of the greatest value; every individual necessarily labours to render the annual revenue of the society as great as he can. He generally, indeed, neither intends to promote the public interest, nor knows how much he is promoting it. By preferring the support of domestic to that of foreign industry, he intends only his own security; and by directing that industry in such a manner as its produce may be of the greatest value, he intends only his own gain, and he is in this, as in many other cases, led by an invisible hand to promote an end which was no part of his intention. By pursuing his own interest he frequently promotes that of the society more effectually than when he really intends to promote it (484–85).

Source: Adam Smith, *An Inquiry into the Nature and Causes of the Wealth of Nations* (Strahan and Cadell, 1776, 5th ed. 1789). Ed. Edwin Cannan, 1904. Reprinted New York: Modern Library, 2000.

3. Excerpts from Alexander Hamilton's *Report on Manufactures* (United States, 1791)

Alexander Hamilton, the first secretary of the treasury of the United States, was a vigorous advocate of manufacturing. In a report presented to Congress on December 5, 1791, Hamilton summarized his reasons for encouraging the expansion of manufacturing, including the advantages of economic diversification, the provision of employment for otherwise idle persons (a category he thought included women and children), the encouragement of immigration into the country, the achievement of economic independence from other countries, and the strengthening of national security by enabling the country to provide for its own needs in time of war. He also answered the objections raised by opponents of his position: That because both labor and capital were scarce and expensive, the resulting manufactures would be costly, a consequence that would make it more beneficial to the country to retain its agricultural character and the clear advantages it offered. Hamilton's *Report on Manufactures* can be seen as the first comprehensive attempt to provide a national economic policy. The following extracts summarize the key elements in the report.

REPORT ON MANUFACTURES

The Secretary of the Treasury, in obedience to the order of the House of Representatives, of the 15th day of January, 1790, has applied his attention, at as early a period as his other duties would permit, to the subject of Manufactures; and particularly to the means of promoting such as will tend to render the United States, independent of foreign nations for military and other essential supplies. And he thereupon respectfully submits the following Report.

The expediency of encouraging manufactures in the United States, which was not long since deemed very questionable, appears at this time to be pretty generally admitted. The embarrassments, which have obstructed the progress of our external trade, have led to serious reflections on the necessity of enlarging the sphere of our domestic commerce: the restrictive regulations, which in foreign markets abridge the vent of the increasing surplus of our Agricultural produce, serve to beget an earnest desire, that a more extensive demand for that surplus may be created at home: And the complete success, which has rewarded manufacturing enterprise, in some valuable branches ... justify a hope, that the obstacles to the growth of this species of industry are less formidable than they were apprehended to be, ...

... the cultivation of the earth—as the primary and most certain source of national supply—as the immediate and chief source of subsistence to man—as the principal source of those materials which constitute the nutriment of other kinds of labor—as including a state most favourable to the freedom and independence of the human mind—one, perhaps, most conducive to the multiplication of the human species–has intrinsically a strong claim to pre-eminence over every other kind of industry.

But, that it has a title to any thing like an exclusive predilection, in any country, ought to be admitted with great caution. That it is even more productive than every other branch of Industry requires more evidence than has yet been given.... That its real interests, precious and important as ... they truly are, will be advanced, rather than injured by the due encouragement of manufactures, may, it is believed, be satisfactorily demonstrated. And it is also believed that the expediency of such encouragement ... may be shown to be recommended by the most cogent and persuasive motives of national policy.

. . .

But without contending for the superior productiveness of Manufacturing Industry, ... but to evince in addition that the establishment and diffusion of manufactures have the effect of rendering the total mass of useful and productive labor, in a community, greater than it would otherwise be. In prosecuting this discussion, it may be necessary briefly to resume and review some of the topics ...

... and to enumerate the principal circumstances, from which it may be inferred—that manufacturing establishments not only occasion a positive augmentation of the Produce and Revenue of the Society, but that they contribute essentially to rendering them greater than they could possibly be, without such establishments; These circumstances are–

1. The division of labour.
2. An extension of the use of Machinery.
3. Additional employment to classes of the community not ordinarily engaged in the business.
4. The promoting of emigration from foreign Countries.
5. The furnishing greater scope for the diversity of talents and dispositions which discriminate men from each other.
6. The affording a more ample and various field for enterprize.
7. The creating in some instances a new, and securing in all, a more certain and steady demand for the surplus produce of the soil.

Each ... has a considerable influence upon the total mass of industrious effort in a community: Together, they add ... a degree of energy and effect.... Some comments upon each of them, ... may serve to explain their importance.

I.... The Division of Labour

It has justly been observed, that there is a scarcely any thing of greater moment in the economy of a nation than the proper division of labour. The separation of occupations causes each to be carried to a much greater perfection, than it could possibly acquire, if they were blended.

II.... The Use of Machinery

The employment of Machinery forms an item of great importance in the general mass of national industry. 'Tis an artificial force brought in aid of the natural force of man; and, to all the purposes of labour, is an increase of hands; an accession of strength, unencumbered too by the expence of maintaining the laborer ... those occupations, which give greatest scope to the use of this auxiliary, contribute most to the general Stock of industrious effort, and, in consequence, to the general product of industry....

[M]anufacturing pursuits are susceptible in a greater degree of the application of machinery, than those of Agriculture.... [A]ll the difference is lost to a community, which, instead of manufacturing for itself, procures the fabrics requisite to its supply from other Countries. The substitution of foreign for domestic manufactures is a transfer to foreign nations of the advantages accruing from the employment of Machinery....

The Cotton Mill, invented in England, within the last twenty years, is a signal illustration of [this] general proposition.... In consequence of it, all the different processes for spinning Cotton are performed by means of Machines, which are put in motion by water, and attended chiefly by women and Children; and by a smaller number of persons, ... than are requisite in the ordinary mode of spinning. And it is an advantage of great moment, that the operations of this mill continue with convenience during the night as well as through the day.... To this invention is to be attributed essentially the immense progress, which has been so suddenly made in Great Britain, in the various fabrics of cotton.

III.... The Additional Employment of Classes of the Community

This is not among the least valuable of the means, by which manufacturing institutions contribute to augment the general stock of industry and production. In places where those institutions prevail, besides the persons regularly engaged in them, they afford occasional and extra employment to industrious individuals and families, who are willing to devote the leisure resulting from the intermissions of their ordinary pursuits to collateral labours, as a resource for multiplying their acquisitions or their enjoyments. The husbandman ... experiences a new source of profit and support; from the increased industry of his wife and daughters; invited and stimulated by the demands of the neighboring manufactories.

Besides this advantage of occasional employment to classes having different occupations, there is another, ... the employment of persons who would otherwise be idle (and in many cases a burthen on the community) either from ... temper, habit, infirmity of body, or some other cause, indisposing or disqualifying them for the toils of the Country.... [I]n general, women and Children are rendered more useful, and the latter more early useful by manufacturing establishments, than they would otherwise be. Of the number of persons employed in the Cotton Manufactories of Great Britain, it is computed that four sevenths nearly are women and children; of whom the greatest proportion are children, and many of them of a very tender age.

IV.... The Promoting of Emigration from Foreign Countries

Men reluctantly quit one course of occupation and livelihood for another, unless invited to it by very apparent and proximate advantages. Many who would go from one country to another, if they had a prospect of continuing with more benefit the callings, to which they have been educated, will often not be tempted to change their situation, by the hope of doing better, in some other way.

Manufacturers, who, listening to the powerful invitations of a better price for their fabrics, or their labour, of greater cheapness of provisions and raw materials, of an exemption from the chief part of the taxes, burthens and restraints, which they endure in the old world, of greater personal independence and consequence, under the operation of a more equal government, and of what is far more precious than mere religious toleration—a perfect equality of religious privileges; would probably flock from Europe to the United States to pursue their own trades or professions, if they were once made sensible of the advantages they would enjoy, and were inspired with an assurance of encouragement and employment, will, with difficulty, be induced to transplant themselves, with a view to becoming Cultivators of Land.

V.... Furnishing Greater Scope for the Diversity of Talents and Dispositions

This is a much more powerful means of augmenting the fund of national Industry than may at first sight appear. It is a just observation, that minds of the strongest and most active powers for their proper objects fall below mediocrity and labour without effect, if confined to uncongenial pursuits.... [T]hence ... the results of human exertion may be Immensely increased by diversifying Its objects. When all the different kinds of industry obtain in a community, each individual can find his proper element, and can call into activity the whole vigour of his nature. And the community is benefited by the services of its respective members ... in which each can serve it with most effect.

VI.... Affording a More Ample and Various Field for Enterprise

This also is of greater consequence in the general scale of national exertion, ... and has effects not altogether dissimilar from those of the circumstance last noticed. To cherish and stimulate the activity of the human mind, by multiplying the objects of enterprise, is not among the least considerable of the expedients, by which the wealth of a nation may be promoted. Even things in themselves not positively advantageous, sometimes become so, by their tendency to provoke exertion.

VII.... Creating, in Some Instances, a New, and Securing in All a More Certain and Steady Demand for Surplus Produce of the Soil

This is among the most important of the circumstances which have been indicated. It is a principal means, by which the establishment of manufactures contributes to an augmentation of the produce or revenue of a country, and has an immediate and direct relation to the prosperity of Agriculture.

...

[A] domestic market is greatly to be preferred to a foreign one; because it is in the nature of things far more to be relied upon. It is a primary object of the policy of nations, to be able to supply themselves with subsistence from their own soils; and manufacturing nations, as far as circumstances permit, endeavor to procure from the same source, the raw materials necessary for their own fabrics.... [N]ations who have neither mines nor manufactures, can only obtain the manufactured articles of which they stand in need, by an exchange of the products of their soils; and that, if those who can best furnish them with such articles are unwilling to give a due course to this exchange, they must of necessity, make every-possible effort to manufacture for themselves; the effect of which is that the manufacturing nations abridge the natural advantages of their situation, through an unwillingness to permit the Agricultural countries to enjoy the advantages of theirs, and sacrifice the interests of a mutually beneficial intercourse to the vain project of selling every thing and buying nothing.

But it is also a consequence of the policy ... that the foreign demand for the products of Agricultural countries is, in a great degree, rather casual and occasional, than certain or constant.... [I]t may be safely affirmed, that such interruptions are at times very inconveniently felt, and that cases not unfrequently occur, In which markets are so confined and restricted as to render the demand very unequal to the supply. Independently likewise of the artificial impediments, which are created by the policy in question, there are natural causes tending to render the external demand for the surplus of Agricultural nations a precarious reliance. The differences of seasons, in the countries which are the consumers, make immense differences in the produce of their own soils, in different years; and consequently in the degrees of their necessity for foreign supply. Plentiful harvests with them, especially if similar ones occur at the same time in the countries which are the furnishers, occasion of course a glut in the markets of the latter. Considering how fast and how much the progress of new settlements in the United States must increase the surplus produce of the soil, and weighing seriously the tendency of the system, which prevails among most of the commercial nations of Europe, ... there appear strong reasons to regard the foreign demand for that surplus as too uncertain a reliance, and to desire a substitute for it, in an extensive domestic market.

To secure such a market, there is no other expedient, than to promote manufacturing establishments. Manufacturers who constitute the most numerous class, after the Cultivators of land, are for that reason the principal consumers of the surplus of their labour.

This idea of an extensive domestic market for the surplus produce of the soil is of the first consequence. It ... most effectually conduces to a flourishing state of Agriculture. If the effect of manufactories should be to detach a portion of the hands, which would otherwise be engaged in Tillage, it might possibly cause a smaller quantity of lands to be under cultivation; but, by their tendency to procure a more certain demand for the surplus produce of the soil, they would, at the same time, cause the lands which were in cultivation to be better improved and more productive. And while ... the condition of each individual farmer would be meliorated, the total mass of Agricultural production would probably be increased. For this must evidently depend as much, if not more, upon the degree of improvement than upon the number of acres under culture.

. . .

The foregoing considerations seem sufficient to establish, as general propositions, that it is the interest of nations to diversify the industrious pursuits of the individuals who compose them—that the establishment of manufactures is calculated not only to Increase the general stock of useful and productive labour; but even to improve the state of Agriculture in particular, certainly to advance the interests of those who are engaged in it.

. . .

The objections to the pursuit of manufactures in the United States ... represent an impracticability of success, arising from three causes—scarcity of hands–dearness of labour—want of capital.

The two first circumstances, are to a certain extent real, and, within due limits, ought to be admitted as obstacles to the success of manufacturing enterprise In the United States. But there are various considerations, which lessen their force, and tend to afford an assurance that they are not sufficient to prevent the advantageous prosecution of many very useful and extensive manufactories.

With regard to scarcity of hands, the fact itself must be applied with no small qualification to certain parts of the United States. There are large districts, which may be considered as pretty fully peopled; and ... are thickly interspersed with flourishing and increasing towns. If these districts have not already reached the point, at which the complaint of scarcity of hands ceases, they are not remote from it, and are approaching fast towards it; and having, perhaps, fewer attractions to agriculture than some other parts of the Union, they exhibit a proportionably stronger tendency towards other kinds of industry. In these districts may be discerned no inconsiderable maturity for manufacturing establishments.

But there are circumstances ... that materially diminish, everywhere, the effect of a scarcity of hands ... the great use which can be made of women and children; [and] ... the vast extension given by ... the employment of Machines, which substituting the Agency of fire and water, had prodigiously lessened the necessity of manual labour—the employment of persons ordinarily engaged in other occupations, during the seasons, or hours of leisure; ... may also be ... a resource for obviating the scarcity of hands—lastly the attraction of foreign emigrants ... soon as the United States shall present the countenance of a serious prosecution of Manufactures—as soon as foreign artists shall be made sensible that the state of things here affords a moral certainty of employment and encouragement—competent numbers of European workmen will transplant themselves....

It may be affirmed therefore, in respect to hands for carrying on manufactures, that we shall in a great measure trade upon a foreign Stock, reserving our own for the cultivation of our lands and the manning of our Ships, ... the objection to the success of manufactures, deduced from the scarcity of hands, is alike applicable to Trade and Navigation, and yet these are perceived to flourish, without any sensible impediment from that cause.

As to the dearness of labour (another of the obstacles alleged) this has relation principally to two circumstances, ... the scarcity of hands; [and], the greatness of profits.

As far as it is a consequence of the scarcity of hands, it is mitigated by all the considerations which have been adduced as lessening that deficiency.

. . .

[Machinery]

This circumstance is worthy of the most particular attention. It diminishes immensely one of the objections most strenuously urged against the success of manufactures in the United States.

To procure all such machines as are known in any part of Europe, can only require a proper provision and due pains. The knowledge of several of the most important of them is already possessed. The preparation of them here is, in most cases, practicable on nearly equal terms. As far as they depend on Water, some superiority of advantages may be claimed, from the uncommon variety and greater cheapness of situations adapted to Mill seats, with which different parts of the United States abound.

. . .

To the general allegation, connected with the circumstances of scarcity of hands and dearness of labour, that extensive manufactures can only grow out of a redundant or full population, it will be sufficient, to answer generally, that the fact has been otherwise.... The supposed want of Capital for the prosecution of manufactures in the United States, is the most indefinite of the objections....

It is very difficult to pronounce any thing precise concerning the real extent of the monied capital of a Country, and still more concerning the proportion which It bears to the objects that invite the employment of Capital. It is not less difficult to pronounce how far the effect of any given quantity of money, as capital, ... may be increased by the very circumstance of the additional motion, which is given to it by new objects of employment. That effect, like the momentum of descending bodies, may not improperly be represented, as in a compound ratio to mass and velocity. It seems pretty certain, that a given sum of money, in a situation, in which the quick impulses of commercial activity were little felt, would appear inadequate to the circulation of as great a quantity of industry and property, as in one in which their full influence was experienced.

It is not obvious, why the same objection might not as well be made to external commerce as to manufactures; since it is manifest that our immense tracts of land ... are capable of giving employment to more capital than is actually bestowed upon them. It is certain, that the United States offer a vast field for the advantageous employment of Capital; but it does not follow, that there will not be found, in one way or another, a sufficient fund for the successful prosecution of any species of industry which is likely to prove truly beneficial.

The following considerations are of a nature to remove all inquietude on the score of the want of Capital.

The introduction of Banks, ... has a powerful tendency to extend the active Capital of a Country. Experience of the Utility of these Institutions is multiplying in the United States. It is probable that they will be established wherever they can exist with advantage; and wherever they can be supported, ... they will add new energies to all pecuniary operations.

The aid of foreign Capital may safely, and, with considerable latitude, be taken into calculation. Its instrumentality has been long experienced in our external commerce; and it has begun to be felt in various other modes. Not only our funds, but our Agriculture, and other internal improvements, have been animated by it. It has already in a few instances extended even to our manufactures.

It is a well-known fact, that there are parts of Europe, which have more Capital than profitable domestic objects of employment. Hence, among other proofs, the large loans continually furnished to foreign states. And it is equally certain, that the capital of other parts may find more profitable employment in the United States, than at home. And notwithstanding there are weighty inducements to prefer the employment of capital at home, even at less profit, to an investment of it abroad, though with greater gain, yet these inducements are overruled either by a deficiency of employment or by a very material difference in profit.

   . . .

And, whatever be the objects which originally attract foreign Capital, when once introduced it may be directed towards any purpose of beneficial exertion which is desired. And to detain it among us, there can be no expedient so effectual as to enlarge the sphere within which it may be usefully employed: Though introduced merely with view to speculations in the funds, it may afterwards be rendered subservient to the Interests of Agriculture, Commerce, and Manufactures. But the attraction of foreign Capital for the direct purpose of Manufactures, ought not to be deemed a chimerical expectation. There are already examples of it.... And the examples, if the disposition be cultivated can hardly fail to multiply. There are also instances of another kind, which serve to strengthen the expectation. Enterprises for improving the Public Communications by cutting canals, opening the obstructions in Rivers and erecting bridges have received very material aid from the same source. When the Manufacturing Capitalist of Europe shall advert to the many important advantages, which have been intimated, in the Course of this report, he cannot but perceive very powerful inducements to a transfer of himself and his Capital to the United States.... [I]t cannot escape his observation, ... that the progressive population and improvement of the United States, insure a continually increasing domestic demand for the fabrics which he shall produce.

   . . .

There remains ... an objection to the encouragement of manufactures, of a nature different from those which question the probability of success. This is derived from its supposed tendency to give a monopoly of advantages to particular classes, at the expense of the rest of the community, who, it is affirmed, would be able to procure the requisite supplies of manufactured articles on better terms from foreigners, than from our own Citizens, and who, it is alleged, are reduced to the necessity of paying an enhanced price ... by every measure which obstructs the free competition of foreign commodities.

It is not an unreasonable supposition, that measures, which serve to abridge the free competition of foreign Articles, have a tendency to occasion an enhancement of prices and it is not to be denied that such is the effect, in a number of Cases; but the fact does not uniformly correspond with the theory. A reduction of prices has, in several instances immediately succeeded the establishment of a domestic manufacture. Whether it be that foreign manufactures endeavour to supplant, by underselling our own, or whatever else be the cause, the effect has been such as is stated, and the reverse of what might have been expected.

But though it were true, that the immediate and certain effect of regulations controlling the competition of foreign with domestic fabrics was an increase of Price, it is universally true, that the contrary is the ultimate effect with every successful manufacture. When a domestic manufacture has attained to perfection, and has engaged in the prosecution of it a competant number of Persons, it invariably becomes cheaper. Being free from the heavy charges which attend the importation of foreign commodities, it can be afforded, and accordingly seldom or never fails to be sold Cheaper, in … time, than was the foreign Article for which it is a substitute. The internal competition which takes place, soon does away every thing like Monopoly, and by degrees reduces the price of the Article to the minimum of a reasonable profit on the Capital employed.

. . .

Whence it follows, that it is the interest of a community, with a view to eventual and permanent economy, to encourage the growth of manufactures. In a national view, a temporary enhancement of price must always be well compensated by a permanent reduction of it.

. . .

I. There seems to be a moral certainty, that the trade of a country which is both manufacturing and Agricultural will be more lucrative and prosperous than that of a Country, which is merely Agricultural.

. . .

From these circumstances collectively—two important inferences are to be drawn, one, that there is always a higher probability of a favorable balance of Trade, in regard to countries in which manufactures founded on the basis of a thriving Agriculture flourish, than in regard to those, which are confined wholly or almost wholly to Agriculture; the other (which is also a consequence of the first), that countries of the former description are likely to possess more pecuniary wealth, or money, than those of the latter.

. . .

Not only the wealth, but the independence and security of a Country, appear to be materially connected with the prosperity of manufactures. Every nation, with a view to those great objects, ought to endeavour to possess within itself all the essentials of national supply. These comprise the means of Subsistence, habitation, clothing, and defence.

. . .

One more point of view only remains in which to Consider the expediency of encouraging manufactures in the United States.

It is not uncommon to meet with an opinion that though the promoting of manufactures may be the interest of a part of the Union, it is contrary to that of another part. The Northern & southern regions are sometimes represented as having adverse interests in this respect. Those are called Manufacturing, these Agricultural states; and a species of opposition is imagined to subsist between the Manufacturing and Agricultural interests.

This idea of an opposition between those two interests is the common error of the early periods of every country; but experience gradually dissipates it…. But it is nevertheless a maxim, well established by experience, ... that the aggregate prosperity of manufactures, and the aggregate prosperity of Agriculture are intimately connected.... Perhaps the superior steadiness of the demand of a domestic market for the surplus produce of the soil, is alone a convincing argument of its truth.

. . .

It is a truth as important as it is agreeable, and one to which it is not easy to imagine exceptions, that every thing tending to establish substantial and permanent order in the affairs of a Country, to increase the total mass of industry and opulence, is ultimately beneficial to every part of it.

. . .

But there are more particular considerations which serve to fortify the idea that the encouragement of manufactures is the interest of all parts of the Union. If the Northern and Middle states should be the principal scenes of such establishments, they would immediately benefit the More southern, by creating a demand for productions, some of which they have in common with the other states, and others of which, are either peculiar to them, or more abundant, or of better quality, than elsewhere. These productions, principally, are Timber, flax, Hemp, Cotton, Wool, raw silk, Indigo, iron, lead, furs, hides, skins and coals. Of these articles Cotton and Indigo are peculiar to the southern states, as are hitherto Lead and Coal, Flax and Hemp are or may be raised in greater abundance there, than in the More Northern states; and the Wool of Virginia is said to be of better quality than that of any other state.... The Climate of the south is also better adapted to the production of silk.

The extensive cultivation of Cotton can perhaps, hardly be expected but from the previous establishment of domestic Manufactories of the Article; and the surest encouragement and vent, for the others, would result from similar establishments in respect to them.

If then, it satisfactorily appears, that it is the Interest of the United States, generally, to encourage manufactures, ... there are circumstances which Render the present a critical moment for entering, with Zeal upon the important business. The effort cannot fail to be materially seconded by a considerable and increasing influx of money, in consequence of foreign speculations in the funds—and by the disorders, which exist in different parts of Europe.

The first circumstance not only facilitates the execution of manufacturing enterprises, but it indicates them as a necessary mean to turn the thing itself to advantage.... If useful employment be not found for the Money of foreigners brought to the country to be invested in purchases of the Public Debt, it will quickly be re-exported to defray the expense of an extraordinary consumption of foreign luxuries; and distressing drains of our specie may hereafter be experienced, to pay the interest and redeem the Principal of the Purchased debt.

This useful employment too ought to be of a nature to produce solid and permanent improvements. If the money merely serves to give a temporary spring to foreign commerce; as it cannot procure new and lasting outlets for the products of the Country, there will be no real or durable advantage gained. As far as it shall find its way in Agricultural ameliorations, in opening canals, and in similar improvements, it will be productive of substantial utility. But there is reason to doubt whether in such channels, it is likely to find sufficient employment, and still more whether many of those who possess it, would be as readily attracted to its objects of this nature, as to manufacturing pursuits.

. . .

The disturbed state of Europe, inclining its citizens to emigration, the requisite workmen will be more easily acquired than at another time; and the effect of multiplying the opportunities of employment to those who emigrate, may be an increase of the number and extent of valuable acquisitions to the population, arts, and industry of the Country. To find pleasure in the calamities of other nations would be criminal; but to benefit ourselves, by opening an asylum to those who suffer, in consequence of them, is as justifiable as it is politic.

Source: Alexander Hamilton, *Report on Manufactures,* December 5, 1791. From http://press-pubs. uchicago.edu/founders/documents/v1ch31.html.

4. Excerpts from Thomas Malthus's "Essay on the Principle of Population" (Great Britain, 1798)

Thomas Robert Malthus (1766–1834) published the first version of his "Essay on the Principle of Population" in 1798 as a counterbalance to the optimism about the future of humanity associated with the eighteenth-century Enlightenment. He took particular issue with two writers, the Englishman William Godwin (1756–1836) and the Frenchman the Marquis de Condorcet (1743–1794), who believed in the perfectibility of human beings, a perfectibility that was currently prevented from flowering by badly designed social and political institutions. Neither believed that population growth was anything to be concerned about because progress in science, as well as various social and political reforms based on the supremacy of reason, would ensure that food supplies always would keep pace with population growth.

Malthus, however, was much more pessimistic because he believed that the growth rate of population was much faster than the growth rate of the food supply, his principle of population. At a time when there were few statistical sources, Malthus estimated his own and hypothesized that population increases at a geometric rate, whereas food supplies increase in an arithmetic ratio. Consequently, population could then reach a certain point, the Malthusian ceiling, at which food supplies were inadequate to support the growing population. The resulting starvation and misery would put an end to further population growth.

This type of check, together with wars and plagues, was a positive check to population growth and operated by increasing the death rate. Malthus considered these unfortunate evils as punishment for those who had not had the foresight and moral strength to engage in restraint to lower the birth rate, such as delaying marriage, which was a preventative check to population growth.

An important, and dismal, policy implication occurs here. Any social reorganization of society, which Godwin and Condorcet recommended, could not, in

Malthus's eyes, prevent the working out of these trends because human nature cannot be changed as social natures can be. Hence, if poverty and misery are natural occurrences, poor relief or charity to the poor only will make the problem worse by encouraging the poor to have more children. This conclusion helped influence the passage of the British Poor Law Amendment of 1834, which replaced the previous system of outdoor relief for the able-bodied poor, based on the size of family and the price of bread, with harsh indoor relief. Under the new law, a destitute family was forced to enter a workhouse in which families were separated. The workhouse was deliberately made to be unpleasant, with the expectation that the destitute would rather starve at home than experience the shame of asking for relief by entering it.

As it turned out, Malthus's fears about reaching the Malthusian ceiling were unfounded, at least for those countries experiencing industrialization. The estimates of population growth he used came from scanty evidence from the United States (the first British population census was not taken until 1801); statistics for food production he deduced himself. He seriously underestimated the impact of the agricultural revolution in expanding food supplies and of the revolutionary changes taking place in industry and transportation. That is, improvements in knowledge and methods raised productivity per acre, whereas the nineteenth-century transportation improvements made possible the opening of huge new agricultural areas so that food for urban industrial Europe could be grown anywhere and shipped inexpensively to these markets. (In the modern world, it is not so much lack of available supply that results in famine and death as poor food distribution.) Malthus also underestimated the impact that industrialization and rising income levels would have on lowering the birth rate.

Malthus's views on population, shared to some extent by his friend, economist David Ricardo, present an important exception to the faith in progress characteristic of the nineteenth century. It is due to Malthus that the academic discipline of economics has been dubbed *the dismal science,* a term coined by the philosopher Thomas Carlyle after reading "The Essay on the Principle of Population."

I think I may fairly make two postulates:

First, That food is necessary to the existence of man.

Secondly, That the passion between the sexes is necessary, and will remain nearly in its present state.

These two laws, ever since we have had any knowledge of mankind, appear to have been fixed laws of nature; and, as we have not hitherto seen any alteration in them, we have no right to conclude that they will ever cease to be what they are now, without an immediate act of power in that Being who first arranged the system of the universe; and for the advantage of his creatures, still executes, according to fixed laws, all its various operations.

I do not know that any writer has supposed that on this earth man will ultimately be able to live without food. But Mr. [William] Godwin has conjectured that the passion between the sexes may in time be extinguished. As, however, he calls this part of his work, a deviation into the land of conjecture, I will not dwell longer upon it at present, than to say, that the best arguments for the perfectability of man are drawn from a contemplation of the great progress that he has already made from the savage state, and the difficulty of saying where he is to stop. But towards the extinction of the passion between the sexes, no progress whatever has hitherto been made. It appears to exist in as much force at present as it did two thousand, or four thousand years ago. There are individual exceptions now as there always have been. But, as these exceptions do not appear to increase in number, it would surely be a very unphilosophical mode of arguing, to infer merely from the existence of an exception, that the exception would, in time, become the rule, and the rule the exception.

Assuming, then, my postulata as granted, I say, that the power of the population is indefinitely greater than the power in the earth to produce subsistence for man.

Population, when unchecked, increases in a geometrical ratio. Subsistence only increases in an arithmetical ratio. A slight acquaintance with numbers will show the immensity of the first power in comparison with the second.

By that law of our nature which makes food necessary to the life of man, the effects of these two unequal powers must be kept equal.

This implies a strong and constantly operating check on population from the difficulty of subsistence. This difficulty must fall somewhere; and must necessarily be severely felt by a large portion of mankind.

Through the animal and vegetable kingdoms, nature has scattered the seeds of life abroad with the most profuse and liberal hand. She has been comparatively sparing in the room, and the nourishment necessary to rear them. The germs of existence contained in this spot of earth, with ample food, and ample room to expand it, would fill millions of worlds in the course of a few thousand years, Necessity, that imperious, all-pervading law of nature, restrains them within the prescribed bounds. The race of plants, and the race of animals shrink under this great restrictive law. And the race of man cannot, by any effort of reason, escape from it. Among plants and animals its effects are waste of seed, sickness, and premature death. Among mankind, misery and vice. The former, misery, is an absolutely necessary consequence of it. Vice is a highly probably consequence, and we therefore see it abundantly prevail; but it ought not, perhaps, to be called an absolutely necessary consequence. The ordeal of virtue is to resist all temptation to evil.

This natural inequality of the two powers of population, and of production in the earth, and that great law of our nature which must constantly keep their effects equal, form the great difficulty that to me appears insurmountable in the way to perfectibility of society. All other arguments are of slight and subordinate consideration in comparison of this. I see no way by which man can escape from the weight of this law which pervades all animated nature. No fancied equality, no agrarian regulations in their utmost extent, could remove the pressure of it even for a single century. And it appears, therefore, to be decisive against the possible existence of a society, all the members of which should live in ease, happiness and comparative leisure; and feel no anxiety about providing for themselves and families.

Consequently, if the premises are just, the argument is conclusive against the perfectibility of the mass of mankind.

I have thus sketched the general outline of the argument; but I will examine it more particularly; and I think it will be found that experience, the true source and foundation of all knowledge, invariably confirms its truth.

Source: Thomas Robert Malthus, *An Essay on the Principles of Population as It Affects the Future Improvement of Society* (London, 1798), p. 4–5.

http://www.esp.org/books/malthus/population/malthus.pdf.

5. Combination Acts (Great Britain, 1799, 1800)

The Combination Acts were part of a series of repressive laws prohibiting and penalizing workers from organizing to improve their wages and working conditions. They were passed out of fear that the revolutionary ideas that had led to the French Revolution (1789) and the following backlash against the ancien régime, which deposed the king and led to the confiscation of the nobility's estates, would cross the English Channel and take hold in England. They were repealed in 1824. *See also* Combination Acts.

An Act to repeal an Act, passed in the last Session of Parliament, intitulated, "An Act to prevent Unlawful Combinations of Workmen"; and to substitute other provisions in lieu thereof.

I. Whereas it is expedient to explain and amend an Act [39 Geo. III, c. 81] ... to prevent unlawful combinations of workmen ... be it enacted ... that from ... the passing of this Act, the said Act shall be repealed; and that all contracts, covenants and agreements whatsoever ... at any time ... heretofore made ... between any journeymen manufacturers or other persons ... for obtaining an advance of wages of them or any of them, or any other journeymen manufacturers or workmen, or other persons in any manufacture, trade or business, or for lessening or altering their or any of their usual hours working, or for decreasing the quantity of work (save and except any contract made or to be made between any master and his journeyman or manufacturer, for or on account of the work or service of such journeyman or manufacturer with whom such contract may be made), or for preventing or hindering any person or persons from employing whomsoever he, she, or they shall think proper to employ ... or for controlling or anyway affecting any person or persons carrying on any manufacture, trade or business, in the conduct or management thereof, shall be ... illegal, null and void.

II. No journeyman, workman or other person shall at any time after the passing of this Act make or enter into, or be concerned in the making of or entering into any such contract, covenant or agreement, in writing or not in writing ... and every ... workman ... who, after the passing of this Act, shall be guilty of any of the said offences, being thereof lawfully convicted, upon his own confession, or the oath or oaths of one or more credible witness or witnesses, before any two justices of the Peace ... within three calendar months next after the offence shall have been committed, shall, by order of such justices, be committed to and confined in the common gaol, within his or their jurisdiction, for any time not exceeding 3 calendar months, or at the discretion of such justices shall be committed to some House of Correction within the same jurisdiction, there to remain and to be kept to hard labour for any time not exceeding 2 calendar months.

III. ... Every ... workman ... who shall at any time after the passing of this Act enter into any combination to obtain an advance of wages, or to lessen or alter the hours or duration of the time of working, or to decrease the quantity of work, or for any other purpose contrary to this Act, or who shall, by giving money, or by persuasion, solicitation or intimidation, or any other means, wilfully and maliciously endeavour to prevent any unhired or unemployed journeyman or workman, or other person, in any manufacture, trade or business, or any other person wanting employment in such manufacture, trade or business, from hiring himself to any manufacturer or tradesman, or person conducting any manufacture, trade or business, or who shall, for the purpose of obtaining an advance of wages, or for any other purpose contrary to the provisions of this Act, wilfully and maliciously decoy, persuade, solicit, intimidate, influence or prevail, or attempt or endeavour to prevail, on any journeyman or workman, or other person hired or employed, or to be hired or employed in any such manufacture, trade or business, to quit or leave his work, service or employment, or who shall wilfully and maliciously hinder or prevent any manufacturer or tradesman, or other person, from employing in his or her manufacture, trade or business, such journeymen, workmen and other persons as he or she shall think proper, or who, being hired or employed, shall, without any just or reasonable cause, refuse to work with any other journeyman or workman employed or hired to work therein, and who shall be lawfully convicted of any of the said offences, upon his own confession, or the oath or oaths of one or more credible witness or witnesses, before any two justices of the Peace for the county ... or place where such offence shall be committed, within 3 calendar months ... shall, by order of such justices, be committed to ... gaol for any time not exceeding 3 calendar months; or otherwise be committed to some House of Correction ... for any time not exceeding 2 calendar months.

IV. And for the more effectual suppression of all combinations amongst journeymen, workmen and other persons employed in any manufacture, trade or business, be it further enacted, that all and every persons and person whomsoever (whether employed in any such manufacture, trade or business, or not) who shall attend any meeting had or held for the purpose of making or entering into any contract, covenant or agreement, by this Act declared to be illegal, or of entering into, supporting, maintaining, continuing, or carrying on any combination for any purpose by this Act declared to be illegal, or who shall summons, give notice to, call upon, persuade, entice, solicit, or by intimidation, or any other means, endeavour to induce any journeyman, workman, or other person, employed in any manufacture, trade or business, to attend any such meeting, or who shall collect, demand, ask, or receive any sum of money from any such journeyman, workman, or other person, for any of the purposes aforesaid, or who shall persuade, entice, solicit, or by intimidation, or any other means, endeavour to induce any such journeyman, workman or other person to enter into or be concerned in any such combination, or who shall pay any sum of money, or make or enter into any subscription or contribution, for or towards the support or encouragement of any such illegal meeting or combination, and who shall be lawfully convicted of any of the said offences, upon his own confession, or the oath or oaths of one or more credible witness or witnesses, before any two justices of the Peace … within 3 calendar months … shall … be committed to and confined in the common gaol … for any time not exceeding 3 calendar months, or otherwise be committed to some House of Correction … for any time not exceeding 2 calendar months.

V. [No person shall contribute for any expenses incurred for acting contrary to this Act, or toward the support of any person to induce him not to work, on penalty not exceeding £10, and any person collecting money for such purposes, shall forfeit, not exceeding £5. Offences shall be determined in a summary way before two justices, who, shall fix the penalty, and if not paid, shall cause it to be levied by distress, and if not to be had, shall commit the offender to the common gaol or House of Correction.]

VI. [Sums contributed as subscriptions toward any of the purposes prohibited by this Act to be forfeited.]

VII, VIII. [Concerning the recovery of such contribution money.]

IX. [Offenders may be compelled to give evidence and shall be indemnified from prosecution for any matter relative to their testimony.]

X, XI. [Justices may summon offenders and witnesses and may commit them for nonappearance or refusal to testify.]

XII. [Form of convictions.]

XIII. [Convictions to be transmitted to the next General or Quarter Sessions to be filed, and if appeal be made the justices shall then proceed to hear it.]

XIV. [Act not to abridge powers now given by law to justices touching combinations of manufacturers, etc.]

XV. [Act not to empower manufacturers to employ workmen contrary to the provisions now in force for regulating the conduct of any particular manufacture, without licence from a justice, who may grant the same, whenever the ordinary course of the manufacture is obstructed.]

XVI. [No master in the trade in which any offence is charged to have been committed shall act as a justice under this Act.]

XVII [All contracts between masters or other persons, for reducing the wages of workmen or for altering the usual hours of working, or increasing the quantity of work, shall be void, and masters convicted thereof shall forfeit £20.]

XVIII. And whereas it will be a great convenience and advantage to masters and workmen engaged in manufactures, that a cheap and summary mode be established for settling all disputes that may arise between them respecting wages and work; be it further enacted … that, from and after 1 August … 1800, in all cases that shall or may arise within … England, where the masters and workmen cannot agree respecting the price or prices to be paid for work actually done in any manufacture, or any injury or damage done or alleged to have been done by the workmen to the work, or respecting any delay or supposed delay on the part of the workmen in finishing, the work, or the not finishing such work in a good and workman-like manner, or according to any contract; and in all cases of dispute or difference, touching any contract or agreement for work or wages between masters and workmen in any trade or manufacture, which cannot be otherwise mutually adjusted and settled by and between them, it shall and may be, and it is hereby declared to be lawful for such masters and workmen between whom such dispute or difference shall arise … or either of them, to demand and have an arbitration or reference of such matter or matters in dispute; and each of them is hereby authorised and empowered forthwith to nominate and appoint an arbitrator … to arbitrate and determine such matter or matters in dispute as aforesaid by writing, subscribed by him in the presence of and attested by one witness … and to deliver the same personally to the other party … and to require the other party to name an arbitrator in like manner within two days after such reference to arbitration shall have been so demanded; and such arbitrators so appointed … are hereby authorised and required to … examine upon oath the parties and their witnesses … and forthwith to proceed to hear and determine the complaints of the parties, and the matter or matters in dispute between them; and the award to be made by such arbitrators within the time herein-after limited, shall in all cases be final and conclusive between the parties; but in case such arbitrators so appointed shall not agree to decide such matter or matters in dispute, so to be referred to them as aforesaid, and shall not make and sign their award within the space of three days after the signing of the submission to their award by both parties, that then it shall be lawful for the parties or either of them to require such arbitrators forthwith and without delay to go before and attend upon one of his Majesty's justices of the Peace acting in and for the county … or place where such dispute shall happen and be referred, and state to such justice the points in difference between them … which points … the said justice shall … hear and determine, and for that purpose … examine the parties and their witnesses upon oath, if he shall think fit.

. . .

XIX. [The parties may extend the time limited for making an award.]

XXII. [If either party shall not perform what is directed by the award, he may be committed.]

XXIII. [Any person convicted under this Act may appeal to the General or Quarter Sessions, whose decision shall be final.]

Source: Statutes at Large (39 and 40 Geo. III, c. 106), 53: 847–62, *English Historical Documents, XI, 1783–1832,* ed. A. Aspinall and E. Anthony Smith (New York: Oxford University Press, 1959), 749–52.

6. The Embargo Act (United States, December 22, 1807)

The United States found itself unwillingly drawn into the series of European wars that followed the French Revolution and the rise to power in France of Napoleon Bonaparte. These conflicts began with the French declaration of war on February 1, 1793, on Great Britain, Holland, and Spain. The struggle soon extended to the seas and resulted in the occasional seizure of U.S. ships by both the British and French navies. After 1805, war between Britain and France intensified, and France's continental system and Britain's blockade of French ports further affected U.S. shipping. European interference with U.S. shipping came to a head in 1807, with the *Chesapeake* and *Leopard* incident, which resulted in the passage of the Embargo Act by the U.S. Congress. Shipping was further damaged by the outbreak of war between Britain and the United States in 1812.

Ironically, the long-term economic effect for the United States was positive. Although U.S. shipping dropped off dramatically as a result and the shippers and merchant classes in the major ports saw a reduction in their income, the embargo stimulated a search for new trading partners (especially in Asia) and helped the development of a U.S. textile industry. Because textiles had been imported from Britain, the absence of imported textiles opened up the possibility for growth of an import-substitution industry, especially for the coarser fabrics that found a ready market among U.S. farmers. One of the first to act on this opening was the Boston merchant Francis Cabot Lowell. In 1816, using capital raised from his Boston associates, he opened a textile factory at Waltham, Massachusetts, the largest built in the United States up to that time. This factory became the start of the Waltham-Lowell system.

THE EMBARGO ACT, DECEMBER 22, 1807

Be it enacted by the Senate and House of Representatives of the United States of America in Congress assembled, That an embargo be, and hereby is laid on all ships and vessels in the ports and places within the limits or jurisdiction of the United States, cleared or not cleared, bound to any foreign port or place; and that no clearance be furnished to any ship or vessel bound to such foreign port or place, except vessels under the immediate direction of the President of the United States: and that the President be authorized to give such instructions to the officers of the revenue, and of the navy and revenue cutters of the United States, as shall appear best adapted for carrying the same into full effect: *Provided,* that nothing herein contained shall be construed to prevent the departure of any foreign ship or vessel, either in ballast, or with the goods, wares and merchandise on board of such foreign ship or vessel, when notified of this act.

Sec.2. *And be it further enacted,* That during the continuance of this act, no registered, or sea letter vessel, having on board goods, wares and merchandise, shall be allowed to depart from one port of the United States to any other within the same, unless the master, owner, consignee or factor of such vessel shall first give bond, with one or more sureties to the collector of the district from which she is bound to depart, in a sum of double the value of the vessel and cargo, that the said goods, wares or merchandise shall be relanded in some port of the United States, dangers of the sea excepted, which bond, and also a certificate from the collector where the same may be relanded, shall by the collector respectively be transmitted to the Secretary of the Treasury. All armed vessels possessing public commissions from any foreign power, are not to be considered as liable to the embargo laid by this act.

Source: "Act of December 22, 1807," *U.S. Statutes at Large,* Washington, DC: Congress of the United States, 1807, pp. 451–53.

http://memory.loc.gov/ammem/amlaw/lwcite/html#sl

---

7. Luddite Writings (Great Britain, ca. 1812)

Luddite is the name given to a person opposed to technological change; it derives from a series of scattered outbreaks of machine-breaking in some of the textile areas of England, especially between 1811 and 1816. At this time, there were few mechanisms available for workers to express themselves; union organizing was illegal, and political action was not possible because workers did not yet have the vote. This was also a time when Britain was engaged in fighting the Napoleonic Wars, which had severely interrupted the foreign trade on which many industries, especially the textile industries, depended, and many of these areas were suffering from high unemployment. Although widespread mechanization and the use of steam power were still in the process of being introduced into the industry (which eventually would lead to it being the leading consumer goods industry in the country), many of the skilled manual workers felt threatened by mechanization and, in the absence of any other way to express themselves, resorted to what has been called "collective bargaining by riot." This took the form of groups of men breaking machines and occasionally burning down haystacks in the Midlands. Leadership seemed to be localized; there was no overall effort to coordinate attacks in the different areas, but a possibly mythical General (or Captain) Ludd was reputed to be the leader. Partly because the machine-breakers had real grievances, the general population had sympathy for them.

The first extract is a letter from this General Ludd, indicating potential action against injustices. The second is a poem written in support of the Luddites.

1. A letter from General Ludd to Spencer Perceval Esq. [no date]:

> Sir
>
> The first & most important part of my Duty is to inform you & I request you do the same to all your Colleagues in office, also the Regent; that in consequence of the great sufferings of the Poor whose grievances seem not to be taken *into the least consideration by the Governmint* [*sic*] I shall be under the necessity of again calling into action (not to destroy many more frames) ie but....
>
> My brave sons of Shirewood who are determined & strong to be true and faithful avengers of their Countrys wrongs. I have waited patiently to see if any measures were likely to be adopted by Parliament to alleviate distress in any shape whatever; but that hand of conciliation is shut and my poor suffering country is left without a ray of hope: The Bill for Punish[in]g with death has only to be viewed with contempt & opposed by measures equally strong: & the Gentlemen who framed it will have to repent the act for if one man's life is sacrificed, blood for blood should you be called upon you cannot say I have not given you notice of [problem.]
>
> I have the honor to be
>
> Genl. Ludd

2. A poem in praise of Ned Ludd

This paper was posted up in Nottingham on Saturday morning, May 9, 1812:

Welcome Ned Ludd, your case is good
Make Perceval your aim
For by this bill, 'tis understood
It's death to break a Frame—

With dextrous skill, the Hosiers kill
For they are quite as bad;
And die you must, by this late Bill
Go on my bonny lad!
You might as well be hung for death
As breaking a machine—
So now my lad, your sword unsheathe
And make it sharp and keen—
We are ready now your cause to join
Whenever you may call;
To make foul blood run clear and fine
Of tyrants great and small

Deface this who dare
They shall have tyrants fare
Tossed [?] in everywhere
And can see and hear

Source: Malcolm Thomis, *The Luddites,* New York: Schocken, 1972; letter, 118; poem, 136.

8. Excerpts from the Writings of David Ricardo on Free Trade (Great Britain, 1817)

David Ricardo was a nineteenth-century classical political economist who developed a thoroughgoing, logical analysis of the economic system. He wanted to find the laws regulating the distribution of income between the three classes—industrial capitalists who received profits, landowners who received rents, and workers who received wages—believing that this determined the growth (or not) of the economy. Future growth depended on capital accumulation, which depended on the share of profits in national income: If landowners received too great a share because of protectionist policies increasing the demand for land on which to grow food at home, and if this expensive food then caused wages to rise, profits would be lower and, therefore, growth would be slower or absent. In developing this analysis, he also supported a preference for free trade: Once Ricardo became a member of Parliament, he educated other members about advantages that removing restrictions on trade would have for the country, adding powerful theoretical reasoning to the free-trade movement. The following extracts indicate the theory of comparative advantage (for which he is famous) and show how it links to the advantages of free trade.

Under a system of perfectly free commerce, each country naturally devotes its capital and labour to such employments as are most beneficial to each. This pursuit of individual advantage is admirably connected with the universal good of the whole. By stimulating industry, by rewarding ingenuity, and by using most efficaciously the peculiar powers bestowed by nature, it distributes labour most effectively and most economically: while, by increasing the general mass of productions, it diffuses general benefit, and binds together by one common tie of interest and intercourse, the universal society of nations throughout the civilized world. It is this principle which determines that wine shall be made in France and Portugal, that corn shall be grown in America and Poland, and that hardware and other goods shall be manufactured in England.

Source: David Ricardo, *Works and Correspondence*, ed. Piero Sraffa. London: Cambridge University Press, 1, 1951: p. 133–34.

If, therefore, by the extension of foreign trade, or by improvements in machinery, the food and necessaries of the labourer can be brought to market at a reduced price, profits will rise. If, instead of growing our own corn, or manufacturing the clothing and other necessaries of the labourer, we discover a new market from which we can supply ourselves with these commodities at a cheaper price, wages will fall and profits rise; but if the commodities obtained at a cheaper rate, by the extension of foreign commerce, or by the improvement of machinery, be exclusively the commodities consumed by the rich, no alteration will take place in the rate of profits.

Source: David Ricardo, *Principles of Political Economy and Taxation* [1817] (1821), London: John Murray. 132.

9. "Memoirs" of Prince Metternich (Austria, 1820)

The continent of Europe was periodically the scene of so-called middle-class revolutions in the nineteenth century, characterized by an upsurge of demands for liberal reforms, political representation, constitutional monarchies, nationalism, and an end to repression. In the first half of the century, one of the most influential European statesmen was Prince Metternich (1773–1859), Austria's chief minister, who represented Austria at the Congress of Vienna in 1815. The Congress of Vienna settled Europe after the upheavals of the Napoleonic Wars, establishing boundaries and reaffirming existing power relationships. These agreements were designed to maintain the status quo to prevent the type of revolutionary thinking that had led to the French Revolution and subsequently to war in Europe. Metternich came to represent the old, repressive regimes that the reformers hoped to replace; his conservatism was rooted in eighteenth-century thinking, and the policies he favored were intended to prevent the spread of liberal nationalism, which he feared—rightly, as the redrawing of boundaries after World War I demonstrated—would undermine Austria's position within Europe. Austria was a multicultural, multilingual state in which German speakers, although a minority, were dominant, and it was the most important military power in Germany, though Prussia was beginning to mount a challenge. This excerpt is from Metternich's "Memoirs" (1820) and describes his political faith, the principles underlying his policies.

The progress of the human mind has been extremely rapid in the course of the last three centuries. This progress having been accelerated more rapidly than the growth of wisdom (the only counterpoise to passions and to error); a revolution prepared by the false systems, the fatal errors into which many of the most illustrious sovereigns of the last half of the eighteenth century fall [the Enlightenment], has at last broken out in a country advanced in knowledge and enervated by pleasure, in a country [Italy] inhabited by a people whom one can only regard as frivolous, from the facility with which they comprehend and the difficulty they experience in judging calmly.

Having now thrown a rapid glance over the first causes of the present state of society, it is necessary to point out in a more particular manner the evil which threatens to deprive it, at one blow, of the real blessings, the fruits of genuine civilization, and to disturb it in the midst of its enjoyments. This evil may be described in one word—presumption; the natural effect of the rapid progression of the human mind towards the perfecting of so many things. This it is which at the present day leads so many individuals astray, for it has become an almost universal sentiment.

Religion, morality, legislation, economy, politics, administration, all have become common and accessible to everyone. Knowledge seems to come by inspiration; experience has no value for the presumptuous man; faith is nothing to him; he substitutes for it a pretended individual conviction, and to arrive at this conviction, he dispenses with all inquiry and with all study; for these means appear trivial to a mind which believes itself strong enough to embrace at one glance all questions and all facts. Laws have no value for him, because he has not contributed to make them.... Power resides in himself.... That which, according to him, was required in an age of weakness cannot be suitable in an age of reason and vigor, amounting to universal perfection, which the German innovators designate by the idea, absurd in itself, of the Emancipation of the People! ... Presumption makes every man the guide of his own belief, the arbiter of laws according to which he is pleased to govern himself, or to allow some one else to govern him and his neighbours; it makes him, in short, the sole judge of his own faith, his own actions, and the principles according to which he guides them.

. . .

It is principally the middle classes of society which this moral gangrene has affected, and it is only among them that the real heads of the party are found.

For the great mass of the people it has no attraction and can have none. The labours to which this class—the real people—are obliged to devote themselves are too continuous and too positive to allow them to throw themselves into vague abstractions and ambitions. The people know what is the happiest thing for them: namely, to be able to count on the morrow, for it is the morrow which will repay them for the cares and sorrows of today. The laws which afford a just protection to individuals, to families, and to property, are quite simple in their essence. The people dread any movement which injures industry and brings new burdens in its train.

. . .

There is besides scarcely any epoch which does not offer a rallying cry to some particular faction. This cry, since 1815, has been Constitution. But do not let us deceive ourselves: this word, susceptible of great latitude of interpretation, would be but imperfectly understood if we supposed that the factions attached quite the same meaning to it under different régimes. Such is certainly not the case. In pure monarchies it is qualified by the name of "national representation." In countries which have lately been brought under the representative régime it is called "development," and promises charters and fundamental laws. In the only State which possesses an ancient national representation it takes "reform" as its object. Everywhere it means change and trouble.

. . .

The Governments, having lost their balance, are frightened, intimidated, and thrown into confusion by the cries of the intermediary class of society, which, placed between the Kings and their subjects, breaks the sceptre of the monarch, and usurps the cry of the people…. The evil is plain.

. . .

We are convinced that society can no longer be saved without strong and vigorous resolutions on the part of the Governments still free in their opinions and actions…. By this course the monarchs will fulfil the duties imposed upon them by Him who, by entrusting them with power, has charged them to watch over the maintenance of justice and the rights of all.

. . .

The first principle to be followed by the monarchs, united as they are by the coincidence of their desires and opinions, should be that of maintaining the stability of political institutions against the disorganized excitement which has taken possession of men's minds; the immutability of principles against the madness of their interpretation; and respect for laws actually in force against a desire for their destruction.

. . .

The first and greatest concern for the immense majority of every nation is the stability of the laws and their uninterrupted action—never their change. Therefore let the Governments govern, let them maintain the groundwork of their institutions.

. . .

Let them announce this determination to their people, and demonstrate it by facts.

. . .

Let them be just, but strong; beneficient, but strict.

Let them maintain religious principles in all their purity, and not allow the faith to be attacked and morality interpreted according to the social contract or the visions of foolish sectarians.

Let them suppress Secret Societies, that gangrene of society.

In short, let the great monarchs strengthen their union, and prove to the world that if it exists, it is beneficent, and ensures the political peace of Europe … that the principles which they profess are paternal and protective, menacing only the disturbers of public tranquillity.

Source: Prince Richard Metternich, ed., *Memoirs of Prince Metternich* (1820), trans. Mrs. Alexander Napier; quoted in Raymond Phineas Stearns, *Pageant of Europe* (New York: Harcourt, Brace, 1947), 469–71.

10. The Monroe Doctrine as Expressed in President James Monroe's Annual Message to Congress (United States, 1823)

In the 1820s, Russia claimed Alaska, Great Britain claimed possession of the Columbia River area, and the European powers were threatening to use force to regain possession of Spain's colonies and possibly also to further make advances in the area. Because U.S. military power would not be able to counter such force, President James Monroe, in an address delivered to Congress on December 2, 1823, issued a warning to European powers and expressed a determination to follow an independent policy that became known as the Monroe Doctrine. The size and rapid growth of the internal market meant that industrialization in the United States was much less dependent on export markets than was, for example, Great Britain, and this statement of foreign policy could be seen as the diplomatic counterpart of an independent economic policy. *See also* United States, Industrial Revolution in.

At the proposal of the Russian Imperial Government, made through the minister of the Emperor residing here, a full power and instructions have been transmitted to the minister of the United States at St. Petersburg to arrange by amicable negotiation the respective rights and interests of the two nations on the northwest coast of this continent. A similar proposal had been made by His Imperial Majesty to the Government of Great Britain, which has likewise been acceded to. The Government of the United States has been desirous by this friendly proceeding of manifesting the great value which they have invariably attached to the friendship of the Emperor and their solicitude to cultivate the best understanding with his Government. In the discussions to which this interest has given rise and in the arrangements by which they may terminate the occasion has been judged proper for asserting as a principle in which the rights and interests of the United States are involved, that the American continents, by the free and independent condition which they have assumed and maintain, are henceforth not to be considered as subjects for future colonization by any European powers.

. . .

A strong hope has been long entertained, founded on the heroic struggle of the Greeks, that they would succeed in their contest and resume their equal station among the nations of the earth. It is believed that the whole civilized world take a deep interest in their welfare. Although no power has declared in their favor, yet none, according to our information, has taken part against them. Their cause and their name have protected them from dangers which might ere this have overwhelmed any other people. The ordinary calculations of interest and of acquisition with a view to aggrandizement, which mingles so much in the transactions of nations, seem to have had no effect in regard to them. From the facts which have come to our knowledge there is good cause to believe that their enemy has lost forever all dominion over them; that Greece will become again an independent nation. That she may obtain that rank is the object of our most ardent wishes.

It was stated at the commencement of the last session that a great effort was then making in Spain and Portugal to improve the condition of the people of these countries, and that it appeared to be conducted with extraordinary moderation. It need scarcely be remarked that the result has been so far very different from what was then anticipated. Of events in that quarter of the globe, with which we have so much intercourse, and from which we derive our origin, we have always been anxious and interested spectators. The citizens of the United States cherish sentiments the most friendly in favor of the liberty and happiness of their fellow-men on that side of the Atlantic. In the wars of the European powers in matters relating to themselves we have never taken any part, nor does it comport with our policy so to do. It is only when our rights are invaded or seriously menaced that we resent injuries or make preparations for our defense. With the movements in this hemisphere we are of necessity more immediately connected, and by causes which must be obvious to all enlightened and impartial observers. The political system of the allied powers is essentially different in this respect from that of America. This difference proceeds from that which exists in their respective Governments; and to the defense of our own, which has been achieved by the loss of so much blood and treasure, and matured by the wisdom of their most enlightened citizens, and under which we have enjoyed unexampled felicity, this whole nation is devoted. We owe it, therefore, to candor and to the amicable relations existing between the United States and these powers to declare that we should consider any attempt on their part to extend their system to any portion of this hemisphere as dangerous to our peace and safety. With the existing colonies or dependencies of any European power we have not interfered and shall not interfere. But with the Governments who have declared their independence and maintained it, and whose independence we have, on great consideration and on just principles, acknowledged, we could not view any interposition for the purpose of oppressing them, or controlling in any other manner their destiny, by any European power in any other light than as the manifestation of an unfriendly disposition toward the United States. In the war between those new Governments and Spain we declared our neutrality at the time of their recognition and to this we have adhered and shall continue to adhere, provided no change shall occur which, in the judgment of the competent authorities of this Government, shall made a corresponding change on the part of the United States indispendible to their security.

The late events in Spain and Portugal shew that Europe is still unsettled. Of this important fact no stronger proof can be adduced than that the allied powers should have thought it proper, on any principle satisfactory to themselves, to have interposed by force in the internal concerns of Spain. To what extent such interposition may be carried, on the same principle, is a question in which all independent powers whose governments differ from theirs are interested, even those most remote, and surely none more so than the United States. Our policy in regard to Europe, which was adopted at an early stage of the wars which have so long agitated that quarter of the globe, nevertheless remains the same, which is, not to interfere in the internal concerns of any of its powers; to consider the government de facto as the legitimate government for us; to cultivate friendly relations with it, and to preserve those relations by a frank, firm, and manly policy, meeting in all instances the just claims of every power, submitting to injuries from none. But in regard to these continents circumstances are eminently and conspicuously different It is impossible that the allied powers should extend their political system to any portion of either continent without endangering our peace and happiness; nor can anyone believe that our southern brethren, if left to themselves, would adopt it of their own accord. It is equally impossible, therefore, that we should behold such interposition in any form with indifference. If we look to the comparative strength and resources of Spain and those new Governments, and their distance from each other, it must be obvious that she can never subdue them. It is still the true policy of the United States to leave the parties to themselves, in the hope that other powers will pursue the same course.

Source: James D. Richardson, ed., *A Compilation of the Messages and Papers of the Presidents* (Washington, DC: U.S. Government Printing Office, 1889), 2: 209, 217–18.

11. Report to Parliament of the Sadler Committee on Working Conditions in Textile Mills (Great Britain, 1833)

The use of young children, especially in the textile factories, was common during the Industrial Revolution. In 1832, a British parliamentary committee was set up to investigate the working conditions in these mills, with Michael Sadler as chairman. Following these investigations, Parliament passed the Factory Act of 1833, limiting the hours of work for children. Similar scandalous conditions in mines were the subject of another parliamentary committee, which led to the passage of the Mines Act in 1842, which prohibited the employment of women and boys under the age of 13 in mines. The first factory acts rarely resolved the problems, but after passage of a law in 1836 requiring the registration of births, marriages, and deaths, it was possible to check a child's age; then the problem of underage labor began to be resolved. As economic development proceeded, industrial technology improved, making workers more productive, and as incomes rose so that the earnings of children were less vital to the family's survival, the cost advantage to employers of using children declined, and fewer children were employed. It should be noted that every country beginning an industrialization process, whether in the nineteenth or the twentieth century, has used children as a cheap labor force. *See also* Child Labor and Child Labor Laws.

From the evidence given by Matthew Crabtree:

What age are you?—Twenty-two
What is your occupation?—A blanket manufacturer
Have you ever been employed in a factory?—Yes
At what age did you first go to work in one?—Eight
How long did you continue in this occupation?—Four years
Will you state the hours of labour at the period when you first went to the factory, in ordinary times?—From 6 in the morning to 8 at night
Fourteen hours?—Yes
With what intervals for refreshment and rest?—An hour at noon
When trade was brisk, what were your hours?—From 5 in the morning to 9 in the evening
Sixteen hours?—Yes

How far did you live from the mill?—About two miles

Was there any time allowed for you to get your breakfast in the mill?—No

Did you take it before you left your home?—Generally

During those long hours of labour could you be punctual; how did you awake?—I seldom did awake spontaneously; I was most generally awoke or lifted out of bed, sometimes asleep, by my parents

Were you always in time?—No

What was the consequence if you had been too late?—I was most commonly beaten

Severely?—very severely, I thought

In those mills is chastisement towards the latter part of the day going on perpetually?—Perpetually

So that you can hardly be in a mill without hearing constant crying?—Never an hour, I believe

Do you think that if the overlooker were naturally a humane person it would be still found necessary for him to beat the children, in order to keep up their attention and vigilance at the termination of those extraordinary days of labour?—Yes; the machine turns off a regular quantity of cardings, and of course they must keep as regularly to their work the whole of the day; they must keep with the machine, and therefore however humane the slubber may be, as he must keep up with the machine or be found fault with, he spurs the children to keep up also by various means but that which he commonly resorts to is to strap them when they become drowsy

At the time when you were beaten for not keeping up with your work, were you anxious to have done it if you possibly could?—Yes; the dread of being beaten if we could not keep up with our work was a sufficient impulse to keep us to it if we could

When you got home at night after this labour, did you feel much fatigued?—Very much so

Had you any time to be with yur parents, and to receive instruction from them?—No

What did you do?—All that we did when we got home was to get the little bit of supper that was provided for us and go to bed immediately. If the supper had not been ready directly, we should have gone to sleep while it was preparing

Did you not, as a child, feel it a very grievous hardship to be roused so soon in the morning?—I did

Were the rest of the children similarly circumstanced?—Yes, all of them; but they were not all of them so far from their work as I was

And if you had been too late you were under the apprehension of being cruelly beaten?—I generally was beaten, when I happened to be too late; and when I got up in the morning the apprehension of that was so great, that I used to run, and cry all the way as I went to the mill.

Source: "Report of Committee on Factory Children's Labour," *Parliamentary Papers, 1831–32,* 15: 95–97; quoted in Raymond Phineas Stearns, *Pageant of Europe: Sources and Selections from the Renaissance to the Present Day* (New York: Harcourt, Brace, 1947), 493–94.

12. Excerpts from Alexis de Tocqueville's *Democracy in America* (United States, 1835)

Democracy in America, by Alexis de Tocqueville, was first published in 1835 following de Tocqueville's nine-month journey in the United States. De Tocqueville, who was born on July 29, 1805, came from an aristocratic Norman family that had suffered during the French Revolution. France was still a stratified society, but de Tocqueville believed that democratic institutions and behavior would eventually spread there. He and a friend arrived in the United States in May 1831, and the book describes his impressions of the impact of democracy on various aspects of U.S. society.

He was skeptical about democracy as he saw it, believing that the original desire in the new country for individual liberty was threatened by the trend toward equality and conformity and that majority rule could become a growing tyranny. If these shortcomings could be identified, then safeguards could be installed so that France could reap the benefits of the experience. Although there are many ways in which the book can be criticized—de Tocqueville overgeneralized, he was too subjective at times, and he misread the balance of political power in the country—he was very observant of and reported fairly on many aspects of life, including economic ones. He believed that although the country was predominantly agricultural, Americans would make rapid progress in developing industry because they were ambitious, single-minded in their desire for profits, and concerned with the practical. The following excerpt, from part 2 of the work, illustrates these observations. It is clear that the absence of restrictions played an important role in encouraging Americans to take up new activities.

XIX. WHAT CAUSES ALMOST ALL AMERICANS TO FOLLOW INDUSTRIAL CALLINGS

Agriculture is, perhaps, of all the useful arts, that which improves most slowly amongst democratic nations. Frequently, indeed, it would seem to be stationary, because other arts are making rapid strides towards perfection. On the other hand, almost all the tastes and habits which the equality of condition produces naturally lead men to commercial and industrial occupations.

Suppose an active, enlightened, and free man, enjoying a competency, but full of desires; he is too poor to live in idleness; he is rich enough to feel himself protected from the immediate fear of want, and he thinks how he can better his condition. This man has conceived a taste for physical gratifications, which thousands of his fellow-men indulge in around him; he has himself begun to enjoy these pleasures and he is eager to increase his means of satisfying these tastes more completely. But life is slipping away, time is urgent;—to what is he to turn? The cultivation of the ground promises an almost certain result to his exertions, but a slow one; men are not enriched by it without patience and toil. Agriculture is therefore only suited to those who have already large superfluous wealth, or to those whose penury bids them only seek a bare subsistence. The choice of such a man as we have supposed is soon made; he sells his plot of ground, leaves his dwelling, and embarks in some hazardous but lucrative calling.

Democratic communities abound in men of this kind; and, in proportion as the equality of conditions becomes greater, their multitude increases. Thus, democracy not only swells the number of working-men, but it leads men to prefer one kind of labor to another, and, whilst it diverts them from agriculture, it encourages their taste for commerce and manufacturing.

This spirit may be observed even amongst the richest members of the community. In democratic countries, however opulent a man is supposed to be, he is almost always discontented with his fortune, because he finds that he is less rich than his father was, and he fears that his sons will be less rich than himself. Most rich men in democracies are therefore constantly haunted by the desire of obtaining wealth, and they naturally turn their attention to trade and manufactures, which appear to offer the readiest and most efficient means of success. In this respect, they share the instincts of the poor without feeling the same necessities, say, rather, they feel the most imperious of all necessities, that of not sinking in the world

In aristocracies, the rich are at the same time the governing power. The attention which they unceasingly devote to important public affairs diverts them from the lesser cares which trade and manufactures demand. But if an individual happens to turn his attention to business, the will of the body to which he belongs will immediately prevent him from pursuing it; for, however men may declaim against the rule of numbers, they cannot wholly escape it; and even amongst those aristocratic bodies which most obstinately refuse to acknowledge the rights of the national majority, a private majority is formed which govern the rest.

In democratic countries, where money does not lead those who possess it to political power, but often removes them from it, the rich do not know how to spend their leisure. They are driven into active life by the inquietude and the greatness of their desires, by the extent of their resources, and by the taste for what is extraordinary, which is almost always felt by those who rise, by whatsoever means, above the crowd. Trade is the only road open to them. In democracies, nothing is more great or more brilliant than commerce: it attracts the attention of the public, and fills the imagination of the multitude; all energetic passions are directed towards it. Neither their own prejudices nor those of anybody else can prevent the rich from devoting themselves to it. The wealthy members of democracies never form a body which has manners and regulations of its own; the opinions peculiar to their class do not restrain them, and the common opinions of their country urge them on. Moreover, as all the large fortunes which are found in a democratic community are of commercial growth, many generations must succeed each other before their possessors can have entirely laid aside their habits of business.

Circumscribed within the narrow space which politics leave them, rich men in democracies eagerly embark in commercial enterprise: there they can extend and employ their natural advantages; and indeed, it is even by the boldness and the magnitude of their industrial speculations that we may measure the slight esteem in which productive industry would have been held by them, if they had been born amidst an aristocracy.

A similar observation is likewise applicable to all men living in democracies, whether they be poor or rich. Those who live in the midst of democratic fluctuations have always before their eyes the image of chance; and they end by liking all undertakings in which chance plays a part. They are therefore all led to engage in commerce, not only for the sake of the profit it holds out to them, but for the love of the constant excitement occasioned by that pursuit.

The United States of America have only been emancipated for half a century from the state of colonial dependence in which they stood to Great Britain: the number of large fortunes there is small and capital is still scarce. Yet no people in the world have made such rapid progress in trade and manufactures as the Americans; they constitute at the present day the second maritime nation in the world; and although their manufactures have to struggle with almost insurmountable natural impediments, they are not prevented from making great and daily advances.

In the United States, the greatest undertakings and speculations are executed without difficulty, because the whole population are engaged in productive industry, and because the poorest as well as the most opulent members of the commonwealth are ready to combine their efforts for these purposes. The consequence is, that a stranger is constantly amazed by the immense public works executed by a nation which contains, so to speak, no rich men. The Americans arrived but as yesterday on the territory which they inhabit, and they have already changed the whole order of nature for their own advantage. They have joined the Hudson to the Mississippi, and made the Atlantic Ocean communicate with the Gulf of Mexico, across a continent of more than five hundred leagues in extent which separates the two seas. The longest railroads which have been constructed, up to the present time, are in America.

But what astonishes me in the United States is not so much the marvellous grandeur of some undertakings, as the innumerable multitude of small ones. Almost all the farmers of the United States combine some trade with agriculture; most of them make agriculture itself a trade. It seldom happens that an American farmer settles for good upon the land which he occupies: especially in the districts of the Far West, he brings land into tillage in order to sell it again, and not to farm it: he builds a farm-house on the speculation, that, as the state of the country will soon be changed by the increase of population, a good price may be obtained for it. Every year, a swarm of people from the North arrive in the Southern States, and settle in the parts where the cotton-plant and the sugar-cane grow. These men cultivate the soil in order to make it produce in a few years enough to enrich them; and they already look forward to the time when they may return home to enjoy the competency thus acquired. Thus the Americans carry their business-like qualities into agriculture; and their trading passions are displayed as in their other pursuits.

The Americans make immense progress in productive industry, because they all devote themselves to it at once; and for this same reason, they are exposed to unexpected and formidable embarrassments. As they are all engaged in commerce, their commercial affairs are affected by such various and complex causes, that it is impossible to foresee what difficulties may arise. As they are all more or less engaged in productive industry, at the least shock given to business, all private fortunes are put in jeopardy at the same time, and the state is shaken. I believe that the return of these commercial panics is an endemic disease of the democratic nations of our age. It may be rendered less dangerous, but it cannot be cured; because it does not originate in accidental circumstances, but in the temperament of these nations.

Source: Alexis de Tocqueville, *Democracy in America,* trans. Henry Reeve (New York: D. Appleton, [1835] 1899, 1901), p. 187–192.

13. The Chartists' First Petition to Parliament (Great Britain, 1838)

In the early nineteenth century, it was difficult for workers to organize in unions to push for improvement of their working conditions; some groups began to consider political action to reach the same ends. The London Working Men's Association drew up a petition, called the People's Charter, to present to Parliament in 1838. The petition contained some remarkably modern requests, such as a demand for a secret ballot (to prevent corruption at the polls), payment for members of Parliament (to open up the opportunity for political office to all segments of society, not just the wealthy), universal suffrage (although the Chartists interpreted this as universal male suffrage). The Chartists' movement was not successful, although eventually all but one of their demands—the demand for annual parliaments—were put into place. *See also* Chartism.

Humbly Sheweth,

That we, your petitioners, dwell in a land whose merchants are noted for their enterprise, whose manufacturers are very skilful, and whose workmen are proverbial for their industry. The land itself is goodly, the soil rich, and the temperature wholesome. It is abundantly furnished with the materials of commerce and trade. It has numerous and convenient harbours. In facility of internal communication it exceeds all others. For three and twenty years we have enjoyed a profound peace. Yet, with all the elements of national prosperity, and with every disposition and capacity to take advantage of them, we find ourselves overwhelmed with public and private suffering… We have looked on every side; we have searched diligently in order to find out the causes of distress so sore and so long continued. We can discover none in nature or in Providence…. But the foolishness of our rulers has made the goodness of God of none effect. The energies of a mighty kingdom have been wasted in building up the power of selfish and ignorant men, and its resources squandered for their aggrandisement. The good of a part has been advanced at the sacrifice of the good of the nation. The few have governed for the interest of the few, while the interests of the many have been sottishly neglected, or insolently and tyrannously trampled upon. It was the fond expectation of the friends of the people that a remedy for the greater part, if not for the whole of their grievances, would be found in the Reform Act of 1832. They regarded that Act as a wise means to a worthy end, as the machinery of an improved legislation, where the will of the masses would be at length potential. They have been bitterly and basely deceived…. The Reform Act has effected a transfer of power from one domineering faction to another, and left the people as helpless as before. Our slavery has been exchanged for an apprenticeship to liberty, which has aggravated the painful feelings of our social degradation, by adding to them the sickening of still deferred hope. We come before your honourable house to tell you, with all humility, that this state of things must not be permitted to continue. That it cannot long continue, without very seriously endangering the stability of the throne, and the peace of the kingdom, and that if, by God's help, and all lawful and constitutional appliances, an end can be put to it, we are fully resolved that it shall speedily come to an end. We tell your honourable house, that the capital of the master must no longer be deprived of its due profit; that the labour of the workman must no longer be deprived of its due reward. That the laws which make food dear, and the laws which make money scarce, must be abolished…. That the good of the many, as it is the only legitimate end, so must it be the sole study of the government. As a preliminary essential to these and other requisite changes—as the means by which alone the interests of the people can be effectually vindicated and secured, we demand that those interests be confided to the keeping of the people.... We perform the duties of freemen; we must have the privileges of freemen. Therefore, we demand universal suffrage. The suffrage, to be exempt from the corruption of the wealthy and the violence of the powerful, must be secret. The assertion of our right necessarily involves the power of our uncontrolled exercise. We ask for the reality of a good, not for its semblance, therefore we demand the ballot.... To public safety, as well as public confidence, frequent elections are essential. Therefore, we demand annual parliaments. With power to choose, and freedom in choosing, the range of our choice must be unrestricted. We are compelled, by the existing laws, to take for representatives men who are incapable of appreciating our difficulties, or have little sympathy with them.... The labours of a representative who is sedulous in the discharge of his duty are numerous and burdensome. It is neither just, nor reasonable, nor safe, that they should continue to be gratuitously rendered. We demand that in the future election of members of your honourable house, the approbation of the constituency shall be the sole qualification, and that to every representative so chosen, shall be assigned out of the public taxes, a fair and adequate remuneration for the time which he is called upon to devote to the public service.... May it therefore please your honourable house, to take this our petition into your most serious consideration, and to use your utmost endeavours, by all constitutional means, to have a law passed, granting to every male of lawful age, sane mind, and unconvicted of crime, the right of voting for members of parliament, and directing all future elections of members of parliament to be in the way of secret ballot, and ordaining that the duration of parliament, so chosen, shall in no case exceed one year, and abolishing all property qualifications in the members, and providing for their due remuneration while in attendance on their parliamentary duties.

Source: R. G. Gammage, *History of the Chartist Movement, 1837–1854,* (London 1854; repr. New York: A.M. Kelley, 1969), pp. 87–90.

14. Louis-René Villermé on Poverty ("La Misère") (France, 1840)

The Industrial Revolution in France, as it did elsewhere, created both new wealth and a new appearance of poverty. Poverty always had existed in France, but to French observers the poverty associated with industrial towns somehow seemed worse. It was referred to as *la misère* to describe not just poverty caused by absence of income but also a sociocultural phenomenon, and it shocked those who thought that industrial development also would bring social progress. Louis-René Villermé was a medical doctor who was appointed in 1835 to investigate the conditions in which the industrial working classes lived and worked in order to inform reforms to improve the worst abuses. His findings were that, during good times, working families' incomes were adequate, but a commercial crisis, period of sickness, birth of a third child, or some other normal occurrence could tip the family into penury. He also reported on other aspects of working-class life, deploring intemperance, lax morals, and coarseness of language. His evidence and appeals convinced the French legislature to pass, in 1841, a law limiting the hours of work of children aged 8 to 12 to 8 hours a day and 12 hours for those aged between 12 and 16. Penalties for infraction were nominal fines. No inspectors were authorized to enforce the laws, so they had no real impact.

The following are some extracts from Villermé's reports

I saw lying together individuals of both sexes and very different ages, most without chemises and repulsively filthy. Father, mother, the elderly, children, and adults, pressed and packed together. I will stop here ... the reader must complete the picture for himself; but I warn him, if he is equal to the task his imagination must not falter when confronted by the revolting mysteries that take place in these impure beds amid the darkness and the drunkenness (134).

It is impossible to imagine the appearance of these habitations of the poor if one has not visited them ... grinding poverty—intolerable, murderous ... dark cellars, infected air, walls covered with a thousand forms of filth ... [for beds] dirty, greasy boards ... covered with damp and putrescent straw ... furniture encrusted with grime ... windows always closed ... everywhere piles of garbage, ash, remains of vegetables collected in the streets ... the air, hardly breathable, has a dull, nauseating, slightly acrid smell—the smell of filth, the smell of garbage, the smell of humans (136).

The evil is not new, but it is greater than ever; it results principally from the habitual assembly of workers in large workshops, which are like serails where workers of both sexes and all ages intermingle; and from their stay in cities, especially large cities, where numerous factories create agglomerations of population. It comes also from free competition, that cause of the growth and prodigious expansion of industry, but also of the frequent overproduction of manufactured goods, of bulging warehouses and the collapse of the value of inventories, of the ruin of numerous factory owners, and of the many crises and many oscillations in the rate of salaries that are so injurious to workers (156).

Source: Louis-René Villermé, *Tableau de l'état Physique et Moral des Ouvriers Employés dans les Manufactures de Coton, de Laine, et de Soie* (Paris: Renouard, 1840, reprinted 1989), quoted by James B. Briscoe, "The Debate on the Condition of the Working Class in France circa 1840: A Study in Ideology," in *The Industrial Revolution in Comparative Perspective*, ed. Christine Rider and Mícheál Thompson (Malabar, FL: Krieger, 2000), p. 179–201.

15. Friedrich List Argues for a Protectionist Policy for Germany (Germany, 1841)

Friedrich List was a German economist and political activist who argued strongly for a protectionist policy and national unity to help Germany industrialize, in contrast to the prevailing preference in Britain for free trade and laissez-faire. List argued that a backward country, as Germany was at the beginning of the nineteenth century, would remain forever a backward agricultural economy dependent on manufactured imports from an industrialized economy if it embraced free trade. In this excerpt, he argues forcefully for the establishment of manufacturing, reciprocal preferential trading agreements with other countries, the subsidized establishment of shipbuilding and shipping lines (so as to remove the country's dependence on foreign shipping), and the encouragement of settlements by German nationals in tropical countries (so as to give a preference for German goods that would increase its trade). The development of a strong economy was a prerequisite for the true expression of German talent and skills and essential for the development of a sense of nationhood and a powerful nation.

IF any nation whatever is qualified for the establishment of a national manufacturing power, it is Germany; by the high rank which she maintains in science and art, in literature and education, in public administration and in institutions of public utility; by her morality and religious character, her industry and domestic economy; by her perseverance and steadfastness in business occupations; as also by her spirit of invention, by the number and vigour of her population; by the extent and nature of her territory, and especially by her highly advanced agriculture, and her physical, social, and mental resources.

IV.XXXVI.1

If any nation whatever has a right to anticipate rich results from a protective system adapted to her circumstances, for the progress of her home manufactures, for the increase of her foreign trade and her navigation, for the perfecting of her internal means of transport, for the prosperity of her agriculture, as also for the maintenance of her independence and the increase of her power abroad, it is Germany.

IV.XXXVI.2

Yes, we venture to assert, that on the development of the German protective system depend the existence, the independence, and the future of the German nationality. Only in the soil of general prosperity does the national spirit strike its roots, produce fine blossoms and rich fruits; only from the unity of material interests does mental power arise, and only from both of these national power. But of what value are all our endeavours, whether we are rulers or subjects, nobles or simple citizens, learned men, soldiers, or civilians, manufacturers, agriculturists, or merchants, without nationality and without guarantees for the continuance of our nationality?

IV.XXXVI.3

Meanwhile, however, the German protective system only accomplishes its object in a very imperfect manner, so long as Germany does not spin for herself the cotton and linen yarn which she requires; so long as she does not directly import from tropical countries the colonial produce which she requires, and pay for it with goods of her own manufacture; so long as she does not carry on this trade with her own ships; so long as she has no means of protecting her own flag; so long as she possesses no perfect system of transport by river, canal, or railway; so long as the German Zollverein does not include all German maritime territories and also Holland and Belgium. We have treated these subjects circumstantially in various places in this book, and it is only necessary for us here to recapitulate what we have already thus treated.

IV.XXXVI.4

If we import raw cotton from Egypt, Brazil, and North America, we in that case pay for it in our own manufactured goods; if, on the other hand, we import cotton yarn from England, we have to pay the value of it in raw materials and articles of food which we could more advantageously work up or consume ourselves, or else we must pay for it in specie which we have acquired elsewhere, and with which we could more advantageously purchase foreign raw materials to work up for ourselves, or colonial produce for our own consumption.

IV.XXXVI.5

In the same way the introduction of spinning linen yarn by machinery offers us the means not only of increasing our home consumption of linen, and of perfecting our agriculture, but also of enormously increasing our trade with tropical countries.

IV.XXXVI.6

For the two above-named branches of industry, as well as for the manufacture of woollens, we are as favourably circumstanced as any other nation, by an amount of water power hitherto not utilised, by cheap necessaries of life, and by low wages. What we lack is simply and solely a guarantee for our capitalists and artisans by which they may be protected against loss of capital and want of work. A moderate protective duty of about twenty-five per cent. during the next five years, which could be maintained for a few years at that rate and then be lowered to fifteen to twenty per cent., ought completely to accomplish this object. Every argument which is adduced by the supporters of the theory of values against such a measure, has been refuted by us. On the other hand, we may add a further argument in favour of that measure, that these great branches of industry especially offer us the means for establishing extensive machine manufactories and for the development of a race of competent technical instructors and practical foremen.

IV.XXXVI.7

In the trade in colonial produce Germany, as France and England have done, has to follow the principle—that in respect to the purchase of the colonial produce which we require, we should give a preference to those tropical countries which purchase manufactured goods from us; or, in short, that we should buy from those who buy from us. That is the case in reference to our trade with the West Indies and to North and South America.

IV.XXXVI.8

But it is not yet the case in reference to our trade with Holland, which country supplies us with enormous quantities of her colonial produce, but only takes in return disproportionately small quantities of our manufactured goods.

IV.XXXVI.9

At the same time Holland is naturally directed to the market of Germany for the disposal of the greater part of her colonial produce, inasmuch as England and France derive their supplies of such produce for the most part from their own colonies and from subject countries (where they exclusively possess the market for manufactured goods), and hence they only import small quantities of Dutch colonial produce.

IV.XXXVI.10

Holland has no important manufacturing industry of her own, but, on the other hand, has a great productive industry in her colonies, which has recently greatly increased and may yet be immeasurably further increased. But Holland desires of Germany that which is unfair, and acts contrary to her own interests if rightly understood, inasmuch as she desires to dispose of the greater part of her colonial produce to Germany, while she desires to supply her requirements of manufactured goods from any quarter she likes best. This is, for Holland, an only apparently beneficial and a short-sighted policy; for if Holland would give preferential advantages to German manufactured goods both in the mother country and in her colonies, the demand in Germany for Dutch colonial produce would increase in the same proportion in which the sale of German manufactured goods to Holland and her colonies increased, or, in other words, Germany would be able to purchase so much the more colonial produce in proportion as she sold more manufactured goods to Holland; Holland would be able to dispose of so much more colonial produce to Germany as she purchased from Germany manufactured goods. This reciprocal exchange operation is, at present, rendered impracticable by Holland if she sells her colonial produce to Germany while she purchases her requirements in manufactured goods from England, because England (no matter how much of manufactured goods she sells to Holland) will always supply the greater part of her own requirements of colonial produce from her own colonies, or from the countries which are subject to her.

IV.XXXVI.11

Hence the interests of Germany require that she should either demand from Holland a differential duty in favour of Germany's manufacturing production, by which the latter can secure to herself the exclusive market for manufactured goods in Holland and her colonies, or, in case of refusal, that Germany should impose a differential duty on the import of colonial produce in favour of the produce of Central and South America and of the free markets of the West Indies.

IV.XXXVI.12

The above-named policy would constitute the most effective means of inducing Holland to join the German Zollverein.

IV.XXXVI.13

As matters now stand, Germany has no reason for sacrificing her own manufactories of beetroot sugar to the trade with Holland; for only in case Germany can pay for her requirements of this article by means of her own manufactured goods, is it more to her advantage to supply that requirement by an exchange trade with tropical countries, than by producing it herself at home.

IV.XXXVI.14

Hence the attention of Germany should be at once chiefly directed to the extension of her trade with Northern, Central, and South America, and with the free markets of the West Indies. In connection with that, the following measures, in addition to that above adverted to, appear desirable: the establishment of a regular service of steamships between the German seaports and the principal ports of those countries, the promotion of emigration thither, the confirmation and extension of friendly relations between them and the Zollverein, and especially the promotion of the civilisation of those countries.

IV.XXXVI.15

Recent experience has abundantly taught us how enormously commerce on a large scale is promoted by a regular service of steamships. France and Belgium are already treading in the footsteps of England in this respect, as they well perceive that every nation which is behindhand in this more perfect means of transport must retrograde in her foreign trade. The German seaports also have already recognised this; already one public company has been completely formed in Bremen for building two or three steam vessels for the trade with the United States. This, however, is clearly an insufficient provision. The commercial interests of Germany require not only a regular service of steam vessels with North America, especially with New York, Boston, Charleston, and New Orleans, but also with Cuba, San Domingo, and Central and South America. Germany ought to be behind no other nation in respect to these latter lines of steam navigation. It must certainly not be ignored that the means which are required for these objects will be too great for the spirit of enterprise, and perhaps also for the power of the German seaports, and it seems to us they can only be carried into effect by means of liberal subsidies on the part of the states of the Zollverein. The prospect of such subsidies as well as of differential duties in favour of German shipping, ought at once to constitute a strong motive for these seaports to become included in the Commercial Union. When one considers how greatly the exports of manufactured goods and the imports of colonial produce, and consequently also the customs revenue, of the states of the Zollverein would be increased by such a measure, one cannot doubt that even a considerable expenditure for this object must appear as only a reproductive investment of capital from which rich returns are to be expected.

IV.XXXVI.16

Through the increase of the means of intercourse of Germany with the above-named countries, the emigration of Germans to those countries and their settlement there as citizens would be no less promoted; and by that means the foundation would be laid for future increase of commerce with them. For this object the states of the Zollverein ought to establish everywhere consulates and diplomatic agencies, by means of which the settlement and undertakings of German citizens could be promoted, and especially to assist those states in every practicable way in giving stability to their governments and improving their degree of civilisation.

Source: Friedrich List, *The National System of Political Economy, 1841,* trans. Sampson S. Lloyd (1885), ed. J. Shield Nicholson (London: Longmans, Green, 1909), pp. 341–350.

16. Sir Robert Peel's Speech to the House of Commons Supporting Repeal of the Corn Laws (Great Britain, 1846)

Passed in 1815, the British Corn Laws were a relic of mercantilist commercial policy. Although much loosening of restrictions on trade and commerce had taken place since the eighteenth century, the Corn Laws remained as a symbol of the power of the landed interests to limit the freedom of the new industrial interests. The struggle to repeal them was possibly as much an expression of a political clash between old and new classes as it was an expression of the appeal of laissez-faire ideology. On February 16, 1846, Sir Robert Peel, then prime minister, made the following impassioned speech to the House of Commons in support of repeal. Although the motion passed, it split Peel's Conservation Party, which thereafter was largely in the minority until the 1870s. *See also* Corn Laws.

This night is to decide between the policy of continued relaxation of restriction, or the return to restraint and prohibition. This night you will select the motto which is to indicate the commercial policy of England. Shall it be "advance" or "recede"? Which is the fitter motto for this great Empire? Survey our position, consider the advantages which God and nature have given us, and the destiny for which we are intended. We stand on the confines of Western Europe, the chief connecting link between the old world and the new. The discoveries of science, the improvement of navigation, have brought us within ten days of St. Petersburgh, and will soon bring us to within ten days of New York. We have an extent of coast greater in proportion to our population and the area of our land than any other great nation, securing to us maritime strength and superiority. Iron and coal, the sinews of manufacture, give us advantages over every rival in the great competition of industry. Our capital far exceeds that which they can command. In ingenuity, in skill, in energy, we are inferior to none, Our national character, the free institutions under which we live, the liberty of thought and action, an unshackled press, spreading the knowledge of every discovery and of every advance in science—combine with our natural and physical advantages to place us at the head of those nations which profit by the free interchange of their products. And is this the country to shrink from competition? Is this the country to adopt a retrograde policy? Is this the country which can only flourish in the sickly artificial atmosphere of prohibition? Is this the country to stand shivering on the brink of exposure to the healthful breezes of competition?

Choose your motto. "Advance" or "Recede." Many countries are watching with anxiety the selection you may make. Determine for "Advance," and it will be the watchword which will animate and encourage in every state the friends of liberal commercial policy. Sardinia has taken the lead. Naples is relaxing her protective duties and favouring British produce. Prussia is shaken in her adherence to restriction. The Government of France will be strengthened…. Can you doubt that the United States will soon relax her hostile Tariff, and that the friends of a freer commercial intercourse—the friends of peace between two countries—will hail with satisfaction the example of England?

This night, then—if on this night the debate shall close—you will have to decide what are the principles by which your commercial policy is to be regulated. Most earnestly, from a deep conviction, founded not upon the limited experience of three years alone, but upon the experience of the results of every relaxation of restriction and prohibition, I counsel you to set an example of liberality to other countries, Act thus, and it will be in perfect consistency with the course you have hitherto taken. Act thus, and you will provide an additional guarantee for the continued contentment, and happiness, and well-being of the great body of the people. Act thus, and you will have done whatever human sagacity can do for the promotion of commercial prosperity.

You may fail. Your precautions may be unavailing. They may give no certain assurance that mercantile and manufacturing prosperity will continue without interruption. It seems to be incident to greater prosperity that there shall be a reverse—that the time of depression shall follow the season of excitement and success…Gloomy winters, like those of 1841 and 1842, may again set in. Are those winters effaced from your memory? From mine they never can be.

. . .

When you are again exhorting a suffering people to fortitude under their privations, when you are telling them, "These are the chastenings of an all-wide and merciful Providence, sent for some inscrutable but just and beneficent purpose," … when you are encouraging them to bear without repining the dispensations of Providence, may God grant that by your decision of this night you have laid in store for yourselves the consolation of reflecting that such calamities are, in truth, the dispensations of Providence—that they have not been caused, they have not been aggravated by laws of man restricting, in the hour of scarcity, the supply of food!

Source: Hansard's "Parliamentary Debates," 3rd ser. (1846), London: House of Commons Publications 83: 1041–43.

17. Excerpts from *The Communist Manifesto* by Karl Marx and Friedrich Engels (1848)

Karl Marx and his friend and collaborator Friedrich Engels met in Paris in 1843, at a time when Paris was the center of intellectual discussions of socialism. Both became active in the Communist League. After the failure of the European revolutions of 1848, they produced *The Communist Manifesto,* which describes Marx's idea of history as a history of class struggles that will end with the success of the proletariat; the advent of the classless, Communist society; and the withering away of the state, which up to then had always been an instrument of repression in the hands of the ruling class. To some extent, he was influenced by the Hegelian idea of the evolution of society as the conflict of ideas: In each stage of history, thesis comes into conflict with antithesis, out of which emerges a synthesis appropriate to the new stage of history. But Marx used the method of dialectics in reverse, in which the conflict is one of the materialistic conflict of classes: Each historical stage is characterized by a particular mode of economic production that contains within itself the seeds of its own destruction. In the case of capitalist production, labor (the proletariat) cooperates to produce value, but profits are privately appropriated by capital (the bourgeoisie). As internal contradictions build up, the conflict between the social nature of production and the private control over what is produced becomes too great. *The Communist Manifesto* uses this analysis to become a revolutionary call for action by the proletariat. The following extracts summarize this progression of history, and the conditions that will apply to the classless society.

A spectre is haunting Europe—the spectre of Communism … [because Communism is acknowledged to be a power].

. . .

To this end, Communists of various nationalities have assembled in London , and sketched the following manifesto.

. . .

BOURGEOIS AND PROLETARIANS

The history of all hitherto existing society is the history of class struggles.

Freeman and slave, patrician and plebeian, lord and serf, guild-master and journeyman, in a word, oppressor and oppressed, stood in constant opposition to one another, carried on an uninterrupted, now hidden, now open fight, a fight that each time ended, either in a revolutionary reconstruction of society at large, or in the common ruin of the contending classes.

. . .

The modern bourgeois society that has sprouted from the ruins of feudal society, has not done away with class antagonisms. It has but established new classes, new conditions of oppression, new forms of struggle in place of the old ones.

Our epoch, the epoch of the bourgeoisie, possesses, however, this distinctive feature: It has simplified the class antagonisms. Society as a whole is more and more splitting up into two great camps, into two great classes directly facing each other—the bourgeoisie and proletariat.

. . .

The feudal system of industry, in which industrial production was monopolised by closed guilds, now no longer sufficed for the growing wants of new markets. The manufacturing system took its place. The guild-masters were pushed aside by the manufacturing middle class; division of labour between the different corporate guilds vanished in the face of division of labour in each single workshop.

Meantime the markets kept ever growing, the demand ever rising. Even manufacture no longer sufficed. Thereupon, steam and machinery revolutionised industrial production. The place of manufacture was taken by the giant, modern industry, the place of the industrial middle class, by industrial millionaires—the leaders of whole industrial armies, the modern bourgeoisie.

Modern industry has established the world market, for which the discovery of America paved the way. This market has given an immense development to commerce, to navigation, to communication by land. This development has, in turn, reacted on the extension of industry; and in proportion as industry, commerce, navigation, railways extended, in the same proportion the bourgeoisie developed, increased its capital, and pushed down into the background every class handed down from the Middle Ages.

We see, therefore, how the modern bourgeoisie is itself the product of a long course of development, of a series of revolutions in the modes of production and of exchange.

. . .

The executive of the modern state is but a committee for managing the common afairs of the whole bourgeoisie.

The bourgeoisie has played a most revolutionary rôle in history … has put an end to all feudal, patriarchal, idyllic relations. It has pitilessly torn asunder the motley feudal ties that bound man to his "natural superiors," and has left no other bond between man and man than naked self-interest, than callous "cash payment." … It has resolved personal worth into exchange value, and in place of the numberless indefeasible chartered freedoms, has set up that single, unconscionable freedom— Free Trade. In one word, for exploitation, veiled by religious and political illusions, it has substituted naked, shameless, direct, brutal exploitation.

. . .

The bourgeoisie cannot exist without constantly revolutionising the instruments of production, and thereby the relations of production, and with them the whole relations of society. Conservation of the old modes of production in unaltered form, was, on the contrary, the first condition of existence for all earlier industrial classes. Constant revolutionising of production, uninteruppted disturbance of all social conditions, everlasting uncertainty and agitation distinguish the bourgeois epoch from all earlier ones.… All that is solid melts into air, all that is holy is profaned, and man is at last compelled to face with sober senses his real conditions of life and his relations with his kind.

. . .

The bourgeoisie has through its exploitation of the world market given a cosmopolitan character to production and consumption in every country.… In place of the old wants, satisfied by the production of the country, we find new wants, requiring for their satisfaction the products of distant lands and climes. In place of the old local and national seclusion and self-sufficiency, we have intercourse in every direction, universal inter-dependence of nations.

. . .

The bourgeoisie, during its rule of scarce one hundred years, has created more massive and more colossal productive forces than have all preceding generations together. Subjection of nature's forces to man, machinery, application of chemistry to industry and agriculture, steam-navigation, railways, electric telegraphs, clearing of whole continents for cultivation, canalisation of rivers, whole populations conjured out of the ground—what earlier century had even a presentiment that such productive forces slumbered in the lap of social labour?

. . .

Modern bourgeois society with its relations of production, of exchange and of property, a society that has conjured up such gigantic means of production and of exchange [can no longer control these forces].... The productive forces at the disposal of society no longer tend to further the development of the conditions of bourgeois property; on the contrary, they have become too powerful for these conditions, by which they are fettered, and no sooner do they overcome these fetters than they bring disorder into the whole of bourgeois society, endanger the existence of bourgeois property.

. . .

But not only has the bourgeoisie forged the weapons that bring death to itself; it has also called into existence the men who are to wield those weapons—the modern working class—the proletarians.

In proportion as the bourgeoisie, i.e., capital, is developed, in the same proportion is the proletariat, the modern working class, developed—a class of labourers, who live only so long as they find work, and who find work only so long as their labour increases capital. These labourers, who must sell themselves piecemeal, are a commodity, like every other article of commerce, and are consequently exposed to all the vicissitudes of competition, to all the fluctuations of the market.

. . .

The proletariat goes through various stages of development. With its birth begins its struggle with the bourgeoisie. At first the contest is carried on by individual labourers, then by the workpeople of a factory, then by the operatives of one trade, in one locality, against the individual bourgeoise who directly exploits them.

. . .

But with the development of industry the proletariat not only increases in number; it becomes concentrated in greater masses, its strength grows.... Thereupon the workers begin to form combinations (trade unions) against the bourgeoisie.

. . .

This organisation of the proletarians into a class, and consequently into a political party, is continually being upset again by the competition between the workers themselves.

. . .

Finally, in times when the class struggle nears the decisive hour, the process of dissolution going on within the ruling class, in fact within the whole range of old society, assumes such a violent, glaring character, that a small section of the ruling class cuts itself adrift, and joins the revolutionary class, the class that holds the future in its hands.

. . .

Of all the classes that stand face to face with the bourgeoisie today, the proletariat alone is a really revolutionary class. The other classes decay and finally disappear in the face of modern industry; the proletariat is its special and essential product.

. . .

All the preceding classes that got the upper hand, sought to fortify their already acquired status by subjecting society at large to their conditions of appropriation. The proletarians cannot become masters of the productive forces of society, except by abolishing their own previous mode of appropriation.... They have nothing of their own to secure and to fortify; their mission is to destroy all previous securities for, and insurances of, individual property.

PROLETARIANS AND COMMUNISTS

. . .

The Communists, therefore, are on the one hand, practically, the most advanced and resolute section of the working class parties of every country.

. . .

The immediate aim of the Communists is the same as that of all the other proletarian parties: formation of the proletariat into a class, overthrow of bourgeois supremacy, conquest of political power by the proletariat.

. . .

Communism deprives no man of the power to appropriate the products of society; all that it does is to deprive him of the power to subjugate the labour of others by means of such appropriation.

. . .

[T]he first step in the revolution by the working class, is to raise the proletariat to the position of ruling class, to establish democracy ... to wrest ... all capital from the bourgeoisie, to centralise all instruments of production in the hands of the state ... and to increase the total of productive forces as rapidly as possible.

. . .

Nevertheless in the most advanced countries, the following will be pretty generally applicable.

1. Abolition of property in land and application of all rents of land to public purposes.
2. A heavy progressive or graduated income tax.
3. Abolition of all right of inheritance.
4. Confiscation of the property of all emigrants and rebels.
5. Centralisation of credit in the hands of the state, by means of a national bank with state capital and an exclusive monopoly.
6. Centralisation of the means of communication and transport in the hands of the state.
7. Extension of factories and instruments of production owned by the state; the bringing into cultivation of waste lands, and the improvement of the soil.
8. Equal obligation of all to work.
9. Combination of agriculture with manufacturing industries; gradual abolition of the distinction between town and country.
10. Free education for all children in public schools. Abolition of child factory labour. Combination of education with industrial production, etc.

In place of the old bourgeois society, with its classes and class antagonisms, we shall have an association, in which the free development of each is the condition for the free development of all.

. . .

Workingmen of all countries, unite!

Source: Karl Marx and Friedrich Engels, *The Communist Manifesto* London: The Communist League. (1848); also in *Marx/Engels Selected Works*, vol. 1 (Moscow: Progress Publishers, 1969), p. 98–137; http://www.gutenberg.org/etext/61.

18. Commodore Matthew Perry's Instructions Regarding His Mission to Japan (United States, 1852)

In Asia, following the Treaty of Nanking between Great Britain and China (1842), the Treaty of Wanghia was negotiated between the United States and China, resulting in the opening of five Chinese ports with extraterritorial rights for trade and residence. The United States took the lead in forcing Japan open to the West, and the threat of force and diplomacy colored Commodore Matthew Perry's mission to Japan. The following are excerpts from the instructions for Commodore Perry that Acting Secretary C. M Conrad sent to Secretary of the Navy J. P. Kennedy on November 5, 1852. *See also* Japan, Industrial Revolution in.

Sir: As the squadron destined for Japan will shortly be prepared to sail, I am directed by the President to explain the objects of the expedition, and to give some general directions as to the mode by which those objects are to be accomplished.

Since the islands of Japan were first visited by European nations, efforts have constantly been made by the various maritime powers to establish commercial intercourse with a country whose large population and reputed wealth hold out great temptations to mercantile enterprise. Portugal was the first to make the attempt, and her example was followed by Holland, England, Spain and Russia; and finally by the United States. All these attempts, however, have thus far been unsuccessful; the permission enjoyed for a short period by the Portuguese to trade with the islands, and that granted to Holland to send annually a single vessel to the port of Nangasaki [*sic*], hardly deserving to be considered exceptions to this remark.

China is the only country which carries on any considerable trade with these islands.

So rigorously is this system of exclusion carried out, that foreign vessels are not permitted to enter their ports in distress, or even to do an act of kindness to their own people.

. . .

When vessels are wrecked or driven ashore on the islands, their crews are subjected to the most cruel treatment.

. . .

Every nation has undoubtedly the right to determine for itself the extent to which it will hold intercourse with other nations. The same law of nations, however, which protects a nation in the exercise of this right imposes upon her certain duties, which she cannot justly disregard. Among those duties none is more imperative than that which requires her to succor and relieve those persons who are cast by the perils of the ocean upon her shores.

. . .

Recent events—the navigation of the ocean by steam, the acquisition and rapid settlement by this country of a vast territory on the Pacific, the discovery of gold in that region, the rapid communication established across the isthmus which separates the two oceans—have practically brought the countries of the east in closer proximity to our own; although the consequences of these events have scarcely begun to be felt, the intercourse between them has already greatly increased, and no limits can be assigned to its future extension.

The duty of protecting those American citizens who navigate those seas is one that can no longer be deferred. In the year 1851, instructions were accordingly given to Commodore Aulick, then commanding our naval forces in the East Indies, to open a negotiation with the government of Japan. It is believed that nothing has been done under these instructions, and the powers conferred on Commodore Aulick are considered as superseded by those now given to Commodore Perry.

The objects sought by this government are—

1. To effect some permanent arrangement for the protection of American seamen and property wrecked on these islands, or driven into their ports by the stress of weather.
2. The permission to American vessels to enter one or more of their ports in order to obtain supplies of provisions, water, fuels, etc., or, in case of disasters, to refit so as to enable them to prosecute their voyage. It is very desirable to have permission to establish a depot for coal, if not on one of the principal islands, at least on some small uninhabited one, of which, it is said, there are several in their vicinity.
3. The permission to our vessels to enter one or more of their ports for the purpose of disposing of their cargoes by sale or barter.

   . . .

   This government, however, does not seek by this expedition to obtain any exclusive commercial advantage for itself, but, on the contrary, desires and expects that whatever benefits may result from it will ultimately be shared by the civilized world.

It is manifest, from past experience, that arguments or persuasion addressed to this people, unless they be seconded by some imposing manifestation of power, will be utterly unavailing.

You will, therefore, be pleased to direct the commander of the squadron to process, with his whole force, to such point on the coast of Japan as he may deem most advisable, and there endeavor to open a communication with the government, and if possible, to see the emperor in person, and deliver to him the letter of introduction from the President with which he is charged.

If after having exhausted every argument and every means of persuasion, the commodore should fail to obtain from the government any relaxation of their system of exclusion, or even any assurances of humane treatment of our shipwrecked seamen, he will then change his tone, and inform them in the most unequivocal terms that is it the determination of this government to insist, that hereafter all citizens or vessels of the United States that may be wrecked on their coasts, or driven by stress of weather into their harbors, shall so long as they are compelled to remain there, be treated with humanity; and that if any acts of cruelty should hereafter be practiced upon citizens of this country, whether by the government or by the inhabitants of Japan, they will be severely chastised. In case he should succeed in obtaining concessions on any of the points above mentioned, it is desirable that they should be reduced into the form of a treaty, for negotiating which he will be furnished with the requisite powers.

. . .

He will bear in mind that, as the President has no power to declare war, his mission is necessarily of a pacific character, and will not resort to force, unless in self defense in the protection of the vessels and crews under his command, or to resent an act of personal violence offered to himself, or to one of his officers.

Source: Senate Executive Documents (751), 33rd Congress, 2nd Session, no. 34, 4–9; in *American Foreign Policy A Documentary Survey, 1776-1960,* ed. Dorothy Burne Goebel (New York: Holt, Rinehart, 1961), pp. 106–107.

19. Excerpt from *Bleak House* by Charles Dickens (Great Britain, 1852–1853)

Nineteenth-century English novelists often were keen observers of the society around them; the work of many of them also brought serious social problems to the attention of those in power. A good example is Charles Dickens (1812–1870), whose concern for social reform is apparent in both his journalism and his novels. *Bleak House,* the novel from which this excerpt is taken, has an incredibly broad sweep—procrastination in the law courts, orphans, sanitary reform, English philanthropists in Africa, female suffrage, slums—illustrating many aspects of English life in the first half of the nineteenth century. The following passage describes a journey from the countryside to the iron country. *See also* Iron Industry.

As he comes into the iron country farther north, such fresh green woods as those of Chesney Wold are left behind; and coal pits and ashes, high chimneys and red bricks, blighted verdure, scorching fires, and a heavy never-lightening cloud of smoke, become the features of the scenery.

. . .

He comes to a gateway in the brick wall, looks in, and sees a great perplexity of iron lying about, in every stage, and in a vast variety of shapes; in bars, in wedges, in sheets; in tanks, in boilers, in axles, in wheels, in cogs, in cranks, in rails; twisted and wrenched into eccentric and perverse forms, as separate parts of machinery; mountains of it broken-up, and rusty in its age; distant furnaces of it glowing and bubbling in its youth; bright fireworks of it showering about, under the blows of the steam-hammer; red-hot iron, white-hot iron; cold-black iron; an iron taste, an iron smell, and a babel of iron sounds.

Source: Charles Dickens, *Bleak House* (Harmondsworth, U.K.: Penguin Books, 1971 [1853]), 901–2.

20. Czar Alexander II's Decree Emancipating the Serfs (Russia, 1861)

The Crimean War showed the backwardness of Russia's social, economic, and governmental structure. To try to improve conditions, Czar Alexander II (1855–1881) began a reform program. Although the nobility were violently opposed, Alexander issued a Decree of Emancipation on March 3, 1861, giving the serfs civil freedom, although still leaving them in economic bondage. This reform was carried out in two steps. First, a census of the serfs was taken by the nobles. Then in 1863, the former serfs were required to begin making monetary payments to the nobles, payments that had been determined by the nobles themselves.

Economically speaking, although the ties of feudalism had weakened to a greater or lesser degree in most of the other countries of Europe, the emergence of a free labor force, free from the ties to the land or to old feudal relationships, would be necessary if industrial development was to take place and the economy diversify. Russia's economy was large, but it was far from being modern and its political system not even remotely democratic. The revolutions and progress toward political reform that had taken place in other European countries had had very little impact on Russian society. Czar Alexander's decree did little to change the reality of Russian peasant life. Following are some relevant passages of the decree. *See also* Russia, Industrial Revolution in.

In considering the various classes and conditions of which the State is composed, we came to the conviction that the legislation of the empire having wisely provided for the organization of the upper and middle classes and having defined with precision their obligations, their rights, and their privileges, has not attained the same degree of efficiency as regards the peasants attached to the soil, thus designated because either from ancient laws or from custom they have been hereditarily subjected to the authority of the proprietors, on whom it was incumbent at the same time to provide for their welfare.... In the most favourable cases this state of things has established patriarchal relations founded upon a solicitude sincerely equitable and benevolent on the part of the proprietors, and on an affectionate submission on the part of the peasants; but in proportion as the simplicity of morals diminished … those bonds of mutual goodwill slackened, and a wide opening was made for an arbitrary sway, which weighed upon the peasants, and was unfavourable to their welfare.

. . .

We thus came to the conviction that the work of a serious improvement of the condition of the peasants was a sacred…mission which, in the course of events, Divine Providence called upon us to fulfill.

. . .

It is to the nobles themselves, conformable to their own wishes, that we have reserved the task of drawing up the propositions for the new organization of the peasants—propositions which make it incumbent upon them to limit their rights over the peasants, and to accept the onus of a reform which could not be accomplished without some material losses.

. . .

[T]he peasants attached to the soil will be invested within a term fixed by the law with all the rights of free cultivators.

The proprietors retaining their rights of property on all the land belonging to them, grant to the peasants for a fixed regulated rental the full enjoyment of their close [enclosure]; and, moreover, to assure their livelihood and to guarantee the fulfillment of their obligations towards the Government, the quantity of arable land is fixed by the said dispositions, as well as other rural appurtenances. But, in the enjoyment of these territorial allotments, the peasants are obliged, in return, to acquit the rentals fixed by the same dispositions to the profit of the proprietors. In this state, which must be a transitory one, the peasants shall be designated as "temporarily bound."

At the same time, they are granted the right of purchasing their close, and, with the consent of the proprietors, they may acquire in full property the arable lands and other appurtenances which are allotted to them as a permanent holding. By the acquisition in full property of the quantity of land fixed, the peasants are free from their obligations towards the proprietors for land thus purchased, and they enter definitively into the condition of free peasants—landholders.

By a special disposition concerning the domestics, a transitory state is fixed for them.... On the expiration of a term of two years ... they shall receive their full enfranchisement and some temporary immunities.

. . .

Although these dispositions ... have been ... adapted to economical necessities and local customs, nevertheless, to preserve the existing state where it presents reciprocal advantages, we leave it to the proprietors to come to amicable terms with the peasants, and to conclude transactions relative to the extent of the territorial allotment and to the amount of rental to be fixed in consequence, observing, at the same time, the established rules to guarantee the inviolability of such agreements.

. . .

Russia will not forget that the nobility, acting solely upon its respect for the dignity of man and its love for its neighbour, has spontaneously renounced rights given to it by serfdom actually abolished, and laid the foundation of a new future , which is thrown open to the peasants.

Source: [state papers in] *The London Annual Register ... 1861* (London: J. Dodsley), pp. 207–11; quoted in Raymond Phineas Stearns, *Pageant of Europe: Sources and Selections from the Renaissance to the Present Day* (New York: Harcourt, Brace, 1947), pp. 663–665.

21. Excerpt from *London Labour and the London Poor* by Henry Mayhew (Great Britain, 1861)

Henry Mayhew was a journalist who accepted an assignment to report on the poor in London for the *Morning Chronicle.* He interviewed each subject about their daily life and the struggles of life in Victorian London. These stories shocked middle-class readers. The articles were collected and published in four volumes in 1861 under the title *London Labour and the London Poor. See also* Wealth and Poverty in the Industrial Revolution.

A VAGRANT'S STORY

A cotton spinner (who had subsequently been a soldier), whose appearance was utterly abject, was the next person questioned. He was tall, and had been florid-looking (judging from his present complexion). His coat—very old and worn, and once black—would not button, and would have hardly held together if buttoned. He was out at elbows, and some parts of the collar were pinned together. His waistcoat was of a match with his coat, and his trousers were rags. He had some shirt, as was evident by his waistcoat, held together by one button. A very dirty handkerchief was tied carelessly round his neck. He was tall and erect, and told his adventures with heartiness.

"I am thirty-eight," he said, and have been a cotton-spinner, working at Chorlton-upon Medlock. I can neither read nor write. When I was a young man, twenty years ago, I could earn 2l. 10s clear money, every week, after paying two piecers and a scavenger. Each piecer had 7s. 6d a week—they are girls; the scavenger—a boy to clean the wheels of the cotton-spinning machine—had 2s. 6d. I was master of them wheels in the factory. This state of things continued until about the year 1837. I lived well and enjoyed myself, being a hearty man, noways a drunkard, working every day from half-past five in the morning till half-past seven at night—long hours, that time, master. I didn't care about money as long as I was decent and respectable. I had a turn for sporting at the wakes down there. In 1837, the "self-actors" (machines with steam power) had come into common use. One girl can mind three pairs—that used to be three men's work—getting 15s. for the work which gave three men 7l. 10s. Out of one factory 400 hands were flung in one week, men and women together. We had a meeting of the union, but nothing could be done, and we were told to go and mind the three pairs, as the girls did, for 15s a week. We wouldn't do that. Some went for soldiers, some to sea, some to Stoppard (Stockport) where the "self-actors" weren't agait. The masters there wouldn't have them—at least, some of them. Manchester was full of them: but one gentleman in Hulme still won't have them, for he says he won't turn the men out of bread. I 'listed for a soldier in the 48th. I liked a soldier's life very well until I got flogged—100 lashes for selling my kit (for a spree and 150 for striking a corporal, who called me an English robber. He was an Irishman. I was confined five days in the hospital after each punishment. It was terrible. It was like a bunch of razors cutting at your back. Your flesh was dragged off by the cats. Flogging was then very common in the regiment. I was flogged in 1840. To this day I feel a pain in the chest from the triangles. I was discharged from the army about two years ago, when the reduction took place. I was only flogged the times I've told you. I had no pension and no friends. I was discharged in Dublin. I turned to, and looked for work. I couldn't get any, and made my way for Manchester. I stole myself aboard of a steamer, and hid myself till she got out to sea, on her way from Dublin to Liverpool. When the captain found me there, he gave me a kick and some bread, and told me to work, so I worked for my passage twenty-four hours. He put me ashore at Liverpool.

I slept in the union that night—nothing to eat and nothing to cover me—no fire; it was winter. I walked to Manchester, but could get nothing to do there, though I was twelve months knocking about. It wants a friend and a character to get work. I slept in unions in Manchester, and had oatmeal porridge for breakfast, work at grinding logwood in the mill, from six to twelve, and then turn out. That was the way I lived chiefly; but I got a job sometimes in driving cattle, and 3d. for it,—or 2d. for carrying baskets in the vegetable markets; and went to Shoedale Union at night. I would get a pint of coffee and half-a-pound of bread, and half-a-pound of bread in the morning, and no work. I took to travelling up to London, half-hungered on the road—that was last winter—eating turnips out of this field, and carrots out of that, and sleeping under hedges and haystacks. I slept under one haystack, and pulled out the hay to cover me, and the snow lay on it a foot deep in the morning. I slept for all that, but wasn't I froze when I woke? An old farmer came up with his cart and pitchfork to load hay. He said: "Poor fellow! have you been here all night?" I answered, "Yes." He gave me some coffee and bread, and one shilling. That was the only good friend I met with on the road. I got fourteen days of it for asking a gentleman for a penny; that was in Stafford. I got to London after that, sleeping in unions sometimes, and begging a bite here and there. Sometimes I had to walk all night. I was once forty-eight hours without a bite, until I got hold at last of a Swede turnip, and so at last I got to London. Here I've tried up and down everywhere for work as a labouring man, or in a foundry. I tried London Docks, and Blackwall, and every place; but no job. At one foundry, the boiler-makers made a collection of 4s. for me. I've walked the streets for three nights together. Here, in this fine London, I was refused a night's lodging in Shoreditch and in Gray's-inn-lane. A policeman, the fourth night, at twelve o'clock, procured me a lodging, and gave me 2d. I couldn't drag on any longer. I was taken to a doctor's in the city. I fell in the street from hunger and tiredness. The doctor ordered me brandy and water' 2s. 6d., and a quartern loaf, and some coffee, sugar, and butter. He said, what I ailed was hunger. I made that run out as long as I could, but I was then as bad off as ever. It's hard to hunger for nights together. I was once in "Steel" (Coldbath-fields) for begging. I was in Tothill-fields for going into a chandler's shop, asking for a quartern loaf and half a pound of cheese, and walking out with it. I got a month for that. I have been in Brixton for taking a loaf out of a baker's basket, all through hunger. Better a prison than to starve. I was well treated because I behaved well in prison. I have slept in coaches when I had a chance. One night on a dunghill, covering the stable straw about me to keep myself warm. This place is a relief, I shave the poor people and cut their hair, on a Sunday. I was handy at that when I was a soldier. I have shaved in public-houses for halfpennies. Some landlords kicks me out. Now, in the days, I may pick up a penny or two that way, and get here of a night. I met two Manchester men in Hyde Park on Saturday, skating. They asked me what I was. I said, "A beggar." They gave me 2s. 6d., and I spent part of it for warm coffee and other things. They knew all about Manchester, and knew I was a Manchester man by my talk.

Source: Henry Mayhew, *London Labour and London Poor* (New York: A. M. Kelley, 1967 [1861]); http://www.victorianlondon.org/mayhew29htm.

22. Report on the Fabian Society by George Bernard Shaw (Great Britain, 1896)

In 1883, the same year that Karl Marx died, the Fabian Society was founded in England by a group of people who were interested in socialism. From the outset, the Fabians rejected the revolutionary implications of Marxian socialism, based as it was on the inevitability of class conflict and violence bringing about the overthrow of capitalism. Instead, they believed that the abuses that industrial capitalism had created could be ameliorated by political action and by the steady evolution of capitalism into socialism. The playwright George Bernard Shaw joined the society in 1884 and wrote this report in 1896, summarizing the aims and methods of Fabian socialism. Perhaps appropriately given the state of political development in Britain at that time, the Fabians emphasized peaceful parliamentary procedures but did not intend to become a political party, hoping instead to influence voters from all classes through the Society's educational activity. The following are extracts from the report.

I. THE MISSION OF THE FABIANS

The object of the Fabian Society is to persuade the English people to make their political constitution thoroughly democratic and so to socialize their industries as to make the livelihood of the people entirely independent of private capitalism.

The Fabian Society endeavors to pursue its Socialist and Democratic objectives with complete singleness of aim. For example ....

It has no distinctive opinions on the Marriage Question, Religion, Art, abstract Economics, historic Evolution, Currency, or any other subject than its own special business of practical Democracy and Socialism.

It brings all the pressure and persuasion in its power to bear on existing forces, caring nothing by what name any party calls itself, or what principles, Socialist or other, it professes, but having regard solely to the tendency of its actions, supporting those which make for Socialism and Democracy, and opposing those which are reactionary.

It does not propose that the practical steps towards Social-Democracy should be carried out by itself, or by any other specially organized society or party.

It does not ask the English people to join the Fabian Society.

II. FABIAN ELECTORAL TACTICS

The Fabian Society does not claim to be the people of England, or even the Socialist party, and therefore does not seek direct political representation by putting forward Fabian candidates at elections. But it loses no opportunity of influencing elections and inducing constituencies to select Socialists as their candidates.
. . .

III. FABIAN TOLERATION

The Fabian Society, far from holding aloof from other bodies, urges its members to lose no opportunity of joining them and permeating them with Fabian ideas as far as possible. Almost all organizations and movements contain elements making

for Socialism, no matter how remote the sympathies and intentions of their founders may be from those of the Socialists. On the other hand, unintentionally reactionary proposals are constantly being brought forward in Socialist bodies. Fabians
are therefore encouraged to join all other organizations, Socialist or non-Socialist,
in which Fabian work can be done.

IV. FABIAN CONSTITUTIONALISM

The Fabian Society is perfectly constitutional in its attitude; and its methods are
those usual in political life in England.

The Fabian Society accepts the conditions imposed on it by human nature and
by the national character and political circumstances of the English people. It sym-
pathizes with the ordinary citizen's desire for gradual, peaceful changes, as against
revolution, conflict with the army and police, and martyrdom. It recognizes the
fact that Social-Democracy is not the whole of the working-class program, and that
every separate measure towards the socialization of industry will have to compete
for precedence with numbers of other reforms.... The Fabian Society therefore
begs those Socialists who are looking forward to a sensational historical crisis to join
some other Society.

V. FABIAN DEMOCRACY

Democracy, as understood by the Fabian Society, means simply the control of the
administration by freely elected representatives of the people. The Fabian Society
energetically repudiates all conceptions of Democracy as a system by which the technical work of government administration, and the appointment of public officials,
shall be carried on by referendum or any other form of direct popular decision.
Such arrangements may be practical in a village community, but not in complicated
industrial civilizations which are ripening for Social-Democracy.

. . .

VI. FABIAN COMPROMISE

The Fabian Society, having learned from experience that Socialists cannot have
their own way in everything any more than other people, recognizes that in a Democratic community Compromise is a necessary condition of political progress.

VI. FABIAN SOCIALISM

Socialism, as understood by the Fabian Society, means the organization and conduct of the necessary industries of the country, and the appropriation of all forms
of economic rent and capital by the nation as a whole, through the most suitable
public authorities, parochial, municipal, provincial, or central.

The Socialism advocated by the Fabian Society is State Socialism exclusively. The
foreign friends of the Fabian Society must interpret this declaration in view of the
fact that since England now possesses an elaborate democratic State machinery,
graduated from the Parish Council or Vestry up to the central Parliament, and
elected under a franchise which enables the working-class vote to overwhelm all
others, the opposition which exists in the Continental monarchies between the

State and the people does not hamper English Socialists. For example, the distinction made between State Socialism and Social-Democracy in Germany, where the municipalities and other local bodies are closed against the working class, has no meaning in England. The difficulty in England is not to secure more political power for the people, but to persuade them to make any sensible use of the power they already have.

VIII. FABIAN INDIVIDUALISM

The Fabian Society does not suggest that the State should monopolize industry as against private enterprise or individual initiative further than may be necessary to make the livelihood of the people and their access to the sources of production completely independent of both. The freedom of individuals to test the social value of new inventions; to initiate improved methods of production; to anticipate and lead public enterprise in catering for new social wants; to practise all arts, crafts, and professions independently; in short, to complete the social organization by adding the resources of private activity and judgment to those of public routine, is, subject to the above conditions, highly valued by the Fabian Society as Freedom of Speech, Freedom of the Press, or any other article in the charter of popular liberties.

IX. FABIAN FREEDOM OF THOUGHT

The Fabian Society strenuously maintains its freedom of thought and speech with regard to the errors of Socialist authors, economists, leaders, and parties, no less than to those of its opponents. For instance, it insists on the necessity of maintaining as critical an attitude towards Marx and Lasalle, some of whose views must by this time be discarded as erroneous or obsolete, as these eminent Socialists themselves maintained towards their predecessors, St. Simon and Robert Owen.
. . .

XII. FABIAN NATURAL PHILOSOPHY

The Fabian Society endeavors to rouse social compunction by making the public conscious of the evil condition of society under the present system. This it does by the collection and publication of authentic and impartial statistical tracts, compiled, not from the works of Socialists, but from official sources.... The first volume of Karl Marx's *Das Kapital,* which contains an immense mass of carefully verified facts concerning modern capitalistic civilization, and practically nothing about Socialism, is probably the most successful propagandist work ever published. The Fabian Society, in its endeavors to continue the work of Marx in this direction, has found that the guesses made by Socialists at the condition of the people almost invariably flatter the existing system instead of, as might be suspected, exaggerating its evils. The Fabian Society therefore concludes that in the natural philosophy of Socialism, light is a more important factor than heat.

XIII. FABIAN REPUDIATIONS

The Fabian Society discards such phrases as "the abolition of the wage system," which can only mislead the public about the aims of Socialism. Socialism does not involve the abolition of wages, but the establishment of standard allowances for the maintenance of all workers by the community in its own service, as an alternative to wages fixed by the competition of destitute men and women for private employment, as well as to commercial profits, commissions, and all other speculative and competitive forms of remuneration. In short, the Fabian Society, far from desiring to abolish wages, wishes to secure them for everybody.

The Fabian Society resolutely opposes all pretensions to hamper the socialization of industry with equal wages, equal hours of labor, equal official status, or equal authority for everyone. Such conditions are not only impracticable, but incompatible with the equality of subordination to the common interest which is fundamental in modern Socialism.

The Fabian Society steadfastly discountenances all schemes for securing to any person, or any group of persons, "the entire product of their labor." It recognizes that wealth is social in its origin, and must be social in its distribution, since the evolution of industry has made it impossible to distinguish the particular contribution that each person makes to the common product, or to ascertain its value.

The Fabian Society desires to offer to all projectors and founders of Utopian communities in South America, Africa, and other remote localities, its apologies for its impatience of such adventures. To such projectors, and all patrons of schemes for starting similar settlements and workshops at home, the Society announces emphatically that it does not believe in the establishment of Socialism by private enterprise.

XIV. FINALLY

The Fabian Society does not put Socialism forward as a panacea for the ills of human society, but only for those produced by defective organization of industry and by a radically bad distribution of wealth.

Source: George Bernard Shaw, *Report on Fabian Policy and Resolutions,* Fabian Tract no. 70 (London: Fabian Society, 1896); reproduced in *Readings in Western Civilization,* 3rd ed., ed. George H. Knoles and Rixford K. Snyder (Philadelphia: Lippincott, 1960), 2: pp. 663–666.

23. Samuel Gompers on the Principles of the American Federation of Labor (United States, 1903, 1914, 1920)

The history of labor in the United States was one of short-lived and usually idealistic attempts to organize. Although a few craft-based organizations did appear, it was not until after 1870, a period coinciding with the most rapid phase of U.S. industrialization, that unions became a permanent if strongly resisted feature of U.S. life. Success at that time lay with local, craft-based unions, but with improvements in transportation and communications breaking down local and regional barriers, such isolation, as well as jurisdictional conflicts between unions, increased the need for some national organization that would coordinate the activities of different unions.

The result was the foundation in 1886 of the American Federation of Labor (AF of L), a loose confederation of craft-based unions. Under the influence of its first, and longest-serving, president, Samuel Gompers, the AF of L strove to make unions respectable, a conservative force for good working conditions within the capitalist system. Gompers's three-pronged philosophy influenced the working of the AF of L for many years and justified its claim to be the voice of labor. The first part of Gompers's philosophy, represented by the first excerpt below, was that unions should be based on crafts, on the skills of the workers, rather than on the industry. The second part, illustrated by the second excerpt, was a focus on economic improvement, that unions should concentrate on improving workers' wages, working conditions, and bargaining with employers, rather than relying on legislation to achieve these goals. The third part, represented by the last excerpt, was political nonpartisanship; Gompers did not want the union movement to be directly allied to one particular political party but rather to support those candidates for office who would help further labor's cause and deny support to those who opposed it.

Initially, this approach was successful, but the rise of large mass-production industries and continuing technological progress blurred once-clear lines between specific skills, and the formation of industrial unions created divisions within the union movement. These divisions were healed when the Congress of Industrial Organizations (CIO)—which had been expelled from the AF of L in 1937—reunited with the AF of L in 1955. Also, over the years, the original exclusivity of the union movement evolved to more accurately reflect the diversity of U.S. workers.

GOMPERS' OPPOSITION TO INDUSTRIAL UNIONISM, 1903

The attempt to force the trade unions into what has been termed industrial organization is perversive to the history of the labor movement, runs counter to the best conceptions of the toilers' interests now, and is sure to lead to the confusion which precedes dissolution and disruption. It is time for the American Federation of Labor solemnly to call a halt.

. . .

The advocates of the so-called industrial system of labor organizations urge that an effective strike can be conducted only when all workmen, regardless of trade, calling, or occupation, are affected.

That this is not borne out by the history of strikes in the whole labor movement is easily demonstrable. Though here and there such strikes have been temporarily successful, in the main they have been fraught with injury to all. The so-called industrial system of organization implies sympathetic strikes, and these time and experience have demonstrated as a general proposition should be discarded, while strikes of particular trades or callings have had the largest number of successes and the minimum of defeats. Quite apart from these considerations, however, are the splendid advantages obtained by the trade unions without the necessity of strikes or the interruption of industry. No one will attempt to say that a sympathetic strike shall under no circumstances occur. Under certain conditions it may be not only justifiable but practical and successful, even if only as an empathic protest against a great injustice or wrong; but generally and normally considered, such strikes cannot be of advantage.

One feature in connection with a system of industrial organization and its concomitant, the sympathetic strike, has been overlooked. By its methods any one of our international organizations could be financially drained and actually ruined in a very brief period in an effort to sustain the members involved; while, on the other hand, in a well-formulated trade union movement, a large number of men of different crafts, belonging to their own international trade unions, could be indefinitely sustained financially and victory achieved. At least the organizations could be maintained, not only to continue that battle, but to take up the cudgels in defense of their members elsewhere.

Reprinted in *Readings in Western Civilization*, ed. George H. Knowles and Rixford K. Snyder (Philadelphia: Lippincott, vol. 2), pp. 667–668.

THE VALUE OF ECONOMIC ORGANIZATION, 1914

The principle that has directed and controlled all policies of the A.F. of L. is that organization in industry is the key to the betterment of conditions for the workers. Organization for the purpose of making united effort to remedy wrongs that affect the work and the lives of all has been the instrumentality that has brought cheer and hope and betterment to the workers.

Economic organization gives power—power to protect the workers against industrial exploitation and injustice; power to secure for them things that will make life sane, whole, and good; power to bring into their lives something of beauty and pleasure; power to secure political representation for their ideals and recognition of their demands in legislation. The influence of organization in industry and its infinite number of contacts with other organizations constitute an intricate force that is the most powerful single force in society. The power of Labor is commensurate with its unity, solidarity, and federation.

Economic organization is that upon which we justly concentrate our thought and effort. When economic organization is achieved, every other good thing becomes possible for the workers. But because of the great power attaching to this agency, many other movements or forces seek to destroy or to use them. For this reason, the A.F. of L. early adopted the policy of avoiding entangling alliances. This policy has been consistently pursued during all these years. But with great success and increased growth come additional power. Many and tempting will be the avenues for activity and the associations open to the A.F. of L. Increasingly difficult will it be to distinguish the things which are most important and vital for the continuous development of the Federation—the things which make for life rather than mere power. Ever must be held up the policy, the organization—federation, that is the thing.

Source: *Report of the Executive Council, American Federation of Labor Proceedings, 1914,* reprinted in *Readings in Western Civilization,* ed. George H. Knowles and Rixford K. Snyder (Philadelphia: Lippincott vol. 2), p. 668.

POLITICAL NON-PARTISANSHIP, 1920

The partisanship of Labor is a partisanship of principle. The American Federation of Labor is not partisan to a political party, it is partisan to a principle, the principle of equal rights and human freedom. We, therefore, repeat: stand faithfully by our friends and *elect* them. Oppose our enemies and *defeat* them; whether they be candidates for President, for Congress, or for other offices; whether Executive, Legislative, or Judicial.

The experiences and results attained through the non-partisan political policy of the American Federation of Labor cover a generation. They indicate that through its application the workers of America have secured a much larger measure of fundamental legislation, establishing their rights, safeguarding their interests, protecting their welfare and opening the doors of opportunity than have been secured by the workers of any other country.

. . .

In these nearly forty years of actively taking part in the making of the economic and political history of this nation our Federation has witnessed the birth, the struggle for life, and the passing away of all sorts of political movements designed to save the republic from varying degrees of destruction; it has been coddled and mauled, petted and cajoled by the cohorts of particular brands of Liberty; it has been assailed by isms and ologies without number; it has been baited with sugared doses of economic chills and political fevers; it has heard the dirge and attended the last sad rites over many a promising political corpse. It has been courted by all the allurements of the partisan politician; all of the thralling visions of the emotional enthusiast have been pictured for its enticement; all the arts of the crafty self-seeker have been practiced to tempt it. But, despite all these, the American Federation of Labor has never been swerved from its non-partisan political course.

Source: American Federation of Labor, *Forty Years of Action;* reprinted in *Readings in Western Civilization,* ed. George H. Knoles and Rixford K. Snyder (Philadelphia: Lippincott, 1960), 2: p. 668.

24. Excerpts from John Mitchell's *Organized Labor, Its Problems, Purposes, and Ideals* (United States, 1903)

The early years of union organizing in the United States were not easy ones as unions faced employer resistance and either apathy or outright hostility from the general public. One particularly difficult area was coal mining, in which conditions were especially unpleasant. Workers faced a lack of continuous, regular employment and severe occupational hazards, and the prevalence of company towns linked residency to employment, making labor mobility difficult. Union organizing also was difficult because employers opposed unions, refused to accept them as legitimate bargaining agencies for workers, and actively recruited immigrants, and the proliferation of different nationalities and languages made worker unity harder to achieve. Several unions had been started, but the last decade of the nineteenth century and the beginning of the twentieth century saw real progress.

The United Mine Workers Union (UMW) was formed in 1890 through the amalgamation of the National Progressive Union (originally founded in 1888) and several mine locals that had been associated with the Knights of Labor, an idealistic union; it subsequently became affiliated with the American Federation of Labor. John Mitchell (1870–1919) was UMW president from 1899 to 1908, and under his leadership, work hours were reduced, wages increased, and the UMW accepted as a legitimate bargaining body. The union achieved a high degree of respectability during the contentious, 163-day strike in 1902 in the Pennsylvania anthracite fields. Although the coal companies refused to deal with Mitchell, their intransigence, Mitchell's attitude of cooperation, plus the importance of coal to the economy got President Theodore Roosevelt involved in negotiations to end the strike. Although the union did not achieve all that it had hoped for, the workday was reduced to nine hours, wages were increased by 10 percent, and the UMW was recognized as the de facto bargaining body by the arbitration board established by the president to resolve difficulties (because the company owners refused to deal with the union negotiators face-to-face).

Mitchell subsequently wrote a book, from which this extract is taken, about the U.S. labor movement; his attitude is conciliatory and similar in tone to that adopted by the AF of L's Samuel Gompers. After Mitchell stepped down as UMW president, he was succeeded by John Lewis, who was one of the original organizers of the Committee (later Congress) of Industrial Organizations (CIO).

The average wage earner has made up his mind that he must remain a wage earner. He has given up the hope of a kingdom to come, where he himself will be a capitalist, and he asks that the reward for his work be given to him as a workingman. Singly, he has been too weak to enforce his just demands and he has sought strength in union and has associated himself into labor organizations.

Labor unions are for the workman, but against no one. They are not hostile to employers, not inimical to the interests of the general public. They are for a class, because that class exists and has class interests, but the unions did not create and do nor perpetuate the class or its interests and do not seek to evoke a class conflict.

There is no necessary hostility between labor and capital. Neither can do without the other; each has evolved from the other. Capital is labor saved and materialized; the power in labor is in itself a form of capital. There is not even a necessary, fundamental antagonism between the laborer and the capitalist. Both are men, with the virtues and vices of men and each wishes at times more than his fair share. Yet, broadly considered, the interest of the one is the interest of the other, and the prosperity of the one is the prosperity of the other.

. . .

The trade unions stand for the principle of united action and for the policy of a living wage earned under fair living conditions. In union there is strength, justice, and moderation; in disunion, nothing but an alternating humility and insolence, a state of industrial despotism tempered by futile and passing revolutions. Unions stand for the right of association, self-government, and free speech, for the dignity and self-respect of the workman, for the mutual esteem of capitalist and wage earner, and for a wide, far-seeing, open-minded, democratic conduct of industry.

Source: John Mitchell, *Organized Labor, Its Problems, Purposes, and Ideals, and the Present and Future of American Wage Earners* (Philadelphia: American Book and Bible House, 1903), reprinted in *Readings in Western Civilization.* Ed. George H. Knowles and Rixford K. Snyder (Philadelphia: Lippincott. Vol. 2), p. 667.

25. Excerpt from Louis D. Brandeis's *Other People's Money and How the Bankers Use It* (United States, 1914)

Toward the end of the nineteenth century, it became clear, especially in the United States, that the trend toward the increasing scale of industrial operations was threatening competitive conditions in the economy. The formation of trusts and other combinations implied that business decision-making was cooperative rather than competitive. Louis D. Brandeis (1856–1941) was a Progressive Democrat and noted jurist who viewed this trend with alarm. After a successful career representing small companies against large ones, he was appointed to the Supreme Court by President Woodrow Wilson in 1916. His judicial philosophy was activist, and he believed that the law should be used to improve the conditions of everyday life; his experience in many railroad freight-rate and public-utility cases gave him an insight into the connections between big business and big money.

In 1914, Brandeis published a book entitled *Other People's Money and How the Bankers Use It,* in which he made a strong case for competition, not only because it was beneficial for the economy but also because of its implications for the well-being of local communities. The chapter from which the following excerpt is taken, "Big Men and Little Business," begins with a refutation of J. P. Morgan's claim that U.S. financial backing was crucial to initiating new industry. Brandeis points out that the early establishment of new enterprises was usually financed by the owners themselves or a close circle of supporters and that there were few examples of investment-banker financing. He then follows by giving examples (not included here) of the development of several industries—railroads, steamships, the telegraph, harvesting machinery, steel, the telephone, electrical machinery, and the automobile—that began that way, but once they had become established, drew the interest of big banks. Once this happened, the development of various combinations and trusts that limit competition and new inventions was encouraged, and, in Brandeis's eyes, the connection between the (New York) financiers and the industrialists limited the ability of local communities to control their own destinies. In this extract, Brandeis uses the example of the United States Steel Corporation to illustrate industrial concentration through merger and the example of the General Electric Company to illustrate the influence one company can have through interlocking directorates and its control over subsidiary companies in many different activities. Some of the abuses he mentions here were subsequently the target of later antitrust laws.

HOW BANKERS ARREST DEVELOPMENT

But "great banking houses" have not merely failed to initiate industrial development: they have definitely arrested development because to them the creation of the trusts is largely due. The recital in the Memorial addressed to the President by the Investors' Guild in November, 1911, is significant:

"It is a well-known fact that modern trade combinations tend strongly toward constancy of process and products, and by their very nature are opposed to new processes and new products originated by independent inventors, and hence tend to restrain competition in the development and sale of patents and patent rights; and consequently tend to discourage independent inventive thought, to the great detriment of the nation, and with injustice to inventors whom the Constitution especially intended to encourage and protect in their rights."

And more specific was the testimony of the *Engineering News:*

"We are today something like five years behind Germany in iron and steel metallurgy, and such innovations as are being introduced by our iron and steel manufacturers are most of them merely following the lead set by foreigners years ago.

"We do not believe this is because American engineers are any less ingenious or original than those of Europe, though they may indeed be deficient in training and scientific education compared with those of Germany. We believe the main cause is the wholesale consolidation which has taken place in American industry. A huge organization is too clumsy to take up the development of an original idea. With the market closely controlled and profits certain by following standard methods, those who control our trusts do not want the bother of developing anything new.

"We instance metallurgy only by way of illustration. There are plenty of other fields of industry where exactly the same condition exists. We are building the same machines and using the same methods as a dozen years ago, and the real advances in the art are being made by European inventors and manufacturers."

To which President Wilson's statement may be added:

"I am not saying that all invention had been stopped by the growth of trusts, but I think it is perfectly clear that invention in many fields has been discouraged, that inventors have been prevented from reaping the full fruits of their ingenuity and industry, and that mankind has been deprived of many comforts and conveniences, as well as the opportunity of buying at lower prices.

"Do you know, have you had occasion to learn, that there is no hospitality for invention, now-a-days?"

TRUSTS AND FINANCIAL CONCENTRATION

The fact that industrial monopolies arrest development is more serious than even the direct burden imposed through extortionate prices. But the most harm-bearing incident of the trusts is their promotion of financial concentration. Industrial trusts feed the money trust. Practically every trust created has destroyed the financial independence of some communities and of many properties; for it has centered the financing of a large part of whole lines of business in New York, and this is usually with one of a few banking houses. This is well illustrated by the Steel Trust, which is a trust of trusts: that is, the Steel Trust combines in one huge holding company the trusts previously formed in the different branches of the steel business. Thus the Tube Trust combined 17 tube mills, located in 16 different cities, scattered over 5 states and owned by 13 different companies. The wire trust combined 19 mills; the sheet steel trust 26; the bridge and structural trust 27; and the tin plate trust 36; all scattered similarly over many states. Finally, these and other companies were formed into the United States Steel Corporation, combining 228 companies in all, located in 127 cities and towns, scattered over 18 states. Before the combinations were effected, nearly every one of these companies was owned largely by those who managed it, and had been financed, to a large extent, in the place, or in the state, in which it was located. When the Steel Trust was formed all these concerns came under one management. Thereafter, the financing of each of these 228 corporations (and some which were later acquired) had to be done through or with the consent of J.P. Morgan & Co. *That was the greatest step in financial concentration ever taken.*

STOCK EXCHANGE INCIDENTS

The organization of trusts has served in another way to increase the power of the Money Trust. Few of the independent concerns out of which the trusts have been formed, were listed on the New York Stock Exchange, and few of them had financial offices in New York. Promoters of large corporations, whose stock is to be held by the public, and also investors, desire to have their securities listed on the New York Stock Exchange. Under the rules of the Exchange, no security can be so listed unless the corporation has a transfer agent and registrar in New York City. Furthermore, banker-directorships have contributed largely to the establishment of the financial offices of the trusts in New York City. That alone would tend to financial concentration. But the listing of the stock enhances the power of the Money Trust in another way. An industrial stock, once listed, frequently becomes the subject of active speculation; and speculation feeds the Money Trust indirectly in many ways. It draws the money of the country to New York. The New York bankers handle the loans of other people's money on the Stock Exchange; and members of the Stock Exchange receive large amounts from commissions. For instance: There are 5,084,952 shares of United States Steel common stock outstanding. But in the five years ending December 31, 1912, speculation in that stock was so extensive that there were sold on the Exchange an average of 29,380,888 shares a year; or nearly six times as much as there is Steel common in existence. Except where the transactions are by or for the brokers, sales on the Exchange involve the payment of twenty-five cents in commission for each share of stock sold; that is, twelve and one-half cents by the seller and twelve and one-half cents by the buyer. Thus the commission from the Steel common alone afforded a revenue averaging many millions a year. The Steel preferred stock is also much traded in; and there are 138 other industrials, largely trusts, listed on the New York Stock Exchange.

TRUST RAMIFICATIONS

But the potency of trusts as a factor in financial concentration is manifested in still other ways; notably through their ramifying operations. This is illustrated forcibly by the General Electric Company's control of water-power companies which has now been disclosed in an able report of the United States Bureau of Corporations:

"The extent of the General Electric influence is not fully revealed by its con-solidated balance sheet. A very large number of corporations are connected with it through its subsidiaries and through corporations controlled by these subsidiar-ies or affiliated with them. There is a still wider circle of influence due to the fact that officers and directors of the General Electric Company and its subsidiaries are also officers or directors of many other corporations, some of whose securities are owned by the General Electric Company.

"The General Electric Company holds in the first place all the common stock in three security holding companies: the United Electric Securities Co., the Electrical Securities Corporation, and the Electric Bond and Share Co. Directly and through these corporations and their officers the General Electric controls a large part of the water power of the United States.

. . .

"The water-power companies in the General Electric group are found in 18 states. These 18 states have 2,325,757 commercial horsepower developed or under construction, and of this total the General Electric group includes 939,115 h.p. or 40.4 per cent. The greatest amount of power controlled by the companies in the General Electric group in any state is found in Washington. This is followed by New York, Pennsylvania, California, Montana, Iowa, Oregon, and Colorado. In five of the states ... the water-power companies included in the General Electric Group control more than 50 per cent of the commercial power, developed and under con-struction. The percentage of power in the States included in the General Electric group ranges from a little less than 2 per cent in Michigan to nearly 80 per cent in Pennsylvania. In Colorado they control 72 per cent; in New Hampshire 61 per cent; in Oregon 58 per cent; and in Washington 55 per cent.

Besides the power developed and under construction water-power concerns included in the General Electric group own in the States shown in the table 641,600 h.p. undeveloped.

This water-power control enables the General Electric group to control other public service corporations:

"The water-power companies subject to General Electric influence control the street railways in at least 16 cities and towns; the electric-light plants in 78 cities and towns; gas plants in 19 cities and towns; and are affiliated with the electric light and gas plants in other towns. Though many of these communities, particu-larly those served with light only, are small, several of them are the most impor-tant in the States where these water-power companies operate. The water-power companies in the General Electric group own, control, or are closely affiliated with, the street railways in Portland and Salem, Ore.; Spokane, Wash.; Great Falls, Mont,; St. Louis, Mo.; Winona, Minn.; Milwaukee and Racine, Wis.; Elmira, N.Y.; Asheville and Raleigh, N.C., and other relatively less important towns. The towns in which the lighting plants (electric or gas) are owned or controlled include Portland, Salem, Astoria and other towns in Oregon; Bellingham and other towns in Washington; Butte, Great Falls, Bozeman and other towns in Montana; Lead-ville and Colorado Springs in Colorado; St. Louis, Mo.; Milwaukee, Racine and several small towns in Wisconsin; Hudson and Rensselaer, N.Y.; Detroit, Mich.; Asheville and Raleigh, N.C.; and in fact one or more towns in practically every community where developed water power is controlled by this group. In addition to the public-service corporations thus controlled by the water-power companies subject to General Electric influence, there are numerous public-service corporations in other municipalities that purchase power from the hydroelectric developments controlled by or affiliated with the General Electric Co. This is true of Denver, Colo., which has already been discussed. In Baltimore, Md., a water-power concern in the General Electric Group, namely, the Pennsylvania Water & Power Co., sells 20,000 h.p to the Consolidated Gas, Electric Light & Power Co., which controls the entire light and power business of the city. The power to operate all the electric street railway systems of Buffalo, N.Y., and vicinity, involving a trackage of approximately 375 miles, is supplied through a subsidiary of the Niagara Falls Power Co."

And the General Electric Company, through the financing of public service companies, exercises a like influence in communities where there is no water power:

"It, or its subsidiaries, has acquired control of or an interest in the public-service corporations of numerous cities where there is no water-power connection, and it is affiliated with still others by virtue of common directors…. This vast network of relationship between hydro-electric corporations through prominent officers and directors of the largest manufacturer of electrical machinery and supplies in the United States is highly significant.

. . .

"It is possible that this relationship to such a large number of strong financial concerns, through common officers and directors, affords the General Electric Company an advantage that may place rivals at a corresponding disadvantage. Whether or not this great financial power has been used to the particular disadvantage of any rival water-power concern is not so important as the fact that such power exists and that it might be so used at any time."

THE SHERMAN LAW

The Money Trust cannot be broken, if we allow its power to be constantly augmented. To break the Money Trust, we must stop that power at its source. The industrial trusts are among its most effective feeders. Those which are illegal should be dissolved. The creation of new ones should be prevented. To this end the Sherman Law should be supplemented both by providing more efficient judicial machinery, and by creating a commission with administrative functions to aid in enforcing the law. When that is done, another step will have been taken toward securing the New Freedom. But restrictive legislation alone will not suffice. We should bear in mind the admonition with which the Commissioner of Corporations closes his review of our water-power development:

"There is … presented such a situation in water powers and other public utilities as might bring about at any time under a single management the control of a majority of the developed water power in the United States and similar control over the public utilities in a vast number of cities and towns, including some of the most important in the country."

We should conserve all rights which the Federal Government and the States now have in our natural resources, and there should be a complete separation of our industries from railroads and public utilities.

Source: Louis D. Brandeis, *Other People's Money and How the Bankers Use It* (New York: Stokes, 1914), ch. 7.

✀⅌

26. Allied Armistice Demands for Ending Fighting on the Western Front (November 10, 1918)

The outcome of World War I was influenced by the entry of the United States on the side of the Allies on April 16, 1917. Even before a German U-boat destroyed American lives by sinking the British passenger liner *Lusitania,* which also was carrying munitions, on May 7, 1915, the United States had provided the Allies with supplies, though not with troops. This position changed with the resumption of unrestricted submarine warfare on Allied shipping in January 1917. Suffering from a British blockade of European ports, and hoping that the upsurge in military action would bring a quick victory to the Central Powers, Germany resumed submarine attacks on the assumption that the United States would remain a noncombatant.

Previous years had seen Germany and its allies fighting a war on two fronts: the Eastern Front, against Russia, and the Western Front, against Britain, France, and the other Allies. After 1915, however, the situation in Russia was deteriorating badly. The Russian army was desperately short of munitions and supplies, yet the incompetent czarist government did little to calm internal dissatisfactions. Winter 1916–1917 saw workers in Petrograd ignore an order to return to work; soldiers sent to force the strikers back to work joined them. The Duma (parliament) was ordered to go home, but it refused and set up a provisional reformist government instead, though this attempt failed. Alexander Kerensky set up a government of moderate socialists but faced opposition from the minority Bolsheviks, led by Vladimir Ilyich Ulyanov, better known as Nikolai Lenin, and Leon Trotsky (also known as Lev Bronstein). In November 1917 (October, according to the old calendar), a second revolution occurred, with Kerensky being overthrown by Lenin. Given the exhausted state of the Russian economy, Lenin agreed to a truce with Germany, and in March 1918 the Treaty of Brest-Litovsk was signed between Russia and Germany and her allies. Because Germany had the upper hand, the conditions of the treaty split the Russian empire, ceded Poland and Lithuania to Germany and Austria-Hungary, removed Bessarabia from Russian control to be eventually transferred to Romania, gave parts of Armenia to Turkey, and established Finland, Estonia, and Livonia as independent states separate from Russia and under the protection of Germany. At the same time, Romania was isolated by Russia's defection, so it also sued for peace and agreed to terms with the Central Powers under the Treaty of Bucharest of March 1918. Romania yielded Dobruya to Bulgaria and some mountain passes to Austria-Hungary and, in return for cooperation with the Central Powers, was promised Bessarabia.

These actions effectively collapsed the Eastern Front, permitting Germany to concentrate on strengthening the Western Front. But the tide had turned in the

Allies' favor, thanks to ships, food, arms, and, in 1918, men from the United States; the German U-boat campaign was weakening, though the British blockade was preventing food and supplies from reaching Germany and the subject peoples of Austria-Hungary were growing increasingly disaffected. Major Allied victories in summer 1918 were followed by the collapse of Austria-Hungary in October, when various Balkan states declared their independence. Negotiations for peace then ensued, leading to the following terms for an armistice, which took effect on November 11, 1918.

When the Allies finally presented the draft of a peace treaty to Germany on May 7, 1919, it was significantly harsher than what had been outlined in the armistice or in President Woodrow Wilson's "Fourteen Points," which had been publicly declared as the Allies' war aims; the final version of the treaty led John Maynard Keynes to publish his objections in "The Economic Consequences of the Peace" (see the following document). Some minor adjustments were made, and the treaty finally was signed in June. Peace treaties were signed with Austria (September 1919), Bulgaria (November 1919), Hungary (June 1920), and Turkey (August 1920), but this last one never went into effect.

The warnings of British economist Keynes were more accurate than had been anticipated. The requirements that Germany make reparations in kind led to less work for corresponding French and British industry; Germany also found it difficult to make money payments, given the restrictions on her trade, which stymied her efforts to export and thus earn foreign exchange. Germany stopped making payments in 1922, and in spite of efforts, such as the Dawes Plan of 1924, the Young Plan of 1929–1930, and a temporary moratorium in 1932, which was conditional on the United States forgiving war debts owed to it, the entire system of reparations and payments of Allied war debts collapsed in 1932. The United States refused to forgive these debts, so the Allied countries, which had been counting on receiving payments from Germany, in turn refused to pay their debts to the United States, effectively wiping the slate clean.

The following terms were set by the victorious Allied powers for the armistice after World War I; they were accepted by Germany on November 11, 1918.

1. Effective six hours after signing.
2. Immediate clearing of Belgium, France, Alsace-Lorraine, to be concluded within 14 days. Any troops remaining in these areas to be interned or taken as prisoners of war.
3. Surrender 5000 cannon (chiefly heavy), 30,000 machine guns, 3000 trench mortars, 2000 planes.
4. Evacuation of the left bank of the Rhine, Mayence, Coblence, Cologne, occupied by the enemy to a radious of 30 kilometers deep.
5. On the right bank of the Rhine a neutral zone from 30 to 40 kilometers deep, evacuation within 11 days.
6. Nothing to be removed from the territory on the left bank of the Rhine, all factories, railroads, etc. to be left intact.

7. Surrender of 5000 locomotives, 150,000 railway coaches, 10,000 trucks.
8. Maintenance of enemy occupation troops through Germany.
9. In the East all troops to withdraw behind the boundaries of August 1, 1914, fixed time not given.
10. Renunciation of the Treaties of Brest-Litovsk and Bucharest.
11. Unconditional surrender of East Africa.
12. Return of the property of the Belgian Bank, Russian and Romanian gold.
13. Return of prisoners of war without reciprocity.
14. Surrender of 160 U-boats, 8 light cruisers, 6 Dreadnoughts [large, heavily-armed battle-ships]; the rest of the fleet to be disarmed and controlled by the Allies in neutral or Allied harbors.
15. Assurance of free trade through the Cattegat Sound; clearance of mine-fields and occupation of all forts and batteries, through which transit could be hindered.
16. The blockade remains in effect. All German ships to be captured.
17. All limitations by Germany on neutral shipping to be removed.
18. Armistice lasts 30 days.

Source: Web site The First World War at http://www.firstworldwar.com/features/armistice/htm (accessed February 12, 2007).

27. Excerpts from John Maynard Keynes's *The Economic Consequences of the Peace* (Great Britain, 1919)

British economist John Maynard Keynes (1883–1946), who was sent by the British treasury as its principal representative at the Paris Peace Conference following the end of World War I, objected strongly to the conditions imposed on Germany. (He in fact resigned his civil service post to write *The Economic Consequences of the Peace,* from which these extracts are taken.) Keynes felt that a spirit of vindictiveness had influenced these requirements, which would have the result of impoverishing Germany by stripping its economy of its industrial strength, ultimately making it impossible both to fulfill the demands for material and financial reparations and to meet the needs of the German population. No account was taken of Germany's ability to pay nor, in fact, of the impact that reparation payments would have on the receiving countries.

Keynes summarized the three main elements of the prewar German economy: its overseas commerce, the exploitation of its coal and iron resources and the industries based on them, and the transport and tariff system. He then stated that the treaty aimed to systematically destroy these elements. The demands of the treaty were (in brief): all vessels over 1,600 tons, half those between 1,000 and 1,600 tons, and one-quarter of all trawlers and fishing boats to be ceded to France; German shipyards will build up to 200,000 tons annually for five years for the Allies if required; all German overseas possessions (including those owned by German nationals) to be ceded; the provinces of Alsace and Lorraine to be ceded to France, with no compensation for personal property so taken; approximately 45 percent of net German coal output (about 60 million tons) to be paid as reparations in kind to France, Belgium, Italy, and Luxembourg over the next 10 years; favorable (most favored nation) status to be given to Germany's trading partners, who are under no obligation to grant this status to Germany; surrender of some railroad equipment; and the principal waterways of Germany to be placed under the management of international commissions.

These provisions went far beyond what originally had been proposed. Full repayment would have required a flourishing economy and an export surplus, but the treaty's demands created a severe energy shortage resulting from the coal reparations preventing the rebuilding of industry. The trade provisions and loss of most of the merchant marine put most overseas markets out of reach. As it turned out, Keynes was correct in his predictions: The outflow of monetary reparations from Germany and the requirements placed on German industry were insupportable, the chain of reparation payments and war debt obligations of the Allies was extremely fragile, and the humiliation experienced by the German people helps explain the later rise of German nationalism designed to restore the country's sense of honor. In spite of various plans to restructure reparation payments, the whole scheme eventually collapsed.

World War I marked a dramatic turning point in the economic history of the world. Britain had lost its economic dominance, whereas the United States emerged as the world's largest and strongest economy; however, unlike Britain after the Napoleonic Wars, the United States did not take on a significant international role at that time. In the opinion of many observers, the aftermath of the war contained within it the seeds of the next: The impositions on Germany helped the rise to power of the National Socialists and Adolf Hitler. This lesson, and the experiences of the next two decades, helped influence the decisions taken at the end of World War II, which aimed to strengthen the international order and unify rather than divide Europe.

I believe that it would have been a wise and just act to have asked the German Government at the Peace Negotiations to agree to a sum of $10,000,000,000 in final settlement, without further examination of particulars. This would have provided an immediate and certain solution, and would have required from Germany a sum which, if she were granted certain indulgences, it might not have proved entirely impossible for her to pay. This sum should have been divided up amongst the Allies themselves on a basis of need and general equity.

But the case was not settled on its merits.

THE CONFERENCE AND THE TERMS OF THE TREATY

I do not believe that, at the date of the Armistice [November 11, 1918], responsible authorities in the Allied countries expected any indemnity from Germany beyond the cost of reparation for the direct material damage which had resulted from the invasion of Allied territory and from the submarine campaign. At that time there were serious doubts as to whether Germany intended to accept our terms, which in other respects were inevitably very severe. It would have been thought an unstatesmanlike act to risk the continuance of the war by demanding a money payment which Allied opinion was not then anticipating and which probably could not be secured in any case. The French, I think, never quite accepted this point of view; but it was certainly the British attitude; and in this atmosphere the pre-Armistice conditions were framed.

A month later the atmosphere had changed completely. We had discovered how hopeless the German position really was, a discovery which some, though not all, had anticipated, but which no one had dared reckon on as a certainty. It was evident that we could have secured unconditional surrender if we had determined to get it.

. . .

On December 6, the [British] Prime Minister [Lloyd George] issued a statement of policy and aims in which he stated, with significant emphasis on the word *European,* that "All the European Allies have accepted the principle that the Central Powers must pay the cost of the war up to the limit of their capacity."

. . .

His Final Manifesto ... [and] I quote it in full:

"1. Trial of the Kaiser
2. Punishment of those responsible for atrocities
3. Fullest indemnities from Germany
4. Britain for the British, socially and industrially
5. Rehabilitation of those broken in the war
6. A happier country for all"

Here is food for the cynic. To this concoction of greed and sentiment, prejudice and deception, three weeks of the [political electoral] platform had reduced the powerful governors of England, who but a little while before had spoken not ignobly of Disarmament and a League of Nations and of a just and lasting peace which should establish the foundations of a new Europe.

. . .

[The Prime Minister] had pledged himself and his government to make demands of a helpless enemy inconsistent with solemn engagements on our part, on the faith of which this enemy had laid down his arms. There are few episodes in history which posterity will have less reason to condone—a war ostensibly waged in defense of the sanctity of international engagements ending in a definite breach of one of the most sacred possible of such engagements on the part of the victorious champions of these ideals.

. . .

Apart from other aspects of the transaction, I believe that the campaign for securing out of Germany the general costs of the war was one of the most serious acts of political unwisdom for which our statesmen have ever been responsible. To what a different future Europe might have looked forward to if either Mr. Lloyd George or Mr. Wilson [President of the United States] had apprehended that the most serious of the problems which claimed their attention were not political or territorial but financial and economic, and that the perils of the future lay not in frontiers or sovereignties but in food, coal, and transport. Neither of them paid adequate attention to these problems at any stage of the Conference.... The hopes to which the Prime

Minister had given rise not only compelled him to advocate an unjust and unworkable economic basis to the Treaty with Germany, but set him at variance with the President, and on the other hand with competing interests to those of France and Belgium. The clearer it became that but little could be expected from Germany, the more necessary it was to exercise patriotic greed and "sacred egotism" and snatch the bone from the juster claims and greater need of France or the well-founded expectations of Belgium. Yet the financial problems which were about to exercise Europe could not be solved by greed. The possibility of *their* cure lay in magnanimity.

Europe, if she is to survive her troubles, will need so much magnanimity from America, that she must herself practice it. It is useless for the Allies, hot from stripping Germany and one another, to turn for help to the United States to put the States of Europe, including Germany, on to their feet again.... I still believe that before the main Conference, or very early in its proceedings, the representatives of Great Britain should have entered deeply, with those of the United States, into the economic and financial situation as a whole, and that the former should have been authorized to make concrete proposals on the general lines (1) that all interallied indebtedness be canceled outright; (2) that the sum to be paid by Germany be fixed at $10,000,000,000; (3) that Great Britain renounce all claim to participation in this sum and that any share to which she proves entitled be placed at the disposal of the Conference for the purpose of aiding the finances of the New States about to be established; (4) that in order to make some basis of credit immediately available an appropriate proportion of the German obligations representing the sum to be paid by her should be guaranteed by all parties to the Treaty; and (5) that the ex-enemy Powers should also be allowed, with a view to their economic restoration, to issue a moderate amount of bonds carrying a similar guarantee. Such proposals involved an appeal to the generosity of the United States. But that was inevitable; and in view of her far less financial sacrifices, it was an appeal which could fairly have been made to her. Such proposals would have been practical. There is nothing in them quixotic or Utopian. And they would have opened up for Europe some prospect of financial stability and reconstruction.

. . .

The Treaty includes no provisions for the economic rehabilitation of Europe—nothing to make the defeated Central Empires into good neighbors, nothing to stabilize the new States of Europe, nothing to reclaim Russia; nor does it promote in any way a compact of economic solidarity amongst the Allies themselves; no arrangment was reached at Paris for restoring the disordered finances of France and Italy, or to adjust the systems of the Old World and the New.

The Council of Four paid no attention to these issues ... [French Premier] Clemenceau [determined] to crush the economic life of his enemy, Lloyd George to do a deal and bring home something which would pass muster for a week, the President to do nothing that was not just and right. It is an extraordinary fact the fundamental economic problems of a Europe starving and disintegrating before their eyes was the one question in which it was impossible to arouse the interest of the Four. Reparation was their main excursion into the economic field, and they settled it as a problem of theology, of politics, of electoral chicane, from every point of view except that of the economic future of the States whose destiny they were handling.

. . .

[I shall briefly consider] the present situation of Europe, as the War and the Peace have made it; and it will no longer be part of my purpose to distinguish between the inevitable fruits of the War and the avoidable misfortunes of the Peace.

The essential facts of the situation, as I see them, are expressed simply. Europe consists of the densest aggregation of population in the history of the world. This population is accustomed to a relatively high standard of life…. In relation to other continents Europe is not self-sufficient; in particular, it cannot feed itself. Internally the population is not evenly distributed, but much of it is crowded into a relatively small number of dense industrial centers. This population secured for itself a livelihood before the war, without much margin of surplus, by means of a delicate and immensely complicated organization, of which the foundations were supported by coal, iron, transport, and an unbroken supply of imported food and raw materials from other continents. By the destruction of this organization and the interuption of the stream of supplies, a part of this population is deprived of its means of livelihood. Emigration is not open to the redundant surplus…. The danger confronting us, therefore, is the rapid depression of the standard of life of the European populations to a point which will mean actual starvation for some (a point already reached in Russia and approximately reached in Austria). Men will not always die quietly. For starvation, which brings to some lethargy and a helpless despair, drives other temperaments to the nervous instability of hysteria and to a mad despair. And these in their distress may overturn the remnants of organization, and submerge civilization itself in their attempts to satisfy desperately the overwhelming needs of the individual. This is the danger against which all our resources and courage and idealism must now cooperate.

· · ·

What then is to be done? The tentative suggestions of this chapter may appear … inadequate. But the opportunity was missed at Paris during the six months which followed the Armistice, and nothing we can do now can repair the mischief wrought at that time. Great privation and great risks to society have become unavoidable. All that is now open to us is to redirect … the fundamental economic tendencies which underlie the events of the hour, so that they promote the reestablishment of prosperity and order, instead of leading us deeper into misfortune.

· · ·

The events of the coming year will not be shaped by the deliberate acts of statesmen, but by the hidden currents, flowing continually beneath the surface of political history, of which no one can predict the outcome. In one way only can we influence these hidden currents—by setting in motion those forces of instruction and imagination which change *opinion*. The assertion of truth, the unveiling of illusion, the dissipation of hate, the enlargement and instruction of men's hearts and minds, must be the means.

· · ·

We have been moved already beyond endurance, and need rest. Never in the lifetime of men now living has the universal element in the soul of man burnt so dimly.

Source: John Maynard Keynes, *The Economic Consequences of the Peace* (1919), from http://www. gutenberg.org/files/15776/15776 8.txt (accessed February 13, 2007). Also: *The Collected Works of John Maynard Keynes, vol. 2: The Economic Consequences of the Peace* (London: Palgrave Macmillan, 1971).

28. Excerpts from R. H. Tawney's *Religion and the Rise of Capitalism* (Great Britain, 1926)

The relationship between ideas and economic activity long has been of interest to historians, economists, and sociologists. One of the most interesting discussions has been over the connection between capitalism (the pursuit of profit, monetary gain, and capital accumulation) and the rise of Protestantism, which began with the protestations of Martin Luther in Germany and continued with the teachings of John Calvin in Switzerland. Later, in England, a modified version, Anglicanism (from which various groups of nonconformists, including the Calvinist Puritans, dissented), completed the break with Rome and Roman Catholicism.

The start of the discussion of the connection between capitalism and Protestantism came with Max Weber's *The Protestant Ethic and the Spirit of Capitalism* (1904), which was intended as an exploratory essay on this relationship. Weber maintained that although the material conditions for the emergence of capitalist activity had existed elsewhere, it flourished in the West only after the development of a spirit of capitalism or rationalist economic ethic, which he linked to Martin Luther's concept of the calling and to the Calvinist-Puritan emphasis on worldly asceticism. Hence, when both are present in the right environment, the result is an encouragement of capitalist activity. In England, R. H. Tawney picked up on this idea (in *Religion and the Rise of Capitalism,* 1926) but also pointed out that reality was much more complex and that it may well be heterodoxy rather than specifically Protestantism that is the key to understanding the connection. This thesis stirred up a considerable controversy.

As Jacob Bronowski and Bruce Mazlish point out in their comment on the Weber-Tawney thesis, "what men think and feel is of the utmost importance; but thoughts and feelings must always be related to the circumstances surrounding them. Thus, changes in religious ethos are complementary to and go hand in hand with developments in other areas.... Cause and effect in such matters are interwoven and hard to distinguish, and the specific nature of the religious-economic link in the seventeenth century is a subject for empirical investigation" (Jacob Bronowski and Bruce Mazlish, *The Western Intellectual Tradition* [New York: Harper & Row, 1960], note 20, 96–98). Although Bronowski and Mazlish think that Weber and Tawney probably overstated their case, they believe that there is a valid connection, which may have more to do with a heterodox group's sense of mission and isolation in the larger society that influences their activity in some new area, in this case, economic development. (For many minority groups, certain activities will not be open to them, hence the concentration in certain other areas.) They also make the interesting point that greater tolerance could well be a by-product of this link. In seventeenth-century England, it became obvious that persecution was incompatible with prosperity if those being persecuted were the ones responsible for generating greater wealth and prosperous conditions in the country. The following extract is taken from a long footnote in Tawney's book in which he answers some of the critics of Weber and also points out what he considers to be flaws in Weber's argument.

Weber's ... main thesis—that Calvinism, and in particular English Puritanism ... played a part of ... importance in creating moral and political conditions favourable to the growth of capitalist enterprise ... is certainly one of the most fruitful examinations of the relations between religion and social history ... [but] there are several points on which Weber's arguments appear ... to be one-sided.

. . .

(i) ... Weber seems to me to explain by reference to moral and intellectual influences developments which have their principal explanation [elsewhere].... There was plenty of the 'capitalist spirit' in the fifteenth-century Venice or Florence, or in South Germany and Flanders, for the simple reason that these areas were the greatest commercial and financial centres ... though all were, at least nominally, Catholic. The development of capitalism in Holland and England ... was due, not to the fact that they were Protestant powers, but to large economic movements, in particular the Discoveries and [its] results.... Of course material and psychological changes went together, and of course the second reacted on the first. But it seems a little artificial to talk as though capitalist enterprise could not appear till religious changes had produced a capitalist spirit.

. . .

(ii) Weber ignores ... intellectual movements, which were favourable to the growth of business enterprise ... but which had little to do with religion. The political thought of the Renaissance.... The speculations of businessmen and economists on money, prices, and the foreign exchange.... Both contributed to the ... single-minded concentration on pecuniary gain.

. . .

(iii) He appears ... to oversimplify Calvinism itself ... he apparently ascribes to the English Puritans ... the conception of social ethics held by Calvin ... [and] he speaks as though all English Puritans ... held much the same view of social duty and expediency. Both views are misleading.

. . .

Both 'the capitalist spirit' and 'Protestant ethics,' ... were a good deal more complex.... What is true and valuable ... is ... that the commercial classes ... were the standard-bearers of a particular conception of social expediency, which ... found expression in religion, in politics, and ... in social and economic conduct and policy.

Source: R. H. Tawney, *Religion and the Rise of Capitalism* (Harmondsworth, U.K.: Penguin, 1926), note 32, 311–13.

ANNOTATED BIBLIOGRAPHY

This bibliography is intended to provide a supplementary list of general reference sources for the Industrial Revolution and related topics; readers are encouraged to refer to the works appearing at the end of each entry for specific sources. Emphasis is given to published books, but readers also should pay attention to the various journals in the field, which often present newer or more specialized details and ideas than are found in books.

General

Cambridge Economic History. Cambridge: Cambridge University Press, 1941–. This multivolume set is comprehensive, worth checking, and useful because it includes Russia and the Far East as well as the usual focus on Europe.

Cipolla, Carlo M., ed. *The Fontana Economic History of Europe*. Harmondsworth, U.K.: Penguin, 1972–1976. This is another useful comprehensive series.

Diamond, Jared. *Guns, Germs and Steel: The Fates of Human Societies*. New York: Norton, 1997. Offering a controversial approach to the development of human societies, Diamond uses an environmental argument to explain differences in nations' economic and social development, especially focusing on the ease or difficulty of (productive) farming.

Dillard, Dudley. *Economic Development of the North Atlantic Community*. Englewood Cliffs, NJ: Prentice Hall, 1967. A general economic history textbook with an international focus on industrialization that can provide a useful introduction to the subject.

Hughes, Jonathan. *Industrialization and Economic History: Theses and Conjectures*. New York: McGraw-Hill, 1970. An interesting approach to the study of industrial development, focusing on the role of institutions, markets, migration, trade, and technological change.

Jones, E. L. *The European Miracle: Environments, Economies and Geopolitics in the History of Europe and Asia*. 2nd ed. Cambridge: Cambridge University Press, 1987. Analyzes the influences that resources, technology, and institutions have on economic growth.

Landes, David S. *The Unbound Prometheus: Technological Change and Industrial Development in Western Europe from 1750 to the Present*. Cambridge: Cambridge University Press, 1969.

Covers the modernization of industry in several countries and links technological change to the economic, institutional, and political changes that occurred in the same time period.

North, Douglass C. *Structure and Change in Economic History*. New York: Norton, 1981. This volume focuses on the changes societies have made over time to deal with the organization of their economic system, with a particular emphasis on property rights.

Polanyi, Karl. *The Great Transformation: The Political and Economic Origins of Our Time*. New York: Rinehart, 1944. Describes the emergence of the market society and describes the painful social changes caused by industrialization in England.

Rider, Christine. *An Introduction to Economic History*. Cincinnati, OH: South-Western, 1995. Another general economic history textbook with chapters on industrialization that can serve as useful introductory reading on the subject.

Rosenberg, Nathan, and L. E. Birdsell Jr. *How the West Grew Rich: The Economic Transformation of the Industrial World*. New York: Basic Books, 1986. Explains the economic development of Western countries in terms of political pluralism and flexible institutions rather than in terms of technological change.

Toynbee, Arnold. *Lectures on the Industrial Revolution in England*. Newton Abbot: David & Charles, [1884] 1969. Toynbee, a nineteenth-century political economist, is credited with development of the idea of the Industrial Revolution in Britain, and his lectures relating economists' ideas to their historical environment are still worth reading.

Historical Statistics

Historical statistics for the United States may be found in *Historical Statistics of the United States: Colonial Times to 1957*. Washington, DC: U.S. Government Printing Office, 1960. Historical statistics for France in Gille, Bertrand. *Les Sources Statistiques de l'Histoire de France des Enquêtes du XVIIe Siècle à 1870*. Geneva, Switzerland: Droz, 1964. And for Great Britain in Mitchell, B. R., and Phyllis Deane. *Abstracts of British Historical Statistics*. London: Cambridge University Press, 1962. The latter is a pioneering work that presents the basic raw material for analyzing British economic growth in the aggregate. Remember, however, that the collection and compilation of national statistics is a predominantly twentieth-century undertaking and that the farther back in history one goes, the less accurate and comprehensive any statistical series will be. It is important to read the notes accompanying the statistics to get a better idea of how the statistics were collected, how they can be used, and how they can be interpreted.

Science and Technology

Bronowski, Jacob. *The Ascent of Man*. Boston: Little Brown, 1975. A well-illustrated, very readable print version of the 1973 BBC television series.

Burke, James. *Connections*. Boston: Little Brown, 1978. Started life as a BBC television series (and is now on DVD); it explores the ideas, inventions, and coincidences that led to major technological advances.

Habakkuk, H. J. *American and British Technology in the Nineteenth Century: Search for Labor-Saving Inventions*. Cambridge: Cambridge University Press, 1962. A classic work on the subject of technological change.

Musson, A. E., and E. Robinson. *Science and Technology in the Industrial Revolution*. Manchester, U.K.: Manchester University Press, 1969. A classic work on the role of science and technology in the industrialization process.

Singer, Charles J., ed. *A History of Technology*. 5 vols. Fair Lawn, NJ: Oxford, 1954–1958. A comprehensive survey.

Europe

Clapham, John H. *The Economic Development of France and Germany, 1815–1914*. 4th ed. Cambridge: Cambridge University Press, [1921] 1936. An early classic comparative study.

Henderson, W. O. *The Industrial Revolution in Europe, 1815–1914*. Chicago: Quadrangle Books, 1961. A general survey of the issues.

Kiesewetter, Hubert. "Competition for Wealth and Power: The Growing Rivalry between Industrial Germany and Industrial Britain 1815–1914." *Journal of European Economic History* 20, pp. 271–299 (1991). An interesting study of different approaches to industrialization that influenced the political and military history of the twentieth century.

Milward, Alan S., and S. B. Saul. *The Economic Development of Continental Europe, 1780–1870*. Totowa, NJ: Rowman and Littlefield, 1973. Another good general survey of issues.

Tilly, Richard. *The Regional Development of the German Economy*. Middletown, CT: Wesleyan University Press, 1978. Introduces more social factors in the author's explanation of German development.

Trebilcock, Clive. *The Industrialization of the Continental Powers, 1780–1914*. London: Longmans, 1981. Trebilcock was the author of one of the first comparative studies of European industrialization.

Great Britain

Ashton, T. S. *The Industrial Revolution, 1760–1830*. New York: Oxford University Press, 1998. A concise volume that emphasizes the benefits the Industrial Revolution produced.

Chambers, J. D. *The Workshop of the World: British Economic History 1820–1880*. Oxford: Home University Press/Oxford University Press, 1916. Considered a sequel to Ashton's book because it focuses more on the consequences of economic growth after the transition to an industrial society.

Clapham, John H. *An Economic History of Modern Britain*. 2nd ed. 3 vols. London: Cambridge University Press, 1950–1952. Although old, this is probably the most extensive work on British economic history for the period since 1820.

Crouzet, François. *The First Industrialists*. Cambridge: Cambridge University Press, 1985. Concerned with the social origins of the first industrial entrepreneurs.

Deane, Phyllis. *The First Industrial Revolution*. 2nd ed. Cambridge: Cambridge University Press, 1979. A classic, readable presentation that discusses many different aspects of the British industrialization process and evaluates the contribution of different sectors of the economy.

Deane, Phyllis, and W. A. Cole. *British Economic Growth, 1688–1959: Trends and Structure*. Cambridge: Cambridge University Press, 1969. A quantitative study of changes in national income over time.

France

Cameron, Rondo. *France and the Economic Development of Europe, 1800–1914*. Princeton, NJ: Princeton University Press, 1961. Looks at the impact that French industrialization had on other countries in Europe.

Caron, François. *An Economic History of Modern France*. New York: Columbia University Press, 1970. Describes how the development of France was shaped by particular geographic, historical, and demographic factors.

Dunham, Arthur Louis. *The Industrial Revolution in France.* New York: Exposition Press, 1955. A good general discussion.

Kemp, T. *Economic Forces in French History.* London: Dobson, 1971. A useful source.

Kindleberger, Charles. *Economic Growth in France and Britain, 1851–1950.* Cambridge, MA: Harvard University Press, 1964. Offers a comparative view.

Germany

Borchardt, Knut. "The Industrial Revolution in Germany, 1700–1914." In *The Fontana Economic History of Europe,* ed Carlo Cipolla. Harmondsworth, U.K.: Penguin, 1972. Borchardt is an authoritative German economic historian who presents an alternative to the theory of the *Sonderweg* (special path) that German industrialization took.

Borchardt, Knut. *Perspectives on Modern German Economic History and Policy.* Cambridge: Cambridge University Press, 1991. Another good presentation of Borchardt's alternative views on the path of German industrialization.

Russia

Blackwell, William L. *The Beginnings of Russian Industrialization, 1800–1860.* Princeton, NJ: Princeton University Press, 1968.

United States

Atack, Jeremy, and Peter Passell. *A New Economic View of American History.* 2nd. ed. New York: Norton, 1994. Demonstrates the application of economic theory to economic history.

Bruchey, Stuart. *The Roots of American Economic Growth: 1607–1861.* London: Hutchison, 1965. Focuses mainly on the earlier years of U.S. industrialization before the post–Civil War growth spurt.

Lebergott, Stanley. *The Americans: An Economic Record.* New York: Norton, 1984. A good U.S. economic history text.

Ratner, Sidney Ratner, James H. Soltow, and Richard E. Sylla. *The Evolution of the American Economy: Growth, Welfare, and Decision Making.* New York: Basic Books, 1979. Another good U.S. economic history text.

Japan

Allen, George C. *A Short Economic History of Modern Japan, 1867–1937.* London: Allen & Unwin, 1972. Covers the early years of Japan's industrialization after the Meiji Restoration.

The Cambridge History of Japan. 6 vols. Cambridge: Cambridge University Press, 1988–1999. Offers a good compilation of modern views on the history of Japan.

Klein, L., and K. Ohkawa. *Economic Growth: The Japanese Experience since the Meiji Era.* Homewood, IL: Richard D. Irwin, 1968. A good introduction to the early period.

Morishima, Michio. *Why Has Japan 'Succeeded'? Western Technology and the Japanese Ethos.* Cambridge: Cambridge University Press, 1982. Morishima, a noted Japanese economist, emphasizes the technological aspect of the modernization of Japan.

Mercantilism

Coleman, D. C., ed. *Revisions in Mercantilism.* London: Methuen. 1969. Coleman provides some of the defenses and criticisms of Eli Heckscher's views in his classic *Mercantilism.*

Heckscher, Eli. *Mercantilism.* Rev. ed. New York: Macmillan, 1955. The classic work on mercantilism.

Transportation

Bagwell, P. S. *The Transportation Revolution from 1770*. London: Batsford, 1974. Surveys the role of transportation in the first stages of the British industrial revolution.

Fishlow, Albert. *American Railroads and the Transformation of the Antebellum Economy*. Cambridge, MA: Harvard University Press, 1965. Estimates the cost saving to be less than often thought as the main lines duplicated already-established water routes.

Fogel, Robert. *Railroads and American Economic Growth*. Baltimore: Johns Hopkins University Press, 1964. Takes a slightly different approach to the impact of the railroads on U.S. economic growth, which Fogel estimates is less than it is often credited to be.

Gourvish, T. R. *Railways and the British Economy 1830–1914*. London: Macmillan, 1980. Describes the impact of the railroads on different sectors of the British economy.

Taylor, George Rogers. *The Transportation Revolution: 1815–1860*. New York: Holt, Rinehart & Winston, 1951. A good survey of U.S. transportation.

Labor

Beard, Mary R. *A Short History of the American Labor Movement*. New York: Macmillan, 1927. An early classic history of U.S. labor.

Dulles, Foster Rhea. *Labor in America: A History*. 3rd. ed. Arlington Heights, IL: Harlan Davidson, [1949] 1966. Another classic labor history.

Ely, Richard T. *The Labor Movement in America*. New York: Thomas Crowell, 1886. A nineteenth-century view from one of the founders of the American Economic Association.

Engels, Frederick. *The Condition of the Working Class in England in 1844*. London: George Allen, [1892] 1952. The contemporary Marxist classic, maintaining that the experience of industrialization had a brutalizing effect on the working classes.

Mayhew, Henry. *London Labor and the London Poor*. 4 vols. New York: A. M. Kelley [1851] 1967. Mayhew was another contemporary observer whose work describes those who were the losers as society industrialized: the unemployed, vagrants, beggars, and paupers.

Pelling, Henry. *A History of British Trade Unionism*. Harmondsworth, U.K.: Penguin, 1963. Considered a classic on the development of unions in Britain.

Thompson, E. P. *The Making of the English Working Class*. Harmondsworth: Penguin, 1968. First published 1963 by Victor Gollancz. Another classic.

Journals

Although most academic journals are not written for the undergraduate reader, they often invite controversy and publish breakthroughs in and new knowledge of many issues in economic history. Important publications for a study of the Industrial Revolution are the following: *American History Review, Business History Review, Central European History, Economic History Review, Explorations in Economic History, Journal of Economic History, Journal of European Economic History,* and *Journal of Modern History.*

Internet Resources

When using Internet resources, make sure you know the provenance of the Web site and that it is reputable.

Http://eh.net is operated by Economic History Services and is supported by the major academic economic history associations; it provides a wealth of information.

Http://www.si.edu is the Web site of the Smithsonian Institution, Washington, DC, and the starting point for access to the many museums and collections associated with it (such as the National Portrait Gallery, http://www.npg.si.edu, and the National Museum of American History, http://www.americanhistory.si.edu). It is a good source for U.S. history, science and technology, the Civil War, and photographs and other images that are too fragile to be adequately reproduced.

Http://www.loc.gov is the Web site of the Library of Congress, the oldest federal cultural institution, which has more than 110 million items in a variety of formats. Old images that are too fragile to reproduce well can be found through the online catalog and include Civil War images and illustrations of people and things.

Http://www.nmsi.ac.uk and http://www.sciencemuseum.org.uk are the Web sites of the Science Museum in London, which also includes the National Railway Museum and the Museum of Photography. It has an unsurpassed collection of images and artifacts for the history of science, industry, and medicine.

Http://www.victorianlondon.org is a fascinating collection of information about Victorian London.

INDEX

Page numbers in bold indicate encyclopedia entries.

ABOUT THE EDITOR
AND CONTRIBUTORS

Christine Rider is professor emerita, St. John's University, New York. She is the author of *An Introduction to Economic History* (1995) and coeditor of *Socialist Economies in Transition: Appraisals of the Market Mechanism* (1992) and *The Industrial Revolution in Comparative Perspective* (1997). Her research interests include various aspects of international economic development and social economics, and she has published in these areas. She was president of the Association for Social Economics in 1998–1999.

Thomas Aiello is a doctoral candidate in the Department of History at the University of Arkansas, specializing in twentieth-century U.S. intellectual and cultural history. His work has appeared in *Americana: The Journal of American Popular Culture, The Southwestern Review, The McNeese Review, The Neoamericanist,* and *North Louisiana History.*

Steve Bass is a practicing architect in New York City and visiting professor of architecture at Notre Dame University. He has taught and written on proportion in design and is the author of *Proportion in Architecture* (2007).

Jon Bekken is associate professor of communications at Albright College and editor of *The Industrial Worker,* the newspaper of the Industrial Workers of the World. He is coauthor of *The IWW: Its First 100 Years* (2005) and has published extensively on various labor-related issues.

Ivan T. Berend is distinguished professor of history at the University of California–Los Angeles. He has published 25 books, including volumes on the economic history of nineteenth- and twentieth-century Europe, the history of Central and Eastern Europe, and the history of Hungary. He is a member of six European academies of science and has won the Konstantin Jiracek Award for scholarly life achievement from the Südosteuropa-Gesellschaft, Germany, and the Kossuth Prize in Hungary.

David Brown is lecturer in U.S. history at the University of Sheffield. He is the author of *Southern Outcast: Hinton Rowan Helper and "The Impending Crisis of the South"* (2007) and coauthor of *Race in the American South: From Slavery to Civil Rights* (2007).

William E. Burns is a historian in Washington, DC. He is the author of *Science in the Enlightenment* (2003) and *Science and Technology in Colonial America,* (2005) among other books and articles.

Christopher J. Castaneda is professor and chair, Department of History, California State University–Sacramento. He has written extensively on the oil and natural gas industries and is the author of *Invisible Fuel: Manufactured and Natural Gas in America, 1800–2000* (1999) .

Robert C. Chidester is a student in the doctoral program in anthropology and history at the University of Michigan and an affiliate of the Center for Heritage Resource Studies at the University of Maryland. His research has focused on the archaeology, history, and public heritage of Maryland's working class, and he is currently codirecting the Hampden Community Archaeology Project in Baltimore.

Charles M. A. Clark is associate dean, Tobin College of Business, and professor of economics and finance, St. John's University. He is the author or editor of nine books, the most recent being his coedited *Rediscovering Abundance* (2006), and he has contributed extensively to professional journals, especially in the areas of Christian social and economic thought, institutional economics, and social policy.

Raymond L. Cohn is professor of economics at Illinois State University in Normal. He has written extensively on immigration from Europe to the United States during the nineteenth century and is the author of "Immigration to the United States" in *EH.Net Encyclopedia of Economic and Business History.*

Mark J. Crowley is associate lecturer at Cardiff University, Wales. He has published widely on aspects of British employment policy in the period 1900–1945, and his main research interests focus on the ideological tensions between the British political parties and the trade union movement in that period.

Raymond J. Cullen is an adjunct assistant professor of finance at the Tobin College of Business, St. John's University, New York. He works in the financial sector and also has served for the last 10 years as an industry arbitrator for the National Association of Securities Dealers.

Kent G. Deng is reader in economic history, London School of Economics. His main research interest is in premodern and early modern economic growth in East Asia, and he is the author of several books and journal articles focusing especially on China.

Theresa W. Devasahayam is an independent scholar who works as a consultant with international development agencies. She has held research positions in the Centre for Asia Pacific Social Transformation Studies at the University of Wollongong, New South Wales, Australia, and the Asia Research Institute at the National University of Singapore. Her research interests include globalization and the status of women, migration of unskilled female labor, and women's fertility and reproductive health and rights.

Susanne Dobrovolny is affiliated with the Wittgenstein Archive, Cambridge. Her research interests include ecological history, the history of science, and London's environmental problems.

Michael Doyle is a former business representative and organizer for the International Brotherhood of Electrical Workers (IBEW) and for many years was a regular contributor to the national *IBEW Journal*. He is currently a freelance writer and is associated with Skidmore College, Saratoga Springs, New York.

Susan H. Farnsworth is professor of history at Trinity University in Washington. Her research interests center on Victorian politics and the Darwinian Revolution. She is the author of *The Evolution of British Imperial Policy during the Mid-Nineteenth Century: A Study of the Peelite Contribution 1846–1874* (1992).

Grant D. Forsyth is associate professor of economics, Eastern Washington University, Cheney, Washington. He currently serves on the Governor's Council of Economic Advisors in Washington State. His research interests focus on tariff formation in antebellum United States.

Christopher Frank is assistant professor of history at the University of Manitoba. His specialty is industrial relations, popular movements, and the law in nineteenth-century Britain, and he has published extensively in these areas. He was a contributor to *Masters, Servants and Magistrates in Britain and Empire, 1562–1955* (2004).

Donald E. Frey is professor of economics at Wake Forest University, Winston-Salem, North Carolina. He is the author of several articles on historical aspects of the relationships between economics and ethics.

Gerald Friedman is professor of economics at the University of Massachusetts. He is the author of *State-Making and Labor Movements: The United States and France, 1876–1914* (1998) and *Reigniting the Labor Movement* (2007) as well as numerous articles on labor history and political economy.

Antoinette Galotola teaches humanities- and art-based disciplines and art history at Empire State College, State University of New York. Her research interests are nineteenth- and twentieth-century U.S. and European art. She has published in *American Studies International, Encyclopedia of Sculpture, PART: A Society for the Promotion of Interdisciplinary Culture,* and *Parsons School of Design On-Line Journal.*

Joseph A. Giacalone is professor of economics and finance, Tobin College of Business, and holder of the Henry George Chair, St. John's University. His areas of research interest are economic history, health care economics *(The U.S. Nursing*

Home Industry), and collegiate business education. He is coeditor of *The Path to Justice: Following in the Footsteps of Henry George* (2003).

Daniel C. Giedeman is assistant professor of economics, Grand Valley State University, Allendale, Michigan. His research interests include financial and banking history, macroeconomics, and institutional economics, and he is the author of several publications on credit and banking, including "Branch Banking Restrictions and Firm Finance Constraints in Early Twentieth Century America."

Donato Gómez-Díaz is professor of history in the Department of Applied Economics, Almeria University. He has published extensively in economic history and demographic history and is especially interested in technological change.

Casey Harison is associate professor of history at the University of Southern Indiana in Evansville, where he teaches courses on modern French, European, and world history. He has published articles on the French working class in the nineteenth century and on U.S. views of the French Revolution.

Michael J. Hicks is associate professor of economics, Air Force Institute of Technology, and research professor, Marshall University. He has written extensively on the roles of coal and transportation in economic development.

Janet Hunter is Saji Professor of Economic History at the London School of Economics and Political Science. She has published widely on the economic history of modern Japan, particularly on the development of the female labor market and the textile industry. She is the author of *Women and the Labour Market in Japan's Industrialising Economy: The Textile Industry before the Pacific War* (2003).

Richard Jensen is a retired professor of history whose 11 books cover a range of political, economic, and military topics in U.S. and world history. He was the founder of H-Net Humanities and Social Sciences Online.

Noel D. Johnson is a visiting assistant professor at the Hobart and William Smith Colleges, Geneva, New York. His research focuses on the successes and failures of early modern European states in establishing credible property rights. He has published in the *Journal of Economic History, Essays in Business*, and *Economic History*.

Phylis Johnson is associate professor of radio and sound studies at Southern Illinois University, Carbondale. She also is a professional broadcaster with 25 years of experience in commercial radio programming and performance and has written extensively on radio, sound, and cultural diversity.

Feisal Khan is assistant professor of economics at Hobart and William Smith Colleges, New York. His research interests include comparative economic systems (with a particular emphasis on Islamic economics and finance), institutional economics, and the impact of corruption on economic development in the Third World, and he has published extensively in these areas.

Robert Karl Koslowsky is a historian of science and technology based in Santa Rosa, California. He has written extensively on the impact of science and technology on society and is the author of *A World Perspective through 21st Century Eyes* (2004) He also produces a monthly newsletter entitled *A World Perspective.*

Ryan L. Lanham is a doctoral candidate at the Virginia Technical University Center for Public Administration and Policy. His research interests include complex public networks, community development, border and boundary issues, and innovation. He previously has worked in information technology and as an Internet venture entrepreneur.

Frederic S. Lee is a professor of economics at the University of Missouri–Kansas City. He has written extensively on heterodox microeconomics and is the author of *Post Keynesian Price Theory* (1998). He is a member of the Industrial Workers of the World and in 1988 retrieved Joe Hill's ashes from the National Archives for the union.

Stephen G. Marshall is an independent scholar and former administrative law judge. He has published on various issues related to shipping and is currently writing a history of containerization, the rise of Port Newark-Elizabeth, and the fall of the New York City waterfront for the New Jersey Historical Commission.

Daniel C. Marston is a clinical psychologist in private practice in western Pennsylvania. He also is a writer on issues related to economics and psychology and an adjunct professor at Carlow College. His clinical and research interests include the area of poverty and mental health.

Michael Meinberg is an independent historian. He mainly is interested in European political history and World War I.

Daniel J. Meissner is an assistant professor at Marquette University in Milwaukee, Wisconsin, where he teaches East Asian history and Sino-American diplomatic and economic relations. He has published on flour industrialization in China and on the development of the transpacific flour trade.

Patit Paban Mishra is professor of history, Sambalpur University, Orissa, India. He has written extensively on various topics in world history; on the history of Asia, South Asia, and Southeast Asia; and has published extensively in these areas.

Martin Moll is a professor of modern history in the History Department at Graz University, Austria. He has published numerous articles about Nazi Germany, World War II, and Austria-Hungary since 1867. He is the editor of *Führer-Erlass, 1939–1945* and has published many articles on Austria-Hungary.

Monir Hossain Moni is assistant professor, Faculty of Social Sciences and Japan Study Center, University of Dhaka, Bangladesh. His research interests encompass Japan and its political economy and role in development cooperation in Asia-Pacific. He has contributed many research articles to journals in the field.

Ian Morley is an assistant professor of architectural and urban history at Ming Chuan University, Taiwan. He has written extensively on the Victorian model of urban development in Britain and on British civic design in the late Victorian and Edwardian eras.

Jürgen Nautz teaches in the Department of Economics, University of Vienna, Austria. His research interests include the economic history of Austria-Hungary, Germany, and the Netherlands.

Jay Needham is a media artist and producer with a multidisciplinary approach to arts practice. He is assistant professor of the Sonic Arts Program in the College of Mass Communication and Media Arts at Southern Illinois University, Carbondale.

Susan Pashkoff is an independent researcher and economist. Her research interests cover nineteenth-century social policy.

Chad Pearson is at the University at Albany, State University of New York, where he is researching the open-shop movement during the Progressive Era. His research interests are labor and business history, and he has published in the journal *Labor History, The Historical Encyclopedia of American Labor* (2005), *The Encyclopedia of New York State* (2005), and *the Encyclopedia of Cleveland History* (1996).

Greg Dean Petersen is an assistant professor of humanities at the National University of Singapore. He is an interdisciplinary humanist, and his research and publications focus on the intersections between the arts and the human relationship with the arts.

Richard Polt is professor of philosophy at Xavier University in Cincinnati and an expert on the history of typewriters.

John L. Recchiuti is professor of history and director of American studies at Mount Union College. He is the author of *Civic Engagement: Social Science and Progressive Era Reform in New York City* (2007).

Helena Sinoracka is retired from her position as professor of economics, Warsaw School of Economics, Poland. She has published extensively on the problems of the Polish socialist economy, with emphasis on the state-owned monopolistic enterprises. She recently has worked as finance manager for several USAID projects in Poland and elsewhere and has been a volunteer in sub-Saharan Africa.

Vaclav Smil is distinguished professor in the Faculty of the Environment at the University of Manitoba, Canada. He is the author of 24 books and more than 300 journal articles, focusing mainly on energy, environmental issues, food, population, and economic and public policy studies, and he has been consulted on these issues by a variety of national and international institutions. Dr. Smil is a fellow of the Royal Society of Canada (Science Academy), and the first non-American to receive the American Association for the Advancement of Science Award for Public Understanding of Science and Technology.

Keir B. Sterling is command historian, U.S. Army Combined Arms Support Command, Fort Lee, Virginia. His research interests include military logistics and the history of the natural sciences. He was senior editor of the *Biographical Dictionary of American and Canadian Naturalists and Environmentalists* (1997) and author of "American Geographers and the OSS during World War II" in J. L. Bellafaire's *The US Army and World War II: Selected Papers* (1998).

Christopher Tait is a doctoral candidate in history at the University of Western Ontario, London, Canada. His research interest is the historical relationship between Britain and Canada, and he has published on European monarchy and the Canadian identity.

Laura Talamante has taught at Loyola Marymount University, Los Angeles. Her teaching and research interests include European and French history with particular emphasis on the French Revolution, gender, and citizenship. She won the UCLA Center for the Study of Women Mary Wollstonecraft Dissertation Award for *Les Citoyennes Marseillaises: Women and Political Change during the French Revolution, 1789–1794* in 2004.

Frederik Tell is associate professor of management at Linköping School of Management, Linköping University, Sweden. His research interests include management of organizational knowledge and capabilities, innovation and industrial dynamics, and the business history of the heavy electrical engineering industry. He is codirector of the research program EPOK (Enterprising by Projects and Organizational Knowledge) and has been a visiting research fellow or faculty at universities in the United States and the United Kingdom.

Lana Thompson is an independent scholar who specializes in the history of medicine and women's studies. She has taught forensic anthropology at Lynn University in Boca Raton, Florida. Her book, *The Wandering Womb: A Cultural History of Outrageous Beliefs about Women,* was published in 1999 by Prometheus, and she is working on a second book about the history of public anatomies.

Erik Thomson is a member of the Society of Fellows in the Liberal Arts at the University of Chicago. His research interests include the history of economic thought, commercial statecraft, and political culture, and he has published on early modern diplomacy and its relation to the commerce of various European nations.

Carolyn Tuttle is professor of economics and business at Lake Forest College, Lake Forest, Illinois. She has researched and written about child labor for the past twenty years and published *Hard at Work in Factories and Mines: The Economics of Child Labor during the British Industrial Revolution* (1999). She won the Jonathan Hughes Prize for excellence in teaching in 2001.

Jane Weiss is assistant professor of English at Kingsborough Community College of the City University of New York. Her scholarship focuses on nineteenth-century U.S. domesticity and the lives of working women in the northeastern United States.

Roland Wenzlhuemer is research assistant at the Centre for British Studies at Humboldt University, Berlin. He has written extensively on the economic transition of the British crown colony of Ceylon (Sri Lanka) in the late nineteenth century, and his current research concerns the evolution of the international telegraph network in the nineteenth century and its social impact on England.

Robert Whaples is professor of economics at Wake Forest University, Winston-Salem, North Carolina, and director of EH.Net, which provides information on economic history at http://eh.net. He won the Economic History Association's Jonathan Hughes Prize for excellence in teaching in 1999.

Kevin F. Wozniak is an independent researcher and professional financial fraud investigator. He has published on U.S. presidential history; cultural and historical topics, including famous U.S. crimes and trials; and jazz. He is at work on the life of Lee Harvey Oswald and on a critical analysis of U.S. authors Mark Twain and Kurt Vonnegut.

Steven Yamarik is an associate professor of economics at California State University–Long Beach. His research interests focus on state-level economic growth and the link between regional trading arrangements (such as NAFTA) and international trade and development. He has published in journals such as *The Review of Economics and Statistics, Journal of International Economics, Review of International Economics,* and *Economic Letters.*

Translators

V. H. Pinches worked as a simultaneous interpreter for the United Nations, New York.

Sharon L. Reeves is a member of the Department of Foreign Languages and Literatures at Queensborough Community College, City University of New York, Bayside, New York.